NEW MEXICO GEOLOGICAL SOCIETY

Guidebook

of the

RUIDOSO COUNTRY

Edited by

Sidney R. Ash and Leon V. Davis

FIFTEENTH FIELD CONFERENCE

October 16, 17 and 18, 1964

RUIDOSO COUNTRY FORMATIONS

See Lexicon on p. 57 of this guidebook for more detailed description

SYSTEM	STRATIGRAPHIC UNIT	PHYSICAL CHARACTER
QUATERNARY	LITTLE BLACK PEAK BASALT FLOW	Olivine basalt.
	BROKEN BACK BASALT FLOW	Olivine basalt.
TERTIARY	SIERRA BLANCA VOLCANICS	Andesite flow breccia, tuffs, volcanic conglomerate.
	LONE MOUNTAIN STOCK	Nordmarkite.
	JICARILLA MONZONITE	Monzonite porphyry.
?	McRAE FORMATION or CUB MOUNTAIN FORMATION of Bodine (1956)	Sandstone, chert pebble conglomerate, shale.
CRETACEOUS	MESAVERDE GROUP or MESAVERDE FORMATION	Sandstone, shale, coal, marl, lignite.
	MANCOS SHALE	Shale, limestone, sandstone.
	DAKOTA SANDSTONE	Sandstone, shale, siltstone.
TRIASSIC	CHINLE FORMATION	Shale, shaly sandstone.
	SANTA ROSA SANDSTONE	Sandstone, chert pebble conglomerate.
PERMIAN	ARTESIA GROUP, ARTESIA FORMATION, BERNAL FORMATION, CHALK BLUFF FORMATION, or WHITEHORSE GROUP	Gypsum, anhydrite, dolomite, impure limestone, siltstone, shale, sandstone.
	SAN ANDRES LIMESTONE	Limestone, dolomite, siltstone, sandstone, gypsum, anhydrite, shale.
	GLORIETA SANDSTONE, or HONDO SANDSTONE MEMBER OF SAN ANDRES FORMATION	Sandstone, silty limestone, siltstone, gypsum, anhydrite.
	YESO FORMATION	Siltstone, limestone, shale, sandstone, gypsum, salt, anhydrite.
	ABO FORMATION	Sandstone, shale, conglomerate.
	BURSUM FORMATION or LABORCITA FORMATION	Limestone, shale, conglomerate.
PENNSYLVANIAN	MAGDALENA GROUP, MADERA LIMESTONE, SANDIA FORMATION	Limestone, shale, sandstone conglomerate.
PRECAMBRIAN	-	Granite, quartzite.

NEW MEXICO GEOLOGICAL SOCIETY • FIFTEENTH FIELD CONFERENCE

CONTENTS

President's Message	3
Executive and Field Conference Committees	4
Publications of the New Mexico Geological Society	5
Schedule	6
Physiographic Setting	7

ROAD LOGS

Road Logs from Ruidoso to Sierra Blanca Ski Resort Headquarters, Tularosa, Carrizozo, Malpais, and Return First day, Friday, October 16, 1964	11
Road Logs from Ruidoso to Hondo, Capitan, Capitan Iron Deposits, and return to Ruidoso Second day, Saturday, October 17, 1964	27
Road Logs from Ruidoso to Capitan, Carrizozo, White Oaks, Ancho and Gallinas Third day, Sunday, October 18, 1964	37

SUPPLEMENTAL ROAD LOGS

Road Log from Gallinas to Gallinas Peak	47
Road Log from Gallinas to Carrizozo	48
Road Log from Roswell to Hondo	49
Road Log from Hondo to Ruidoso	51
Road Log from Ruidoso to Pajarito Mountain	52
Road Log from Nogal to Nogal Peak and Bonito Lake	54

TECHNICAL PAPERS

Stratigraphy and Paleontology

Lexicon of stratigraphic names used in Lincoln County, New Mexico	Christina Lochman-Balk	57
Precambrian geology of south-central New Mexico	William R. Muehlberger and Rodger E. Denison	62
Southwestern edge of late Paleozoic landmass in New Mexico	George O. Bachman	70
A preliminary range chart of Lake Valley Formation (Osage) conodonts in the southern Sacramento Mountains, New Mexico	Robert C. Burton	73
A stratigraphic section of the Sierra Blanca Volcanics in the Nogal Peak area, Lincoln County, New Mexico	Tommy B. Thompson	76
Glacial deposits on Sierra Blanca Peak, New Mexico	Gerald M. Richmond	79

Areal Studies

Geologic outline of the Jicarilla Mountains, Lincoln County, New Mexico	A. J. Budding	82
Résumé of the geology of the Gallinas Mountains	Ralph M. Perhac	87
Geology of the Little Black Peak quadrangle Socorro and Lincoln Counties, New Mexico	Clay T. Smith	92
Geology of the Carrizozo quadrangle, New Mexico	Robert H. Weber	100

Structural Geology

Tectonics and general geology of the Ruidoso-Carrizozo region, central
New Mexico ....**Vincent C. Kelley** and **Tommy B. Thompson** 110

The Lincoln fold system ....**Campbell Craddock** 122

The Lincoln folds, Lincoln, New Mexico ....**Edward J. Foley** 134

Petrology

Differentiation and alkali metasomatism in dike swarm complex and related
igneous rocks near Capitan, Lincoln County, New Mexico ....**Wolfgang E. Elston** and **Henry I. Snider** 140

Economic Geology

Mineral resources of Lincoln County ....**George B. Griswold** 148

Notes on the mineral deposits of the Gallinas Mountains, New Mexico ....**Ralph M. Perhac** 152

Oil and gas tests in Lincoln County, New Mexico ....**Kay C. Havenor** 155

Water Resources

Water supplies near Carrizozo, New Mexico ....**James B. Cooper** 159

Chemistry of water of a section of the eastern flank of the Sacramento Mountains,
Lincoln and Otero Counties, New Mexico ....**F. R. Hall** 161

Miscellaneous

Some aspects of the natural history of the Capitan and Jicarilla Mountains,
and Sierra Blanca region of New Mexico ....**William C. Martin** 171

Petroglyphs of the Sierra Blanca ....**Robert H. Weber** 177

Caves of the Fort Stanton area, New Mexico ....**Donald E. Hallinger** 181

Abstracts of technical papers 185

Paintings by Peter Hurd 190

IN POCKET

Geologic map of the Little Black Peak Quadrangle, Socorro and Lincoln Counties, New Mexico; by Clay T. Smith

Tectonic map of the Ruidoso-Carrizozo region; compiled by V. C. Kelley and Tommy B. Thompson

A note about the end papers —
Folded laminae (X5) of bituminous calcite and anhydrite from the lower part of the Permian Castile Formation of Texas and southeastern New Mexico. According to R. Y. Anderson and D. W. Kirkland of the University of New Mexico, the folds were probably formed by gravitational adjustment on the original slope of the basin. Photograph by D. W. Kirkland.

NEW MEXICO GEOLOGICAL SOCIETY • FIFTEENTH FIELD CONFERENCE

PRESIDENT'S MESSAGE

Welcome to the Ruidoso country and the Fifteenth Annual Field Conference of the New Mexico Geological Society.

Those of us who have been spoiled by extensive outcrops in barren desert mountains now will appreciate the problems of the tree-dodging geologists who work in these higher elevations of more humid climates. You will see some of the better exposures in the road cuts along the highways of the conference route. Sometime just try to follow the rock units back into the forested areas!

In keeping with the Society's policy to serve the entire spectrum of geology, workers in various fields have been asked to contribute to the trip as leaders and as authors of guidebook articles. Each bit of field evidence that we can digest will make us all better geologists. Increase your background knowledge by reading the articles, and please give your attention to the leaders at the discussions. They will welcome your pertinent questions.

As many of you know the organization, preparation, and execution of such a conference is an enormous task. This year, as in the past, the bulk of the load has fallen on the General Chairman, Walter A. Mourant, and the Guidebook Editors, Leon V. Davis and Sidney R. Ash. Special mention should be made of the Road Log Committee Chairman, Carl Ulvog, who spent several months logging the many miles of roads in this region. On behalf of the Society, I wish to thank them and the other chairman and committee workers for their assistance. They have all given unstintingly of their time and efforts to make the trip a success. I hope that each participant will personally tell the leaders, authors, and workers involved how beneficial the conference was to you. Suggest improvements; we aim to please!

Fortunately our Society field trip month, October, falls between the time when the roads in the Ruidoso area are packed with turf fans during the racing season, and the time when they are packed with snow during the skiing season. Only in recent years have the accommodations in this growing resort community been sufficient to support a large conference. *Ruidoso*, Spanish for "noisy," was meant to describe the rushing currents of the Rio Ruidoso. But wait until rock hounds start banging away!

Don't miss the ride on the new gondola tramway to the observation point near Sierra Blanca Peak on the first day of the conference. (If it's a clear day, and with the aid of a time machine, you may be able to see Dr. Clay T. Smith lecturing atop Socorro Peak at last year's conference.) After this regional survey, we shall descend to highway level and be on our way to see as much geology around the Tularosa-Carrizozo-Hondo triangle as we can in one week-end.

Recalling his famous voyage around the world on the *Beagle* from 1831-1836, Charles Darwin wrote:

"The investigation of the geology of all the places visited was far more important, as reasoning here comes into play. On first examining a new district nothing can appear more hopeless than the chaos of rocks; but by recording the stratification and nature of the rocks and fossils at many points, always reasoning and predicting what will be found elsewhere, light soon begins to dawn on the district and the structure of the whole becomes more or less intelligible . . . ."

Isn't this gem of wisdom applicable in our day and age? Consider it while you are observing the screwed-up mess in the Lincoln fold belt.

One last request — upon your return home let others in your companies and agencies know that a field trip can be informative as well as enjoyable.

Thanks for your interest in our Society. I am looking forward to our meeting on the outcrop.

Sam Thompson III
President, New Mexico Geological
Society, 1964-65

NEW MEXICO GEOLOGICAL SOCIETY • FIFTEENTH FIELD CONFERENCE

EXECUTIVE COMMITTEE

Sam Thompson, III*	President	Humble Oil and Refining Co.
A. J. Budding	President	New Mexico Bureau of Mines and Mineral Resources
	Vice-President	
Fred D. Trauger	Secretary	U.S. Geological Survey, Water Resources Division
James L. Albright	Treasurer	Pubco Petroleum Corp.
Wolfgang E. Elston	Past President	Department of Geology, University of New Mexico

FIELD CONFERENCE COMMITTEES

Walter A. Mourant	General Chairman	U.S. Geological Survey, Water Resources Division

Guidebook Committee

Sidney R. Ash	Co-Editor	U.S. Geological Survey, Ground Water Branch
Leon V. Davis	Co-Editor	U.S. Geological Survey, Paleontology and Stratigraphy Branch

Road Logging Committee

Carl Ulvog	Chairman	Sunray DX Oil Co.
Sam Thompson, III		Humble Oil and Refining Co.
Leroy Corbitt		Sunray DX Oil Co.
Tommy B. Thompson		Department of Geology, University of New Mexico
A. J. Budding		New Mexico Bureau of Mines and Mineral Resources
G. O. Bachman		U.S. Geological Survey

Registration Committee

Roy H. Dubitzky	Chairman	Standard Oil Co. of Texas

Caravan Committee

William E. King	Chairman	Department of Earth Science, New Mexico State University

Advertising Committee

Royce F. Lawson, Jr.	Chairman	Humble Oil and Refining Co.

Finance Committee

James L. Albright		Pubco Petroleum Corp.

*Mr. Thompson resigned on August 17, 1964 to accept an assignment with International Petroleum Company, Ltd. in Bogota, Colombia.

NEW MEXICO GEOLOGICAL SOCIETY • FIFTEENTH FIELD CONFERENCE

PUBLICATIONS OF THE NEW MEXICO GEOLOGICAL SOCIETY

GUIDEBOOKS

1. Guidebook of the San Juan Basin [covering the north and east sides], New Mexico and Colorado; First Field Conference, 1950; edited by Vincent C. Kelley and others; 152 + ii pages, 40 illustrations. (Out of print)

2. Guidebook of the south and west sides of the San Juan Basin, New Mexico and Arizona; Second Field Conference, 1951; edited by Clay T. Smith and Caswell Silver; 163 + iv pages, 71 illustrations. (Out of print)

3. Guidebook of the Rio Grande country, central New Mexico; Third Field Conference, 1952; edited by Ross B. Johnson and Charles B. Read; 126 + iii pages, 50 illustrations. (Out of print)

4. Guidebook of southwestern New Mexico; Fourth Field Conference, 1953; edited by Frank E. Kottlowski and others; 153 + v pages, 70 illustrations. $5.00

5. Guidebook of southeastern New Mexico; Fifth Field Conference, 1954; edited by T. F. Stipp; 209 + viii pages, 76 illustration. $5.00

6. Guidebook of south-central New Mexico; Sixth Field Conference, 1955; edited by J. Paul Fitzsimmons; 193 + vii pages, 66 illustrations, hard binding. Prepared with the copperation of the Roswell Geological Society. (out of print)

7. Guidebook of southeastern Sangre de Cristo Mountains, New Mexico; Seventh Field Conference, 1956; edited by A. Rosenweig; 151 + iii pages, 61 illustrations. $7.00

8. Guidebook of southwestern San Juan Mountains, Colorado; Eighth Field Conference, 1957; edited by Frank E. Kottlowski and Brewster Baldwin; 258 + vi pages, 110 illustrations. $7.00

9. Guidebook of the Black Mesa Basin, northeastern Arizona; Ninth Field Conference, 1958; edited by Roger Y. Anderson and John W. Harshbarger; 205 + vii pages, 106 illustrations; hard binding. Prepared in cooperation with the Arizona Geological Society. $8.50

10. Guidebook of west-central New Mexico; Tenth Field Conference, 1959; edited by James E. Weir, Jr., and Elmer H. Baltz; 162 + iv pages, 91 illustrations; hard binding. $8.50

11. Guidebook of the Rio Chama country [New Mexico and Colorado]; Eleventh Field Conference, 1960; edited by Edward C. Beaumont and Charles B. Read; 129 + vii pages, 35 illustrations, hard binding. $8.50

12. Guidebook of the Albuquerque country [New Mexico]; Twelfth Field Conference, 1961, edited by Stuart A. Northrop; 199 + viii pages, 83 illustrations, hard binding. $9.50

13. Guidebook of the Mogollon Rim region, east-central Arizona; Thirteenth Field Conference, 1962; edited by Robert H. Weber and H. Wesley Pierce; 175 + xi pages, 77 illustrations, hard binding. Prepared with the copperation of the Arizona Geological Society. $9.50

14. Guidebook of the Socorro region, New Mexico; Fourteenth Field Conference, 1963; edited by Frederick J. Kuellmer; 240 + ix pages, 90 illustrations, hard binding. $9.00

15. Guidebook of the Ruidoso country [New Mexico]; Fifteenth Field Conference, 1964, edited by Sidney R. Ash and Leon V. Davis, hard binding. $9.00

These publications are available by mail (please add 25 cents for postage and handling) from the New Mexico Bureau of Mines and Mineral Resources, Campus Station, Socorro, New Mexico. Also over-the-counter sales at the New Mexico Bureau of Mines and Mineral Resources, Socorro; the Department of Geology, University of New Mexico, Albuquerque; Holman's Book Store, Albuquerque, N. Mex.; and Museum of Northern Arizona, Flagstaff. Checks should be made payable to the New Mexico Geological Society. Discounts of 20 percent are available on all guidebooks except Nos. 12, 13, 14, and 15 to members of New Mexico Geological Society and to non-members who purchase one set or more. Dealer's discounts are available on all publications by request.

SPECIAL PUBLICATIONS

1. Bibliography and index of the New Mexico Geological Society Guidebooks, 1950-1963; compiled by Sidney R. Ash. In press.

2. A history of the New Mexico Geological Society; by Stuart A. Northrop. In preparation.

MAPS

Geological maps are available by mail or over the counter from the New Mexico Bureau of Mines and Mineral Resources, Socorro, as follows:

(a) Geologic highway map of New Mexico; compiled by Frank E. Kottlowski and others. $1.25 folded; $1.50 rolled. Also available from the Department of Geology, University of New Mexico, and Holman's Book Store, Albuquerque; and Roswell Map Company, Roswell.

(b) Geologic map of the Sierra County Region, New Mexico; compiled by Vincent C. Kelley; accompanies Guidebook of the Sixth Field Conference, $1.00.

(c) Geologic map of the Rio Chama country; compiled by Clay T. Smith and William R. Muehlberger; accompanies Guidebook of the Eleventh Field Conference. $0.50

(d) Geologic map of the Albuquerque country; compiled by Stuart A. Northrop and Arlette Hill; accompanies Guidebook of the Twelfth Field Conference. $0.50.

(e) Tectonic map of the Ruidoso-Carrizozo region; compiled by V. C. Kelley and Tommy B. Thompson; accompanies Guidebook of the Fifteenth Field Conference. $1.00.

ROAD LOGS

Entry and exit road logs to supplement Guidebook of the Ninth Field Conference. $0.10 each. The Road Logs are available by mail or over the counter from the New Mexico Bureau of Bureau of Mines and Mineral Resources, Socorro, as follows:

(a) Albuquerque to Gallup (N.M.) and return, by E. H. Baltz, Jr. and S. W. West.

(b) Mountainair to Correo (N.M.) and return, by Frank B. Titus, Jr.

(c) Gallup (N.M.) to Cortez (Colo.) and return, by K. G. Smith, W. D. Fenex, et al.

(d) Socorro (N.M.) to Holbrook (Ariz.) and return, by S. Thompson III and O. C. Hutson.

(e) Globe to Showlow and to Sanders (Ariz.) and return, by J. P. Akers and H. W. Pierce.

(f) Monticello (Utah) to Tuba City (Ariz.) and return, by T. L. Britt, E. L. Howard, and W. F. Auer.

(g) Kingman via Grand Canyon Junction to Flagstaff (Ariz.) and return, by W. L. Chenoweth, D. R. Dow, and C. H. Williams.

(h) Flagstaff to Prescott (Ariz.) and return, by D. G. Metzger and F. R. Twenter.

(i) Gap Trading Post (Ariz.) to Kanab (Utah) and return, by J. P. Akers.

———0———

Schedule

Thursday, October 15
5:00 - 10:00 p.m.

Registration at the Chaparral Motor Hotel, Ruidoso Downs, New Mexico.

Friday, October 16

Conferees will assemble on the top of Lookout Mountain near the upper terminal of the Gondola Lift at 10:00 a.m. Note: It is a 25 mile drive from the Chaparral to the Sierra Blanca Ski Lodge Headquarters where the lower terminal of the gondola lift is located (traveling time of about 45 minutes) and the lift (15 minute trip) starts operating at 9:00 a.m. Plan Ahead!

Lunch — conferees will make their own arrangements for lunch today. Dining facilities are available in Ruidoso, Ruidoso Downs, and at Ski Lodge Headquarters.

The Caravan will assemble and leave from the Chaparral Motor Hotel at 1:00 p.m. Please be prompt.

Saturday, October 17

The Caravan will assemble in the valley of the Rio Bonito, 8½ miles northwest of Lincoln, New Mexico at 8:30 a.m. Please be prompt. The assembly point is about 38 miles from the Chaparral (traveling time of about 1 hour).

Lunch — conferees will make their own arrangements for lunch today in Capitan after visiting the Capitan Iron Deposits. Following lunch the caravan will assemble on N.M. 48 on the southern outskirts of Capitan.

Cocktail hour and banquet will be at the Chaparral; time to be announced.

Sunday, October 18

The Caravan will assemble at Indian Divide, on U.S. 380, about 6½ miles northwest of Capitan, New Mexico and leave promptly at 8:30 a.m. The assembly point is about 35 miles from the Chaparral (traveling time of about 1 hour).

Lunch — conferees will bring their own lunches with them today. Box lunches are available at the Chaparral and other restaurants in the Ruidoso area.

PHYSIOGRAPHIC SETTING

The southeastern quarter of New Mexico and immediately adjacent areas include parts of the physiographic divisions, provinces and sections enumerated below. These are based on the Fenneman classification (1930).
INTERIOR PLAINS division
    Great Plains province (13)
        High Plains section (13d)
        Raton section (13g)
        Pecos Valley section (13h)
        Edwards Plateau section (13i)
        Central Texas section (13k)
ROCKY MOUNTAIN SYSTEM division
    Southern Rock Mountains province (16)
INTERMONTANE PLATEAUS division
    Colorado Plateau section (21)
        Datil section (21f)
    Basin and Range province (22)
        Mexican Highland section (22d)
        Sacramento section (22e)

Characteristics of the sections are as follows:

"High Plains section: Broad intervalley remnants of smooth fluviatile plains.

Raton section: Trenched peneplain surmounted by disected, lava-capped plateaus and buttes.

Pecos Valley section: Late mature to old plain.

Edwards Plateau section: Young plateau with mature margin of moderate to strong relief.

Central Texas section: Plateau in maturity and later stages of erosion.

Southern Rock Mountains province: Complex mountains of various types; intermont basins.

Datil section: Lava flows entire or in remnants; volcanic necks.

Mexican Highland section: Isolated ranges (largely dissected block mountains) separated by aggraded desert plains.

Sacramento section: Mature block mountains of gently tilted strata; block-plateaus; bolsons." (Fenneman, 1930).

The general locations and boundaries of these are graphically shown on the sketch map.

Although the areas to be examined during the conference are only a small part of that included in the map, the initial stop will be a vantage point on Lookout Mountain. From there a spectacular view extends for scores of miles in all directions. A lecture on the regional geology at this point will include remarks on most of the physiographic provinces and sections shown on the map and listed above.

The immediate area of the conference is mainly in the Sacramento section of the Basin and Range province. However, excursions will travel as far east as the western margin of the Pecos Valley section of the Great Plains (at the junction of Rio Bonito and Rio Ruidoso) and into the margin of the Mexican Highlands section of the Basin and Range province on the west.

The thriving village of Ruidoso is in the eastern foothills of the great Sierra Blanca volcanic pile that rises above the Sacramento Mountains to the south. An intrusive body of major size, the Capitan Mountains, lies northeast of the Sierra Blanca. The highest point on this mass rises almost 3,500 feet to an elevation of 10,230 feet above the adjacent uplands.

The route of the caravan on the first day of the trip is first southwestward and traverses the north plunging front of the Sacramento Mountains into the Tularosa Basin, a bolson in the Mexican Highlands section of the Basin and Range province. A stop will be made in the vicinity of Carrizozo to examine the land forms that constitute the surface of The Malpais, a Recent lava flow. During the remainder of the first day the route crosses the northern and eastern flanks of the Sierra Blanca volcanic pile.

The entire second day will be spent on the back slope of the Sacramento Mountains. Many interesting karst features, developed in both the San Andres Limestone and the Yeso Formation, will be seen along the route. Visible also are two high erosional surfaces, the Sacramento plain and the Diamond A plain.

The Sacramento plain is the uppermost of these surfaces and is essentially the dissected back slope of the Sacramento Mountains eastward from the crest in the vicinity of Cloudcroft. It is believed to be correlative either with the surface of the High Plains (Mescalero) or with the pre-Ogalalla surface.

The Diamond A plain, in the eastern part of the Sacramento backslope, is approximately 250 feet below the Sacramento surface. These two surfaces appear to merge to the west as the Sacramento escarpment is approached.

On the third and final day of the conference, the route traverses the Jicarillo Mountains, a group of physiographic domes that are the results of intrusion of igneous materials. This area resembles both geomorphically and structurally the classic Little Rocky Mountains of east-central Montana.

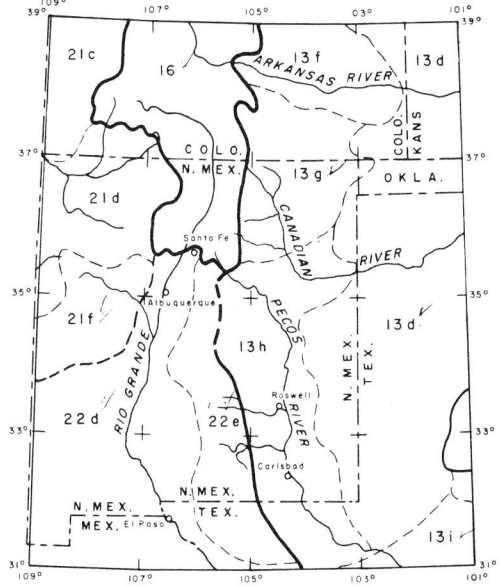

Figure 1. — Physiographic divisions of southeastern New Mexico and adjacent areas (Adapted from Fenneman, 1930).

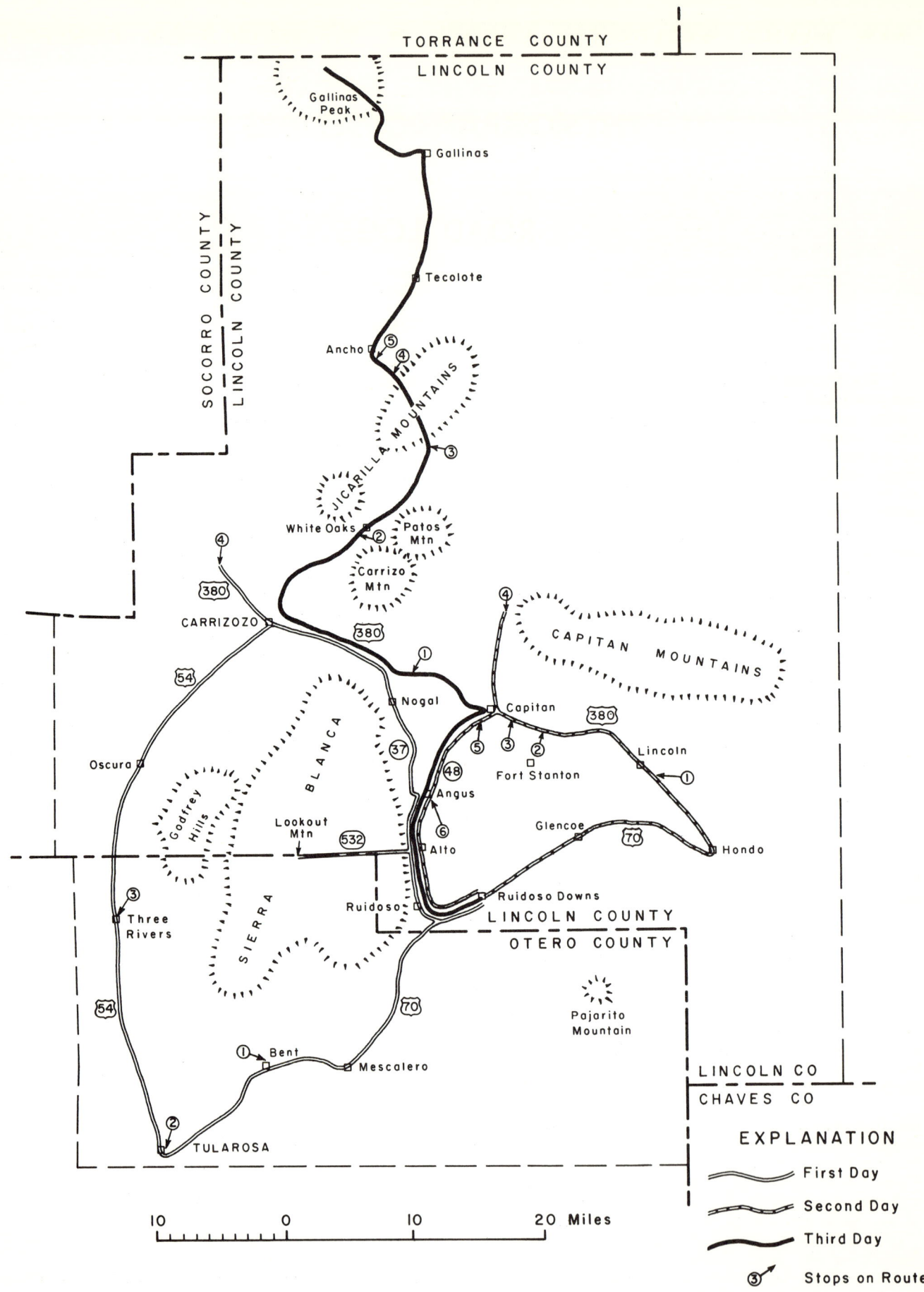

Map showing route of 15th field conference

NEW MEXICO GEOLOGICAL SOCIETY • FIFTEENTH FIELD CONFERENCE

ROAD LOGS

INTRODUCTION

The Ruidoso Country Field Conference road logs are composed and arranged in such a way that they will be useful not only for the conference itself, but also for later visitors to the area. Thus a summary or abstract of planned remarks is provided for some of the caravan stops and each log is presented as an independent unit so that many different route arrangements are possible without extensive cross-references.

All available geologic data relative to the conference area were considered in preparing the logs, including several previously developed road logs as indicated in the references.

The Road Logging Committee is especially indebted to Robert W. Bradley, Jr., for making available an unpublished geological compilation of the area; to George O. Bachman and Walter A. Mourant for assistance in the field and partial checking of the logs; and to A. J. Budding for his contribution to the logging program.

CARL ULVOG, Chairman
Road Logging Committee

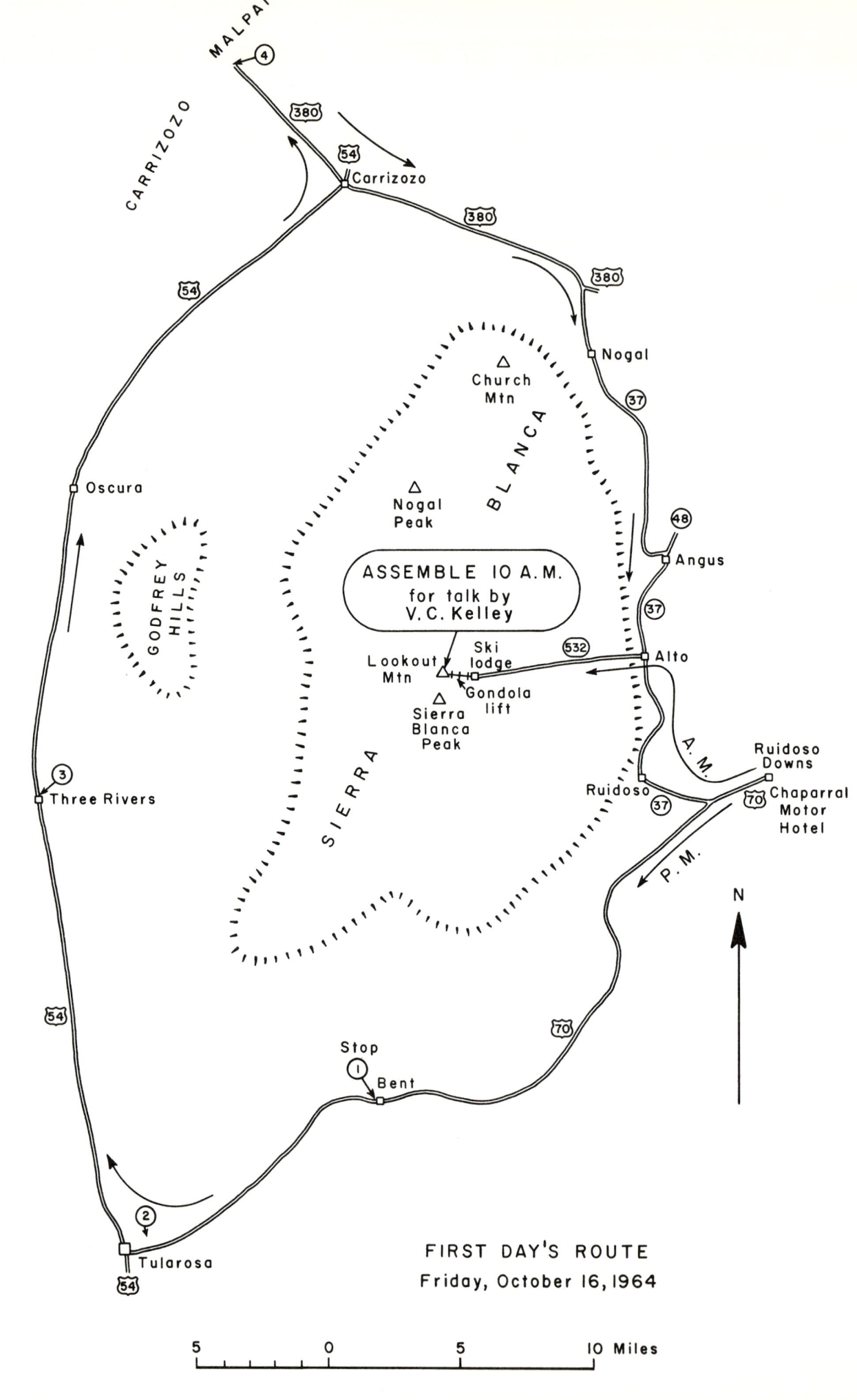

NEW MEXICO GEOLOGICAL SOCIETY • FIFTEENTH FIELD CONFERENCE

Road Logs from Ruidoso to Sierra Blanca Ski Resort Headquarters, Tularosa, Carrizozo, Malpais, and Return

FIRST DAY, FRIDAY, OCTOBER 16, 1964

Distance of Travel: 170.7 miles.
Starting Time: 10:00 a.m.
Assembly Point: On top of Lookout Mountain.

SUMMARY

Conferees will travel individually during the morning of this, the first day of the trip, to Sierra Blanca Ski Resort Headquarters. From there they will take the gondola lift to the top of Lookout Mountain where the field trip will begin with a panoramic view of the Ruidoso Country. At 10:00 a.m. Dr. V. C. Kelley of the University of New Mexico will speak on the regional geology from this point. Then the conferees will return to Ruidoso in time to assemble at the Chaparral Motor Hotel at 1:00 p.m. for the afternoon trip. They will travel in a caravan southwest from Ruidoso on U.S. 70 for closer examinations of structures and stratigraphy, older formations being considered first. Stop 1 is at Bent dome to study Abo in contact with Permian-Pennsylvanian sandstones. (A small inlier of Precambrian mapped by Bachman, 1960, will be discussed here, although the caravan will not visit that feature.) From this point, the trip moves to the most southwesterly locality scheduled for the conference, Stop 2, at the Laborcita bioherms near Tularosa. The remainder of the first day will be devoted to encircling the western and northern ends of the Sierra Blanca uplift and viewing Permian, Triassic, Cretaceous and Tertiary formations. Stop 3, at Three Rivers, affords an excellent view of the great Tertiary igneous complex and other regional structural features. The famed 44-mile long Carrizozo Malpais will be visited at Stop 4, after which the caravan will return to Ruidoso for the night.

Road Log

From Ruidoso to Sierra Blanca Ski Resort Headquarters

Carl Ulvog, Sam Thompson, III, and Tommy B. Thompson
with a note by V. C. Kelley

Note: This road log is for the convenience of those conferees who wish to study the geology from the junction of U.S. 70 and State 37 in Ruidoso to the Ski Resort Headquarters.

Total Mileage

0.0   **Ruidoso, New Mexico, Junction of U.S. 70 and N.M. 37. Proceed west on N.M. 37.**
       0.5

0.5   Slow. Traffic warning light overhead. Sierra Blanca Peak at 1:00.
       1.4

1.9   Side road on left to Carrizo Canyon. Follow N.M. 37.
       0.5

2.4   Yeso exposed in hill on left.
       0.8

3.2   Quarry in Yeso on left.
       0.2

3.4   **Road junction. Turn Right on N.M. 37.**
       0.3

3.7   Road bed is located approximately on northeast-southwest trending fault. San Andres and Yeso upthrown to east, Mesaverde downthrown to west. Progressively younger beds crop out along upthrown side of fault until only Mesaverde is displaced at a point 12 miles to the north-northeast.
       0.3

4.0   Mesaverde exposed on left.
       0.7

4.7   Ruidoso Ranger Station on left.
       0.1

4.8   Road cut on left in Mesaverde.
       0.1

4.9   Sierra Blanca Volcanics (andesite) on left.

11

	1.9
6.8	Side road on left to Alpine Village. Continue on N.M. 37. Road cuts in Mesaverde Formation and Tertiary dikes for next 6 miles ahead.
	0.3
7.1	Volcanic breccia intersected by dikes in road cut.
	0.6
7.7	Road cut in Mesaverde. Transitional zone of purple shales, sandstones and carbonaceous material intruded by Tertiary dikes.
	0.1
7.8	Small northeasterly-trending fault zone with Mesaverde sandstone in juxtaposition with Sierra Blanca Volcanics. The sandstone is cut by several northeasterly-trending mafic dikes.
	0.2
8.0	Sierra Blanca Volcanics (breccia) intersected by dikes on left.
	0.4
8.4	Mesaverde intersected by dikes.
	0.3
8.7	Bridge crossing Eagle Creek. Entering Alto, New Mexico.
	0.1
8.8	Historical Marker.
	"Mon Jeau Lookout, 12 miles. Elevation 10,000 ft. Offers one of the most scenic views in entire southwest. Used by Forest Rangers during fire season. Observation deck open to visitors at all times. Parking space at bottom of lookout tower."
	0.05
8.85	Alto, New Mexico. Slow. Prepare to turn left.
	0.05
8.9	**Junction N.M. 532 and N.M. 37. Turn left (west) on N.M. 532.**
	0.2
9.1	Mafic dike in the road cut on the right.
	0.3
9.4	Road cut in Cub Mountain Formation and Tertiary dikes.
	0.4
9.8	Road junction. Continue straight ahead on N.M. 532. Road on right to Villa Madonna and Mon Jeau Lookout. Sierra Blanca Peak (12,003') at 12:00. It is part of the Three Rivers stock which ranges in composition from monzonite, to syenite, to granite.
	0.6
10.4	Begin series of road cuts in Tertiary intrusives of Sierra Blanca Volcanics (andesite).
	1.2
11.6	Side road on right to Eagle Creek. Continue on pavement.
	0.6
12.2	Side road on left to Mescalero Recreation Area. Continue straight ahead up hill. End of pavement.
	0.1
12.3	Road cut in red and purple, coarse-grained porphyry with large white plagioclase phenocrysts.
	0.3
12.6	Volcanic breccia on left.
	0.3
12.9	Road cut in agglomerate.
	0.1
13.0	Dioritic dike intersecting volcanic breccia.
	0.2
13.2	Excellent exposure of volcanic breccia showing the range in size of breccia fragments.
	0.6
13.8	Sill on right.
	0.4
14.2	Oak Grove Picnic Grounds on right.
	0.2
14.4	Breccia and tuffaceous units showing folding effects due to intrusive action of the Three Rivers stock.
	0.9
15.3	Contact of Three Rivers stock with volcanic breccia. The remainder of this road log will be in intrusive rock.
	0.2
15.5	Mon Jeau Lookout at 3:00.
	0.4
15.9	Mon Jeau Peak at 2:30 across Eagle Creek Canyon. The peak is formed from the Bonita Lake stock. At 11:30 in the canyon is an exposure of the northeastern corner of the Three Rivers stock.

Sierra Blanca Peak (alt. 12,003 ft.) from Ruidoso. U.S. Forest Service, Southwestern Region photograph.

	0.5
16.4	Pajarito Peak on skyline at 9:30.
	1.1
17.5	Cirque on northeast side of Sierra Blanca Peak at 9:00.
	0.7
18.2	Capitan Mountains and Carrizo Mountain on skyline to right (north).
	0.5
18.7	Sierra Blanca Peak at 11:00 with cirque on northeast flank. The north fork of Rio Ruidoso heads into the cirque and flows into the canyon on the left.
	1.8
20.5	Observation Peak (gondola lift) at 9:00.
	1.3
21.8	Sierra Blanca Ski Resort headquarters, elevation 9,700 feet. It is owned and operated by the Mescalero Apache tribe. **PARK AS DIRECTED BY FLAGMAN.** Take tramway to the top of Lookout Peak where Dr. Vincent C. Kelley, Chairman of the Department of Geology, University of New Mexico will give a discussion on the geology of the area at 10:00 a.m. Elevation of Lookout Mountain (near top of gondola lift): 11,400 feet.

The Ruidoso-Carrizozo region is dominated physiographically by Sierra Blanca Peak, the highest mountain of southern or central New Mexico. It surmounts one of two large acidic stocks which intrude related early Tertiary flows and breccias, termed the Sierra Blanca Volcanics. The volcanics aggregate more than 3,000 feet in thickness and were erupted on the site of the previously subsided and eroded Laramide Sierra Blanca basin. To the west of the Sierra Blanca eminence is the long Tularosa-Claunch-Estancia depression. To the west of this depression is a line of uplifts including the San Andres and Oscura tilted fault blocks and the Chupadera Mesa structural bench. To the east of Sierra Blanca is a broad upwarp, herein termed the Mescalero arch, that separates the Tularosa-Sierra Blanca-Claunch sags from the regional Pecos slope into the Delaware basin. This arch approximately follows the crest of the old buried Permian Pedernal Mountains. Also in near coincidence with the Mescalero arch and the old Pedernal Mountains is a northerly-trending group of intrusives, herein termed the Lincoln County Porphyry Belt. — V. C. Kelley

Road Log From Ruidoso To Tularosa

By Carl Ulvog and Sam Thompson, III, with notes by George O. Bachman and Carel Otte

Note: Although conferees will assemble at the Chaparrel Motor Hotel at 1:00 p.m. and travel in a caravan for the remainder of the day, this road log doesn't start until the junction of the U.S. 70 and N.M. 37 is reached on the outskirts of Ruidoso.

Total Mileage	
0.0	**Ruidoso, New Mexico, Junction of U.S. 70 and N.M. 37. Proceed southwest on U.S. 70 which here follows Cherokee Bill Canyon.**
	0.4
0.4	**Junction of U.S. 70 and N.M. 37 (west branch). Continue on U.S. 70.** Valley cuts the Yeso Formation which is overlain by Glorieta and San Andres in the adjacent hills.
	0.9
1.3	Quarry for road material on right (north) side of highway is in the Yeso Formation.
	0.2
1.5	Yeso exposed in road cut.
	0.3
1.8	Leave Lincoln County, enter Otero County.
	0.1
1.9	Historical Marker: "Mescalero Apache Indian Reservation, East Boundary. The Mescalero Apaches, last tribe in the United States to lay down arms, are now a friendly people, living much as they did centuries ago. Their reservation covers 472,320 acres."
	0.2
2.1	Yeso exposed in road cut on right (north); Bear Canyon on left.
	1.2
3.3	Squaw Canyon on left.
	0.4
3.7	San Andres exposure on left.
	0.5
4.2	Road cut in Yeso.
	0.4
4.6	Side road on left (south) in Fence Canyon. U.S. 70 crosses north-south fault.

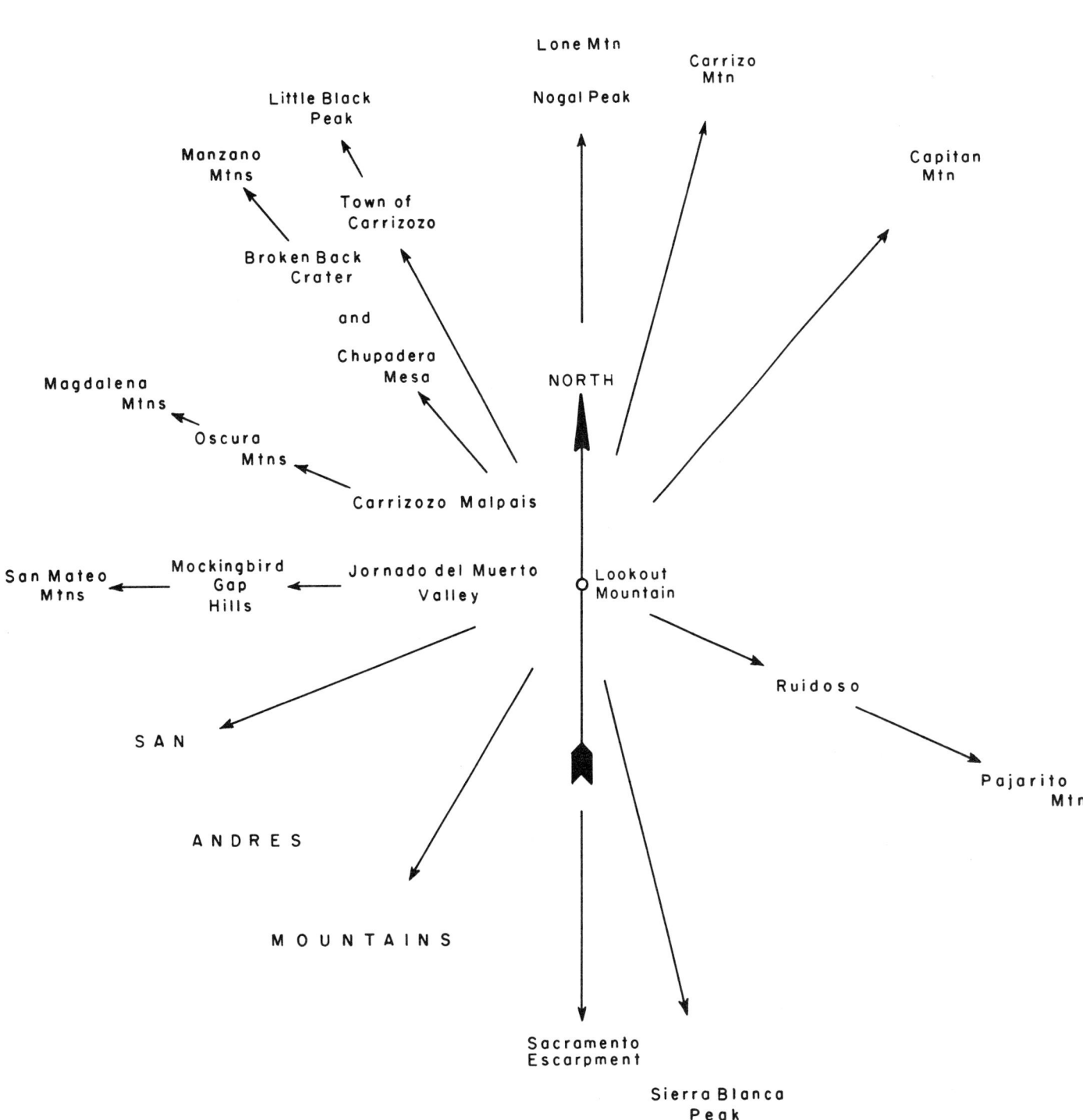

Panoramic index of features seen from Lookout Mountain

	0.1
4.7	Small block of Yeso and Glorieta on upthrown side of fault exposed in road cut on right.
	0.2
4.9	Road cut in San Andres.
	0.4
5.3	Road cut in lower San Andres.
	0.4
5.7	Side road on right. Stay on U.S. 70.
	0.2
5.9	Road cut in San Andres.
	1.1
7.0	Road cut in San Andres.
	0.1
7.1	Side road on right. Stay on U.S. 70 which is now entering Dark Canyon.
	0.1
7.2	North-dipping San Andres exposed on right.
	0.2
7.4	Folded San Andres exposed on left.
	0.3
7.7	San Andres exposed on left.
	0.1
7.8	Road cut in San Andres. Historical Marker.
	"Sierra Blanca (White Mountain) El. 12,003 feet. This great peak easternmost of the west basin-range structures, is the southernmost in the United States towering into the Arctic-Alpine Life Zone. In summer is covered with flowers which attract hummingbirds by the thousands. Sierra Blanca is in the Mescalero Apache Indian Reservation. Elevation at this point is 7,440 feet."
	0.7
8.5	Road cut in San Andres.
	0.7
9.2	Apache Summit. Elevation 7,700 feet. U.S. 70 descends into Tularosa Canyon.
	0.1
9.3	Road cuts in Yeso for next mile ahead.
	2.2
11.5	Road cut in Yeso.
	0.6
12.1	Side road on left leads to Camp Geronimo, privately owned.
	0.1
12.2	Side road on left in Goat Canyon, leads to Rinconada. U.S. 70 crosses the San Andres-Yeso contact.
	0.8
13.0	San Andres cap on ridge at 12:00.
	1.0
14.0	Road cut in San Andres dolomite.
	0.8
14.8	Road cut in Yeso.
	0.6
15.4	Quarry for road material in San Andres dolomite.
	0.6
16.0	Road crosses approximate Yeso-San Andres contact.
	0.2
16.2	**Junction of U.S. 70 and N.M. 26. Stay on U.S. 70.** N.M. 26 leads to the town of Mescalero, Headquarters of Mescalero Apache Indian Reservation. Church at 11:00 was built by Father Albert Braun and several Mescalero Apache Indian helpers as a memorial to Americans killed in World War I. Local stone was used by them and after 20 years of labor the church was dedicated in 1940. Highway traverses Yeso for the next nine miles. San Andres Formation tops adjacent hills.
	0.4
16.6	Overpass. N.M. 26 on left to Cloudcroft.
	0.5
17.1	Junction with road from Mescalero. Continue on U.S. 70.
	0.5
17.6	Historical Marker on left.
	"Blazer's Mill. One of the first fights of the Lincoln County War occurred here on April 5, 1878, when several men of the McSween faction headed by Dick Brewer and Billy the Kid attempted to arrest Buckshot Roberts. In the battle that followed, Roberts and Brewer were killed. George Coe and John Middleton were wounded."

	0.3	
17.9		Big Chief Store on right. Canyon wall ahead has poor exposure of Yeso with Glorieta and San Andres on rim.
	0.5	
18.4		Yeso red beds exposed in canyon on right (north).
	0.3	
18.7		**Road junction. Stay on U.S. 70.**
	0.5	
19.2		Sawmill on left.
	1.0	
20.2		Junction of U.S. 70 and dirt road on left (south) immediately east of Mescalero Indian Reservation.

OPTIONAL SIDE TRIP

0.0	Turn left (south) on dirt road.
0.1	
0.1	Gate
0.1	
0.2	Gate. Bridge crossing Tularosa Creek. Sharp right turn up hill.
0.1	
0.3	Abandoned house. Turn right (west) around shed and follow road back to left. Cross arroyo.
0.1	
0.4	STOP. Precambrian granite exposed in prospect pit about ¼ mile to southwest. Quartzite exposure about ¼ mile to southeast. Retrace route to U.S. 70; allow for side trip mileage.

	0.7	
20.9		Exposure of Pennsylvanian-Permian(?) sandstone in Tularosa Canyon on left side of the highway. These outcrops are on the north side of Bent dome.
	0.2	
21.1		Road cut in Pennsylvanian-Permian(?) sandstone with solution-channel conglomerate at top. Contact with with overlying Abo can be observed on north side of this hill.
	0.3	
21.4		Good exposure of Yeso on west limb of Bent dome at 10:00. **Slow, prepare to turn right.**
	0.1	
21.5		**Road with gate to Mauer Ranch on right.**

SIDE TRIP

0.0	**Turn right (north) off U.S. 70 through Mauer Ranch Gate.**
0.1	
0.1	House on left, continue straight ahead.
0.2	
0.3	**STOP NO. 1. PARK AS DIRECTED BY FLAGMAN.** Bent dome. Abandoned school house; end of road. Conferees will walk about one-quarter mile southeast of the parking area to gray sandstone exposed in a road cut. Sandstone is believed to be a facies of Pennsylvania or Permian (Laborcita Formation). Maroon colored Abo Formation rests on gray sandstone. Note cobbles of quartzite, and rhyolite porphyry at the base of the Abo. Jointed quartzite and granite believed to be of Precambrian age are exposed in arroyos about one mile southeast of this stop. — George O. Bachman **Retrace route back to highway; allow for side trip mileage.**

	0.5	
22.0		Post Office, Bent, New Mexico. Nogal Canyon road on left.

OPTIONAL SIDE TRIP TO VIRGINIA MINE

0.0	Turn left (south) from U.S. 70 onto Nogal Canyon Road.
0.2	
0.2	Gate. Turn left (east).
0.6	
0.8	Road fork; bear left (northeast).
0.2	
1.0	STOP. Bridge. Virginia mine at right. Retrace route to highway and allow for side trip mileage.

	0.4	
22.4		White Sands in the Tularosa Valley at 11:00 o'clock with the San Andres Mountains on the sky line.
	0.3	
22.7		Exposure of Yeso and San Andres at 4:00 and 7:00.

	0.5
23.2	Historical Marker: "Round Mountain. Near the conical peak to the south a small group of Spanish settlers and 7 U.S. Cavalrymen on April 17, 1868, repelled an attack by 200 Indians to close hostilities in this area. Today the event is commemorated annually in Tularosa by Indians and residents alike."
	0.9
24.1	Approximate Yeso-Abo contact. Small butte capped by Yeso dolomite at 9:00. Trail is used by worshippers in ascending to cross at top of butte. High peak in background is Round Mountain.
	0.9
25.0	Bridge crossing Tularosa Canyon. Peat interlaminated with caliche (Quaternary) in canyon walls and in road cut on left.
	0.1
25.1	Abo red beds on left (east). Good exposure of Yeso and San Andres on skyline.
	0.3
25.4	Panoramic view of White Sands and Organ-San Andres Mountains from 11:00 to 2:00. Hembrillo Canyon at 1:00.
	1.4
26.8	Road cut in Abo.
	0.9
27.7	Road cut in Abo.
	0.4
28.1	Tertiary intrusive (diorite?) into Abo on left.
	1.2
29.3	Road cut in Abo.
	1.4
30.7	Abo-Laborcita contact at 3:00.
	1.1
31.8	Side road. Laborcita (Bursum equivalent) in low hill on left.
	0.4
32.2	Water tank on left rests on Laborcita.
	0.2
32.4	**Paved road on left. Follow U.S. 70.**
	0.4
32.8	Divided highway. Entering Tularosa, New Mexico, Elevation 4,520 feet.
	0.4
33.2	**SLOW, PREPARE TO TURN RIGHT.**
	0.2
33.4	**Service station on right. Turn RIGHT (north) on paved road for Tularosa bioherms.**
	0.3
33.7	Bridge crossing Tularosa Creek. Side road, continue straight ahead.
	0.6
34.3	**Road intersection. Turn right.** Laborcita on ridges ahead. Biohermal mounds at 11:00 to 12:00.
	0.3
34.6	Cattle guard. Sierra Blanca Peak at 10:00.
	0.4
35.0	**STOP No. 2. Turn RIGHT on side road and follow directions of flagman for parking.**

From Laborcita Canyon to Domingo Canyon three miles to the north, the upper part of the Holder and the lower two-thirds of the Laborcita Formations form the frontal escarpment. The contact, which in this area is marked by a thin sandy limestone, is about half way up the escarpment. Note persistent limestone markers and relative uniformity of the lithofacies. Certain lithologic sequences appear in a cyclical repetition above and below the contact. Although laterally uniform open marine conditions prevailed in this area, many fluctuations in sea level must have occurred. These conditions persisted throughout Late Pennsylvanian and Early Permian time in this area.

A slightly discordant igneous sill occurs near the mouth of Domingo Canyon. The fine-grained acidic intrusive reaches a thickness of about 200 feet. This sill and the decreasing displacement northward along the frontal system of normal faults prevent the lower portion of the Laborcita Formation from being exposed in the area north of Domingo Canyon. — Carel Otte.

Retrace route to highway. Turn LEFT (west) and allow for mileage to and from parking area.

	0.6
35.6	Cattle guard.
	0.2
35.8	Road junction. Continue straight ahead.
	1.1
36.9	Junction of "Laborcita bioherm" road with U.S. 54. **End of road log from Ruidoso to Tularosa. Field trip participants go to the next road log.**

NEW MEXICO GEOLOGICAL SOCIETY • FIFTEENTH FIELD CONFERENCE

Road Log From Tularosa To Carrizozo

By Carl Ulvog and Sam Thompson, III,
with notes by Tommy B. Thompson, R. H. Weber, and W. A. Mourant

Total Mileage	
0.0	Junction of U.S. 54 with side road from Laborcita bioherms. Proceed north on U.S. 54.
	0.8
0.8	Crest of railroad overpass. San Andres Mountains at 8:00 to 12:30; Mockingbird Gap Hills at 12:30; Oscura Mountains at 1:00.
	1.1
1.9	Bridge crossing arroyo. Sierra Blanca Peak on skyline at 2:00. Exposures of Laborcita, Abo, Yeso, and San Andres in middle distance at 3:00. Series of bridge crossings ahead.
	4.0
5.9	Bridge crossing arroyo. Railroad bridge on right. San Andres limestone with interbedded gypsum in gap at 2:00; San Andres caps ridge at 3:00.
	10.5
16.4	Historical marker.
	(South side)
	"Sierra Blanca (White Mountain) El. 12,003 feet. This great peak, easternmost of the west basin-range structures, is the southernmost in the United States towering into the Artic-Alpine Life Zone. In summer is covered with flowers which attract hummingbirds by the thousands. Sierra Blanca is in the Mescalero Apache Indian Reservation. Elevation at this point is 4,570 feet.
	(North side)
	"Three Rivers Petroglyphs. A mile-long array of pictures pecked into the solid rock walls of a volcanic ridge. They include both geometric and animal forms. Most were made by prehistoric Indians. May be contemporary with nearby Mimbres site, dating from 900-1,000 A.D. Follow road three miles due east."
	0.1
16.5	**STOP NO. 3. THREE RIVERS. Park on the right side of highway as directed by flagmen.**
	Panoramic view: Rose Peak in Godfrey Hills (Tertiary igneous rocks) at 2:00. Petroglyphs on lamprophyre sill on low hills in middle distance at 2:30. Sierra Blanca Peak (intrusive complex) at 3:00. Black Mountain (southwest extension of Sierra Blanca complex) at 4:00. Sacramento Escarpment (folded Paleozoics) at 6:00. Organ Mountains (Tertiary intrusives) at 7:30. San Andres Mountains (west-dipping Paleozoics overlying Precambrian) at 8:00 to 10:00. Salinas Peak capped with Tertiary rhyolite sill at 9:00. Sheep Mountain, Sly Gap and Lady Bug Peak at 9:30. Mockingbird Gap and Mockingbird Gap Hills at 10:00. Oscura Mountains (east-dipping Paleozoics) at 10:30. Phillips Hills (east-dipping San Andres) at 11:30.
	The Godfrey Hills consist of volcanic rocks which overlie the Mesaverde Group and the McRae (Cub Mountain of Bodine, 1956) Formation.
	Black Mountain is a north-northeasterly trending anticline which plunges into the Sierra Blanca basin. The Mesaverde Group forms much of the high ridge of Black Mountain, and it is complexly invaded by dikes and sills. The Black Mountain anticline plunges beneath the Sierra Blanca Volcanics which consist of volcanic breccias and andesites. Sierra Blanca Peak is formed by the Three Rivers stock which intrudes the Sierra Blanca Volcanics. The volcanics along the southern part of the basin dip to the north indicating some subsidence of the basin after the volcanic activity. — Tommy B. Thompson
	1.1
17.6	Bridge crossing arroyo. Carrizozo Malpais in Tularosa Valley at 9:00 to 10:00.
	2.4
20.0	Exposure of Dakota Sandstone, underlain by Chinle, on low hill at 3:00.
	0.5
20.5	Dakota Sandstone on left.
	0.7
21.2	Leave Otero County, enter Lincoln County. Rose Peak in Godfrey Hills at 2:00.
	3.3
24.5	Culvert. Military observation post on Phillips Peak at 9:00. Oscura Mountains on skyline from 10:00 to 11:00.
	2.4
26.9	Side road on left to military observation post. Continue straight ahead on U.S. 54.
	0.9
27.8	**Oscura, New Mexico.** Ridge of Mesaverde Sandstone overlain by Tertiary sill at 1:00. Cub Mountain the rounded peak on the skyline at 2:00. Nogal Peak, a Tertiary igneous complex is the sharp point on the skyline at 2:30.

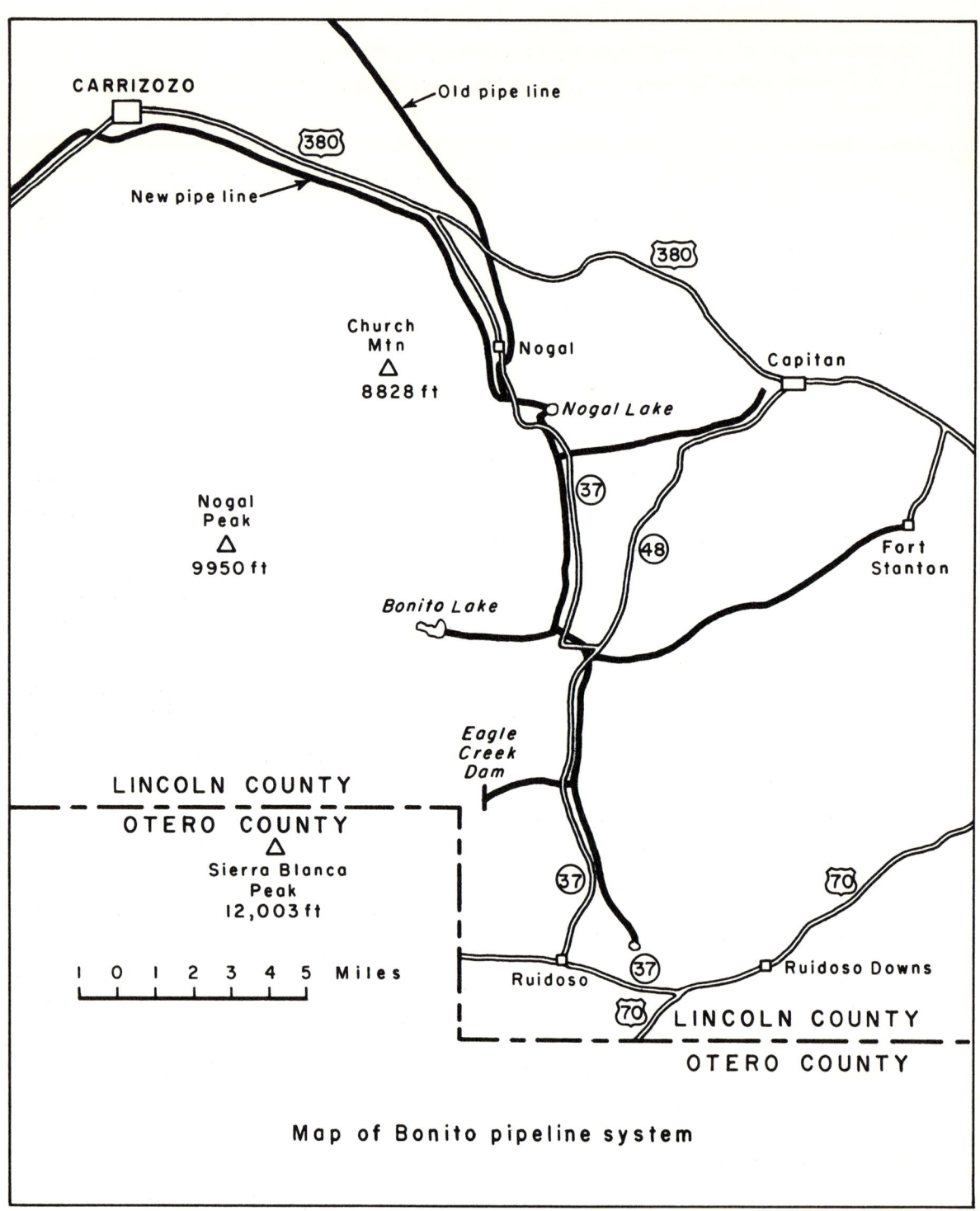

Map of Bonito pipeline system

The old pipeline was built to supply the railroad with soft water for the locomotives to replace the hard water from wells which caused frothing and scaling in the boilers. After conversion to diesel locomotives the railroad no longer needed the pipeline and in 1956 a new pipeline was built to supply Bonito water to Alamogordo and Holloman Air Development Center. At Holloman, water is used as a brake for rocket sleds which are used for experiments on human reactions to acceleration and deceleration. It was at Holloman that Colonel John B. Stapp rode 632 miles per hour on a sled that used water in its braking operation. — W. A. Mourant.

	0.1	
27.9		Side road on left (west) to Oscura Range Camp, White Sands Missile Range. Stay on U.S. 54. Dakota Sandstone dip slope on low hills in middle distance at 9:00 to 11:00.

OPTIONAL SIDE TRIP

	0.0	Junction of U.S. 54 with side road to Oscura Range Camp. Proceed west on dirt road.
	0.9	
	0.9	Cattle guard. Mockingbird Gap at 12:00.
	1.0	
	1.9	Cattle guard. Phillips Hills at 10:00 to 11:00 consist of east-dipping San Andres Formation with narrow band of Yeso at western foot.
	0.4	
	2.3	Passing south end of Bull Gap Ridge. Dakota dip slope at 3:00. Contact with underlying Triassic red beds exposed in west-facing scarp of cuesta.
	0.3	
	2.6	STOP. Road curves to right. Dakota Sandstone with well-developed desert varnish on hill on left side of road ahead. A short walk to the right (north) will permit examination of an undifferentiated sequence of Triassic beds in the western face of Bull Gap Ridge, overlain nonconformably by the Dakota Sandstone. Triassic rocks are prevailingly red to maroon mudstones, siltstones, and sandstones. The Dakota consists of white to buff, friable, coarse- to medium-grained quartz sandstone containing lenses and scattered pebbles and granules of quartzite and sparser chert in the lower portion. Upper beds are thinner bedded and finer grained. Pleistocene deposits exposed in arroyo banks at the southeastern end of Bull Gap Ridge include caliche-capped terraces, spring-deposited travertine aprons and gypsiferous, sandy silts. The latter contains local lenses of minute gastropods, pelecypods, diatoms, and sparse vertebrate remains. The local structure is controlled by the southward-plunging nose of an anticline, of which Bull Gap Ridge forms the eastern limb. The western limb appears to be truncated by a photogeologic fault with Quaternary displacement extending northeastward from the western foot of the Phillips Hills. Its trace is largely concealed to the north by alluvial slope deposits.

	1.3	
29.2		Abandoned coal mine in Mesaverde on right. Lamprophyre sill caps Malagro Hill above mine.
	0.7	
29.9		Begin series of road cuts in Mesaverde.
	1.8	
31.7		Road cut in Mesaverde with Quaternary channel containing Tertiary igneous material.
	0.8	
32.5		Bridge crossing arroyo.
	0.1	
32.6		Tertiary sill at 2:00.
	2.2	
34.8		Oscura Mountains on skyline at 7:00 to 9:00. San Andres and Yeso on Carrizozo anticline in middle distance at 9:00 to 10:00. Carrizozo Malpais on valley floor at 9:00 to 11:00. Little Black Peak at 10:30. Gallinas Mountains, Tecolote Hills, Jicarilla Mountains and Lone Mountain on skyline at 10:30 to 12:00. Carrizo Peak laccolith at 12:30. Willow Hill, capped by sill, at 1:30. Cub Mountain with Nogal Peak in background at 2:00; Sierra Blanca Peak at 3:00; Rose Peak at 4:00.
	2.0	
36.8		Bridge crossing arroyo. Willow Hill at 2:00. Cub Mountain Formation exposed in gap at 2:30. Cub Mountain at 3:00.
	5.9	
42.7		**City limits, Carrizozo, New Mexico.** Historical Marker: "Carrizozo. Founded 1905. Population 1,546. Elevation 5,425 feet. The crossroads of history. Northeast is the ghost town of White Oaks, a once booming mining camp where Emerson Haush lived and laid the scene of his book 'Hearts Desire.' Famous names like Billy the Kid, Pat Garrett and Lew Wallace are closely associated with the area."
	0.5	
42.2		Highway curves to left.
	0.1	
42.3		Fork. Bear RIGHT on U.S. 54.
	0.5	
43.8		**Junction of U.S. 54 with U.S. 380. Carrizozo, New Mexico. End of road log from Tularosa to Carrizozo. Field trip participants go to next road log.**

NEW MEXICO GEOLOGICAL SOCIETY • FIFTEENTH FIELD CONFERENCE

Road Log From Carrizozo To Malpais
By Carl Ulvog and Sam Thompson, III

Total Mileage		
0.0	**Carrizozo, New Mexico. Junction of U.S. 54 and U.S. 380. Proceed west on U.S. 380.** Broken Back Crater (early Quaternary cinder cone) on skyline at 12:30.	
	0.5	
0.5	Side road on left. Continue on U.S. 380.	
	0.4	
0.9	Carrizozo Village limits. Oscura Mountains on skyline at 10:00 to 11:00. Carrizozo anticline in middle distance at 10:00 to 12:30. Carrizozo Malpais in valley at 11:00 to 2:00. Little Black Peak (vent for basalt flow) at 1:30.	
	1.6	
2.5	Inactive copper mill on left.	
	0.8	
3.3	Bridge crossing arroyo.	
	0.1	
3.4	Road cut in Mancos Shale and Tertiary trachytic syenite sill.	
	0.1	
3.5	Edge of basalt flow.	
	0.3	
3.8	Kipuka (island surrounded by lava) of Dakota sandstone at 9:00.	
	0.8	
4.6	Pressure ridge on right.	
	1.0	
5.6	**STOP NO. 4. PARK AS DIRECTED BY FLAGMEN.**	

Historical Marker on right:

"Malpais. This great lava flow is one of the most — perhaps the most recent in the United States. Some of the formations appear as though they had bubbled forth only yesterday."

The Carrizozo Malpais extends southwestward along the floor of the Tularosa Valley for a distance of 44 miles, ranging in width from about one-half mile to more than five miles. At least two Recent flows of alkali olivine basalt issued from a vent marked by Little Black Peak, an intact cinder cone 85 feet in height visible six miles north of this point. The two flow units exposed two miles south of the highway total 162 feet in thickness. Features characteristic of fluidal pahoehoe flows in the immediate vicinity of this stop include highly vesicular, ropy flow surfaces with a glassy crust, tumuli (pressure domes), and collapse structures. A good example of a linear squeeze-up may be seen in a fissure a short distance northwest of the parking area. Pressure ridges are less prominently developed here than along the margins of the flow field and in the narrows 10 to 15 miles down the valley. The malpais provides an island microcosm for a varied and, in some respects, distinctive fauna and flora. Rodents and reptiles are notably melanistic, contrasting sharply with their pale-colored kin in the White Sands dune regions to the south. Deer and bear find the tortured surface of the malpais far more hospitable than it appears to human eyes.

A sweeping view of the Sierra Blanca on the skyline to the southeast and south-southeast highlights the panorama of other geologic features seen bordering the valley. The chain of hills a few miles south of Carrizozo include Willow Hill, Cub Mountain, and Chavez Mountain capped by alkali syenites intrusives into the Mesaverde Group and Cub Mountain Formation. The broad slope extending westward from these hills is underlain by eastward-dipping beds of the Mesaverde and Mancos. Due eastward is the domical intrusive mass of Carrizozo Mountain (syenite porphyry), north of which is Lone Mountain (quartz syenite to granite) girded at the foot by Permian, Triassic, and Cretaceous beds that dip radially away from the intrusive contact. The inactive gold camp of White Oaks lies in the intervening major canyon. The highway to the northwest ascends a dip slope of San Andres limestone and gypsum beds in the eastern limb of the Carrizozo anticline. Standard of Texas' No. 1 Heard-Federal oil test, on the crest of the structure, penetrated an abnormal thickness of 4,265 feet of Yeso Formation, of which 900 feet was salt beds. — R. H. Weber.

End of road log from Carrizozo to Malpais. Field trip participants retrace route to highway and go to next log.

Road Log From Carrizozo To Ruidoso

By Carl Ulvog and Sam Thompson, IIII, with notes and photographs by W. A. Mourant

Total Mileage	
0.0	**Carrizozo, New Mexico. Junction of U.S. 380 and U.S. 54. Proceed southeast on U.S. 380.**
	0.1
0.1	Crest of railroad overpass.
	0.2
0.3	Side road on right. Panoramic view. Lone Mountain at 9:00; Mesaverde overlying Tertiary sill in low rounded hills at 9:30; Carrizo Peak at 10:00; Tucson Mountain at 10:30; Vera Cruz Mountain at 11:00; Gaylord Peak at 1:00; Nogal Peak at 2:00; Cub Mountain at 2:30; Rose Peak at 3:00.
	0.4
0.7	Side road on right to Carrizozo Country Club.
	3.9
4.6	Side road on right. Carrizo Peak, a monzonite laccolith, at 9:00; Tucson Mountain, folded Mesaverde, at 10:00; Vera Cruz intrusive at 11:00; Church Mountain, Tertiary igneous complex, at 2:00; Tertiary extrusives with dikes and sills at 2:00 to 3:00.
	3.6
8.2	**Junction of U.S. 380 and N.M. 37. Turn right (south) on N.M. 37.**
	1.3
9.5	Culvert crossing arroyo. Cub Mountain Formation exposed on left in bottom of arroyo.
	0.6
10.1	Bridge crossing arroyo.
	0.5
10.6	Exposure of conglomeratic sandstone in Mesaverde Formation on left.
	0.1
10.7	Outcrop of purple Cub Mountain Formation on right.
	0.2
10.9	Exposure of Cub Mountain on right.
	0.4
11.3	Bridge crossing arroyo.
	0.4
11.7	Side road on left to Riachuela Ranch.
	0.3
12.0	Exposure of diorite sill on left.
	0.2
12.2	Entering Nogal, New Mexico.
	0.2
12.4	End of pavement, cross Dry Gulch.
	0.3
12.7	Ford Nogal Creek.
	0.2
12.9	Side road on right to Nogal Canyon. Nogal Peak at 2:00 on skyline.
	0.2
13.1	Cattle guard. Entering Lincoln National Forest. Road cuts in rocks of Sierra Blanca igneous complex.
	0.9
14.0	**OPTIONAL STOP.** Top of grade. Road curves to right. Exposure of Cub Mountain Formation on left. Road crosses fault, Cub Mountain Formation downthrown to southeast. Nogal Peak at 9:30. Gaylord Peak at 5:00. Dikes in Cub Mountain Formation exposed in road cuts ahead.
	0.5
14.5	Little Black Peak and Carrizozo Malpais at 3:00.
	0.3
14.8	Top of grade. Carrizo Mountain at 8:00; Vera Cruz Mountain in middle distance at 8:30; Tucson Mountain at 9:00; Capitan Mountains at 10:00.
	0.4
15.2	Side road on left to Nogal Lake and Ranchers' Camp Meeting Grounds. Stay on N.M. 37.

In 1908 the railroad used Nogal Lake for storage of water from the Bonito pipeline. Dorothy Neal states in her book on the Bonito pipeline that: "In order to lessen seepage, almost 600 head of cattle were driven round and round in the bed of the lake to trample the earth." When the lake still leaked excessively they tried grouting by drilling 120 wells around the lake using as much as 1,300 sacks of cement in one well.
— W. A. Mourant

	0.5
15.7	Bridge crossing arroyo.
	0.4
16.1	Cub Mountain Formation exposed on left.
	0.1
16.2	Side road on right to Loma Grande. Loma Grande (part of Sierra Blanca igneous complex) at 3:00.
	0.3
16.5	Road fork. Junction of N.M. 37 with dirt road to Capitan. Bear Right on N.M. 37 towards Ruidoso. Bridge crossing Magado Creek.
	0.4
16.9	Crest of hill. Mon Jeau Peak at 1:30. Sierra Blanca Peak at 2:00.
	0.2
17.1	Bridge. Side road on right to Happy Acres Ranch. Continue straight ahead.

Old pipeline exposed by erosion.   Pine slats and steel banding make a pipeline.

The 116 mile long Bonito pipeline supplied water for railroad and domestic use as far away as Pastura in Guadalupe County.

	1.0
18.1	Exposures of dikes in Cub Mountain Formation on right.
	0.1
18.2	Bridge crossing arroyo.
	1.3
19.5	Exposure of Cub Mountain Formation on left.
	1.2
20.7	Tertiary dike on left. Road cuts in dikes for next 2½ miles ahead.
	0.8
21.5	Exposure of Cub Mountain Formation and Tertiary dikes in arroyo on left. Note prospect pits.
	0.1
21.6	Road fork. Bear left on N.M. 37. Side road on right to Bonito Dam.
	0.5
22.1	Cattle guard.

	0.4
22.5	Bonito, New Mexico.
	0.5
23.0	**Cattle guard. Junction of N.M. 37 with N.M. 48. Turn right on N.M. 37.**
	0.1
23.1	Bridge crossing Bonito Creek. This drainage may mark fault boundary with Cub Mountain Formation downthrown to north and Mesaverde upthrown to south.
	0.2
23.3	Side road on right to Angus, New Mexico. Road cuts in Mesaverde Formation and Tertiary intrusives for next 3½ miles ahead. Note general west dip of Mesaverde.
	3.4
26.7	Side road on right to Sun Valley settlement.
	0.5
27.2	Alto, New Mexico. Roadcut in transition zone between Mesaverde Formation and Cub Mountain Formation. Junction of N.M. 532 with N.M. 37. Stay on N.M. 37. N.M. 37 leads to Mon Jeau Lookout and Sierra Blanca Recreation Area.
	Surface water from Lookout Mountain is impounded and used in snow-making machines for the ski slopes of the recreation area. Eagle Creek water (part of the Bonito pipeline system) is now used by the Eagle Creek Inter-Community Water Supply Association to supply water to Ruidoso, Capitan and Fort Stanton. A 12-million gallon open earthen reservoir has been constructed in Gavilan Canyon to store Eagle Creek water from the pipeline for use by Ruidoso. A storage reservoir on Eagle Creek is planned for future use. — W. A. Mourant.
	1.2
28.4	Crest of hill. Road cut in Mesaverde Formation and Cub Mountain Formation transitional zone of purple shales, carbonaceous material and sandstone intruded by Tertiary dikes.
	0.7
29.1	Approximate contact between Cub Mountain Formation and Mesaverde Formation transitional zone.
	0.3
29.4	Side road on right to Alpine Village. Road traverses along Mesaverde-Mancos contact for next 3.5 miles.
	1.0
30.4	Ruidoso Airport on left in Mancos Shale valley.
	1.0
31.4	Ruidoso Ranger Station on right. Roadbed is on Mancos Shale.
	0.1
31.5	**Ruidoso village limits.** Elevation: 6,875 feet.
	0.5
32.0	Cub Mountain or Mesaverde exposed on right.
	0.4
32.4	Mesaverde exposed on right.
	0.3
32.7	Road crosses Rio Ruidoso, cut into Mancos Shale.
	0.1
32.8	Road junction. Turn left on N.M. 37.
	0.6
33.4	Approximate location of northeast-southwest trending fault with Dakota upthrown to east.
	0.9
34.3	Side road on right to Carrizo Canyon.
	0.1
34.4	Road crosses small fault with Chinle upthrown to east.
	0.1
34.5	Road crosses Carrizo Creek which marks major northeast-southwest trending fault. San Andres Formation on upthrown (east) side.
	1.2
35.7	**Road fork, bear left.** Approximate contacts between San Andres, Glorieta and Yeso.
	0.5
36.2	**Junction of N.M. 37 with U.S. 70.**

END OF ROAD LOG FROM CAPITAN TO RUIDOSO. END OF FIRST DAY'S TRIP! REMEMBER — TOMORROW THE FIELD CONFERENCE WILL ASSEMBLE JUST EAST OF THE TOWN OF LINCOLN AT 8:30 A.M.

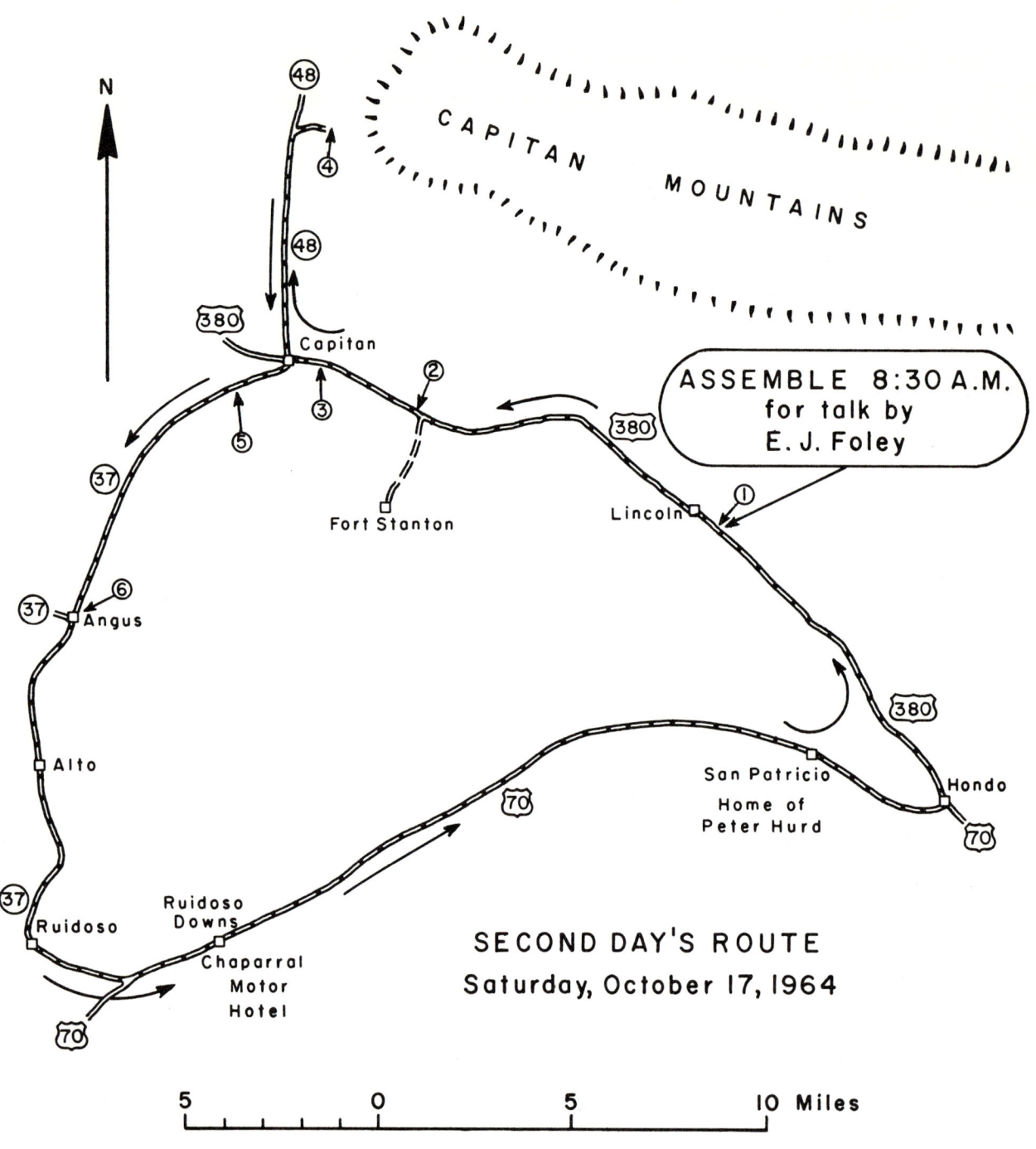

NEW MEXICO GEOLOGICAL SOCIETY • FIFTEENTH FIELD CONFERENCE

Road Logs from Ruidoso to Hondo, Capitan, Capitan Iron Deposits, and return to Ruidoso
SECOND DAY, SATURDAY, OCTOBER 17, 1964

Distance of travel: 85.7 miles
Starting time: 8:30 a.m.
Assembly point: Stop No. 1, 8.1 miles northwest of Hondo

SUMMARY

On the morning of the second day of the conference participants will travel individually to the assembly point 8.1 miles northwest of Hondo on U.S. Highway 380. After members have assembled Ed Foley will lead a discussion of the Lincoln folds at about 8:30 a.m. These folds which involve only the Yeso Formation have been the subject of much interest and controversey. Some of the better exposed Lincoln folds can be seen in the north wall of Bonito Creek in the vicinity of the assembly area. At about 10:00 a.m. the caravan will proceed westward on U.S. 380. Successively younger beds — Glorieta, San Andres and Bernal — are exposed along the route from the assembly point to Stop 2 near historic Fort Stanton. At Stop 2 the Triassic Santa Rosa Sandstone will be examined and discussed. Proceeding westward over the Chinle Formation, the caravan will pause next at Stop 3 on the Cretaceous Dakota Sandstone hogback which marks the eastern rim of the Capitan Coal Basin. After descending into this Basin (Mancos and Mesaverde) the caravan will arrive at the once active mining town of Capitan and then leave the Basin in a northerly direction to study the mineralized San Andres Limestone of the Capitan Iron Deposits at Stop 4. The caravan will return to Capitan for noon lunch, after which the Mesaverde Formation will be examined at Stop 5. The last Stop (No. 6) of the day will be at a point 10 miles south of Capitan for a discussion of the Tertiary Cub Mountain Formation (McRae?). Then the caravan will return to Ruidoso for the night.

Road Log from Ruidoso to Hondo
By Carl Ulvog and Sam Thompson, III

Note: Field trip participants will travel individually to the assembly point at Stop No. 1 which is in the road log from Hondo to Capitan, that follows this road log. This road log is included for those who would like to study the geology of the area between Ruidoso and Hondo.

Total Mileage		
0.0	Ruidoso, New Mexico. Junction of U.S. 70 and N.M. 37. Proceed northeastward on U.S. 70. Yeso Formation outcrops along Rio Ruidoso valley. San Andres forms ridges along valley rim.	
	0.1	
0.1	Hollywood, New Mexico.	
	1.1	
1.2	Ruidoso Downs Racetrack on left.	
	1.4	
2.6	Ruidoso Downs City Limits (east side). Hale Spring, one-half mile south of highway, once fed an Indian acequia or irrigation ditch. This ditch — about 900 years old — skirts the foothills at 2:00 to 3:00 on Agua Fria Estates. Pieces of caliche precipitated from irrigation water in this ditch line driveway entrance to Estates. Hale springs furnishes 225 gallons of water per minute to the town of Ruidoso Downs and Agua Fria Estates.	
	0.6	
3.2	Divided highway ends. Yeso exposed on right.	
	0.2	
3.4	Road cuts in folded Yeso.	
	0.6	
4.0	Dislocated blocks of Yeso and San Andres across Rio Ruidoso at 10:00.	
	1.6	
5.6	Bridge crossing Rio Ruidoso.	
	0.3	
5.9	Road cut on left in Yeso and Tertiary intrusives.	
	0.2	
6.1	Grass covered dissected alluvial fans across valley at 2:00 to 5:00.	
	0.4	

6.5	Road cuts in San Andres slump blocks.
	0.4
6.9	Bridge crossing arroyo.
	0.5
7.4	San Andres exposed on left of highway ahead. Contact with the Glorieta and Yeso covered. (West limb of large syncline.)
	0.2
7.6	East dipping beds of San Andres Limestone and shale in place.
	0.4
8.0	Fox Cave. (Wall-enclosed overhang of San Andres Limestone.)
	0.1
8.1	Turnout on right. San Andres Limestone intruded by Tertiary sills exposed on left. Quaternary gravels abutt against San Andres in vertical contact.
	0.3
8.4	Road cuts in Tertiary sills.
	0.5
8.9	Tertiary sill with spheroidal weathering exposed on left.
	0.4
9.3	Tertiary sills in San Andres Limestone on left.
	0.3
9.6	San Andres exposed on left.
	0.8
10.4	Buckhorn, New Mexico.
	0.3
10.7	Approximate contact (concealed) of San Andres with Yeso. Light colored sills in San Andres Limestone on left.
	0.3
11.0	Road cut on left in Yeso Formation. Yeso outcrops at road level for next 13 miles ahead; San Andres on valley rim.
	0.4
11.4	Yeso dolomite exposed in road cut on left and across Rio Ruidoso at 3:00.
	0.7
12.1	Road cut in Yeso.
	0.9
13.0	Glencoe, New Mexico, Post Office on right.
	0.7
13.7	**Junction of N.M. 214 with U.S. 70. Continue on U.S. 70.** (N.M. 214 leads to Fort Stanton). Road cuts in Yeso. Gravel terrace on ridge ahead is site of prehistoric Indian village excavated in 1956 by Texas Technological College archaeologists.
	0.2
13.9	Dumps of archeological excavations on ridge at 10:00.
	1.3
15.2	Bridge, road cuts in alluvial gravels.
	1.7
16.9	Bridge. San Andres Limestone forms canyon rim; Yeso exposed on lower slopes.
	1.2
18.1	Road cut on left in Yeso gypsum. Fluvial terraces along sides of valley on right.
	2.2
20.3	Entering San Patricio, New Mexico. Home of Peter Hurd, famous artist and ardent polo player, on right across Rio Ruidoso.
	1.1
21.4	Approximate axis of McDaniel anticline as mapped by Mourant, 1963. About 85 irrigation wells yielding as much as 3,500 gallons per minute obtain water from the alluvium in the flat floored valleys of the Rio Ruidoso, Rio Bonito, and Rio Hondo. Ground water is used mainly as a supplement to the surface-water supply. — W. A. Mourant
	0.7
22.1	Road Cut in slide block of San Andres Limestone (displaced at least 300 feet).
	1.6
23.7	Hondo, New Mexico.
	0.4
24.1	Bridge crossing Rio Bonito, which joins Rio Ruidoso one-half mile downstream to form Rio Hondo.
	0.1
24.2	**JUNCTION OF U.S. 70 WITH U.S. 380.**
	End of road log from Ruidoso to Hondo. Conferees turn to the next road log from Hondo to Capitan.

Road Log from Hondo to Capitan

By Carl Ulvog and Sam Thompson, III,
with a note by Edward Foley

Total Mileage	
0.0	**Hondo, New Mexico. Junction of U.S. 70 and 380. Proceed northwest on U.S. 380 toward Lincoln.** Historic Marker: "Historic Lincoln, 10 miles. Lincoln was the county seat of newly created Lincoln County (1869). Its population swollen by discharged soldiers and fortune seekers, it became the focal point of a struggle for economic and policital power — finally erupting into the Lincoln County War. The violence involved settlers, cowboys, merchants, and such people as Pat Garrett and Billy the Kid."
	0.4
0.4	Poorly exposed Yeso across Rio Bonito on left, overlain by San Andres.
	0.7
1.1	Sharply folded Yeso under flat lying San Andres at 9:00.
	0.5
1.6	Fritz's Spring on right. This spring is a source of good water; the aquifer is the Glorieta Sandstone. Many residents of the valley haul water from this spring for cooking beans.
	0.8
2.4	Exposure of Yeso on right.
	0.2
2.6	Folded, steeply dipping Yeso on right.
	0.4
3.0	Side road to left. Begin series of road cuts in Yeso.
	0.7
3.7	Exposure of Yeso, Glorieta and San Andres on right.
	1.6
5.3	Bridge crossing Rio Bonito. Road cut at left exposes red Yeso, yellow Glorieta and gray San Andres.
	1.0
6.3	Gently folded and faulted San Andres limestone across valley at 3:00.
	0.7
7.0	Sharply folded Yeso in lower part of canyon wall at 3:00; note slight deformation of San Andres in upper part of wall.
	0.9
7.9	**Prepare to turn right off of U.S. 380.**
	0.1
8.0	**Side road. Turn right from U.S. 380 through gateway into pasture. Park as directed by flagmen. ASSEMBLY POINT AND STOP NO. 1.** The Lincoln Folds which consists of crumpled Yeso rocks have been explained as drag folds; as landslides; as disharmonic folding; and as having resulted from forceful intrusion of sills related to the Capitan Mountains pluton. Only the Yeso Formation is involved in the folding at Lincoln, and the San Andres Limestone lies more or less flat on the top of the surrounding plateau. The folded zone is bounded on the south side, not by a fault, fold or intrusion, but only by a stream bed. The simplest and most obvious explanation of the Lincoln folds is that they were caused by gravitational slumping, that is, that they are landslides. Similar landslides, though not on such a large scale, are common elsewhere in the valleys of the Rio Bonito, Rio Ruidoso, and the Rio Hondo. This sliding probably took place during Pleistocene or early Recent time, when the Sierra Blanca and Capitan Mountains provided far greater runoff than they do today. — Edward Foley **Return to U.S. 380. Turn right (northwest). Allow for mileage to and from parking area.**
	0.7
8.7	Sharply folded Yeso at 3:00. Capitan Mountains on skyline.
	0.5
9.2	Cemetery on right.
	0.2
9.4	Historic Marker: "Lincoln Town: Turbulent center of the Lincoln County War 1875-1881; historic points include the graves of J. H. Tunstall, whose murder set off hostilities, and Alexander McSween, leader of one of the warring factions; Penfields' Store, formerly owned by McSween; site of the McSween house, where final battle of the War was fought; the adobe walls from whose shelter Billy the Kid shot and killed sheriff Brady; the Ellis House, where Governor Lew Wallace, author of "Ben Hur", conferred with Billy

the Kid in a vain effort to persuade him to accept a pardon and lay down his arms; and the old courthouse, originally the store of Fritz and Murphy, rivals of Tunstall and McSween, and leaders of the opposing faction."

Note anticline across river at 2:00.

    0.3

9.7   Entering Lincoln, New Mexico, historic center of the Lincoln County Cattle War, 1877-1879.

    0.1

9.8   Sharply folded Yeso at 3:00.

    0.5

10.3   Historic Marker:

"Old Lincoln County Court House. Historic House Museum managed by Old Lincoln County Memorial Commission. This adobe structure built in 1874 as Murphy-Dolan store. Served as Court House 1880-1913. Pat Garrett, first sheriff with office in this building, imprisoned Billy The Kid in upstairs room. The young outlaw made a dramatic escape April 28, 1881."

    0.6

10.9   Bridge crossing arroyo. Folded Yeso at 3:00.

    0.5

11.4   Bridge crossing arroyo. Road cuts in steeply dipping Yeso.

    1.0

12.4   Exposure of Yeso, Glorieta and San Andres at 3:00.

    0.5

12.9   Bridge crossing arroyo.

    0.9

13.8   Road cut in Yeso.

    0.2

14.0   Side road to Salazar Canyon on right. Continue on U.S. 380. Capitan Mountains on skyline at 3:00.

    0.1

14.1   Road cut in Yeso and San Andres.

    0.5

14.6   Road cut in Yeso.

    0.1

14.7   Cross contact from Yeso to Glorieta and San Andres.

    0.5

15.2   Old Busy Bee Store on right. Weathered yellowish Glorieta sandstone with overlying San Andres limestone at 3:00. Westerly dips seen here are on east flank on Sierra Blanca structural basin.

    0.4

15.6   Road cut in Yeso, Glorieta and San Andres. Sierra Blanca at 12:00. Optional Stop to examine road cut exposure of the Yeso, Glorieta and San Andres.

    0.2

15.8   Bridge crossing arroyo.

    0.1

15.9   Government Spring on right near double fence posts.

    0.1

16.0   The corrugated-iron covered building on right houses a well which pumps sand from the Glorieta Sandstone.

    0.1

16.1   Feather Cave (also called Dan's Cave and Smetnick Cave) in San Andres at 3:00. The cave has been excavated by archaeological students from the University of New Mexico.

    0.6

16.7   Side road on left to Fort Stanton Cave (also called Government Cave).

    0.2

16.9   Bridge crossing Rio Bonito. Upper San Andres exposed on right.

    0.5

17.4   Culvert crossing for arroyo. Approximate contact of San Andres with Bernal facies of Artesia Group. Orange colored siltstones of Bernal poorly exposed in this locality.

    0.4

17.8   Poorly exposed Bernal in arroyo on left. Hills at 11:00 to 2:00 are capped by Santa Rosa conglomerates.

    0.2

18.0   Prepare to turn left off U.S. 380.

    0.1

18.1   **STOP NO. 2**   **Turn left off of highway into cleared area. Park as directed by flagmen.** This knoll and the knoll north of the highway are capped by a 6-foot bed of pebble conglomerate in the Santa Rosa Sandstone. We are on the east flank of the Sierra Blanca synclinorium. **After stop return to U.S. 380; allow for mileage to and from parking area.**

	0.1
18.2	**Junction of U.S. 380 and N.M. 214; continue on U.S. 380.**
	Historical Marker:
	"Fort Stanton Tuberculosis Hospital 2 miles. Established in 1855, Fort Stanton was a base for U.S. Army Operations against Apache Indians. During the Civil War, the post was abandoned by Union forces and occupied briefly by Confederates. From 1899 to 1953 Fort Stanton was used as a hospital by the U.S. Public Health Service and is now operated by the State Tuberculosis Hospitals' Board."
	0.3
18.5	Exposure of red-orange Bernal in low rounded hills (middle distance) at 3:00.
	0.6
19.1	Exposure of Santa Rosa on low hill at 3:00 with Capitan Gap on skyline.
	1.2
20.3	Rodeo Bar on right. Oil test No. 1 Pearson TD 1,005 feet was drilled in the field on left side of road. See article by Havenor in this guidebook for details.
	0.4
20.7	Side road (dirt) on right to Capitan Gap. Continue on U.S. 380. Dakota Sandstone caps ridge at 3:00.
	0.5
21.2	Outcrop of reddish-purple Chinle on left.
	0.2
21.4	Chinle exposed on left. Dakota Sandstone caps ridge at 3:00.
	0.3
21.7	Exposure of Chinle-Dakota contact in road cut on left.
	0.1
21.8	Side road (dirt) on left to New Mexico Thorium Corporation mill. Road cut in Dakota Sandstone and dikes on east flank of Capitan Coal Basin. Strike valley cut in Mancos Shale ahead. Mesaverde sandstone on low ridges at 10:00 to 1:00. Sierra Blanca Peak skyline at 10:00. Nogal Peak at 11:00.
	0.1
21.9	Prepare to turn left on U.S. 380.
	0.1
22.0	**STOP NO. 3. Turn left off U.S. 380 into pasture. Park as directed by flagmen.**
	The Dakota Sandstone (about 130 feet thick) is intruded here by igneous dikes. Igneous sills and dikes, presumably of Tertiary age, outcrops in the Rio Hondo drainage basin as far east as Tinnie to its western limit at Indian Divide.
	After stop return to U.S. 380; allow for mileage to and from parking area.
	0.1
22.1	Bridge crossing arroyo. Mancos shale and sandstone at 3:00.
	0.2
22.3	Bridge crossing arroyo in Mancos-derived alluvium.
	0.1
22.4	Historic Marker:
	"A little bear cub, his feet badly burned, was rescued from a forest fire near here (in Capitan Gap) in 1950. The cub was nursed back to health and flown to Washington, D.C., to become the living symbol of Smokey the Bear in the U.S. Forest Service's fire prevention program."
	Entering Capitan, New Mexico. Elevation 6,350 feet.
	0.3
22.7	Junction of N.M. 48 with U.S. 380.
	End of road log from Hondo to Capitan. Field conference members go on to the next road log.

Road Log from Capitan to The Capitan Iron Deposits

Carl Ulvog and Sam Thompson, III, with
a note by V. C. Kelley

Total Mileage	
0.0	**Capitan, New Mexico. Junction of U.S. 380 and N.M. 48. Proceed north on N.M. 48.**
	0.1
0.1	Bridge crossing Salado Creek.
	0.3
0.4	Pavement ends. Road follows strike of Mancos Shale valley. Dakota dip slope on right; Mesaverde on left.
	0.4
0.8	Thin dikes form ridge on left. Mesaverde caps ridge in background.

	0.2
1.0	Culvert crossing. Mancos derived alluvium in dry gulley.
	0.1
1.1	Small quarry pit on right marks excavation of limestone lens in Mancos. Ridge of Mesaverde extending into valley from west at 12:00 represents west-plunging synclinal axis. Small hill at 1:00 underlain by Tertiary dike. Trees and knolls in valley mark dike outcrops.
	0.1
1.2	Northeast trending dike on right terminates at road.
	0.9
2.1	Mesaverde on ridge at left. Mancos valley and dip slope of underlying Dakota on right in middle distance. Capitan Mountains on skyline at 1:00 to 3:00. Capitan Gap at 2:00.
	0.1
2.2	Culvert. Abandoned lumber mill on right.
	1.1
3.3	Ranch house on left. Titsworth Dome at 2:30. (Westwardly dipping Dakota Sandstone on west flank).
	0.4
3.7	Draw. East-west valley underlain by Mancos Shale on downthrown side (south) of Taylor Ranch fault. Timbered hills in foreground underlain by west dipping San Andres limestone on upthrown side of fault. West dipping sequence of Bernal, Dockum, Dakota, Mancos and Mesaverde from 11:00 to 10:00. Tucson Mountain (Mesaverde sandstone) on skyline at 10:00.
	0.1
3.8	Side road on left to ranches. Continue on N.M. 48. Three miles west of here oil test Western Ranchers No. 1 Beecher was drilled to a total depth of 1,342 feet. See the article by Havenor for details.
	0.5
4.3	Road curves to right, crossing east-west trending Taylor Ranch fault. San Andres on upthrown (north) side.
	0.1
4.4	Cattle guard. Entering Lincoln National Forest. Road forks, bear left. Note switchback on West Mountain Road at 12:00.
	0.1
4.5	San Andres outcrop on left.
	0.1
4.6	San Andres exposed on right.
	0.6
5.2	**Prepare to turn right.**
	0.2
5.4	**Turn right (northeast) off main road.**
	0.2
5.6	Roadbed on San Andres Limestone.
	0.4
6.0	Road curves right and crosses under power line. Power line road on left.
	0.2
6.3	Gypsum (alabaster) in Bernal exposed in lower part of ridge at 9:00. The alabaster was mistakenly quarried from the base of this ridge for "marble" tombstones. Dakota on skyline.
	0.3
6.6	Road forks; bear right, down hill.
	0.7
7.3	Prospect pit in San Andres on right.
	0.1
7.4	Road forks; bear right. Road on left follows ridge of principal Capitan Iron Deposit.
	0.1
7.5	Prospect pit on right.
	0.1
7.6	Gate. Capitan Iron Deposits on ridge to east.
	0.1
7.7	**STOP NO. 4. PARK AS DIRECTED BY FLAGMEN.**

The Capitan deposit is in nearly flat-lying limestone of the San Andres Formation (Permian) and near the western end of the large early Tertiary aplitic intrusive of the Capitan Mountains. The ore, which is largely magnetite, forms nearly a ring about 1,300 feet in diameter; the average width of outcrop is 100 feet. Although only two very small sills of aplite crop out near the deposit, an unusually large quantity of silicates has formed in the limestone, especially inside the ring of ore. The principal silicate minerals are epidote phlogopite, and tremolite which are arranged in concentric zones outward in the order given. Magnetite forms the fourth or outer zone. All the minerals are present in the inner zone, but the characterizing mineral of a zone is not present in an outer zone. The deposits, which are genetically related to the intrusive, are located in a secondary breccia in the limestone. Solution by groundwater, probably in early Triassic time, created a spongelike cavernous condition in the limestone which crushed gradually to form what is termed a collapse breccia. — V. C. Kelley

End of Road Log from Capitan to the Capitan Iron Deposits.
After stop, retrace route to Capitan and go to the next Road Log.

Road Log from Capitan to Ruidoso
By Carl Ulvog and Sam Thompson, III

Total Mileage

0.0	**Capitan, New Mexico. Junction U.S. 380 with N.M. 48 (Lincoln Avenue). Proceed south on N.M. 48.**
	0.3
0.3	Highway curves right. Road bed is on Mancos. Mesaverde forms ridges at 11:00.
	0.5
0.8	Paved side road on right. Continue on N.M. 48.
	0.3
1.1	Cattle guard. Sierra Blanca Peak at 11:30. Road crosses northeast-southwest trending fault with only Mesaverde displaced at this point. Progressively older beds crop out along upthrown side of fault such that about nine miles to the southwest, San Andres is faulted against Mesaverde.
	0.3
1.4	Road cut in Mesaverde.
	0.5
1.9	Road cut (on right) in Mesaverde.
	0.6
2.5	Culvert crossing.
	0.2
2.7	Cattle guard. Road cut on left is in contorted Mesaverde. Nogal Peak at 12:30.
	0.3
3.0	Road cut in upper Mesaverde Formation. Lithology is transitional with Cub Mountain Formation.
	0.1
3.1	Prepare to stop.
	0.1
3.2	**STOP NO. 5. PARK ON RIGHT SIDE OF HIGHWAY AS DIRECTED BY FLAGMEN.** Good exposure of Mesaverde buff sandstone and purple shale in road cut. In this area it is about 600 feet thick and consists of quartzose sandstone, thin beds of limestone, siltstone, shale and coal. The Mesaverde is transitional with the overlying Cub Mountain and at this stop the pebbles seen here may be from the pebble conglomerate of the Cub Mountain Formation.
	0.1
3.3	Begin 1.2 mile long series of road cuts in Mesaverde displaying transitional-type lithology.
	0.4
3.7	Side road on right to Nogal. Westwardly-dipping Dakota Sandstone on conical hill at 11:00.
	0.3
4.0	Bridge crossing arroyo.
	0.6
4.6	Road on left to Ferguson Ranch. Highway crosses north-south trending fault with upper Mesaverde Formation upthrown to east and Cub Mountain Formation downthrown to west.
	0.1
4.7	Cub Mountain Formation(?) on right.
	0.1
4.8	Road cut in Cub Mountain Formation.
	0.2
5.0	Bridge crossing Magado Creek.
	0.2
5.2	Road cut on left in Cub Mountain Formation. Tertiary dike along crest of hill.
	0.1
5.3	Ranch house on right.
	0.2
5.5	Dike on left.
	0.1
5.6	Cub Mountain Formation and Tertiary intrusives exposed in road cuts for next one-half mile.
	1.7

Sierra Blanca from Mon Jeau Lookout. New Mexico State Tourist Bureau photograph.

7.3	Cattle guard.	
	0.5	
7.8	Side road on right to ranch.	
	0.4	
8.2	Cattle guard.	
	0.8	
9.0	Cattle guard.	
	0.3	
9.3	Road cut in Cub Mountain Formation and Tertiary intrusives. **Prepare to stop.**	
	0.1	
9.4	End of N.M. 48. Join N.M. 37. **STOP NO. 6. PARK AS DIRECTED BY FLAGMEN.** These purple siltstones intruded by igneous rocks are typical of the Cub Mountain Formation. The Cub Mountain Formation consists of white sandstone, multicolored siltstone and varied igneous rocks which are usually light in color.	
	0.1	
9.5	Bridge crossing Bonito Creek. This drainage may mark fault boundary with Cub Mountain Formation downthrown to north and Mesaverde upthrown to south.	
	0.2	
9.7	Side road on right to Angus, New Mexico. Road cuts in Mesaverde Formation and Tertiary intrusives for next 3½ miles ahead. Note general west dip of Mesaverde.	
	3.4	
13.1	Side road on right to Sun Valley settlement.	
	0.5	
13.6	Alto, New Mexico. Roadcut in transition zone between Cub Mountain Formation and Mesaverde Formation. Junction of N.M. 532 with N.M. 37. Stay on N.M. 37. N.M. 532 leads to Mon Jeau Lookout and Sierra Blanca Recreation Area.	
	1.2	
14.8	Optional stop. Crest of hill. Road cut in Mesaverde Formation and Cub Mountain Formation transitional zone of purple shales, carbonaceous material and sandstone intruded by Tertiary dikes.	
	0.7	
15.5	Approximate contact between Cub Mountain Formation and Mesaverde Formation (transitional zone).	
	0.3	
15.8	Side road on right to Alpine Village. Road traverses along Mesaverde/Mancos contact for next 3.5 miles ahead.	
	1.0	
16.8	Ruidoso Airport on left in Mancos shale valley.	
	1.0	
17.8	Ruidoso Ranger Station on right. Roadbed is on Mancos shale.	
	0.1	
17.9	Ruidoso village limits. Elevation: 6,875 feet.	
	0.5	
18.4	Cub Mountain Formation(?) or Mesaverde Formation(?) exposed on right.	
	0.4	
18.8	Mesaverde Formation exposed on right.	
	0.3	
19.1	Road crosses Rio Ruidoso, cut into Mancos shale.	
	0.1	
19.2	Road junction. Turn left on N.M. 37.	
	0.6	
19.8	Approximate location of northeast-southwest trending fault with Dakota upthrown to east.	
	0.5	
20.7	Side road on right to Carrizo Canyon.	
	0.1	
20.8	Road crosses small fault with Chinle upthrown to east.	
	0.1	
20.9	Road crossed Carrizo Creek which marks major northeast-southwest trending fault. San Andres Formation on upthrown (east) side.	
	1.2	
22.1	**Road fork, bear left.** Approximate contacts between San Andres, Glorieta and Yeso.	
	0.5	
22.6	**JUNCTION OF N.M. 37 WITH U.S. 70. END OF ROAD LOG FROM CAPITAN TO RUIDOSO AND END OF SECOND DAYS FIELD TRIP.**	

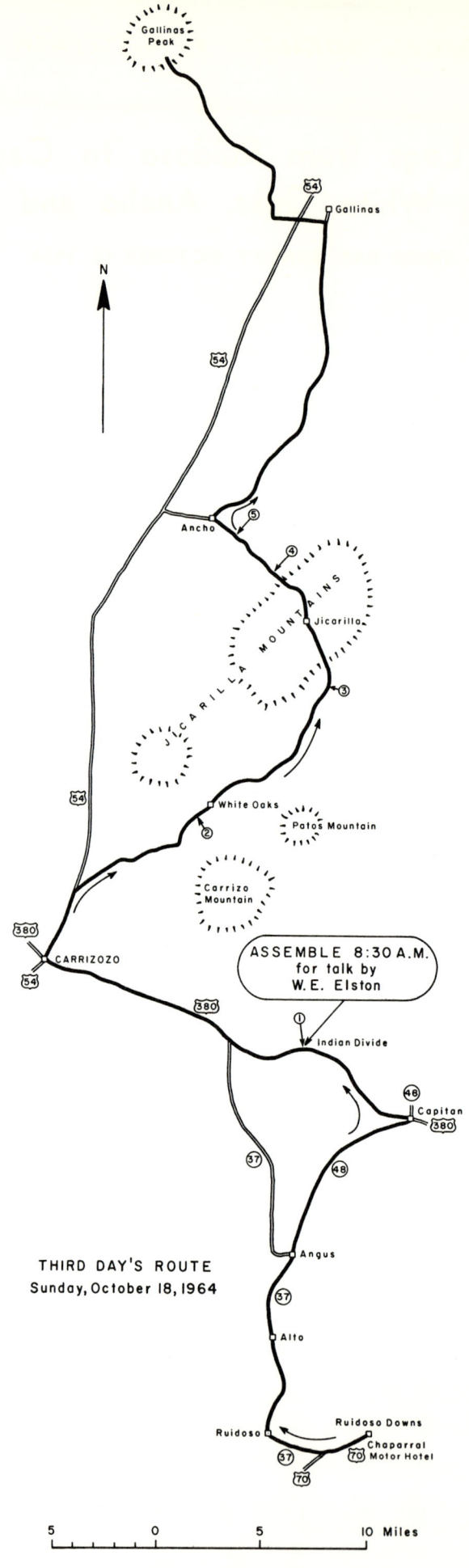

THIRD DAY'S ROUTE
Sunday, October 18, 1964

Road Logs from Ruidoso to Capitan, Carrizozo, White Oaks, Ancho and Gallinas

THIRD DAY, SUNDAY, OCTOBER 18, 1964

Distance of Travel: 101.7 miles
Starting Time: 8:30 a.m.
Assembly point: Stop No. 1, Indian Divide, 6.5 miles northwest of Capitan, New Mexico.

For the last day's trip the caravan will assemble at Indian Divide (Stop 1). This is a complex area of faulting and extensive Tertiary igneous activity with excellent exposures of the Mesaverde and Cub Mountain Formations with their many dikes. From here the road leads northward away from the Sierra Blanca igneous complex into the Tularosa Basin to the historic White Oaks gold mining area. Stop 2 provides an opportunity to observe and discuss the Cretaceous beds and Tertiary igneous intrusives which caused the gold-tungsten mineralization. At Stop 3 the contact of Bernal with San Andres will be studied and the Jicarilla pluton discussed. The trip will continue on through the one-time placer mining center of Jicarilla, New Mexico and at Stop 4 the Dakota, San Andres and the Bernal will be discussed. After this stop the conferers will continue traveling north to Stop 5 near Ancho, New Mexico where exposures of the San Andres and Bernal will be examined. The conference will then proceed across successively older rocks until the Glorieta may be observed at Gallinas, New Mexico. The Field Conference will officially end at this point. Conferees may then embark on various unguided tours using the supplementary logs or return to their homes.

Road Log from Ruidoso to Capitan

By Carl Ulvog and Sam Thompson, III

Note: Field trip participants will travel individually to the assembly point at STOP NO. 1 which is in the road log from Capitan to Carrizozo that follows this road log. This road log is included for those who would like to study the geology of the area between Ruidoso and Capitan.

Total Mileage	
0.0	**Ruidoso, New Mexico. Junction of U.S. 70 and N.M. 37. Proceed west on N.M. 37.**
	0.5
0.5	Road fork, bear right. Approximate locations of contacts between the San Andres, Glorieta and Yeso.
	1.2
1.7	Road crosses Carrizo Creek which marks major northeastward-trending fault. San Andres Formation on upthrown (east) side.
	0.1
1.8	Road crosses small fault with the Chinle upthrown to the east.
	0.1
1.9	Side road on left to Carrizo Canyon.
	0.9
2.8	Approximate location of northeastward-trending fault with Dakota upthrown on the east side of fault.
	0.5
3.3	Prepare to turn right.
	0.1
3.4	**Road junction, turn right on N.M. 37.**
	0.1
3.5	Road crosses Rio Ruidoso cut into the Mancos Shale.
	0.3
3.8	Mesaverde Formation exposed on left.
	0.4
4.2	Cub Formation or Mesaverde Formation exposed on right.
	0.4
4.6	Ruidoso village limits. Elevation: 6,875 feet.
	0.1
4.7	Ruidoso Ranger Station on left. Roadbed is on Mancos Shale.

                1.0
5.7   Ruidoso Airport on right in valley cut into the Mancos Shale.
                1.1
6.8   Side road on left to Alpine Village.
                0.3
7.1   Approximate contact between the Cub Mountain Formation and Mesaverde Formation.
                0.7
8.7   Bridge crossing Eagle Creek. Entering Alto, New Mexico.
                0.1
8.8   Historical Marker.
         "Mon Jeau Lookout, 12 miles. Elevation 10,000 feet. Offers one of the most scenic views in entire Southwest. Used by Forest Rangers during fire season. Observation deck open to visitors at all times. Parking space at bottom of lookout tower."
                0.1
8.9   Alto, New Mexico, Post Office on left. Junction of N.M. 532 with N.M. 37. Continue on N.M. 37. N.M. 532 leads to Monjeau Lookout and Sierra Blanca Recreation Area. Roadcut ahead in Mesaverde sandstone.
                0.6
9.5   Side road on left to Sun Valley settlement.
                3.4
12.9   Side road on left to Angus, New Mexico. Mesaverde Formation exposed in roadcut shows general west dip.
                0.2
13.1   Bridge crossing Rio Bonito. This drainage may mark fault with Mesaverde upthrown to south and Cub Mountain Formation downthrown to north.
                0.1
13.2   **Junction of N.M. 37 with N.M. 48. Go straight ahead on N.M. 48.** N.M. 37 on left leads to Nogal and Carrizozo, New Mexico. Begin series of road cuts in Cub Mountain Formation and Tertiary intrusives.
                1.1
14.3   Cattle guard.
                0.4
14.7   Side road on left to ranch. Road cuts in Cub Mountain Formation and Tertiary intrusives for next 3.5 miles ahead.
                2.9
17.6   Bridge crossing Magado Creek.
                0.4
18.0   Side road on right to Ferguson Ranch. Highway crosses north-south trending fault with upper Mesaverde Formation upthrown to east and Cub Mountain Formation downthrown to west. Begin series of roadcuts in Mesaverde Formation.
                0.6
18.6   Bridge crosses arroyo.
                0.3
18.9   Side road on left to Nogal, New Mexico. Capitan Mountain at 11:00 to 2:00. Capitan Gap at 12:30.
                0.5
19.4   Road cut in Mesaverde buff sandstone and purple shale.
                0.2
19.6   Road cut in upper Mesaverde Formation; lithology transitional with Cub Mountain Formation.
                0.3
19.9   Cattle guard. Road cut on right in contorted Mesaverde.
                1.6
21.5   Cattle guard. Highway crosses northeast-southwest trending fault with only Mesaverde displaced at this point.
                0.2
21.7   Capitan, New Mexico, city limits. Elevation 6,350 feet.
                0.1
21.8   **Side road (paved) on left, continue straight ahead on N.M. 48.**
                0.5
22.3   New Mexico Thorium Corporation mine at 12:00. Highway curves sharp left.
                0.3
22.6   **Junction of N.M. 48 with U.S. 380. End of road log from Ruidoso to Capitan; conferees go to next road log.**

Road Log from Capitan to Carrizozo

By Carl Ulvog and Sam Thompson, III, with a note by W. E. Elston

Total Mileage	
0.0	**Capitan, New Mexico. Junction of N.M. 48 with U.S. 380. Proceed west on U.S. 380.**
	0.1
0.1	Smokey Bear Museum on right. Historic Marker: "Smokey Bear Museum. The Smokey Bear Museum was built by the people of Capitan, New Mexico. It opened July 1, 1960, to perpetuate the claim of Capitan as the birthplace of Smokey the Bear, rescued from a fire in the Capitan Mountains in 1950, and to help prevent forest fires. It features exhibits of the natural resources of Lincoln County."
	0.5
0.6	Leaving Capitan, entering Capitan coal fields. Old mine dumps at 2:00. Reserves of bituminous coal in the Capitan area have been estimated at 2 million tons. Mines operated here at the turn of the century produced over 600,000 tons of coal. Approximate contact between Mancos Shale and Mesaverde Formation. The Mesaverde, consisting of sandstones, shales and coal beds, is nearly 600 feet thick in this area.
	0.6
1.2	Outcrop of andesite sill (Tertiary) on right.
	0.7
1.9	Bridge crossing Oso Creek. Mesaverde sandstones in westward dipping ridges contains numerous fossils. White sandstone, cut by streams, contain shells of giant clams and another bed, 150 feet upstream from the bridge, is composed almost entirely of small oyster shells.
	0.3
2.2	Road cut in Mesaverde sandstone and andesite dike. Hills on skyline at 10:00 are Tertiary volcanics which overlie sediments at axis of Sierra Blanca synclinorium. Highway traverses northern edge of this once active volcanic area.
	0.5
2.7	Road cut in Mesaverde Formation.
	0.3
3.0	Road cut in Tertiary dikes and purple siltstones of Cub Mountain Formation.
	0.3
3.3	Road cut in Cub Mountain Formation and small dikes.
	0.3
4.1	Culvert crossing over Salado Creek.
	0.2
4.3	Road cut in Cub Mountain Formation intruded by west-dipping rhyolite sill. Road cuts for next 1½ miles in Cub Mountain Formation and Tertiary dikes.
	1.8
6.1	Side road on left to Ranchman's Camp Meeting and Nogal Lake Campground. Road cut in Cub Mountain Formation.
	0.2
6.3	Road cut in Indian Divide Fault Zone. Cub Mountain Formation downthrown to east and Mesaverde Formation upthrown to west with at least 200 feet of displacement indicated. Tertiary dikes intruded along fault zone. (Note: Road construction planned for 2.6 miles of new highway ahead beginning approximately at this point. Road log follows route as of May 1, 1964, prior to new construction.)
	0.1
6.4	**Prepare to turn right off U.S. 380.**
	0.1
6.5	**ASSEMBLY POINT AND STOP NO. 1. TURN RIGHT OFF U.S. 380 AND FOLLOW DIRECTIONS OF FLAGMEN.** Indian Divide elevation 6,996 feet.
	Road cuts provide the best exposure of the northeastward-trending Tertiary dike-swarm complex, which extends from Sierra Blanca 40 miles into the Jicarilla Mountains. Each major exposure is a composite dike made up of several rock types. Rock types are in order of age: (1) labradorite - olivine diabase porphyry, (2) olivine diabase porphyry, (3) diabase, (4) hornblende - biotite diabase, (5) rhyolite, (6) latite grading to trachyte and (7) phonolite. Rhyolite tends to form sills rather than dikes and may be contemporaneous with the granitoid rocks of the Carrizo, Capitan, Patos, and Vera Cruz Mountains. Alteration characteristically includes the conversion of labradorite in diabase to oligoclase by sodium betasomation. — W. E. Elston.
	Return to U.S. 380 and allow for side trip mileage.

Igneous Dikes in Cub Mountain Formation near Indian Divide, Lincoln County, New Mexico.
Photograph by W. A. Mourant.

	0.1	
6.6	Begin series of road cuts in Mesaverde Formation and Tertiary dikes. Nogal Peak of Sierra Blanca igneous complex at 11:30.	
	0.1	
6.7	Sierra Blanca Peak at 9:00.	
	0.5	
7.2	Road cut in coal-bearing Mesaverde shales intruded by Tertiary dikes.	
	0.7	
7.9	Road cut on right exposes gradational contact of Mesaverde (yellowish sandstone) with overlying Cub Mountain Formation (purplish siltstone and white sandstone).	
	0.4	
8.3	Road cut in Cub Mountain sandstone intruded by Tertiary dikes.	
	0.2	
8.5	Side road on left to ranch. Continue on U.S. 380.	
	0.4	
8.9	Boundary of Lincoln National Forest. Church Mountain, Tertiary igneous complex, at 10:00.	

(Note: According to planned re-routing of highway, distance from "total mileage point 6.3" above to Lincoln National Forest boundary at "total mileage point 8.9" will be shortened approximately 0.5 mile. At "total mileage point 7.2" above construction plans call for incorporation of old highway into new route with a correction of –0.3 mile. Remaining –0.2 mile correction is cumulative over balance of rerouting.)

	0.5	
9.4	Road cut through Tertiary rhyolite dike which forms high northerly-trending ridge (part of the Vera Cruz Mountain complex).	
	0.9	
10.3	Mesaverde exposure on right.	
	0.4	
10.7	Side road on right to abandoned mine workings on Vera Cruz Mountain, small laccolite at 3:00.	
	1.2	
11.9	Bridge crossing Nogal Creek. Carrizo Mountain laccolith at 3:00; Tucson Mountain (folded Mesaverde) at 4:00.	
	0.4	
12.3	**Junction of U.S. 380 with N.M. 37. Continue on U.S. 380.**	
	7.5	
19.8	Side road on left to Carrizozo Country Club.	
	0.2	
20.0	Carrizozo Village Limits. Historical Marker:	

"Carrizozo. Founded 1905, population 1,546. Elevation 5,425 feet. The crossroads of history. Northeast is the ghost town of White Oaks, a once booming mining camp where Emerson Haush lived and laid the scene of his book "Hearts Desire". Famous names like Billy the Kid, Pat Garrett and Lew Wallace are closely associated with the area."

Panoramic view: Salinas Peak in San Andres Mountains at 10:00; Mockingbird Gap at 10:30; Oscura Mountains at 11:00 to 12:00; Carrizozo anticline in San Andres Formation in middle distance at 11:30 to 12:30; Carrizozo Malpais in Tularosa Valley at 10:00 to 2:00, with Little Black Peak at 1:30; Gallinas Mountains on skyline at 2:30; Tecolote Hills at 3:00; Lone Mountain laccolith at 3:30; Carrizo Mountain laccolith at 4:00; Tucson Mountain (folded Mesaverde) at 5:00; Vera Cruz Mountain laccolith at 5:30; Church Mountain (igneous complex) at 7:00; Gaylord Peak at 7:30; Nogal Peak at 8:00; Cub Mountain at 8:30; Willow Hill at 9:00 with Rose Peak in Godfrey Hills in background.

	0.3	
20.3	Railroad overpass.	
	0.2	
20.5	**Carrizozo, New Mexico. Intersection of U.S. 380 and U.S. 54. End of Road Log from Capitan to Carrizozo; conferees go to next road log.**	

Road Log from Carrizozo to White Oaks, Ancho, and Gallinas
By A. J. Budding

0.0   **Carrizozo, New Mexico. Intersection of U.S. 380 and U.S. 54. Proceed north on U.S. 54.**
In this vicinity, the Tularosa Basin has a synclinical structure, with a gentle, southward plunge. Road is on Quaternary, probably underlain by Mesaverde Formation.
         0.1

0.1   Historic marker on left. Panoramic view: Baxter Mountain at 12:00; low rounded hills of Mesaverde at 12:30; Carrizo Mountain at 1:00; Tucson Mountain at 2:00; Nogal Peak at 4:00; Cub Mountain at 4:30; Oscura Peak at 8:00; Carrizozo mailpais stretches between 8:00 and 10:00, with Little Black Peak at 10:00; Gallinas Mountains at 11:00; and Lone Mountain at 11:30.
         1.3

1.4   Culvert over arroyo. The few exposures of shale in arroyo bottom belong to the Mesaverde sequence.
         1.9

3.3   **Turn right off U.S. 54 onto N.M. 349 to White Oaks.** Marker of Old Lincoln County Memorial Commission reads:
"White Oaks 6 miles. Dominated Lincoln County in 1880's. Nucleus of and main producer in gold mining area since early Spanish times. Prosperous and politically powerful in territorial days after 1879 gold discovery. Activity diminished since World War I."
         0.1

3.4   **CAUTION;** Cross Southern Pacific Railroad tracks.
         0.3

3.7   On top of rise, the following panoramic view: Lone Mountain at 11:00, Baxter Mountain at 11:45, Patos Mountain at 12:30, Carrizo Mountain at 1:00, Tucson Mountain at 2:30. Road traverses plain, popularly known as "Yucca Flats."
         2.2

5.9   Low grass-covered hills from 1:00 to 3:00 expose face slope of alternating shale and sandstone of the Upper Cretaceous Mesaverde Group.
         1.7

7.6   Low ridge in front of Lone Mountain at 10:00 is dip slope of Dakota Sandstone, dipping away from the Lone Mountain pluton. From 10:30 to 12:00 valley in Mancos Shale and ridges of sandstone beds in the Mesaverde Group.
Lone Mountain is made up of rocks of syenitic composition. Along much of its borders, the syenite is in contact with limestones of the San Andres Formation, and locally contact-metasomatic deposits of magnetite and hematite, with accompanying silicates, have been formed. A few of such deposits have produced iron ore in the past.
         1.1

8.7   Cattle guard. Sandstones of Mesaverde Group cap ridge on left.
         0.1

8.8   One-way bridge.
         0.6

9.4   One-way bridge. Toreva block of Mesaverde sandstone at 9:00. Due to southerly dip of beds, older Cretaceous formations are exposed further ahead. Baxter Mountain at 11:30.
         0.5

9.9   From this point on, several steeply dipping dikes are visible on the southeast slope of Baxter Mountain.
         0.1

10.0   Cattle guard.
         0.3

10.3   **STOP NO. 2. FOLLOW DIRECTIONS OF FLAGMEN.** After parking walk about 100 yards to the edge of the arroyo to left of road for a discussion of Cretaceous sequence, Tertiary igneous rocks and gold mineralization of Baxter Mountain (White Oaks District). The gold mines of the White Oaks district are clustered northeast of Baxter Mountain, in Baxter Gulch. The lode deposits were discovered in the late 1870's, and the district underwent a brief period of prosperity, which lasted until the beginning of the 20th century. The gold-tungsten mineralization forms fracture fillings in the Mancos Shale and in the numerous dikes of monzonitic and lamprophyric composition.
         0.6

10.9   Cedarvale cemetery, on right, contains graves of prominent citizens of White Oaks.
         0.2

11.1   Tailing dumps and foundations of old mills across arroyo to left. Bedrock is Mancos Shale.
         0.2

11.3   Cattle guard and bridge.

	0.1
11.4	Broad valley opening to north is partly cut along a fault zone, which exposes Mancos Shale, Dakota Sandstone and Dockum Group on the west, and Mesaverde Group downthrown to the east. Baxter Gulch is behind the ridge on left.
	0.4
11.8	White Oaks, a booming mining town at the turn of the century, lies ahead. Besides the ruins of adobe buildings, note the two prominent houses, one of red brick to the right and a white wooden house with red roof to the left of the road. These houses are relics of the rich mining years.
	0.2
12.0	Cattle guard. Keep straight ahead. Mesaverde sandstone caps the ridge ahead.
	0.3
12.3	Mesaverde Formation crops out on both sides of the road.
	0.2
12.5	Mesaverde sandstone in road cut to right shows slickensided surfaces, indicating a north trending fault, about following the road. Displacement along this fault is small, and probably does not exceed a few tens of feet.
	0.1
12.6	Bridge across arroyo. To left in arroyo bottom outcrops of Mesaverde sandstone. This is part of the lowermost sandstone of the Mesaverde Group, from here on road traverses soil derived from the Mancos Shale.
	1.1
13.7	Monzonite sill in road cut on left. Several such sills and dikes traverse the Mancos Shale in this vicinity, giving the shale a hornfelsic appearance, with in places highly sericitized knots of andalusite. Plain to right is on Mancos Shale, which has been badly eroded by gullying. Sandstone ridge in slope leading to Patos Mountain is lower sandstone of Mesaverde Group.
	0.3
14.0	Bridge. Ridge at 9:00 is underlain by Mancos Shale and monzonite sills.
	0.5
14.5	Cattle guard; boundary of Lincoln National Forest. Low ridge at this stop is underlain by Mancos Shale cut by lamprophyre (spessartite) dikes. Patos Mountain, at 12:00 to 1:00 (southeast), is a dome of trachy-andesite-trachyte-rhyolite composition.
	0.9
15.4	Road on Mancos Shale.
	0.4
15.8	View of Jicarilla Mountains from 9:30-11:00. Jack's Peak at 10:30. Road has climbed slightly, and the Mancos-Mesaverde contact is in the trees to the right of the road.
	0.4
16.2	**Junction; continue straight ahead to Jicarilla and Ancho.**
	0.1
16.3	Cattle guard; windmill at left of road is site of Vaughn No. 1 Crenshaw (T.D. 400 feet). Tree covered low ridge from 9:00-12:00 is dipslope of Dakota Sandstone.
	0.8
17.1	Cattle guard; outcrop of Dakota Sandstone, cut by lamprophyre dike, to left of road. Southward dip of sandstone is about 20°, indicating proximity of the Jicarilla pluton to the north. Ridge on skyline at 3:00 exposes Dakota-Mancos-Mesaverde sequence. Sandstones of the Mesaverde Formation form the dipslope.
	0.1
17.2	Road descends onto red colored soil derived from the siltstones of the Triassic Chinle Formation. Grey ridges in middle distance ahead are underlain by San Andres Limestone. Jicarilla intrusive on skyline.
	0.4
17.6	Cattle guard.
	0.1
17.7	Slight rise in road is underlain by Santa Rosa Sandstone of Dockum Group, here consisting of brown, impure sandstones with chert pebble conglomerate layers.
	0.2
17.9	Road is on Bernal (?) Formation.
	0.8
18.7	**STOP NO. 3. FOLLOW DIRECTIONS OF FLAGMEN.** At this point outcrops of the San Andres Limestone, dipping south and away from the Jicarilla pluton. Contact between the San Andres and Bernal is exposed in nearby road cut. To east of the road a large decoiffement (gravitational gliding) block of Dakota Sandstone.
	0.2
18.9	Grey limestone of San Andres Formation is exposed in road cut on left.
	0.7

19.6	Monzonite exposed near road. These outcrops form part of an offshoot of the main pluton, as further ahead we will again encounter San Andres Limestone. The Jicarilla pluton, which consists mainly of quartz monzonite porphyry and monzonite porphyry, has barely been deroofed by erosion, and at the surface Permian limestones and sandstones alternate irregularly with monzonite outcrops.
	0.5
20.1	Cattle guard. Crossing a limestone roof pendant in the monzonite.
	0.2
20.3	Cattle guard. Foster Ranch on left. Road is now in monzonite of the Jicarilla pluton, and this will be the dominating rock for the next several miles.
	0.2
20.5	Good outcrop of monzonite to left of road.
	1.1
21.6	Picnic area to right.
	0.2
21.8	Dark dike cuts monzonite.
	0.5
22.3	Highest point on road. Descend into Jicarilla.
	0.8
23.1	Sideroad to Benge Ranch; continue straight ahead.
	0.8
23.9	Jicarilla, N. M., center of placer gold mining in the 1840's and again during the 1930's. Most of the placer gold is reported to have occurred in the lowermost 6 inches of the alluvial valley fill, which in many arroyos amounts to 30 to 40 feet in thickness. This fact, combined with the lack of water at this elevation, makes placer mining an unprofitable undertaking at the present time. The placer gold has presumably been derived from small vein deposits, which follow joints in the monzonite porphyry, or occur near the contact of the intrusive and the Permian limestone.
	0.1
24.0	Bridge across Ancho Gulch. Still in monzonite.
	0.2
24.2	Gallina Mountains at skyline at 11:30. Tecolote Hills at 12:00.
	0.2
24.4	Permian sandstone (Glorieta?) in road cut on right, dipping north.
	0.1
24.5	San Andres Limestone exposed in road cut, also dipping away from the Jicarilla intrusive, which has been traversed.
	0.2
24.7	Valley to right of road has been "Sampled with bulldozer" during the summer of 1960. A big trench, about 40 feet deep extends just across the fence, and was made to sample the placer potentialities of the alluvium. Jack's Peak at 2:00.
	0.7
25.4	Blocks of San Andres Limestone along the road.
	0.5
25.9	San Andres Limestone exposed in road cut on right.
	0.5
26.4	Old milling equipment, used in placer mining during the 1930's to be seen on left of road.
	0.1
26.5	Gypsum of uppermost beds of San Andres Formation, exposed in road cut to right.
	0.1
26.6	Recent effort at mining placer gold on right.
	0.2
26.8	Small stock of monzonite underlies hills to right and left.
	0.4
27.2	Valley to right is in Chinle formation, which also underlies the lower slope of hills at 3:00. Capping the hills is a thin layer of consolidated gravels, probably belonging to the Pliocene Ogallalla formation.
	0.2
27.4	**STOP NO. 4 AT ROAD JUNCTION. FOLLOW DIRECTIONS OF FLAGMEN FOR PARKING.** Dakota Sandstone at 2:00. San Andres Limestone and Bernal Sandstone to left of road, at 8:30.
	0.3
27.7	Cattle guard; Dakota Sandstone at right.
	0.1
27.8	Dakota (?) Sandstone in road cut at left, Chinle Formation in valley to right.
	0.3
28.1	Cattle guard; Dakota Sandstone, exposed in hills at 1:00, is part of a north-trending, doubly-plunging syncline.

0.4

28.5 Dakota (?) Sandstone, road cut on left.

0.4

28.9 Cattle guard; hills from 6:30 to 12:30 are underlain by San Andres Limestone, domed by Tertiary intrusives.

0.3

29.2 Low hills on right expose Dakota Sandstone on purple mudstones of Chinle Formation.

0.5

29.7 Constriction in valley, San Andres Limestone on left, Dakota Sandstone on right, note old mine workings half way up the slope near Dakota Sandstone.

0.3

30.0 San Andres Limestone outcropping in road cut on left. At 4:00 breach in Dakota ridge forming rim of doubly-plunging syncline.

0.2

30.2 Gypsum on left of road, indicates proximity of San Andres-Bernal.

0.6

30.8 Northeast-trending dike crosses road at this point.

0.2

31.5 **STOP NO. 5. FOLLOW DIRECTIONS OF FLAGMEN FOR PARKING.** At 8:30 good section of gypsum member of San Andres Limestone and yellow and red fine-grained sandstones of the Bernal(?) Formation.

0.1

31.1 Cattle guard; hill on left exposes interbedded limestone and gypsum of the upper part of the San Andres Limestone.

0.2

31.3 Caution. Cross Southern Pacific Railroad tracks. Keep left. Enter Ancho, N. M. Turn right (north) on old U.S. 54. Road is on Bernal (?) Formation.

0.9

32.2 Mesas at 10:30 are capped by Dakota Sandstone.

0.8

33.0 Scattered outcrops of Santa Rosa Sandstone, here intruded by several lamprophyre dikes, such as exposed on low knob across railroad tracks. Slope ahead is made up of red Chinle mudstones, capped by Dakota Sandstone, and forms part of doubly plunging syncline, mentioned previously.

1.0

34.0 Road is on Chinle Formation.

0.2

34.2 Across railroad tracks note small fault, which has downthrown the east-dipping Dakota Sandstone.

0.5

34.7 Cattle guard; entering Luna, N. M.

0.1

34.8 Road to right leads to outcrops of Ogallalla gravels on Chinle Formation.

0.4

35.2 Santa Rosa Sandstone in road cut on left.

0.6

35.8 Notch in ridge at 8:00 is contact between Dakota Sandstone (left) and San Andres Limestone (right). The proximity of these two beds in the field is explained as the result gravitational gliding (décoiffement) from a dome-shaped structure to the north (see Budding, 1963).
Prominent notch at 9:00 is made by Red Hill Canyon.

0.9

36.7 Road crosses Red Hill Canyon.

0.6

37.3 San Andres Limestone outcrops along the road.

0.4

37.7 Cattle guard; Glorietta Sandstone ahead on right.

0.1

37.8 Brown soil color indicates presence of Yeso sandstone.

0.2

38.0 Low ridge at 1 - 3:00 exposes Yeso Formation, capped by Gloiretta Sandstone.

0.6

38.6 Yeso Limestone beds to left of road have been tilted steeply by intrusion to the west.

0.2

38.8 Glorieta Sandstone.

0.9

39.7 Tecolote, N. M.

          0.3
40.0   Side road to left; continue straight ahead.
          0.7
40.7   Glorieta Sandstone in road cut on left.
          1.3
42.0   Ranchhouse; road on left leads through Tecolote hills to U.S. 54. These hills are underlain by intrusive rocks of Tertiary age. For the next few miles, the road is on Glorieta Sandstone.
          2.2
44.2   Crossroad, continue straight ahead. Hills to right on skyline are in San Andres Limestone.
          1.2
45.4   Glorieta Sandstone exposed on both sides of road.
          0.4
45.8   San Andres Limestone crops out from beneath the Glorieta Sandstone.
          0.7
46.5   Crossing El Paso Natural Gas Company pipeline.
          2.0
48.5   **Turn left (west) on side road.** Gallinas Mountains from 1:00 - 2:00. Gallinas, N. M., 0.3 mile ahead (north).
          0.1
48.6   Blocks of San Andres Limestone next to road.
          1.2
49.8   **Junction U.S. 54.**
END OF ROAD LOG FROM CARRIZOZO TO GALLINAS. END OF 15TH FIELD CONFERENCE. WE HOPE YOU HAVE ENJOYED THE TRIPS AND WILL BE ABLE TO PARTICIPATE IN NEXT YEAR'S FIELD CONFERENCE OF THE NEW MEXICO GEOLOGICAL SOCIETY.
HASTA LA VISTA.

SUPPLEMENTAL ROAD LOGS
By Carl Ulvog and Sam Thompson, III

Road Log from Gallinas to Gallinas Peak

Total Mileage		
0.0		Junction of U.S. 54 and Red Canyon road, 1½ miles west of Gallinas, New Mexico. **Proceed west on dirt road toward Red Cloud Picnic Area.** South Mesa and Rough Mountain in Gallinas Mountains at 1:00 to 2:00.
	1.3	
1.3		Cattleguard. **Follow sharp turn right (north). Continue on road toward Gallinas Lookout.** Yeso underlies low timbered ridge on left (west).
	0.8	
2.1		Small Glorieta outlier caps low hill on right.
	0.1	
2.2		Side road on left to Fuller Ranch. South Mesa (Tertiary porphyritic trachyte intrusive, with Glorieta and Yeso Formation on east side) at 9:00 to 10:30.
	1.3	
3.5		Junction of Corona-Bates Ranch road with Gallinas Lookout-Red Cloud Picnic Area road. **Turn left (west) toward Gallinas Lookout.**
	1.5	
5.0		Cattle guard. Roadbed on Yeso Formation. Rough Mountain (tree-covered Yeso) at 2:00.
	1.3	
6.3		Road crosses draw. Prospect pit in metamorphosed Yeso on ridge at right. Road follws north-south trending fault downthrown to west. Rough Mountain Mining District has numerous prospect pits and mines of fluorite and copper mineralization.
	0.1	
6.4		Side road on left to South Canyon. Follow main road which curves left, crossing north-south fault. On upthrown side (east) is small fault block of Precambrian and Abo.
	0.3	
6.7		Large mine excavation in altered (metamorphosed) Yeso Formation on right.
	0.1	
6.8		Porphyritic trachyte dike and steeply dipping Yeso on right.
	0.1	
6.9		Large mine excavation on right.
	1.3	
8.2		Red Cloud Picnic Ground. Perhac (1961) maps small block of Precambrian immediately west of road. Complex area of Glorieta and Yeso with trachyte intrusives.
	1.9	
10.1		Curve to left (west). Road on Glorieta and Yeso. Duran Mesa to north.
	2.1	
12.2		Junction with road from Corona on right. Follow road ahead to Gallinas Lookout. Approximate contact of Yeso with main Gallinas Peak intrusive. Road ahead on Tertiary porphyritic rhyolite.
	0.9	
13.1		Road fork. Bear right (north) to Gallinas Lookout.
	1.8	
14.9		Gallinas Lookout. Elevation 8,615'. Gallinas Peak (elevation 8,637') is Tertiary porphyritic rhyolite pluton intruding Glorieta and Yeso. Panoramic view: Duran Mesa at 2:00; Chameleon Hill at 2:30; Capitan Mountain at 4:30; Jicarilla Mountains and Tecolote Hills at 5:00; Lone Mountain and Sierra Blanca Peak on skyline at 6:00; Oscura Mountains at 7:30; Fra Cristobal Mountains at 8:00; San Mateo Mountains at 8:30; Los Pinos Mountains at 9:00; Manzano Mountains at 10:00 Sandia Mountains at 10:30; Chupadera Mesa in middle distance at 8:00 to 10:00. Retrace route to U.S. 54. (Road junction at total mileage point 13.1 provides alternate route to highway). **End of road log from Gallinas to Gallinas Peak.**

Road Log from Gallinas to Carrizozo

Total Mileage	
0.0	**Junction of U.S. 54 and Red Canyon road 1½ mile west of Gallinas, New Mexico. Proceed south on N.M. 54.** South Mesa, Tertiary porphyritic trachyte intruded into Yeso and Glorieta, at 3:00. Rough Mountain, faulted and mineralized Yeso, at 4:00. Gallinas Peak Lookout on skyline at 3:30. Capitan Mountains on skyline at 10:00 to 10:30. Jacks Peak in Jicarilla Mountains at 10:30. Tecolote Hills in middle distance at 10:00 to 11:00. Tecolote Peak at 11:00.
	1.3
1.3	Lincoln Compressor Station, El Paso Natural Gas Company.
	1.5
2.8	Glorieta exposed along side of highway.
	0.3
3.1	Crest of hill. Begin series of road cuts in San Andres. Tecolote Peak, Tertiary intrusive, at 10:00. Yeso, Glorieta and San Andres on lower slopes. Jicarilla Mountains at 10:30; Carrizo Peak at 11:00; Lone Mountain at 11:30; Sierra Blanca Peak on skyline at 11:00.
	1.2
4.3	Side roads on right and left.
	0.8
5.1	Road cuts in San Andres. Erratic dips possibly due to slumping.
	0.3
5.4	Cross approximate contact between San Andres and Bernal.
	0.1
5.5	Road cut on left in Bernal red beds.
	0.3
5.8	Culvert crossing. Santa Rosa Sandstone caps ridge on left.
	1.2
7.0	Side road on left to Tecolote Hills. Side road on right to Dimmit Bond ranch. San Andres on ridges at 1:00 to 5:00. Bernal exposed along highway ahead for next 7½ miles.
	4.1
11.1	Bernal forms mesa at 8:30. Jacks Peak in Jicarilla Mountains at 9:00. Santa Rosa — downfaulted to east — forms ridge on left in middle distance.
	0.8
11.9	Bridge crossing Largo Canyon. Highway enters northeast corner of Little Black Peak quadrangle.
	1.6
13.5	Ancho Truck Stop on right.
	1.4
14.9	San Andres exposed in drainage on right.
	0.3
15.2	Side road on left to Ancho, side road on right to ranch.
	0.4
15.6	Begin series of road cuts in Santa Rosa sandstones, red shales and conglomerates.
	1.5
17.1	Cross approximate contact between Santa Rosa and Chinle.
	1.1
18.2	Dakota Sandstone forms ridge on left.
	1.3
19.5	Side road on right to Knight ranch. Small outlier of Dakota at 2:00.
	1.0
20.5	Road cut in Dakota. Highway crosses west edge of Dakota Sandstone ridge.
	0.7
21.2	Junction of N.M. 10 with U.S. 54. Historical Marker: "Gran Quivira National Monument 39 miles northwest. The spectacular ruins of two early Spanish Missions; first Mission was built in 1627 and the larger one with Convents in 1659. Adjoining the Missions are the ruins of a large prehistoric Indian village." Highway is on Chinle Formation. Dakota Sandstone ridge on left.
	1.2
22.4	Road cut on right in Chinle Formation.
	0.9
23.3	Culvert crossing arroyo. Outliers of Dakota on right.
	0.4

23.7	Bridge crossing Coyote Canyon drainage. Lone Mountain at 10:00. (Tertiary monzonite intrusive surrounded by concentric ridges of San Andres, Bernal, Santa Rosa, Chinle and Dakota.)
	0.3
24.0	Side road on left to Pat Dunning ranch.
	0.5
24.5	Contact of Chinle with overlying Dakota exposed on right.
	0.2
24.7	Road cut exposure of Dakota/Chinle contact.
	0.1
24.8	Panoramic view: Jicarilla Mountains at 9:00 to 10:00. Lone Mountain at 10:00, Carrizo Peak at 11:00, Nogal Peak and Sierra Blanca Peak at 11:30, Cub Mountain at 12:30, San Andres Mountains at 1:00, Mockingbird Gap at 2:00, Oscura Mountains at 2:00 to 3:00, Carrizozo anticline in San Andres Formation at 1:00 to 2:00 in middle distance, Carrizozo Malpais in Tularosa Valley at 1:30 to 2:30, Little Black Peak at 2:00.
	0.3
25.1	Culvert crossing arroyo. Approximate contact of Dakota with Mancos. Highway on Mancos for next 6 miles ahead.
	0.1
25.2	Side road on left to Coyote, New Mexico.
	0.5
25.7	Road cut in Mancos shale, limestone, and Tertiary diabase (basalt?) sill.
	0.3
26.0	Side road on right to ranches.
	5.4
31.4	Bridge crossing White Oaks Canyon. Approximate contact of Mancos with Mesaverde Formation. Mesaverde sandstone forms low hill ahead.
	2.7
34.1	Side road on left (N.M. 349) to White Oaks, New Mexico. Low rounded hills (Tertiary sills in Mesaverde) at 8:00 to 9:00.
	3.1
37.2	Carrizozo Village Limits.
	0.1
37.3	Historical Marker: "Carrizozo. Founded 1905, population 1,546. Elevation 5,425'. The crossroads of history. Northeast is the ghost town of White Oaks, a once booming mining camp where Emersan Haush lived and laid the scene of his book **Hearts Desire**. Famous names like Billy the Kid, Pat Garret and Lew Wallace are closely associated with the area."
	0.1
37.4	Intersection of U.S. 54 with U.S. 380.

End of road log from Gallinas to Carrizozo.

Road Log from Roswell to Hondo

Total Mileage

0.0	**Roswell, New Mexico. Intersection of U.S. 70-380 (2nd Street) with U.S. 285 (Main Street). Proceed west on U.S. 70-380.**
	3.4
3.4	National Guard Armory on right.
	0.4
3.8	New Mexico State Highway Department on right.
	1.8
5.6	Roadcut in San Andres Formation on right.
	0.3
5.9	Crest of Six Mile Hill structure. Pajarito Peak at 11:00. Sierra Blanca at 12:00, Capitan Mountain at 1:00. Hill crest is approximately on axis of Six Mile Hill structure—a broad anticline broken by faults. Note reversal of dip in San Andres limestone in roadcuts ahead.
	1.0
6.9	Divided highway ends.
	0.4
7.3	Bridge crossing arroyo.

	5.3
12.6	Bridge crossing arroyo.
	0.2
12.8	Begin series of roadcuts in San Andres Formation.
	0.2
13.0	Side road on left to Two Rivers Reservoir.
	0.4
13.4	Roadside Park. Chisum Trail Marker: "John Chisum, owner of the famous South Spring River Ranch, trailed several herds of cattle from the Pecos Valley to the San Carlos Indian Reservation in Arizona, under government contract, in the early 1870's. The trail left the Pecos at Seven Rivers, and swung westward to follow roughly the present route of U.S. 70 in Arizona."
	0.8
14.2	Roadcut in San Andres.
	4.0
18.2	Roadside Park. Sierra Blanca at 12:00 o'clock, Capitan Mountain at 2:00, Border Hills (ridge in middle distance) at 11:00 to 3:00.
	0.9
21.1	Side road on right to Walker AFB Aux. Site 579-10.
	0.1
21.2	Leave Chaves County, enter Lincoln County. Roadcuts in San Andres for next 9.5 miles ahead.
	3.1
24.3	Road ascends Border Hills structure. (Narrow faulted anticline trending 35 miles northeast-southwest).
	0.4
24.7	Quarry in San Andres limestone on left. (Strike: N 40°E, dip: 35°SE.)
	0.2
24.9	Roadcut exposes steeply dipping San Andres on left. Approximate axis of Border Hills structure.
	0.4
25.3	Rest area on right.
	1.0
26.3	Road on left to crest of Border Hills (where San Andres displays 30 to 40° SE dip on southeast limb of structure.)
	3.4
29.7	Rest area on left.
	0.4
30.1	Side road on right to Walker AFB Aux. Site 579-9.
	0.6
30.7	Picacho Hills. Highway descends to Rio Hondo Valley. Approximately 400 feet of San Andres limestone exposed in roadcuts over next 1.5 miles ahead.
	0.3
31.0	Roadcut exposes contact of San Andres with underlying Glorieta Sandstone (Hondo Sandstone Member of some geologists).
	0.8
31.8	Bridge crossing arroyo.
	0.7
32.5	Riverside, New Mexico.
	0.2
32.7	Roadcut exposes yellowish Glorieta sandstone between limestones.
	0.9
33.6	Sunset, New Mexico.
	0.7
34.3	Roadcut in Yeso Formation; Glorieta Sandstone in cliffs on right. Yeso exposed in roadcuts over next 8 miles ahead.
	4.1
38.4	Picacho, New Mexico. San Andres on hills, Yeso at highway level.
	2.5
40.9	Approximate axis of Picacho anticline, large closed structure trending north-south. Two wells drilled on this anticline (National Exploration Co., sec. 21, T. 11 S., R. 18 E.; and Stanolind Oil and Gas Co., sec. 10, T. 12 S., R. 18 E.) were dry and both reported Precambrian above 3,000'.
	1.1
42.0	"Adobe Hacienda," home of Louise Massey, song writer, on left.
	1.5
43.5	Tinnie, New Mexico.

	0.5
44.0	Junction of N.M. 368 with U.S. 70-380. N.M. 368 follows north-south axis of Tinnie Fold belt to Arabela in Capitan Mountains. Continue on U.S. 70-380.
	0.6
44.6	Roadcut in Yeso and gray porphyritic sill.
	0.4
45.0	Junction of N.M. 395 with U.S. 70-380. Continue on U.S. 70-380.
	0.6
45.6	Steep easterly dipping monoclinal bend in Yeso and San Andres at 2:30.
	1.5
47.1	Hondo, New Mexico Post Office.
	0.1
47.2	Routes divide. U.S. 70 (left) to Ruidoso and U.S. 380 (right) to Lincoln. **End of Road Log from Roswell to Hondo.**

Road Log from Hondo to Ruidoso

Total Mileage

0.0	**Hondo, New Mexico. Junction of U.S. 380 and U.S. 70. Proceed west on U.S. 70.**
	0.1
0.1	Bridge crossing Rio Bonito, which joins Rio Ruidoso one-half mile downstream to form Rio Hondo.
	0.5
0.6	Church on left. San Andres caps ridge on left, valley cut in Yeso Formation.
	1.5
2.1	Road cut in slide block of San Andres limestone (minimum displacement 300 feet).
	0.7
2.8	Approximate axis of McDaniel anticline as mapped by Mourant in 1963.
	0.7
3.5	San Patricio, home of Peter Hurd — famous artist and poloist.
	0.2
3.7	Begin series of road cuts in Yeso Formation.
	2.4
6.1	Road cut on right in Yeso gypsum. Fluvial terraces along sides of valley on left.
	1.2
7.3	Bridge crossing arroyo. San Andres limestone forms canyon rim, Yeso exposed on lower slopes.
	1.7
9.0	Bridge. Roadcuts in alluvial gravels.
	1.3
10.3	Gravel terraces on ridge at right is site of prehistoric Indian village excavated in 1956 by Texas Technological College archaeologists.
	0.2
10.5	Bridge crossing arroyo. Junction of N.M. 214 with U.S. 70. N.M. 214 leads to Fort Stanton. Continue on U.S. 70. Road cut in Yeso.
	0.7
11.2	Glencoe, New Mexico, Post Office on left.
	0.3
11.5	Roadcut in Yeso.
	1.3
12.8	Yeso dolomite exposed in road cut on right and across valley at 9:00.
	0.3
13.1	Road cut in Yeso Formation and Tertiary intrusives.
	0.3
13.4	Approximate contact of Yeso with San Andres, on east limb of large syncline. Road cuts in San Andres Formation for next 3.5 miles ahead. Note light colored sills in San Andres on right.
	0.4
13.8	Buckhorn, New Mexico.
	0.1
13.9	San Andres exposed on right. Begin series of road cuts in San Andres Formation.
	0.5
14.4	Tertiary sills in San Andres exposed on right.
	0.5

14.9	Road cut in Tertiary sills displaying spheroidal weathering.
	1.2
16.1	San Andres limestone with Tertiary sills exposed on right. Quaternary gravels abutt against San Andres in vertical contact.
	0.1
16.2	Fox Cave. (Wall-enclosed overhang of San Andres limestone.)
	0.3
16.5	East dipping San Andres limestone and shale in place.
	0.4
16.9	San Andres exposed on right. Contact with Glorieta and Yeso obscured.
	0.4
17.3	Bridge crossing arroyo. Alluvial fans on left across valley.
	0.3
17.6	Road cut in San Andres slump blocks.
	0.2
17.8	Road cut in Yeso.
	0.6
18.4	Yeso exposed in excavation on right.
	0.2
18.6	Bridge crossing Rio Ruidoso.
	1.6
20.2	Dislocated blocks of Yeso and San Andres across Rio Ruidoso at 3:00.
	0.6
20.8	Road cut in folded Yeso.
	0.2
21.0	Divided highway begins.
	0.5
21.5	Entrance to Agua Fria Estates on left. Hale Spring, one-half mile south of highway, once fed an Indian acequia (irrigation ditch). This ditch — about 900 years old — skirts foothills on left. Pieces of caliche precipitated from irrigation water in this ditch line driveway entrance.
	0.1
21.6	Ruidoso Downs City Limit. Elevation 6,400'.
	1.4
23.0	Ruidoso Downs racetrack on right.
	1.1
24.1	Ruidoso, New Mexico City Limits.
	0.1
24.2	Junction of N.M. 37 with U.S. 70.
	End of Road Log from Hondo to Ruidoso.

Road Log from Ruidoso to Pajarito Mountain

Total Mileage

0.0	**Ruidoso, New Mexico. Junction of U.S. 70 with N.M. 37. Proceed southwest on U.S. 70.**
	4.5
4.5	Turn left (south) on side road (gravel) to Fence Canyon and White Tail.
	0.1
4.6	Cattle guard.
	0.3
4.9	Roadcuts in San Andres for next 9 miles ahead.
	2.6
7.5	Side road on right to quarry in San Andres. Continue on main road ahead.
	2.9
10.4	Road curves to right.
	0.2
10.6	Crest of hill. High parts of surrounding hills are part of Sacramento plain, the highest surface on the east slope of the Sacramento Mountains. Pray and Allen believe this may be of Pliocene age and that stripping of Cretaceous rocks from the region provided some of sediments for Ogallala Formation to the east.
	0.3
10.9	Quarry in San Andres on left; water well and tank on right.
	1.4

12.3	Side road on right to house.	
	1.4	
13.7	Road junction. Bear left toward White Tail. San Andres outcrops along left side of road.	
	0.4	
14.1	Exposure of Glorieta in gulley on right side of road. (White Tail community ahead in valley floored by Glorieta Sandstone.)	
	0.9	
15.0	School buildings on right.	
	0.5	
15.5	Bear right and follow main road.	
	1.8	
17.3	Road curves to left.	
	0.3	
17.6	Cattle guard.	
	0.3	
17.9	Approximate contact of San Andres with Glorieta.	
	0.4	
18.3	Pajarito Mountain at 12:00.	
	0.6	
18.9	Road descends into open valley with Glorieta sandstone floor.	
	1.4	
20.3	Water well on right. Stratigraphic log of this well shows igneous rock encountered at depth of 250'.	
	0.4	
20.7	Road fork, bear left. Glorieta exposed in draw on right.	
	0.6	
21.3	San Andres exposed on left.	
	0.1	
21.4	Road junction, turn right toward Pajarito Lookout.	
	0.9	
22.3	Small sink hole on left. Cross old telephone line. Pajarito Lookout Tower at 11:00 on San Andres Limestone. Note west dip of San Andres to left of tower. Beds are dipping away from central part of Pajarito intrusion.	
	0.4	
22.7	Bear right. Large sink hole on left.	
	0.4	
23.1	Large sink hole on left. Follow old telephone line.	
	1.0	
24.1	Enter wooded area.	
	0.1	
24.2	Gate, bear right.	
	0.1	
24.3	Note west dip of San Andres.	
	0.2	
24.5	Glorieta outcrop.	
	0.3	
24.8	Roadcut in contorted Yeso.	
	0.5	
25.3	Gate, sharp turn. Park you car and walk 20 yards along gulley east of sharp turn to see contact zone of intrusion. Glorieta sandstone, in contact with hornblende granite, is yellowish-red and purple, possibly due to metamorphism. Granite contains quartz grains, possibly through assimilation of silica from Glorieta.	
	0.2	
25.5	Roadcut in Yeso redbeds.	
	0.3	
25.8	San Andres carbonate exposed.	
	0.5	
26.3	Pajarito Lookout. Top of Pajarito Mountain (Elevation 8,014') in San Andres formation. Tertiary granite intrusive exposed on east side of mountain. Panoramic view: Sierra Blanca intrusive at 9:00 to 9:30; Jicarilla Mountains in distance at 10:30; Capitan Mountain intrusives at 11:00 to 1:00; south end of Sacramento Mountains in middle distance with Guadalupe Mountains in background at 4:30; Sacramento plain on San Andres formation at 6:00 to 9:00; the Diamond A plain extending eastward to constructional terraces adjoining Pecos River at 1:00 to 4:30; flat grassy area at 2:00 to 4:30 in foreground outlines structural bench with numerous sink holes.	

Following information taken from W. S. Motts and Robert Gaal (1960). Ridge descending from Pajarito Mountain in an easterly direction is mainly an igneous outcrop with small prominence at 2:30 composed of silicious limestones. At the base of Pajarito Mountain, one mile to east-southeast is a small gray to reddish-gray exfoliation dome in an igneous outcrop. Immediately east of this dome are cuestas formed by east dipping Glorieta with San Andres on back slope.

At the contact of igneous and sedimentary rocks in this area, the igneous rock is granitic in composition with medium to large amounts of quartz. At a distance from the contact zone and nearer the central part of the intrusive, quartz disappears as a constitutent and monzonites and syenites predominate thus suggesting assimilation of silica from the country rock, i.e., the Glorieta sandstone. Small outcrops of olivine diabase occur in central parts of the intrusive, probably representing a dike type of intrusion. Interesting metamorphic effects are displayed in small saddle just below the crest and on this side of the low peak ½ mile away at 2:00.

Retrace route to U.S. 70.

End of Road Log from Ruidoso to Pajarito Mountain.

Road Log from Nogal to Nogal Peak and Bonito Lake

**Modified from log by George B. Griswold
in the guidebook of the 14th Field Conference of New Mexico Geological Society**

Note: Road is very rough and a 4-wheel drive vehicle is recommended for this trip.

Total Mileage

0.0		Village of Nogal. This was once the trading center for gold-silver-lead-zinc-copper mines located in Dry Gulch about 2½ miles west of here. Current mining is nearly at a standstill.
	0.4	
0.4		Dry Gulch crossing.
	0.1	
0.5		Nogal Creek crossing. Here we cross the contact between the Cub Mountain Formation and the overlying Sierra Blanca volcanic pile.
	0.3	
0.8		SLOW, turn off State 37 onto Nogal Creek Road. The road from here to the Rialto molybdenum prospect will soon demonstrate the complex volcanic-intrusive relationships of the Sierra Blanca "igneous complex." A swarm of north-trending monzonite(?) dikes have invaded the basaltic andesite flows in this particular area.
	0.4	
1.2		Monzonite exposed on left side of road.
	0.5	
1.7		Cattle guard.
	0.5	
2.2		Highly altered volcanic rocks which were originally basaltic andesite.
	1.1	
3.7		Cattle guard. Both canyon walls are now underlain by basaltic andesite.
	0.7	
4.4		Ford across to north side of canyon.
	0.3	
4.7		Monzonite exposed at right.
	0.2	
4.9		Rockford Canyon to right leads to gold prospects which are believed to have been one of the earliest ore discoveries in Lincoln County.
	0.3	
5.2		Ford over to south side of creek.
	0.2	
5.4		Truck trail to left, bear right. Monzonite porphyry exposed on north side of creek.
	0.1	
5.5		Ford back to north side of creek.
	0.1	
5.6		Altered volcanics exposed along road.
	0.1	
5.7		Prospect pit in altered volcanics at right.

5.8		Short tunnel into andesite. For the next ¾ of a mile both canyon walls expose fairly unaltered basaltic andesite volcanics.
	0.8	
6.6		Ford over to west side of creek. This is the northeastern margin of the Nogal Peak monzonite stock. Here the rock is brownish-gray in color, equigranular, and relatively unaltered. The creek follows the contact between the stock and altered volcanics to the north.
	0.4	
7.0		Bear right. Road to left leads over ridge into Tanbark Canyon.
	0.2	
7.2		Ford back to north side of creek.
	0.2	
7.4		A tongue from the stock extends from the south across the creek here. The tongue is about 500 feet wide and extends north for 1,000 feet.
	0.1	
7.5		Indian Creek to the right. Continue on main road.
	0.3	
7.8		Ford to south side of creek.
	0.3	
8.1		Road Fork. Turn sharply to the left. Road to right ends at the base of Nogal Peak. Our road will start to climb up onto the south ridge of Nogal Creek. Go in first gear and keep your engine "revved." We are now on the northwestern edge on the Rialto stock. The stock will be well exposed in the road cut for the next mile. Note that hydrothermal alteration is evident and tends to increase as we proceed up the ridge.
	1.0	
9.1		Fulmer Tunnel has the only significant exposure of molybdenum mineralization in the Nogal Peak district.
	0.2	
9.3		Walk from here over altered monzonite outcrop on the ridge crest.
	0.1	
9.4		Cross through gate. Start descent into Tanbark Creek. The road is rough and steep — use first gear.
	0.2	
9.6		Contact between monzonite and altered volcanics. This is the eastern margin of the Rialto stock.
	0.1	
9.7		Road junction, turn right.
	0.5	
10.2		Parsons Gold Mine. Gold was mined from a breccia pipe during the early 1900's.
	1.6	
11.8		Parsons Hotel.
	0.5	
12.3		Silver Bar mine.
	0.3	
12.6		Bonito Creek Junction. Turn left. Outcrops here are thick basaltic andesite flows complexly invaded by later diorite, monzonite and latite.
	0.6	
13.2		Prospect tunnel into altered volcanics.
	0.2	
13.4		Canyon to left leads to Martha Washington silver mine.
	0.5	
13.9		High peak right of road is Grizzly Peak. The peak is underlain by monzonite and diorite and is on the eastern edge of Bonito Lake.
	0.2	
14.1		Contact of Bonito Lake stock. This stock covers at least 6 square miles surrounding Bonito Lake.
	0.6	
14.7		Cattle guard. Then ford to south side of Bonito Creek.
	0.9	
15.6		Ford to north side of Bonito Creek.
	0.1	
15.7		Bonito Lake. This artificial reservoir was built by the Southern Pacific Railroad for use in their steam locomotives. Water was transported by pipeline as far as Vaughn, New Mexico. The reservoir now supplies water to the city of Alamogordo. The road around the lake exposes outcrops of monzonite.
	1.2	
16.9		Bonito Dam. Outcrop of dioritic facies of Bonito Lake stock across from dam.
	0.4	
17.3		Eastern margin of Bonito Lake stock. Outcrops from here east will be mostly altered basaltic andesite with occasional monzonite dikes and sills which extend out into the volcanics.

	0.1
17.4	Prospect tunnel into pyritized volcanics.
	1.0
18.4	Bonito Cafe. Outcrop of monzonite at left is a sill in the basaltic andesite volcanics.
	1.6
20.0	Road junction. Turn left for Nogal.
	End of road log from Nogal Peak to Bonito Lake.

SELECTED REFERENCES

Allen, J. E. and Kottlowski, F. E., 1958, Roswell-Capitan-Ruidoso and Bottomless Lakes Park, New Mexico: N. Mex. Inst. Min. and Tech., State Bur. of Mines and Min. Res. Scenic Trips to Geologic Past, No. 3, 47 p.

Bachman, G. O., 1960, Southwestern edge of late Paleozoic landmass in New Mexico: U.S. Geol. Survey Prof. Paper 400-B, p. B239-B241.

Budding, A. J., 1963, Origin and age of superficial structures, Jicarilla Mountains central New Mexico: Geol. Soc. America Bull., v. 74, p. 203-208, 2 figs.

Griswold, B. B., 1959, Mineral deposits of Lincoln County, New Mexico: N. Mex. Inst. Min. Tech., State Bur. Mines and Min. Res. Bull. 67, 117 p. Also see the article by Griswold in this guidebook.

Kelley, V. C., 1949, Geology and economics of New Mexico iron ore deposits. Univ. N. Mex., Pub. Geol. No. 2.

Motts, W. S., and Gaal, Robert, 1960, Geology of Pajarito Mountain area, Otero County, New Mexico: Am. Assoc. Petroleum Geologists Bull., v. 44, p. 108-111, 2 figs.

Mourant, W. A., 1963, Water resources and geology of the Rio Hondo drainage basin, Chaves, Lincoln and Otero Counties, New Mexico: N. Mex. State Engineer Tech. Rept. 28, 85 p.

Neal, D. J., 1961, Captive mountain waters: Texas Western Univ. Press, 103 p.

New Mexico Geological Society, 1963, Guidebook of the Socorro Region, New Mexico — Fourteenth Field Conference, R. W. Foster, Chairman.

Perhac, R. M., 1961, Geology and mineral resources of Gallinas Mountains, New Mexico: Unpublished doctoral dissertation, Univ. Michigan. Also see the two articles by Perhac elsewhere in this guidebook.

Permian Basin Section, Society of Economic Paleontologists and Mineralogists, and Roswell Geological Society, 1959, Guidebook of the Sacramento Mountains of Otero County, New Mexico. Carl Ulvog, Frank Packard, and Sam Thompson, III, Chairmen.

Roswell Geological Society, 1951, Guidebook to the Capitan-Carrizozo-Chupadera Mesa region — Fifth Field Conference, T. F. Stipp, Chairman.

————1952, Guidebook of the Pedernal positive element and the Estancia Basin — Seventh Field Conference, E. J. Foley, Chairman.

————1958, Giudebook of Hatchet Mountains and Cooks Range — Florida Mountain areas — Eleventh Field Conference, G. R. Washburn, Chairman.

LEXICON OF STRATIGRAPHIC NAMES USED IN LINCOLN COUNTY, NEW MEXICO

Christina Lochman-Balk

New Mexico Institute of Mining and Technology
Socorro, New Mexico

This lexicon is an alphabetical listing and brief discussion of the stratigraphic names which have been used in Lincoln County, New Mexico, for units that are Pennsylvanian through Quaternary in age. The form used is as follows:

Unit name (formation or group)—system or period. Names printed entirely in capitals are currently accepted by the U.S. Geological Survey. Names printed in caps and lower case are used locally or have been recently proposed.

1) Areal distribution given in original description.
2) Reference in which unit was first defined or mentioned.
3) Type locality.
4) Short lithologic description and thickness at type locality or in the type area.
5) Age to stage; contacts; emending or redefining descriptions; additional information on areal distribution and thickness, lithology, and character of the beds in the area of the field conference.

ABO FORMATION — Permian

1) Central New Mexico
2) W. T. Lee, 1909; redescribed by Needham and Bates, 1943.
3) Abo Canyon, south end of Manzano Mountains, Socorro Co.
4) Dark red, purple, coarse-grained ss., cgl. at base, some sh., 300 to 800 feet thick.
5) Wolfcampian — Leonardian; conformable and gradational on Bursum Fm., disconformable (?) on upper Madera Ls.; overlain conformably and gradationally by Yeso Fm. (Pray and Otte 1954). Abo is transitional with Bursum in northern Sacramento Mtns.; in southern Sacramento Mtns. Early Wolfcampian is absent and Abo or equivalent marine beds of late Wolfcampian age lie unconformably on Pennsylvanian or older rocks. Abo is 1,400 feet thick in the north and thins abruptly to 250 feet in the central Sacramento Mtns. Farther south it is composed of two tongues separated by, and transitional with southward thickening brackish-marine Hueco Fm.; basal tongue is the Powwow Cgl. and upper tongue is Deer Mountain red sh. Widespread in New Mexico and in the subsurface of West Texas.

ARTESIA GROUP — Permian

1) Eastern New Mexico and West Texas.
2) D. B. Tait, and others, 1962, p. 504.
3) Humble Federal Bogle well No. 1, sec. 30, T. 16 S., R. 30 E., Eddy Co.
4) A sequence of shelf rocks composed of anhydr., dolo., ss., siltst. and red sh. 1,710 feet thick in the Type wall.
5) Upper Guadalupian; unconformably lies on San Andres Fm.; overlain unconformably by Triassic rocks in northeastern New Mexico, and overlain disconformably on the shelf and conformably in the Delaware Basin by the Ochoan series. The group extends from the top of the Tansill Fm., down through the Yates Fm., Seven Rivers Fm., Queen Fm., and Grayburg Fm., including the basal or Premier sand; it is traceable both in the surface and in the subsurface of southeastern and east-central New Mexico. All units thin northwestward across the shelf and top units are missing because of erosion; traced into West Texas and southwestern Oklahoma where marker beds thin and disappear and predominate clastic facies pass into the Whitehorse Group; to the south group units pass into the Capitan and Goat Seep reefs of the Delaware Basin. The authors do not comment on the use of the term "Artesia red sand" from 1929-1953 for the upper mbr. of the Queen Fm. in the Artesia oil field, Eddy Co., New Mexico.

BERNAL FORMATION — Permian

1) Central-northern New Mexico.
2) G. O. Bachman, 1953.
3) Section at Bernal Butte, near Chapelle, T. 13 N., R. 16 E.
4) Red, red-orange siltst. with 11-foot thick gyp. bed approximately 35 feet above the base. The formation is 165 feet thick.
5) Upper Guadalupian; lies disconformably on karst surface of the San Andres Fm.; in field conference area, also disconformably on the Glorieta Ss. mbr. of the San Andres Ls.; overlain unconformably by the Triassic Santa Rosa Ss. Thickness ranges from 30 to 355 feet. Originally was upper clastic mbr. of the San Andres Fm. In the field conference area it is red-brown to yellow-brown siltst., clayst. and fine ss., with a basal buff ss., a few gyp. beds, local crossbedding and many lenses, and is rather friable. It is the lateral equivalent to the Artesia Gp. (Tait, and others, 1962).

Broken Back Basalt Flow — Quaternary

1) Near Broken Back Crater.
2) Used by R. H. Weber, 1963, and defined by C. T. Smith, 1964.

3) Broken Back Crater, Broken Back Crater quadrangle, Lincoln Co.
4) Gray-green to black alkali olivine basalt.
5) Post-Pleistocene(?); rests unconformably on the San Andres Ls., Bernal Fm., or Santa Rosa Fm., overlain(?) disconformably by the Little Black Peak flow.

BURSUM FORMATION — Permian

1) Central, New Mexico.
2) R. H. Wilpolt, and others, 1946.
3) NE½ sec. 1, T. 6 S., R. 4 E., Socorro Co., (E. A. Lloyd, 1949, designated a new type section in NE½ sec. 14, T. 2 N., R. 4 E.).
4) Dark purple-red and green sh. interbedded with arkose, arkosic cgl. and gray ls. Locally there is a reworked rubbly nodular ls. at the base. It is 28 to 234 feet thick.
5) Late Virgilian and Early Wolfcampian; gradationally and transitionally overlies the arkosic mbr. of the Madera Ls., gradationally and transitionally overlain by the Abo; local erosional disconformities at base of clastic lenses, of intertonguing terresterial to brackish-water red beds and of marine ls. with fusulinid fauna (*Triticites* and *Schwagerian*) of both Pennsylvanian and Permian aspect. In the northern Sacramento Mtns. the Laborcita Formation of Otte (1954, 1959) is equivalent to the Bursum and represents continental near-short deposits across the Pennsylvanian-Permian boundary; near Tularosa it contains huge algal bioherms and wedges out unconformably a few miles to the southeast. Occurs throughout central and southeastern New Mexico.

CHALK BLUFF FORMATION — Permian

1) The Pecos Valley area of southeastern New Mexico.
2) W. B. Lang, 1937.
3) Section at Chalk Bluff, on eastern bank of the Pecos River, southeast of Artesia.
4) Anhydr., dolo. anhydr., ss., dolo., ls., beds of green bentonite. It is a back-reef fm. 1,000 feet thick and consists of, in ascending order, the Queen Ss., the Seven Rivers gypsif. Mbr., and the Three Twins Mbr.
5) Upper Guadalupian; lies unconformably on the San Andres Fm. and is conformably overlain by the Salado Fm. (Tait, and others, 1962). It is equivalent to the evaporite facies of the Artesia Gp. The top of Lang's Carlsbad Ls. is the top of the Tansill Fm., but the base of the Dog Canyon Ls. is not known. "Chalk Bluff" not adequate as originally defined, will not be redefined as it is only one facies (evaporite) of the units of the Artesia Gp.; use restricted to the Artesia area of the Pecos River Valley.

CHINLE FORMATION — Upper Triassic

1) Northern Arizona, Southern Utah.
2) H. E. Gregory, 1915.
3) Chinle Valley in northeastern Arizona.
4) Four units — red sh. and shly. ss., lenses of ls. cgl., and red sh., variegated sh. with ls. cgl., dark-brown sdy. sh. (named Divisions A, B, C, D). The Chinle is 400 to 1,000 feet thick.
5) In the conference area it overlies unconformably the Santa Rosa Ss., is unconformably overlain by Tertiary sediments and volcanics and consists of a single unit 200 to 400 feet thick. Here it is composed of interbedded dark-red, purple, chocolate-brown silst., clayst. and mudst. with some thin beds of ss. and ls. peb. cgl.; soft, friable, contains some fossil wood.

Cub Mountain Formation — Early Tertiary

1) Central New Mexico, peripheral to Sierra Blanca.
2) Used without definition by M. W. Bodine, Jr., 1956, p. 8-11; and defined by R. H. Weber, 1964. Also see Kelley and Thompson, 1964, for remarks concerning the Cub Mountain Fm.
3) Sanders Canyon, from SW¼SW¼ sec. 16 to SW¼SW¼ sec. 24, T. 9 S., R. 10 E.
4) White to gray, yellow, buff, brown, massive to thin-bedded, fine- to coarse-grained, poorly sorted, arkosic ss. Contains cross-laminations and channels. Interbedded with variegated montmor. clayst., mudst., siltst., and fine ss., thin cgl. lenses in lower part; upper part contains coarse-grained graywacke ss. It is 2,400 feet thick.
5) Latest Upper Cretaceous(?) — Eocene(?); apparently lies conformably to disconformably on the Mesaverde Gp.; overlain unconformably by the Sierra Blanca Volcanics. The upper contact is sharp. Thought to be lithologic and stratigraphic equivalent of the Baca Fm.; upper mbr. possibly equivalent to Spears Mbr. of the Datil Fm.

DAKOTA SANDSTONE — Upper Cretaceous

1) Nebraska and Kansas.
2) F. B. Meek and F. V. Hayden, 1862, p. 419-420.
3) Hills back of the town of Dakota, Dakota Co., Nebraska.
4) Yellow, red and white ss. interbedded with variegated clays and lignite. About 400 feet thick.
5) In the field conference area it overlies unconformably the Triassic (Chinle or Dockum) and is overlain conformably by the Mancos Sh.; elsewhere some units of the Dakota contain fossils and are now known to be of Early Cretaceous age. In the conference area the Dakota is 144 to 182 feet thick. It is usually divided into 3 units: a lower white qtz., massive-bedding, coarse ss., a middle carbonaceous sh. (locally thin coal beds) siltst., mudst., and an upper interbedded fine-med. grained ss. and sh.; gradational into the Mancos Shale.

DOCKUM GROUP — Upper Triassic

1) Texas Panhandle.
2) W. F. Cummins, 1890, p. 189.
3) Vicinity of Dockum, western Dickens Co., Texas.

4) Red, red-brown ss., white qtz. peb. cgls., siltst. and clays; very lenticular; contains silicified wood, reptile bones and *Unio*.
5) Possibly equivalent to interval C of the Chinle; unconformably overlies Permian to Precambrian rocks and is overlain unconformably by the Dakota Ss.; occurs in northeastern to southeastern New Mexico and Oklahoma and Texas Panhandle; locally two or more fms. recognized; equivalence not known; in central New Mexico the Dockum is divided into the Santa Rosa Ss. the overlying Chinle Fm.; 500 to 600 feet thick in the field conference area.

GLORIETA SANDSTONE — Permian
1) Central northern New Mexico.
2) C. R. Keyes, 1915, p. 257, 262.
3) South-central part of T. 15 N., R. 12 E., on Glorieta Mesa, 1 mile west of the village of Rowe, San Miguel Co. as designated by Needham and Bates (1943).
4) White-gray, medium-coarse grained qtzitic. ss., beds 2-6 feet thick, cliff-former; at the base is a 20-foot thick buff-white, thin-bedded ss. It is 12 to 300 feet thick.
5) Leonardian; conformably overlies the Yeso Fm., and is conformably overlain by the San Andres Fm. Occurs in central and southeastern New Mexico, the subsurface of West Texas. It is stratigraphic equivalent of the Hondo Ss. Mbr.

HONDO SANDSTONE MBR. (of the San Andres Fm.) — Permian
1) Pecos Valley area of southeastern New Mexico.
2) W. B. Lang, 1937.
3) Probably along the base of the Algerita escarpment, on the east side of Big Dog Canyon, Tps. 23 and 24 S., R. 20 E.
4) Coarse white qtz. ss. grains streaked with yellow or red-brown, cemented by iron and lime. 50± feet thick.
5) Leonardian; conformably rests on the Yeso Fm., conformably overlain by the San Andres Fm.; a stratigraphic equivalent of the Glorieta Ss.; Pray (1961) uses unit in Sacramento Mtns. for beds of clean, qtz. ss. with rounded, frosted grains. Occurring within typical San Andres Ls. 60 to 120 feet above the top of the Yeso Fm.; the Hondo Ss. is now not used as originally defined by Lang as a mbr. of the Chupadera Fm. (abandoned).

Jicarilla Monzonite — Tertiary(?)
1) From the vicinity of the village of Jicarilla east to the vicinity of Jack's Peak.
2) A. J. Budding, 1964.
3) Vicinity of the village of Jicarilla, Lincoln Co.
4) Leucocratic, gray to buff, monzonite porphyry, varying amounts of qtz.
5) Latest Upper Cretaceous-pre-Pliocene.

Little Black Peak Basalt Flow — Quaternary
1) 4½ miles to south and west of Little Black Peak.
2) C. T. Smith, 1964.
3) Little Black Peak, Little Black Peak quadrangle, Lincoln Co.
4) Dense, fine-grained to aphanitic olivine basalt, trachyte texture.
5) Post-Pleistocene to Recent; lies disconformably on Quaternary fill in Recent topographic valleys.

Lone Mountain Stock — Tertiary
1) Lone Mtn., Lincoln Co.
2) C. T. Smith, 1964.
3) Lone Mtn.
4) Nordmarkite, 80 percent potash feldspar, 8 percent qtz., 5 percent dark minerals; plagioclase feldspar almost absent.
5) Middle Tertiary; regional discordant, local, concordant.

McRae Formation — Upper Cretaceous to Early Tertiary
1) Caballo Mtns. and Dona Ana Co.
2) V. C. Kelley and C. Silver, 1952, p. 115-120.
3) Eastern shore of Elephant Butte Reservoir for several miles north of dam.
4) At base pebble to boulder cgls. interbedded with sh. and siltst., some breccia, overlain by interbedded sh. and ss., cgl. thin and rare, sh. redbrown to purple, ss. gray-green or pink, arkose common; *Triceratops* in lower beds. More than 3,000 feet thick.
5) Latest Upper Cretaceous to Eocene; overlies the Mesaverde Gp. conformably and gradationally to unconformably; unconformably overlain by younger Tertiary sediments and volcanics.

MADERA LIMESTONE (of Magdalena group) — Pennsylvanian
1) Bernalillo Co.
2) C. R. Keyes, 1903.
3) Eastern slope of the Sandia Mtns.
4) Blue to gray ls. 300 feet thick.
5) Desmoinesian-Virgilian; conformably and gradationally overlies the Sandia Fm.; overlain conformably or disconformably by the Bursum or Abo; interbedded ls. and gray calcareous sh., ls. thickest and most common in lower two-thirds, sh., little ss. with arkose, and red beds predominate in upper one-third of the formation. It is 1,000 to 2,500 feet thick in the field conference area. Widespread in New Mexico.

MAGDALENA GROUP — Pennsylvanian
1) Central New Mexico.
2) C. H. Gordon, 1907.
3) Magdalena Mtns. — no type section designated.
4) Divided into two formations. The upper is the Madera Ls. It is 300 to 700 feet thick and is composed of dark-blue ls.; the lower is the Sandia Fm., 500 to 700 feet thick. It consists of blue and black clay sh., dense earthy ls., and cgl. ss. or qtzite. The Magdalena has a maximum thickness of 1,400 feet.

5) Restricted to Pennsylvanian; rests disconformably on Mississippian ls., and is disconformably or conformably overlain by Permian rocks; widespread in New Mexico and West Texas. The Magdalena Group is 900 to 2,700 feet thick in the field conference area.

MANCOS SHALE — Upper Cretaceous

1) Western Colorado.
2) C. W. Cross, 1899.
3) Mancos Valley near town of Mancos, in southwestern Colorado.
4) Dark-gray sdy. sh. with ss. lenses and fossiliferous calcareous sh. and thin ls. lenses. 2,000 feet thick.
5) Montanan and Coloradoan; conformably or disconformably overlies the Dakota Ss. It is overlain conformably and gradationally by the Mesaverde Gp. or unconformably by Tertiary sediments; gray to black calcareous fissile sh. interbedded with a few thin beds of ls., near top thin beds of buff, qtzose. ss.; 4,600 to 4,700 feet thick in the field conference area. Widespread in New Mexico.

MESAVERDE GROUP — Upper Cretaceous

1) Western Colorado and northwestern New Mexico.
2) W. H. Holmes, 1877.
3) Mesa Verde, Montezuma Co., Colorado.
4) Divided into three units which in descending order are: an upper ss. (190 feet of massive ss.), a middle coal-bearing group of 800 to 900 feet of ss., sh. marl and lignite, and a lower ss. consisting of 120 feet of massive ss. The Mesaverde has a total thickness of about 1,200 to 1,500 feet.
5) Carlile to Pierre; rests conformably on the Dakota Ss. or Mancos Sh.; overlain conformably and gradationally by latest Upper Cretaceous and/or early Tertiary rocks including the McRae Fm. and the Cub Mountain Fm.; or disconformably overlain by these fms.; three units recognized in field conference area, and has a total thickness of 500 to 550 feet. The Mesaverde is widespread in New Mexico.

OGALLALA FORMATION — Upper Miocene and Pliocene

1) Kansas and Colorado into Nebraska.
2) N. H. Darton, 1898.
3) Feldt Ranch, in the vicinity of Ogallala, Keith Co., Nebraska designated by C. J. Hesse, 1935.
4) Calcareous grit or soft ls., sdy. clay, ss., with local basal cgl. About 150 to 300 feet thick in the type area; Elias, 1931, restricted the Ogallala to the interbedded buff to pink, unsorted ss. and gravel with fine clay and siltst. that underlie the "Plains marls" and other Pleistocene units.
5) In the field conference area it lies unconformably on the San Andres Fm. up to the Dakota (?) Fm.; overlain unconformably by Quaternary sediments or volcanics; poorly cemented cgl. with fine-grained sdy., calcareous matrix and about 50 feet thick in field conference area. Lateral equivalent of the "Panhandle Fm."

SAN ANDRES FORMATION — Permian

1) San Andres Mtns. of central New Mexico.
2) W. T. Lee, 1909; also see Needham and Bates, 1943 and Kottlowski, and others, 1956.
3) Rhodes Canyon, San Andres Mtns., in sec. 29, T. 12 S., R. 2 E.
4) Lt. to drk. gray, massive-bedded, often cherty, poorly fossiliferous ls. About 600 feet thick.
5) Leonardian; rests conformably on the Glorieta Ss.; disconformably overlain by the Bernal Fm. or its stratigraphic equivalents; lower 350 feet of ls., a few beds of dolo. with interbeds of qtz. ss. (15-30 feet thick) and siltsts., upper 400 feet composed of interbedded dark petroliferous ls., dolo, and gyp.; widely distributed in southeastern, central, and north-central New Mexico.

SANDIA FORMATION (of Magdalena group) — Pennsylvanian

1) Central New Mexico.
2) C. L. Herrick, 1900.
3) Southern end of the Sandia Mtns. — no type section.
4) Ss., cgl., and sh. with occasional sdy. ls., about 150 feet thick.
5) Morrowan — Desmoinesian; unconformably rests on Mississippian ls. or Precambrian rocks, conformably and gradationally overlain by Madera Ls., Sandia Fm. is now used as defined by C. H. Gordon, 1907 (see Magdalena Gp.); widespread in New Mexico.

SANTA ROSA SANDSTONE (of Dockum Group) — Upper Triassic

1) Northeastern New Mexico.
2) D. Hager and A. E. Robitaille, 1919; defined by N. H. Darton, 1922.
3) Along Pecos River at Santa Rosa, Guadalupe Co.
4) Coarse-grained, gray, massive-bedded, cliff-forming ss.; cgl. at base. 50 to 100 feet thick near type locality.
5) Equivalent to interval C of the Chinle Fm.; unconformably overlies Bernal Fm., conformably and gradationally or disconformably overlain by Chinle Fm.; red to red-brown, coarse to medium-grained, cross-bedded ss. and peb. cgl. with clayst. and siltst. partings; locally there is a buff-white coarse-grained ss. at the top of the unit. 150 to 250 feet thick in the field conference area.

Sierra Blanca Volcanics — Tertiary

1) Lincoln Co. and Otero Co., New Mexico.
2) T. B. Thompson, 1964, and R. H. Weber, 1964.
3) Northern Sierra Blanca.
4) Interbedded andesite and basaltic andesite flow breccias, flows, tuff breccias, and lapilli tuffs,

gray, bluish-gray, purple-gray, pink to red, some volcanic cgl.
5) Miocene(?); lies unconformably on the Cub Mountain Fm. (McRae? Fm.); unconformably overlain by younger latites; possible equivalent of the basal part of the Datil Fm. according to Weber, 1964.

YESO FORMATION — Permian

1) Central New Mexico.
2) W. T. Lee, 1909.
3) 11.2 miles N. 46° E. of Socorro, at point where eastern edge of the Socorro quadrangle intersects the 34°10' parallel; from this point northeast in secs. 4 and 5, T. 2 S., R. 2 E., and in sec. 33, T. 1 S., R. 2 E., Socorro Co.
4) Variegated ss., soft, coarse-grained, friable to hard, fine-grained, pink-yellow, often gypsif. sh., earthy ls., massive white beds of gyp. In field conference area the Yeso is 1,000 to 2,000 feet thick.
5) Leonardian; rests conformably and gradationally on the Abo Fm., conformably and gradationally or disconformably overlain by the Glorieta Ss.; 4,255 feet of Yeso encountering in Standard of Texas-Heard Oil test including over 1,000 feet of halite beds as well as a thick gypsum section; Carrizozo dome probably the site of a persistant evaporite basin during Yeso time (Kottlowski, 1963); widespread in New Mexico and subsurface of West Texas.

REFERENCES CITED

Bachman, G. O., 1953, Geology of a part of northwestern Mora County, New Mexico: U.S. Geol. Survey Oil and Gas Inv. Map OM 137.
Bodine, M. C., 1956, Geology of Capitan coal field Lincoln County, New Mexico: N. Mex. Inst. Min. and Tech., State Bur. Mines and Min. Res. Circ. 35.
Budding, A. J., 1964, Geologic outline of the Jicarilla Mountains: New Mexico Geol. Soc., 15th Field Conf., Guidebook of the Ruidoso Country, [New Mexico], 1951.
Cross, W., 1899, Description of the Telluride quadrangle: U.S. Geol. Survey Geol. Atlas, Folio 57.
Cummins, W. F., 1890, The Permian of Texas and its overlying beds: Texas Geol. Survey, 1st Ann. Rept., p. 189.
Darton, N. H., 1898, Preliminary report on the geology and water resources of Nebraska west of the one hundred and third meridian: U.S. Geol. Survey 19th Ann. Rept., pt. 4, p. 719-785, pls. 74-118.
_____ 1922, Geologic structure of parts of New Mexico: U.S. Geol. Survey Bull. 726E, p. 183.
Elias, M. K., 1931, The geology of Wallace County, Kansas: Kansas Geol. Survey Bull. 18, 254 p., 7 figs., 42 pls.
Gordon, C. H., 1907, Notes on the Pennsylvanian formations in the Rio Grande Valley, New Mexico: Jour. Geol., v. 15, p. 805-816.
Gregory, H. E., 1916, The Navajo country, a geographic and hydrographic reconnaissance of parts of Arizona, New Mexico, and Utah: U.S. Geol. Survey Water-Supply Paper 380.
Hager, D. and Robitaille, A. E., 1919, Geologic report on oil possibilities in eastern New Mexico: unpublished report.
Herrick, C. L., 1900, The geology of the White Sands of New Mexico: Jour. Geol., v. 8, p. 112-128.
Hesse, C. J., 1935, A vertebrate fauna from the type locality of the Ogallala Formation: Kansas Univ. Sci. Bull., v. 22, no. 5, p. 79-118, 8 pls.

Holmes, W. H., 1877, Report [on the San Juan district, Colorado]: U.S. Geol. Geog. Survey Terr. (Hayden), 9th Ann. Rept., p. 237-276, 1 map.
Kelley, V. C., and Thompson, T. B., 1964, Tectonics and general geology of the Ruidoso-Carrizozo region, central New Mexico: New Mexico Geol. Soc., 15th Field Conf., Guidebook of the Ruidoso country [New Mexico].
Kelley, V. C., and Silver, C., 1952, Geology of the Caballo Mountains with special references to regional stratigraphy and structure and to mineral resources, including oil and gas: N. Mex. Univ. Pub. Geol., no. 4, 286 p., 19 pls., 26 figs.
Keyes, C. R., 1903, Geological sketches of New Mexico: Ores and Minerals, v. 12, p. 48.
_____ 1915, Conspectus of the geologic formation of New Mexico: Des Moines, 12 p.
Kottlowski, F. E., 1963, Pennsylvanian rocks of Socorro County: New Mexico Geol. Soc., 14th Field Conf., Guidebook of the Socorro [New Mexico] region, p. 102-111, 2 figs.
Kottlowski, F. E., Flower, R. H., Thompson, M. S., and Foster, R. W., 1956, Stratigraphic studies of the San Andres Mountains, New Mexico: N. Mex. Inst. Min. and Tech., State Bur. Mines and Min. Res. Mem. 1.
Lang, W. T. B., 1937, The Permian formations of the Pecos Valley of New Mexico and Texas: Am. Assoc. Petroleum Geologists Bull., v. 21, p. 833-898, 29 figs.
Lee, W. T., 1909, The Manzano Group of the Rio Grande Valley, New Mexico: U.S. Geol. Survey Bull. 389.
Lloyd, E. R., 1949, Pre-San Andres stratigraphy and oil-producing zones in southeastern New Mexico, a progress report: N. Mex. School Mines, State Bur. Mines and Min. Res. Bull. 29, 79 p.
Meek, F. B., and Hayden, F. V., 1862, Descriptions of new Cretaceous fossils from Nebraska Territory: Acad. Nat. Sci. Phia. Proc., v. 13, p. 419-420.
Needham, C. E., and Bates, R. L., 1943, Permian type sections in central New Mexico: Geol Soc. America Bull., v. 54, p. 1653-1667.
Otte, Carel, Jr., 1954, Late Pennsylvanian and Early Permian stratigraphy of the northern Sacramento Mountains, Otero County, New Mexico: Doctor's Thesis, Calif. Inst. Tech.
_____ 1959, Late Pennsylvanian and Early Permian stratigraphy of the northern Sacramento Mountains, Otero County, New Mexico: N. Mex. Inst. Min. Tech., State Bur. Mines and Min. Res. Bull. 50, 111 p., 14 pls., 15 figs.
Pray, L. C., 1961, Geology of the Sacramento Mountains escarpment, Otero County, New Mexico: N. Mex. Inst. Min. Tech., State Bur. Mines Min. Res. Bull. 35, 144 p., 34 figs., 3 pls.
Pray, L. C., and Otte, Carel, Jr., 1954, Correlation of the Abo Formation of south-central New Mexico [Abs.]: Geol. Soc. America Bull., v. 65, p. 1296.
Smith, C. T., 1964, Geology of the Little Black Peak quadrangle, Socorro and Lincoln Counties, New Mexico. New Mexico Geol. Soc., 15th Field Conf., Guidebook of the Ruidoso Country [New Mexico].
Tait, J. L., and others, 1962, Artesia Group (Upper Permian) of New Mexico and West Texas: Am. Assoc. Petroleum Geologists Bull., v. 46, p. 504-517, 4 figs.
Thompson, T. B., 1964, A stratigraphic section of the Sierra Blanca Volcanics in the Nogal Peak area, Lincoln County, New Mexico: New Mexico Geol. Soc., 15th Field Conf., Guidebook of the Ruidoso Country [New Mexico].
Weber, R. H., 1963, Cenozoic volcanic rocks of Socorro County, New Mexico: New Mexico Geol. Soc., 14th Field Conf., Guidebook of the Socorro region [New Mexico], p. 132-143, 1 fig.
_____ 1964, Geology of the Carrizozo quadrangle: New Mexico Geol. Soc., 15th Field Conf., Guidebook of the Ruidoso Country [New Mexico].
Wilpolt, R. H., and others, 1946, Geologic map and stratigraphic sections of Paleozoic rocks of Joyita Hills, Los Pinos Mountains, and northern Chupadera Mesa, Valencia, Torrance, and Socorro Counties, New Mexico: U.S. Geol. Survey Oil and Gas Map 61.

PRECAMBRIAN GEOLOGY OF SOUTH-CENTRAL NEW MEXICO

William R. Muehlberger and Rodger E. Denison

Department of Geology and Crustal Studies Laboratory
The University of Texas, Austin, Texas

INTRODUCTION

The Ruidoso country contains no Precambrian outcrops and no wells in the region to penetrate to it. To interpret the Precambrian geology of the actual field trip area we have therefore selected the larger area shown in figure 1, which gives sufficient regional control for interpolation into the Ruidoso country. The extensive outcrop belt of the San Andres Mountains, Sierra Oscura, Los Pinos and southern Manzano Mountains form the western flank; the exposures in southern Torrance County as well as the numerous wells in that area form the northern; a line of wells along the western margins of some of the Precambrian belts in eastern New Mexico forms the eastern flank; the southern line has been drawn in Otero County north of the Tertiary intrusive rocks that extend into Trans-Pecos Texas. This contribution furnishes petrographic descriptions of basement well and outcrop samples (Denison) and a synthesis of Precambrian history in the map area (both authors).

PREVIOUS WORK AND PRESENT PROJECT

Numerous studies have touched on various aspects of the map area. The most complete general references include individual studies on outcrop belts in the southern Manzano (Stark, 1956), Los Pinos (Stark and Dapples, 1946), San Andres (Kottlowski and others, 1956, Kottlowski, 1959), and Organ Mountains (Dunham, (1961), and Flawn (1956).

The basement rocks in this area can be placed into petrographically allied rock groups. Some of the state-1935); Bent dome (Bachman, 1960); and regional subsurface studies by Foster (1959), Foster and Stipp ments made concerning these groups are defensible only in light of our larger study to make a geologic map of the buried basement of North America. This project is an outgrowth of the AAPG Basement Rocks Committee project to prepare a map at a scale of 1:5,000,000 showing the wells that penetrate the basement, contours on the surface of the buried basement, and gross lithology of the exposed basement. We are making a petrographic study of sample materials from each basement well, and isotopic age determinations of selected samples in order to work out the geologic history of the Precambrian.

ACKNOWLEDGEMENTS

Our sincere thanks to Roy W. Foster, New Mexico

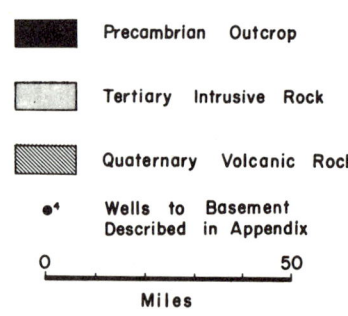

Figure 1. Map of south-central New Mexico showing locations of wells to basement, Precambrian outcrops, Tertiary intrusive rock and Quaternary volcanic rock.

Bureau of Mines and Mineral Resources, who picked the sample materials from the wells and collected samples from the Sierra Oscura and San Andres Mountains. In addition we have obtained samples from various company files and individuals which have made isotopic age determinations possible. In areas of such sparse control and complex geology, each basement well is valuable and needed. Isotopic age determinations for our program have been made by members of the Isotope Geology Branch, U.S. Geological Survey, S. S. Goldich, Chief. This work has been performed under Contract AF 49 (638)-1115 of the Air Force Office of Scientific Research as part of the Advanced Research Projects Agency Project VELA UNIFORM.

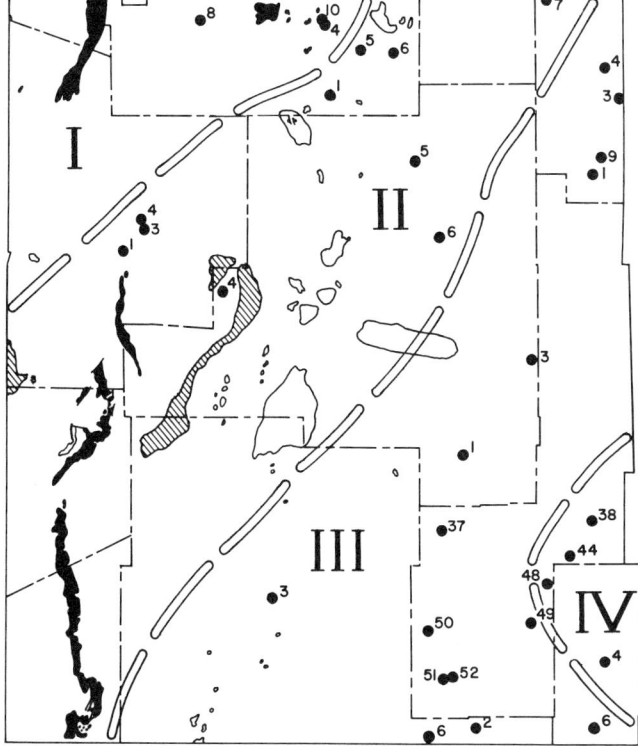

Figure 2. Map of south-central New Mexico showing Precambrian subdivisions described in text: 1, Northwest metamorphic area; II, Central granite belt; III, Sediment and diabase belt; IV, Southeast granite gneiss area.

REGIONAL STATEMENT

The Precambrian rocks of the map area are divisible into four geologic units.

1. *Northwest metamorphic area (I).*— This includes the southern Manzano and Los Pinos Mountains (the band of black shown in fig. 1) in northeastern Socorro County, and most of southern Torrance County. The basement rocks are dominantly metasedimentary and metavolcanic with minor intrusive granitic masses.

2. *Central granite belt (II).*—The area north of a line drawn from the southwest to the northeast corner of the map area and south of the Northwest metamorphic area includes practically all of the Precambrian outcrops in the San Andres Mountains and Sierra Oscura and the wells in Torrance and Lincoln Counties that penetrated either granite, granite gneiss, or granodiorite gneiss. This also includes metasedimentary rock exposed in the San Andres Mountains in a band straddling the Sierra-Dona Ana county lines.

3. *Sediment and diabase belt (III).*—The belt south of the central diagonal and also possibly the area of the field conference are underlain by Precambrian sedimentary rocks that have been extensively intruded and contact metamorphosed by sills and dikes of diabase. The sequence consists largely of quartzite and siltstone, and in a small portion of the area impure limestone. Some of these rocks also crop out in the San Andres Mountains where they overlie the older metamorphic rocks and underlie the Bliss Sandstone (Kottlowski, 1959, p. 261). This Precambrian sedimentary sequence resembles those found in the Franklin Mountains near El Paso (Harbour, 1960) and in the Van Horn region of Trans-Pecos Texas (King and Flawn, 1953). The total thickness is unknown but is probably not great.

4. *Southeast granite gneiss area (IV).*—A group of wells penetrate granite gneisses in southern Chaves and northwest Eddy Counties. This is the western edge of a complex igneous-metamorphic suite of basement rocks in southeast New Mexico.

DESCRIPTION OF INDIVIDUAL AREAS

Northwest metamorphic area (I).—The Los Pinos and southern Manzano Mountains have been mapped and described by Stark and Dapples (1946) and Stark (1956). The following summary is abstracted from their work. The trend of metamorphic rocks essentially parallels the length of the range. The Precambrian stratigraphic sequence consists of a lower metaclastic series unconformably overlain by about 7,000 feet of quartzite, muscovite schist, and quartzite in ascending stratigraphic order. These have been named Sais Quartzite, Blue Springs Muscovite Schist, and White Ridge Quartzite, respectively. This sequence is in turn overlain unconformably by the Sevilleta Rhyolite, which is at least 4,000 feet thick. All of these units have been tightly folded into an asymmetric syncline whose axis strikes northeast across the range. Regional cleavage was developed during this folding episode. Cross folding, faulting and small crenulations were later developed on earlier schistosity. Granitic rocks that intruded this metasedimentary sequence have been divided into a gray equigranular biotitic granite and a younger porphyritic pink granite that is gneissic in places. Granitic rocks of this character have an isotopic age of about 1.35 b.y. in the Sandia Mountains near Albuquerque (Tilton, Wetherill, and Davis, 1962).

Southern Torrance County includes the southernmost portion of the Estancia basin wherein most wells have penetrated metasedimentary rocks that are very similar to the Precambrian rocks in the Los Pinos and Manzano Mountains. The Pedernal uplift consists of granitic rocks flanked by these metasedimentary units. The trend of this belt appears to be south-southwestward under the Jornada del Muerto and may well connect with the metasedimentary rocks of the central San Andres Mountains. North of the map area this metasedimentary terrane extends under the Galisteo basin and is exposed in the high mountains of the upper Pecos River drainage.

Central granite belt (II).—The San Andres Mountains and Sierra Oscura are dominantly underlain by Precambrian rocks that are described by Kottlowski (1959, p. 261) as follows:

> "Red to gray granites, including roof-pendants of various schists and gneisses, and cut by pegmatite and diabase dikes, occur in the northern and southern parts of the mountains. From Sulphur Canyon to south of Hembrillo Canyon a thick series of metamorphic rocks is exposed including mica and quartz-feldspar schists, quartzites, amphibolites, phyllites, talc schist, talc, and dolomite, intruded by diabase and aplite dikes and by small masses of granite. Foliation of the metamorphic rocks along Hembrillo Canyon strikes N. 30-45°W. and dips steeply westward."

Samples furnished by Foster from this outcrop belt and from wells to the north of the Sierra Oscura demonstrate similar lithologies, the rocks being either granite, granite gneiss, or granodiorite gneiss. Some of these are porphyroblastic granite or porphyroblastic gneiss. Foster suggests (written communication, 1963) that the gray biotite granite has been intruded by pink two-mica granite. Similar appearing granite and granite gneiss are found in southeastern Torrance and northern Lincoln Counties. Isotopic age determinations in this belt of granitic rocks are somewhat variable and suggest two thermal events. Samples from the Sun #1 Bingham State (Socorro 1) give 1.57 b.y. by the rubidium-strontium method on feldspar and 1.35 b.y. by potassium-argon on biotite. This suggests that the rock had an original age near the feldspar age and was reheated at about the time of the biotite age. Determination by rubidium-strontium methods on samples from the southern Sierra Oscura in sec. 5, T. 9 S., R. 6 E., gave a total rock age of 1.30 b.y. and gave 1.43 b.y. on a sample of granodiorite gneiss from sec. 3, T. 13 S., R. 4 E., in east-central Sierra County. Isotopic determinations to the southwest in Dona Ana County suggest ages near 1.30 b.y. with no evidence of two thermal events. Farther south in west Texas ages near 1.00 b.y. have been reported (Wasserburg, and others, 1962).

The variations in isotopic ages in this belt suggest two successive thermal events for at least the northwestern portion of the area. Two ages of metamorphism, or at least two ages of shearing, can be demonstrated in much of the outcrop belt in the Manzano and Los Pinos Mountains. These events may well be those recorded by the isotopic ages determined on samples from the Sun #1 Bingham State well. The total rock age in central Sierra County is apparently an average of the two ages in the Sun well. The other isotopic dates suggest that no record of this early event remains in the minerals used in isotopic age determinations.

Sediment and diabase belt (III).—Most of the map area south of the central granite belt contains Precambrian quartzite and siltstone and in some cases impure limestone. These have been extensively intruded and contact metamorphosed by dikes and sills of diabasic rock. Similar sedimentary rocks are exposed in the Central San Andres Mountains where they are intruded by dikes of pale pink aplite (Kottlowski, 1959, p. 261). These aplite dikes are truncated by the basal beds of the Bliss Sandstone.

This nearly unmetamorphosed sedimentary section which underlies the Bliss Sandstone is very similar in general character to the Precambrian rocks exposed in the Franklin Mountains and may well be correlative with them. The presence of lithic fragments of what appears to be rhyolite indicates a rhyolite source in the near vicinity. There are two of these: the Panhandle volcanic terrane to the east, with isotopic age of about 1.2 b.y.; the Franklin Mountains rhyolite to the south which gave a total rock age of 0.99 b.y. by rubidium-strontium techniques on a sample from 4,850 feet south, 500 feet west of 31°52'30"N, 106°30'W. It is not known which of these was the source although the presence of diabase suggests that the sediments are younger than the Panhandle Rhyolite and older than the Franklin Mountains rhyolite.

The curious occurrence of albite in the basic rock in six of the wells, as well as its generally femic-poor character makes these rocks distinctive. Strongly amygdaloidal textures and devitrified volcanic glass in some of these basic rocks suggest that the diabases may be part of an extrusive-intrusive complex that was contemporaneous with deposition of the clastic sediments. No physical connection is known, nor have isotopic age determinations been made to corroborate this suggestion.

The exposure of these rocks nearest to the field trip area is at Bent Dome (Bachman, 1960) where Precambrian quartzite, granitic rock, and associated diorite underlie the Paleozoic rocks at the south end of the Pedernal uplift.

Tertiary igneous rocks occupy much of the Pedernal uplift today and obscure the Precambrian. In addition the Precambrian crystaline basement is downwarped out of sight in the broad Laramide basin extending from Sierra Blanca northward to the Jicarilla Mountains, but the late Precambrian sedimentary rocks are preserved along the southeast flank of this basin.

Southeast granite gneiss area (IV).— Four wells in the southeast corner of the map area penetrate banded granitic gneisses. Detailed petrographic study show these to be gneisses of metamorphic origin rather than primary flow-banded intrusive granitic rocks. They are of high rank metamorphic grade and are the extension of an area of similar rocks lying immediately to the east. The Eddy County well, however, penetrated two distinct rock types: a coarse biotite granite, and a rock similar to the granitic gneisses previously described. These rocks are similar in age to those of the central granite belt although those to the southeast toward the Central basin platform are somewhat younger.

SUMMARY

A thick Precambrian sedimentary and rhyolitic sequence was deposited, folded, and then intruded and metamorphosed by granitic rocks about 1.57 b.y. ago. Igneous activity again occurred about 1.35 b.y. ago followed by a long period of erosion. Limestone, sandstone, and siltstone were deposited across the deeply eroded surface of these older rocks and diabasic rocks were intruded and extruded. If these rocks are related to those in the Franklin Mountains their minimum age is 1.0 b.y. The Precambrian history of the area as presently interpretable ended with the basal Paleozoic deposition of the Bliss Sandstone. Hopefully a study of Laramide intrusions will furnish information on the general composition of the underlying crustal layers, and inclusions within the igneous rocks may preserve sufficient material to indicate the nature and composition of the Precambrian basement rocks that underlie the eruptive centers.

REFERENCES CITED

Bachman, G. O., 1960, Southwestern edge of late Paleozoic landmass in New Mexico: Geol. Survey Prof. Paper 400-B, p. B239-B241.

Dunham, K. C., 1935, The geology of the Organ Mountains, with an account of the geology and mineral resources of Dona Ana County, New Mexico: N. M. Sch. Mines, State Bur. Mines & Min. Res. Bull. 11, 272 p.

Flawn, P. T., 1956, Basement rocks of Texas and southeast New Mexico: Univ. Texas Publ. No. 5605, 261 p.

Foster, R. W., 1959, Precambrian rocks of the Sacramento Mountains and vicinity: Permian Basin Sec. SEPM, and Roswell Geol. Soc., Guidebook for Joint Field Conference in Sacramento Mountains of Otero County, New Mexico, p. 137-153.

Foster, R. W., and Stipp, T. F., 1961, Preliminary geologic and relief map of the Precambrian rocks of New Mexico: N. Mex. Bur. Mines & Min. Res. Circular 57, 37 p.

Harbour, R. L., 1960, Precambrian rocks at North Franklin Mountain, Texas: Bull. Amer. Assoc. Petroleum Geol., v. 44, p. 1785-1792.

King, P. B., and Flawn, P. T., 1953, Geology and mineral deposits of Precambrian rocks of the Van Horn area, Texas: Univ. Texas Publ. No. 5301, 218 p.

Kottlowski, F. E., 1959, Sedimentary rocks of the San Andres Mountains: Permian Basin Sec. SEPM, and Roswell Geol. Soc., Guidebook for Joint Field Conference in Sacramento Mountains of Otero County, New Mexico, p. 259-277.

Kottlowski, F. E., Flower, R. H., Thompson, M. L., and Foster, R. W., 1956, Stratigraphic studies of the San Andres Mountains, New Mexico: N. Mex. Inst. Min. Tech., State Bur. Mines and Min. Res. Mem. 1, 132 p.

Pray, L. C., 1961, Geology of the Sacramento Mountains Escarpment, Otero County, New Mexico: N. Mex. Inst. Min. Tech., State Bur. Mines and Min. Res. Bull. 35, 144 p.

Stark, J. T., 1956, Geology of the South Manzano Mountains, New Mexico: N. Mex. Inst. Min. Tech., State Bur. Mines and Min. Res. Bull. 34, 46 p.

Stark, J. T., Dapples, E. C., 1946, Geology of the Los Pinos Mountains, New Mexico: Geol. Soc. America Bull., v. 47, p. 1121-1172.

Tilton, G. R., Wetherill, G. W., and Davis, G. L., 1962, Mineral ages from the Wichita and Arbuckle Mountains, Oklahoma, and the St. Francis Mountains, Missouri: Jour. Geophys. Res., v. 67, p. 4011-4019.

Wasserburg, G. J., Wetherill, G. W., Silver, L. T., and Flawn, P. T., 1962, A study of the ages of the Precambrian of Texas: Jour. Geophys. Res., v. 67, p. 4021-4047.

APPENDIX

Petrographic descriptions of basement samples in the area of figure 1. For data concerning depth to basement, total penetration, etc. see Foster and Stipp (1961). County well numbers are those of Foster and Stipp. Mineral percentages are given only for rocks which were suitable for modal analysis.

CHAVES COUNTY

Chaves 37: Humble #1 State N; 35-14S-17E. Thin sections: 2610-2700'; 2700-2770'; 2770-2790'; 2790-2830'; 3880-4010'.

Flawn (1956, p. 210) described cores at 3476', 3500-3503', 3804-3809', 3835', 3936', 3939' as diabase, microgranodiorite, and metaquartzite and suggested the possibility of a Tertiary age for the igneous rocks. The later interpretation of Foster (1959) indicated a Precambrian age for the overlying sediment (thought to be Permian by Flawn) and appears to fit the general pattern to the west. The upper intervals are generally medium-grained quartzites and arkoses in part argillaceous and thin bedded. There are no identified crystalloblastic minerals, and micaceous minerals are interpreted as detrital. The diabases are unaltered with clear plagioclase laths and subophitic pyroxenes. Some olivine is present and olivine diabase is probably the best general name to apply to all of the intrusions. No microgranodiorite was identified in any of the above intervals.

Chaves 38: Magnolia #1 Turney; 23-14S-22E. Thin sections: 4920-5000'; 5150-5200'; 5245-5280'; 5290-5340'.

A difficult well to interpret—Flawn (1956) considered the rock at 5321-24' to be an albite granodiorite gneiss and epidote chlorite oligoclase gneiss. The rock from 4920' through 5200' is a rather coarse diabase with local granophyric patches in the upper interval. The diabase contains some fresh pyroxene, plagioclase, opaque minerals and various alterations. The lower intervals are characterized by exceptionally erratic texture and uneven quartz distribution. Some parts appear gneissic with preferentially oriented chlorite and a rude banding of quartz-poor and granophyric material. It is possible that the rock is banded by primary flowage but similarities to the rock in Chaves 44 support a metamorphic origin. In any case the grade of metamorphism is comparatively high grade. The feldspars appear to be perthitic and are uniformly clouded with alterations and hematite dust. The diabase intrudes the granitic rock; however, if the features of the granitic rock are metamorphic and not primary igneous then the diabase is also post metamorphic.

Chaves 44: Humble #1 Gorman; 30-15S-22E. Thin section: 5805-5825'.

This rock appears to be a banded granite gneiss. Some chips are composed of plagioclase, quartz and preferentially oriented chlorite; others are a mosaic of clear microcline, quartz and plagioclase in a typically metamorphic granoblastic texture. The plagioclase is sodic oligoclase and contains both sericite shreds and uniform clouding accompanied by hematite dust. One cutting chip contains biotite with minor chlorite alterations which suggests that the chlorite in other chips is retrograded from biotite. Epidote, a strongly colored variety, is associated with chlorite. The general character of the material in this well supports a metamorphic origin for the rock in Chaves 38.

Chaves 48: Black #1 Shildneck; 24-16S-20E. Thin sections: 6740-6780'; 6830-6850'; 6890-6910'; 6970-6990'.

The first interval is a well defined granite gneiss. Partly chloritized biotite appears to have a fair preferential orientation and is set in a granoblastic mosaic of clear microcline, quartz and plagioclase. Smaller amounts of opaque minerals, sphene, zircon and apatite are present. The lower three thin sections are of diabase which is fairly uniformly altered. The upper diabase is considerably finer grained and undoubtedly younger than the granite gneiss and is post metamorphic. Most of the plagioclase has numerous micaceous alterations uniformly distributed. Chlorite and epidote replace portions of the pyroxene. Cutting chips in the lower interval contain patches of finer material rich in apatite and stained a reddish color by hematite. This reddish material may be but a residual potash feldspar and is unusual.

Chaves 49: Magnolia #1 Black Hills Unit; 31-17S-20E. Thin sections: 5915-5940'; 6000-6045'; 6065-6085'.

Quartzitic and arkosic sandstones are associated with argillaceous intervals. The argillaceous material appears to have no preferred orientation and is somewhat silty and highly siliceous. The interval from 6000-6045' contains delicately bedded chloritic-carbonaceous shaly intervals and dirty sand. At least one chip in this interval contains abundant fine-grained carbonate. Sparse glauconite is found in the sandy beds. The quartzites have abundant feldspar or feldspar alterations and some lithic (rhyolitic?) detritus. This interval is very well cemented by secondary growth and is essentially nonporous.

Chaves 50: Gulf #1 Chaves "U"; 10-18S-16E. Thin section: 3100'±.

The thin section is in the Texas Bureau of Economic Geology collection and was described by Flawn (1956, p. 208) as a tuff or flow. This may be a correct interpretation but the evidence is not strong. Foster and Stipp (1961, p. 147) reports a section of dolomite and talc above this interval. Pray (1961, p. 26) believes the Precambrian interval in this well to be several hundred feet of relatively pure dolomite and some igneous intrusive rocks that have created contact metamorphic minerals. The rock is exceptionally fine grained, containing sparse sand-size grains of microsline, quartz and other feldspars set in a sub-microscopic matrix that in plane light has a tuffaceous appearance. However it is most unusual for a devitrified tuff material to have no crystalline structure in polarized light and the matrix may be clay-like material. Small porphyroblasts in the goundmass have anomalous interference colors near the cores, are slightly zoned, contain abundant inclusions, and are tentatively identified as scapolite. Abundant disseminated carbonate is present in some areas of the slide. The well is possibly related to the metacarbonate sequence in Otero 6. We interpret the rock in this well as of clastic sedimentary origin rather than a tuff.

Chaves 51: Sun #1 Pinon Unit; 19-19S-17E. Thin sections: 1732-1761'; 1800-1823'; 1848-1883'; 1897-1911'.

The entire interval appears to be an altered albite andesite porphyry as reported by Flawn (1956, p. 213). The interval and chips within intervals vary slightly but the general character is comparatively uniform. The only primary minerals are albite occurring as both phenocrysts and groundmass material and opaque material. Epidote replaces them extensively throughout as aggregates of crystals, abundant discrete crystals in albite and in amygdules. Chlorite and vermicular biotite masses replace the former femic mineral. Chlorite, quartz and albite are amygdaloidal minerals. It is suggested that the rock has been metamorphosed rather than simply epidotized and hydrothermally altered. Biotite appears crystalloblastic and unlike simple secondary (alteration) biotite. Some phenocrysts are up to 4 mm in diameter.

Chaves 52: Sun #2 Pinon Unit; 20-19S-17E. Thin section: 1650-1659'.

This is a meta-albite andesite containing phenocrysts of albite (near An_9) set in a recrystallized groundmass of quartz, biotite-chlorite and micaceous alterations; some cutting chips contain hematite, which masks the character of the minerals. Epidote is common in some chips but is never as abundant as in Chaves 51 and is in fine granular aggregates — never well crystallized. Sparse zircons are striking and unusual in this type rock. The albite phenocrysts are partly altered with mottled micaceous material. The groundmass is finely granoblastic with olive-green biotite as the most crystalline mineral. Rounded quartz aggregates may be a reconstitution of amygdules. This porphyry is considered to be metamorphosed to middle greenschist facies in the groundmass while the phenocrysts remain as igneous relicts.

DE BACA COUNTY

DeBaca 1: Transcontinental #1 McWhorter; 6-3S-22E. Thin sections: 4360-4370'; 4636-4768'.

The upper interval is a diabase containing laths of slightly zoned calcic plagioclase, relict pyroxene mostly calcitized and chloritized, opaque minerals, and tremolitic amphibole, biotite, and generally indeterminant feldspar alterations. The fabric is subophitic. Samples from the lower interval are exceptionally poor—the largest cutting chip is less than 1 mm. in length. On the basis of the partial textures seen in the larger chips the rock is interpreted as a slightly metamorphosed clastic sediment. Quartz appears to be the most abundant detritus and certain chips may be derived from quartzite beds within this interval. Argillaceous and silty argillaceous material is also present in abundance.

DeBaca 3: Katz #1 Marble Field; 13-1N-22E. Thin sections: 5390-5490'; 5490-5550'; 5550-5580'.

The nearly two hundred feet of penetration appears to be totally in altered albite basalt (spilite?). The rock is now composed chiefly of plagioclase and its alteration products, chlorite and opaque minerals. There are numerous amygdules filled with chlorite, hematite-stained plagioclase, and chalcedonic quartz. The general character of a devitrified semiopaque basaltic glass, partially well-defined pilotaxitic texture and development of amygdules strongly suggest an extrusive basalt flow. The rock has undergone no metamorphic events of any sort since extrusion as shown by the undisturbed devitrified glass. The alteration of the feldspars either to calcite or an indeterminate clay-mica-zeolite mixture is considered deuteric. The alteration may be associated with the albitization of a more calcic plagioclase.

DeBaca 4: Pair #1 Overton-Federal; 20-2N-22E. Thin section: 5410-5420'.

This is an amygdaloidal albite basalt containing chiefly plagioclase, chlorite, and opaques. The plagioclase appears to be intermediate albite but is extensively and uniformly clouded with alterations and disseminated hematite dust. All primary femic minerals have been converted to chlorite. Calcite is found as thin veinlets. Numerous tiny apatite needles are present. This rock is similar to that found in DeBaca 3 and the sodic character of the plagioclase in both wells is distinctive.

DeBaca 7: South Basin #1 Good; 5-4N-20E. Thin sections: 4670-4730'; 4730-4770'.

Both intervals appear to be essentially the same type of rock, a metamorphosed clastic sediment. The common crystalloblastic minerals are chlorite, sericite-muscovite and epidote, and all are preferentially oriented. In at least one chip the mineral assemblage includes a blue-green amphibole, biotite, epidote, quartz and feldspar, and suggests a metabasic rock. The crystalloblastic micas and epidote vary extensively in proportions in cutting chips and are set in a quartz or quartz-feldspar mosaic, again varying from cutting chip to cutting chip. This rock is interpreted to have been an argillaceous silty sediment in which a diabase was injected and then metamorphosed to a greenschist facies assemblage in the quartz-albite-muscovite-chlorite subfacies.

DeBaca 9: Talbert #1 Andree; 20-2S-22E. Thin section: 5110-5340'.

This well penetrated silty iron-rich argillites and fine arkosic sandstones. The argillaceous material is hematite-rich, and one chip contains abundant fine carbonate. The hematite-rich areas are local and at least one has a tuffaceous appearance. The fine arkosic sandstone chips average about 0.1 mm in grain size and contain abundant intergranular carbonate. The mineral detritus is largely quartz with feldspars of various types and some lithic debris possibly rhyolitic in origin. Opaque minerals are common in the sandstones, apparently as detrital grains. The well is interpreted to be in an essentially unmetamorphosed sequence of bedded sandstones and argillites and is not dissimilar to rocks penetrated in surrounding wells.

EDDY COUNTY

Eddy 4: Magnolia #1 Tres Ranchos Unit; 10-19S-23E. Thin section: 10,000-10,010'.

This rock is granitic but appears to be of two types. One is a coarse biotite granite containing plagioclase, microcline and strained quartz with a typical hypidiomorphic (igneous) texture. The grain size is generally greater than 3 mm. Minor amounts of hornblende, magnetite, sphene, apatite, zircon, sphene-leucoxene, epidote and chlorite-calcite replacing biotite are present. Alteration of feldspars is minor. The finer grained chips are equigranular about 1 mm. in size. In the other rock type the texture is not typical of igneous rock and is very similar to gneissic granites. In the finer cutting chips chlorite shows a very modest preferential orientation, some associated with muscovite. Microcline is generally fresh. Plagioclase, near An_{10}, is more altered and contains small sericite flakes. Quartz in both coarse and fine chips is generally strained. Tentatively the rock is interpreted as a banded granite gneiss possibly derived from the metamorphism of normal granite.

Eddy 6: Magnolia #1 State W; 16-21S-22E. Thin sections: 11,230-11,250'; 11,280-11,290'; 11,312' (core).

The first interval contains chips of relatively pure quartzite. The quartz contains secondary overgrowths and is associated with minor amounts of feldspar, opaque minerals, and lithic detritus that mostly appears to be rhyolitic. A material identified as collophane occurs as common, apparently detrital, grains. All other chips are of diabasic rock. The plagioclase is calcic albite and is in lath shapes associated with chlorite, well crystallized epidote, opaque minerals and calcite. The lowest interval is a quartz-epidote rock with smaller amounts of chlorite, opaque minerals and sphene. The alteration of the diabase and indeed the original rock are very similar to those in Chaves 51 and 52. The rock in this well is interpreted as an albite diabase intruding a quartzite and later metamorphosed or hydrothermally altered.

LINCOLN COUNTY

Lincoln 1: Stanolind #1 Picacho; 10-12S-18E. Thin sections: 2538-2603'; 2682-2759'.

This rock is a feldspathic quartzite containing coarse material about 1 mm. in size and fairly well sorted sand averaging 0.15-0.2 mm in diameter. No new metamorphic minerals are noted but calcite-siderite has replaced other minerals along grain boundaries in some cutting chips. Most of the detritus is quartz with considerable feldspar, microcline, plagioclase and perthite. Rock fragments appear to be metamorphic in origin and many of the large quartz grains are extensively strained. Minor sphene, zircon, chlorite, opaque minerals, and feldspar alterations are present. This rock is similar to many sediments in the basement of eastern New Mexico.

Lincoln 3: Texam #1 Boyle; 11-9S-20E. Thin sections: 3100-3160'; 3270-3300'; 3400-3440'; 3500-3520'.

About 470 feet of albite diabase were penetrated in this well. The alteration is erratic but in general the albite laths are uniformly clouded and locally replaced by fine alterations. Brownish pyroxene has been almost completely replaced by chlorite and opaque minerals or epidote. Hematite-magnetite is common. Chlorite is present as femic pseudomorphs and amygdule-like fillings. Masses of epidote together with minor chalcedony and quartz replace portions of the original rock completely. Some intervals are porphyritic and amygdaloidal with chlorite-calcite-epidote and one is filled with well-crystallized brilliant apple-green pumpellyite. The rock name suggests an intrusive rock although the porphyritic and amygdaloidal character indicates an extrusive albite basalt.

Lincoln 4: Standard of Texas #1 Heard; 33-6S-9E. Thin sections: 7790-7840'; 8010-8040'; 8040' (core).

The rock in this well is, strictly speaking, a troctolite (olivine plagioclase rock). Troctolites, however, connote a large differentiated mass of gabbroic rock and this may not be the origin of this rock. Pyroxene occurs as thin rims around olivine and minor crystals. Olivine contains cracks filled by opaque minerals along which variable alteration has taken place. Very bright reddish biotite is well crystallized but present only in small amounts. Plagioclase contains mottled alterations but is generally fresh and well twinned. The core is the most altered of the three samples, and contains a sheared zone with a very mildly pleochroic yellowish biotite, calcite and chlorite. Most olivine has been replaced by chlorite-iddingsite. Plagioclase contains masses of a colorless amphibole. An approximate mode of the freshest material in percent is: 58.2, plagioclase; 19.7, olivine; 8.0, plagioclase alterations; 7.2, opaque minerals; 4.1, olivine alterations; 2.2, pyroxene; 0.6, biotite.

Lincoln 5: Malcom and Morrow #1 Franks; 23-2S-15E. Thin section: 2040-2100'.

This is a granodiorite containing minerals in the following percentages: 40.9, plagioclase; 32.4, quartz; 14.3, microcline; 5.0, plagioclase alterations; 3.0, chlorite; 2.8, epidote; 1.6, calcite; and traces of opaque minerals, sphene-leucoxene. The rock has a generally altered appearance with calcite and hematite veinlets in some chips. Epidote is well crystallized and abundant. Microcline is clear and unaltered; plagioclase is turbid with alterations, hematite dust and abundant discrete sericite flakes. The plagioclase appears to be intermediate oligoclase. Quartz is mildly strained to unstrained. Chlorite replaces a former femic mineral, probably biotite, and is accompanied by sphene-leucoxene as an alteration byproduct.

Lincoln 6: Elliot Production #1 Federal; 10-5S-16E. Thin sections: 2590-2660'; 2710-2760'; 2760-2770'; 2910-2970'; 3190-3250'; 3380-3420'.

This well penetrated about 850 feet of granite gneiss cut by abundant diorite dikes. The granite gneiss has a sheared appearance with relict eyes of plagioclase and microcline set in a biotite-rich quartz-feldspar mosaic. Some chips have a typical hypidiomorphic texture but most are gneissic. Plagioclase is slightly zoned and all feldspars are fresh except in some lower intervals where there is relatively uniform alteration. The diorite contains minor late intergranular quartz. Plagioclase laths are calcic andesine, are generally fresh, and near cores contain dustlike particles that may be rutile. Pyroxene contains schiller opaque minerals. Large red-brown biotite crystals are common but not abundant. A pale green amphibole appears to replace large parts of the pyroxene. The well is interpreted as intergranular granite gneiss intruded by diorite of unknown age. The diorite does not have a definite metamorphic imprint and no similar rocks are found in basement rocks of this area.

Lincoln: outcrop sample, Sierra Oscura; SE 1/4, 5-9S-6E.

This is a coarse-grained red granite with the following mineral percentages: 34.0, microcline; 31.0, quartz; 28.9, plagioclase and plagioclase alterations; 2.6, muscovite; 1.6, chlorite; 1.0, biotite; 0.6, epidote; 0.2, opaque minerals; and traces of sphene-leucoxene and zircon. Large microcline crystals contain poikilitically enclosed plagioclase and quartz. Microcline is generally fresh. Plagioclase is sodic oligoclase in composition and is turbid with alterations. Large porphyroblasts of muscovite are found as intergranular crystals and as smaller crystals enclosed in plagioclase. Quartz is moderately strained but there are no mortar textures or shear lineations. Biotite is partly converted to chlorite with attendant sphene-leucoxene and epidote. A rubidium-strontium isotopic age on a whole rock sample gave 1.30 b.y.

OTERO COUNTY

Otero 2: Standard of Texas #1 Scarp; 18-21S-18E. Thin sections: 2630-2635'; 2655-2660'.

Flawn (1956, p. 228) interpreted the lower interval as an analcitic syenogabbro, and the other rocks as gabbro. The rock in our thin sections is gabbroic with no positively identified potash feldspar and we favor the rock name diabase for the entire drilled interval. The freshest rock has a sub-ophitic texture with reddish-brown pigeonitic pyroxene, sericitized plagioclase, primary opaque minerals, femic alterations, reddish-brown biotite near the opaque minerals, and a blue-green amphibole as well as a pale tremolitic amphibole replacing primary femic minerals. Epidote is common as a replacement mineral. Some sheared chips are noted. Numerous cracks in plagioclase are filled with a white virtually non-birefringent mica. The rock is fairly coarse grained with relict crystals to about 4 mm. in diameter.

Otero 3: Southern Production #1 Cloudcroft; 5-17S-12E. Thin sections: 4520-4530'; 4530-4540'; 4558-4561'; 4582-4593'; 4593-4602'; 4602-4607'; 4607-4620'; 4620-4631'; 4631-4643'; 4665-4672'; 4684-4686'; 4686-4697'; 4697-4702'.

The fourteen thin sections from this well show a quartzite and argillaceous quartzite sequence cut by diabasic dikes at 4558-4561', 4607-4631', and 4686' to total depth. Most intervals contain moderately well sorted and rounded quartzites and have only small amounts of lithic and feldspathic detritus. Some intervals around 4665' have quartz-feldspar detritus in a sericite matrix that appears to have been reconstituted. The interval from 4675-4680' contains masses of what appears to be fine-grained biotite with small enclosed grains; these masses are of unknown origin but are possibly reconstituted glauconite. The diabases range from exceptionally fine-grained indeterminate semiopaque devitrified glass with sericitized plagioclase laths to medium crystalline rock (4607-4631') containing fresh calcic plagioclase and mostly altered pyroxene. Apatite needles are common.

Otero 6: LeFors #1 Federal; 22-21S-16E. Thin sections: 2230-2250'; 2240-2250(2)'; 2255'.

Diverse metamorphic rocks were penetrated in this comparatively short interval. The four thin sections are all slightly different; however, some generalizations can be made. Several chips are epidote-feldspar rock with slight banding. Epidote locally is virtually the sole mineral. Wollastonite in radiating fibrous mats, very mildly anisotropic garnets, calcite and tremolite are the main rock forming minerals. The rock is interpreted as a contact metamorphosed impure limestone. The impurities are probably clays and silica with some dolomite. Several other minerals may be present but the fine character of the rock does not lend itself to confident determinations. Diabasic intrusion or the syenites found to the south may be the metamorphic agent.

SIERRA COUNTY

Sierra: outcrop sample, north side of Rhodes canyon; SW 1/4, 3-12S-4E.

This is a granodiorite gneiss with the following mineral percentages: 32.2, plagioclase; 19.0, quartz; 17.9, biotite; 16.6, microcline; 10.3, feldspar alterations; 1.7, sphene; 1.2, opaque minerals; 0.3, apatite; 0.3, hornblende; and traces of zircon, epidote, and chlorite. The foliation is outlined by a rude but persistent preferred orientation of the biotite associated with minor amounts of blue-green hornblende. Abundant well-crystallized sphene is associated with biotite and opaque minerals. Microcline is generally fresh with very delicate twinning. Plagioclase is intermediate oligoclase and contains extensive mottled alterations. Small amounts of myrmekite are present. Apatite is in large well-formed crystals. Quartz is mildly strained. Microcline crystals exceed 5 mm. Isotopic age on whole rock by rubidium-strontium methods is 1.43 b.y.

SOCORRO COUNTY

Socorro 1: Sun #1 Bingham State; 23-5S-5E. Thin section: 3139-3140' (core).

This is a granite gneiss with the following mineral percentages: 35.3, microcline; 27.7, plagioclase; 26.9, quartz; 7.4, biotite; 1.0 opaque minerals; 0.9, muscovite; 0.5, chlorite; 0.3, epidote; traces of zircon and apatite. The plagioclase is near An_{10} incomposition, though faintly zoned and containing general disseminated alterations. The microcline is clear and in part well twinned. The quartz is generally strained. Olive-green biotite is strongly pleochroic and has good preferred orientation. Chlorite replaces small amounts of the biotite. Muscovite is generally associated with biotite. The composition of this rock is essentially a "perfect" igneous granite. The rock is therefore interpreted as metamorphosed rock of igneous granitic composition. The microcline was dated at 1.57 b.y. by the rubidium-strontium method and the biotite was dated at 1.36 b.y. by the potassium-argon method.

Socorro 3: Lockhart #2 Lockhart; 33-4S-6E. Thin section: 2700-2800'; 2800-2850'.

This is a granodiorite gneiss containing uniformly sericitized feldspar; the few fresh chips do contain microcline. Both hornblende and biotite are common and are preferentially oriented. Chlorite replaces some biotite, sphene is well crystallized, and large epidote masses replace some feldspar. One quartz crystal contains over twenty included or partly included zircons. The plagioclase also occurs in crystals larger than 4 mm., and is calcic albite in composition. Average grain size is slightly larger than 1 mm. The interpretation is an igneous granodiorite metamorphosed by a later event, possibly that reflected in the Sun #1 Bingham State.

Socorro 4: Lockhart #1 Lockhart Federal; 28-4S-6E. Thin section: 2975' (core).

This is a granite or granodiorite gneiss with the following mineral percentages: 40.2, plagioclase and alterations; 28.7, quartz; 27.2, microcline; 1.2, biotite; 1.1, chlorite; 0.6, opaque minerals; 0.6, epidote; 0.4, muscovite; traces of zircon, sphene, and apatite. It is a crudely banded rock containing concentrations of biotite-chlorite showing modest preferred orientation along planes. The concentration of biotite is accompanied by an impoverishment of microcline. This suggests metamorphic differentiation of a rock, possibly very similar to that found in Socorro 1. The plagioclase, near An_{20}, is turbid with alterations and intensely altered near biotite-rich bands. Microcline is clear, containing very minor alterations. Epidote and muscovite are concentrated in the biotite-poor areas. Sphene is concentrated near biotite-rich zones.

Socorro: outcrop sample; 23-2N-3E, in Sevilleta Grant.

This is a pink granite gneiss with the following mineral percentages: 46.6, microcline; 41.4, quartz; 8.5, plagioclase; 1.7, biotite; 1.3, muscovite; 0.2, fluorite; 0.2, opaque minerals; and traces of sphene, feldspar alterations, and epidote. The general character is a highly siliceous gneissic granite containing only modest amounts of accessory minerals. The gneissic characters are mortared boundaries, aggregate quartz and biotite-muscovite preferentially aligned along planes. The biotite has a very unusual bright apple-green color and is associated with sphene. Microcline is fresh and slightly perthitic. The plagioclase is calcic albite and contains abundant fine sericite flakes. The quartz also occurs as large extensively strained crystals. This is probably a phase of the Los Pinos Granite of Stark and Dapples (1946).

TORRANCE COUNTY

Torrance 1: Lubbock Machine #1 Colbaugh; 12-1N-12E. Thin sections: 981-1000'; 1055-1075'; 1102-1126'.

This is a granite gneiss and sheared granite gneiss(?) containing roughly equal microcline, plagioclase and quartz with small amounts of biotite. The upper interval contains about five percent biotite having a moderate preferred orientation. The general character is very similar to rocks from wells to the southwest in Socorro County. The intermediate interval appears to be in part slightly coarser but has been brecciated and sheared to obscure many original characteristics. The lowest interval is similar to the upper interval but contains virtually no biotite. The sequence is interpreted as a granite gneiss possibly crudely banded and containing local shear zones that are probably not associated with a Precambrian event but with Paleozoic or younger tectonism.

Torrance 4: Stewart #1 Lemmons; 3-3N-12E. Thin sections: 190-234'; 352-414'; 614-701'.

These three intervals appear to be in the same type of rock: a muscovite-quartz-feldspar schist. Relicts(?) of quartz, plagioclase and potash feldspar are set in a finely granoblastic quartzo-feldspathic groundmass containing lepidoblastic muscovite. Rare micrographic material was noted and interpreted as relict. Minor opaque minerals including zircon and sphene-leucoxene and feldspar alterations are present. Replacement calcite is significant in some chips. The rock is tentatively called a rhyolite porphyry. One chip is a quartz-muscovite schist which does not support a rhyolite origin, but this may be a local band or other inhomogeneity in the rock.

Torrance 5: Associated #1 Luna-Federal; 25-3N-13E. Thin section: 546-568'.

The cuttings are composed of single mineral fragments, all smaller than 0.7 mm in maximum dimension. The fragments are quartz, microcline, plagioclase, biotite, opaque minerals, feldspar alterations, chlorite and epidote. The general composition and relative abundances correspond to a granitic rock. The lack of finer grained fragments suggest it may be a granitic rock and not a mineralogic equivalent such as metarhyolite. No interpretation of rock type is justified on the basis of the fine cuttings.

Torrance 6: Duran Dome #1 State; 31-3N-15E. Thin sections: 1457'.

There are only three small cutting chips on this slide and all appear to be granite gneiss. Microcline, plagioclase and quartz are common, myrmekite is locally developed. The biotite is strongly pleochroic and preferentially oriented. Microcline is clear with only minor alterations while primary plagioclase is mottled with extensive alterations. Small amounts of epidote and opaque minerals are present. This rock is tentatively correlated with the gneisses in Socorro County.

Torrance 8: Eidal #1 Mitchell; 33-4N-8E. Thin sections: 3518-3542'; 3557-3580'.

The upper interval is a hematite-rich muscovitic phyllite.

Most of the rock is hematite in ragged anhedral grains with abundant fine muscovite and quartz. Small amounts of tourmaline in smoky blue-green crystals and sphene are present. Minor feldspar may be associated with the quartz but the fine-grained character (finer than 0.7 mm) does not permit resolution of most of the rock. The lower interval is an amphibolite containing a pale green, mildly pleochroic amphibole, chlorite, epidote, sphene, opaque minerals, quartz, sericite, apatite, and minor indeterminate feldspar. Calcite replaces portions of the rock. Biotite was not identified. The texture is granoblastic with no apparent preferred orientation. The rocks are interpreted to be a pelitic rock and basaltic rock later metamorphosed to greenschist facies.

Torrance 10: Rogers and Poynor #1 Federal; 34-4N-12E. Thin section: 250-265'.

This is a muscovite schist containing granoblastic quartz-feldspar with lepidoblastic muscovite. There is a former abundant mineral now replaced by calcite rimmed by what appears to be a yellowish-red hematite stain. This stain also is found in linear bands in certain cutting chips. Small amounts of smoky blue-green tourmaline are present in sun bursts. Opaque minerals in discrete crystals and ragged anhedra, zircon, and feldspar alterations make up the remainder of the rock. The rock is interpreted to be a metamorphosed argillaceous feldspathic sandstone or may possibly have been derived from a volcanic rock although all relict textures have been destroyed.

SOUTHWESTERN EDGE OF LATE PALEOZOIC LANDMASS IN NEW MEXICO

George O. Bachman

Denver, Colorado
United States Geological Survey Professional Paper 400B*

At many localities in central New Mexico, Permian strata lie directly on Precambrian rocks. The surface on the Precambrian rocks is highly irregular, being locally diversified with hills, ridges, and even mountains. Thompson (1942) said that "these pre-Cambrian rocks probably represent the buried remnants of a large land area of the Ancestral Rocky Mountains," and he named this positive element the Pedernal landmass. It is difficult, if not impossible, to determine the exact extent of the Pedernal landmass; in many parts of New Mexico evidence on this point can be obtained only from widely spaced outcrops and drill holes. It has been shown, however, that during parts of Pennsylvanian and Permian time this landmass extended north-south at least 150 miles in central New Mexico.

The remarkable influence of the Pedernal landmass on Pennsylvanian and Permian sedimentation has been discussed by other workers (Read and Wood, 1947; Cline, 1959; Otte, 1959).

During reconnaissance geologic mapping in 1954, R. L. Sutton and I discovered exposures in northern Otero County, N. Mex., where the Abo formation of Permian age lies on rocks of Precambrian age (Bachman, 1954; Dane and Bachman, 1958). These exposures are near Bent, which is about 12 miles northeast of Tularosa, in secs. 25 and 26, T. 13 S., R. 11 E., and sec. 30, T. 13 S., R. 12 E. The outcrops are on the east flank of a small dome, here called Bent dome. I have since mapped these exposures in more detail (fig. 1). They are the southernmost exposures in New Mexico, so far as I know, in which this relation may be observed at the surface, and they are of particular interest because in the Sacramento Mountains, about 20 miles to the south of Bent dome, pre-Permian Paleozoic rocks attain a thickness of about 5,500 feet (Pray, 1959, p. 88).

The Precambrian rocks on Bent dome consist chiefly of light-gray quartzite. At one small exposure (sec. 25, T. 13 S., R. 11 E.) the quartzite appears to be intruded by coarsely crystalline granite, which closely resembles that forming cobbles and pebbles in the Abo formation on Bent dome and in areas to the west. The Abo formation contains cobbles and pebbles of quartzite that resembles Precambrian quartzite in texture but not in color, being generally dark gray, maroon, or purple whereas the quartzite of the Precambrian exposures is light gray.

Diorite exposed on the west side of Bent dome (sec. 26, T. 13 S., R. 11 E.) may also be of Precambrian age (Foster, 1959, p. 143), but its age is uncertain. This diorite is very similar to Tertiary diorite found elsewhere in the region; and, moreover, it is not intricately jointed as are the rocks known to be Precambrian, and no pebbles of diorite like that on Bent dome have been identified in the Abo formation.

On the west side of Bent dome, and also in the vicinity of the Virginia Mine and at a locality on U.S. Highway 70 one mile east of Bent, there are exposures of light-gray, medium-grained, well-sorted sandstone beds thought to be of Pennsylvanian age. The Abo formation overlies these beds unconformably. The supposedly Pennsylvanian beds are estimated to be about 200 feet thick near the Virginia Mine, but they are absent on the east side of the dome and are presumed to wedge out eastward from the mine. The high degree of sorting indicates that these beds may have been deposited before major uplift of the Pedernal landmass.

The Abo formation on Bent dome consists of poorly consolidated dark-red shale, arkose, and conglomerate. Cobbles of granite and quartzite as much as 10 inches in diameter have been observed at the base of the formation, and also some pebbles of a distinctive brownish-red rhyolite porphyry. The formation is 220 feet thick on the southeastern part of the dome (fig. 2). On the eastern flank of the dome the Abo is apparently thinner and it may be no more than 100 feet thick where it overlies the highest points on the surface of Precambrian rocks (NW1/4SW1/4 sec. 30, T. 13 S., R. 12 E.). About 6 miles west of Bent dome the Abo formation is about 1,400 feet thick (Pray, 1959, p. 118) and rests on rocks of Late Pennsylvanian and early Permian age.

The unconformity at the base of the Abo sandstone and the onlap of the Abo on pre-Permian rocks of various ages in the Sacramento Mountains have long been known (Pray, 1949, p. 1914-1915). Early Permian folding and faulting are indicated throughout the length of the Sacramento Mountains and are directly related to uplift of the Pedernal landmass. The exposures at Bent dome provide a point of geographic control for the southwestern part of the landmass and probably represent a part of the early Permian tectonic system of the Sacramento Mountains.

REFERENCES

Bachman, G. O., 1954, Reconnaissance map of an area southeast of Sierra Blanca in Lincoln, Otero, and Chaves Counties, New Mexico, in New Mexico Geol. Soc. Guidebook, 5th Field Conf., 1954: p. 94b.

Cline L. M., 1959, Preliminary studies of the cyclical sedimentation and paleontology of upper Virgil strata of the La Luz area, in Permian Basin Sec. Soc. Econ. Paleontologists and Mineralogists and Roswell Geol. Soc. Guidebook, Sacramento Mtns., 1959: p. 172-185.

Dane, C. H., and Bachman, G. O., 1958, Preliminary geologic map of the southeastern part of New Mexico: U.S. Geol. Survey Misc. Geol. Inv. Map I-256.

---

*Permission to publish obtained by Field Trip Chairman from author.

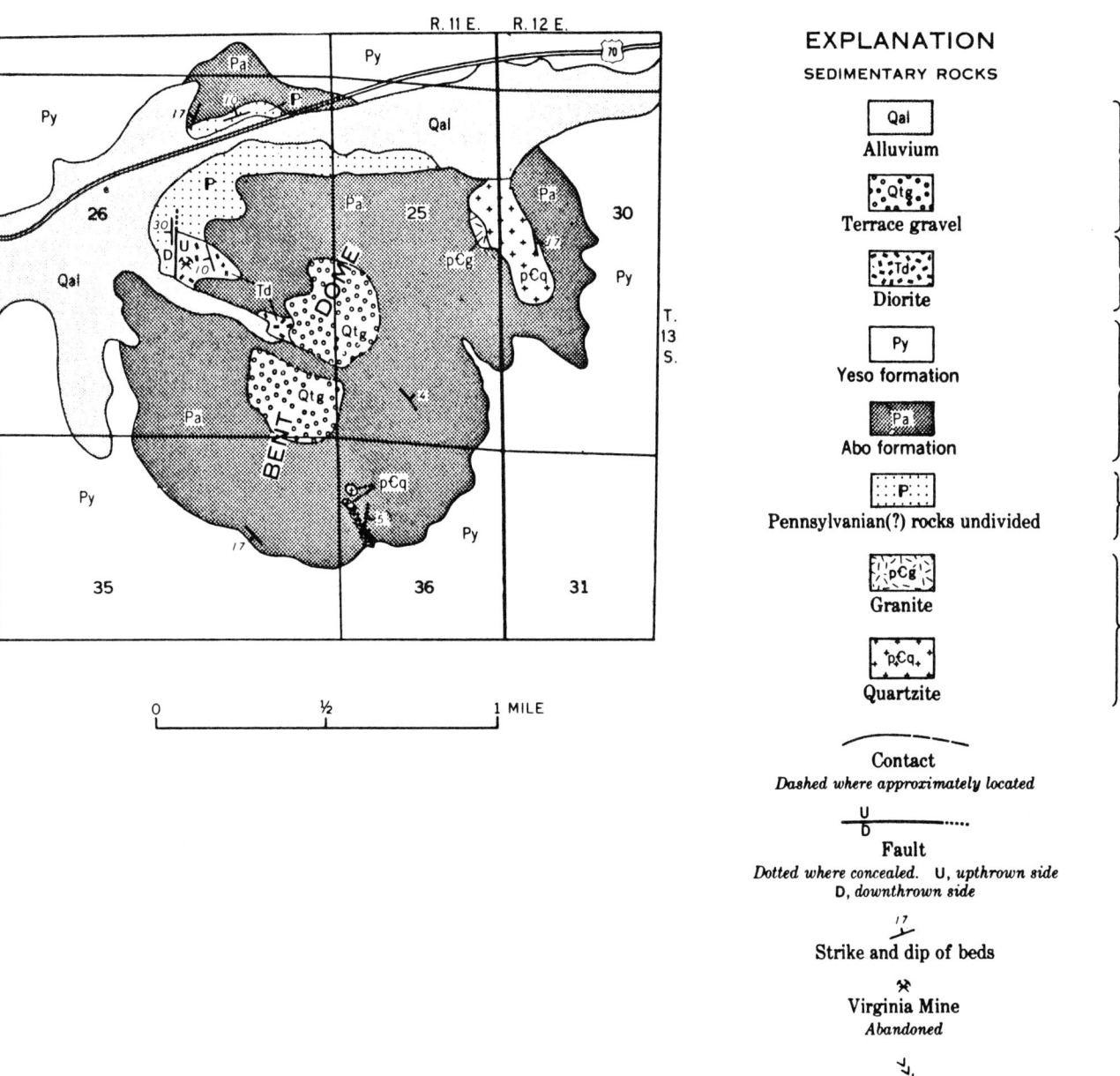

Figure 1. — Geologic map of Bent dome, Otero County, N. Mex.

Foster, R. W., 1959, Precambrian rocks of the Sacramento Mountains and vicinity, in Permian Basin Sec. Soc. Econ. Paleontologists and Mineralogists and Roswell Geol. Soc. Guidebook, Sacramento Mtns., 1959: p. 137-153.

Otte, Carel, Jr., 1959, Late Pennsylvanian and early Permian stratigraphy of the northern Sacramento Mountains, Otero County, New Mexico: New Mexico Inst. Min. Tech., State Bur. Mines and Min. Res. Bull. 50, p. 21-58.

Pray, L. C., 1949, Pre-Abo deformation in the Sacramento Mountains, New Mexico [abs.]: Geol. Soc. America Bull., v. 60, no. 12, p. 1914-1915.

──────, 1959, Stratigraphy and structure of the Sacramento Mountains, in Permian Basin Sec. Soc. Econ. Paleontologists and Mineralogists and Roswell Geol. Soc. Guidebook, Sacramento Mtns., 1959: p. 86-130.

Read, C. B., and Wood, G. H., Jr., 1947, Distribution and correlation of Pennsylvanian rocks in late Paleozoic sedimentary basins in northern New Mexico: Jour. Geology, v. 55, no. 3, p. 220-236.

Thompson, M. L., 1942, Pennsylvanian System in New Mexico: New Mexico School Mines, State Bur. Mines and Min. Res. Bull. 17, p. 12-13.

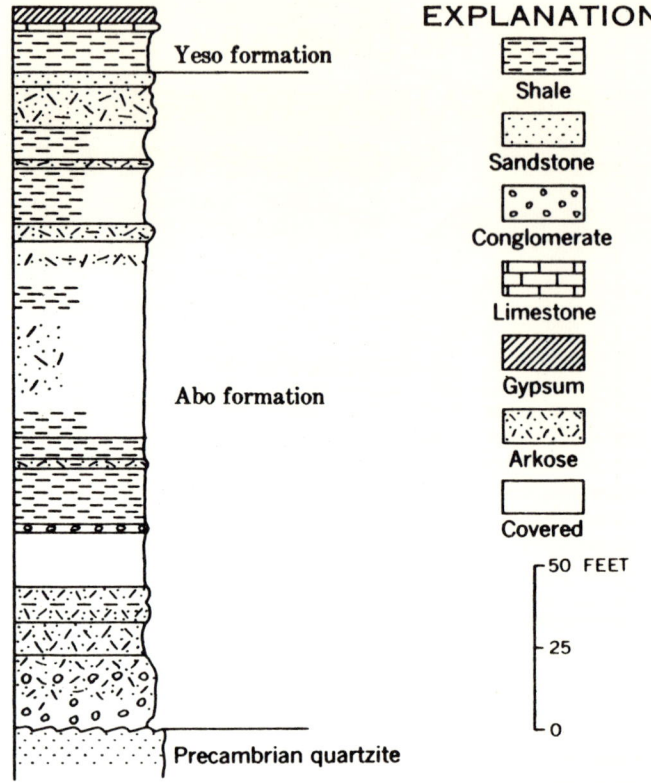

Figure 2. — Graphic section of Abo formation and adjacent rocks at Bent dome NW¼ sec. 36, T. 13 S., R. 11 E.

A PRELIMINARY RANGE CHART OF LAKE VALLEY FORMATION (OSAGE) CONODONTS IN THE SOUTHERN SACRAMENTO MOUNTAINS, NEW MEXICO

Robert C. Burton
West Texas State University
Canyon, Texas

INTRODUCTION

The Lake Valley Formation in the Alamo Canyon area of the southern Sacramento Mountains contains a large, well preserved conodont fauna. In this paper some stratigraphic implications of several species found in the Lake Valley are discussed and a chart is included to graphically illustrate their stratigraphic ranges. The material presented here is based on information obtained during a four-year study of Mississippian conodonts in the southern Sacramento Mountains.

Mississippian rocks in the Sacramento Mountains are marine and consist (descending) of the Helms (Chester); Rancheria (Meramac); Lake Valley (Osage); and Caballero (Kinderhook) Formations. Each of the formations yielded conodonts; however, faunas recovered from the Helms Formation and the Rancheria Formation are small and reworked and thus are of limited stratigraphic value. Although both the Lake Valley Formation and the Caballero Formation yield large, well preserved, indigenous faunas, the Lake Valley fauna contains more distinctive species of definable stratigraphic range and geographic distribution. Therefore, because of its greater potential for zonation and correlation, species from the Lake Valley conodont fauna are presented here.

In the Sacramento Mountains, the Lake Valley Formation is about 400 feet thick (Pray, 1961, p. 59) and is divided into six members. They are (descending) the Dona Ana, Arcente, Tierra Blanca, Nunn, Alamogordo and Andrecito Members. The Lake Valley Formation consist mostly of crinoidal limestone and small amounts of calcareous siltstone and shale. However, in the central part of the Sacramento Mountains, near Alamogordo, the Lake Valley contains a number of biohermal structures. According to Pray (1961, p. 60), these are the best exposures of Mississippian bioherms known in North America.

PROCEDURE

The conodonts discussed here were obtained from five collecting localities associated with the bioherms exposed in the Alamo Canyon area southeast of Alamogordo (fig. 1). At locality one the type Dona Ana, Arcente, and Alamogordo Members of the Lake Valley are exposed in a biohermal flank facies. Locality four also extends across the flank facies of a bioherm. At both of these localities conodonts were obtained from the Dona Ana, Tierra Blanca, Alamogordo and Andrecito Members of the Lake Valley. Collecting localities two and five are within the core facies of two bioherms and conodonts were obtained from the time equivalents of the Tierra Blanca, Nunn and Alamogordo Members. Locality three extends across an "interreef" facies where conodonts were extracted from the Tierra Blanca, Alamogordo and Andrecito Members. In general the Dona Ana, Tierra Blanca, Alamogordo and Andrecito Members consistently yielded conodonts wherever sampled, whereas the Arcente Member was always barren. The Nunn member usually is covered in this area and was not sampled although its equivalent was collected in the core facies of the bioherms at localities two and five.

One-half kilogram chip samples were taken continuously along a locality, with each sample being composed of chips from each one-foot interval. The samples were digested in a 15 percent acetic acid and the conodonts were picked from the residue. About 4,200 identifiable conodonts were extracted from 450 samples.

FAUNAL EVALUATION

Locally the Andrecito and Dona Ana Members faunas, which represent pre- and post-reef deposition respectively, vary in assemblage composition only with respect to the rare (less than 10 specimens per kilogram) species. The Alamogordo and Tierra Blanca Members faunas, which are contemporaneous to the biohermal structures, are equally consistent through the local facies i.e., core, flank, and "interreef."

Eleven of the 12 conodont species making up the *Bactrognathus communis* Zone of Hass (1959) in the Chappel Limestone of south-central Texas are present in and restricted to the Tierra Blanca Member fauna. The remaining species of the *B. communis* Zone, i.e., *Pseudopolygnathus multistriata* Mehl and Thomas, 1947, occurs only in the Alamogordo Member fauna. Further, 6 of the 8 species which constitute Hass's *Gnathodus punctatus* Zone are found in the Andrecito and Alamogordo Members faunas, thus indicating the eastward regional distribution of this part of the Lake Valley fauna.

It is impossible to make other regional comparisons because of the lack of published information regarding Mississippian conodont occurrences in the Southwest. However, the author is presently engaged in a study of faunas of similar age in the Big Hatchet Mountains, Hidalgo County, New Mexico. Large conodont faunas are indicated and species which are identical to forms previously found in the Lake Valley Formation in the southern Sacramento Mountains are present. Although the study is not sufficiently advanced to make meaningful comparisons these early results are suggestive of a close correlation between the faunas of the two areas.

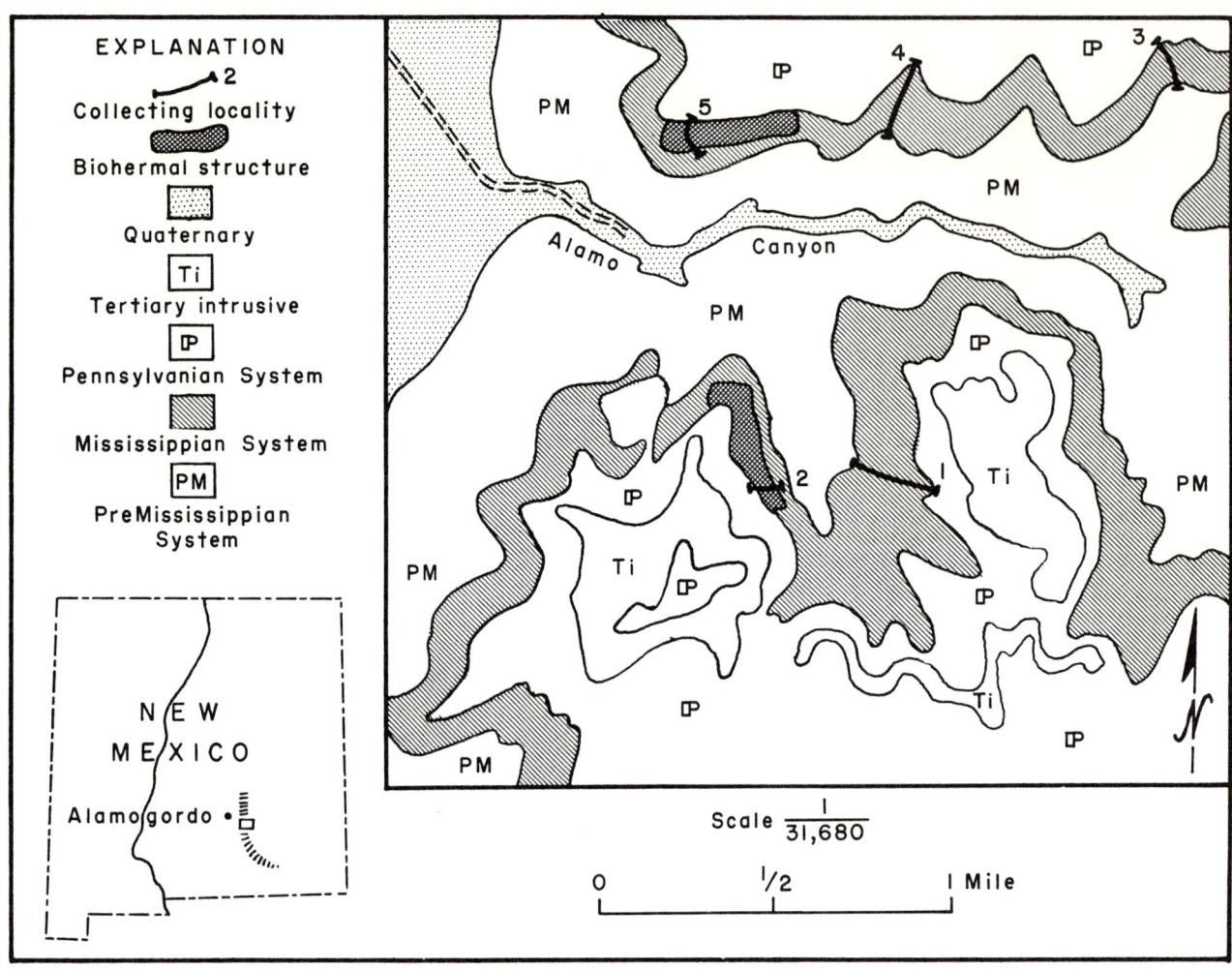

Figure 1. — Index map showing location of collecting localities in Alamo Canyon. Map adapted from Pray, 1961, pl. 1.

The interregional and intercontinental relationships of the Lake Valley Formation conodont fauna are much more complex because of assemblage variations both real and taxonomic — a matter which cannot be resolved in this preliminary range chart. However, in spite of the ramifications, some of these relationships are mentioned below.

CHART INTERPRETATION

Apatognathus lipperti Bischoff, 1956 is restricted to the Alamogordo Member. It is rare (less than 10 specimens per kilogram), delicate, and of short stratigraphic range locally. This form has been reported previously only from Germany (Bischoff, 1956; Bischoff and Ziegler, 1956). Thus it is of local and intercontinental correlative value.

Bactrognathus communis Hass, 1959; *B. penehamata* Hass, 1959; *B. distorta* Branson and Mehl, 1941a, are restricted to the Tierra Blanca and Alamogordo Members. *B. penehamata* and *B. communis* have been reported previously only from Texas (Hass, 1959), but this restriction may be taxonomic because of the occurrence of *B. distorta* and forms closely resembling *B. communis* and *B. penehamata* in Missouri. The three species are considered to be of local, regional, and interregional stratigraphic importance.

Bryantodus sp. Flugel and Ziegler, 1957 is found in the middle one-third of the Tierra Blanca Member. It is a sturdy, distinctive, and common (10-25 specimens per kilogram) form. It has been recorded previously only from German localities (Bischoff and Ziegler, 1957) and therefore is at present thought to be of local and intercontinental correlative value.

Doliognathus lata Branson and Mehl, 1941a; and *D. excavata* Branson and Mehl, 1941a are represented on the range chart by *D. lata*. Distinguishing between the two species is of little stratigraphic value locally because the range and abundance of each is essentially the same throughout the Tierra Blanca Member. *Doliognathus* has been recorded in Texas (Hass, 1959), in Missouri (Branson and Mehl, 1941a), and the Harz Mountains in Germany (Branson and Mehl, 1941b). This form is conspicuously absent from Mississippian rocks in the upper Mississippi Valley. Although found in Kinderhook and Osage rocks in Missouri in the Texas and New Mexico region it is restricted to the Osage.

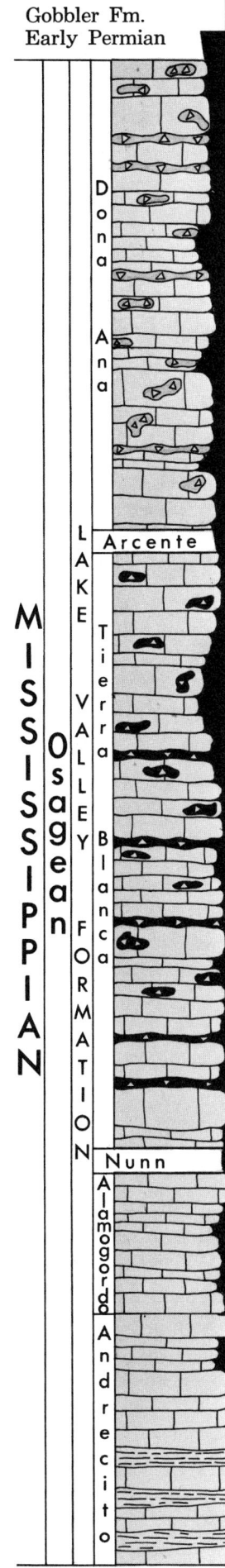

Gnathus texanus Roundy, 1926; *G. delicatus* Branson and Mehl, 1938; and *G. punctatus* Cooper, 1939 occur in greatest abundance in the approximate position shown on the chart. Of the three species only *G. delicatus* is confined to the Lake Valley Formation. The presence of transitional Gnathodids complicates regional, interregional, and intercontinental use. However, recognition of a particular species coupled with the reversal of dominance between Gnathodids and *Polygnathus communis* Branson and Mehl, 1934 can be used to locally divide the Lake Valley Formation.

Hindeodella segaformis Bischoff, 1957 is confined to the Tierra Blanca Member of the Lake Valley Formation. Although this form is subject to extreme breakage it is so distinctive that even small fragments can be identified with certainty. *H. segaformis* has been reported only from Germany (Bischoff, 1957) until now thus limiting it to local and intercontinental use.

Polygnathus communis Branson and Mehl, 1934 is not restricted to the Lake Valley Formation. It ranges from the Caballero Formation (Kinderhook) through the Rancheria Formation (Meramac). Zonation based on variations in the blade to platform dimensions and differences in platform ornamentation are possible to the specialists thereby permitting regional, interregional, and intercontinental correlations. A 2 to 1 dominance of Polygnathids over Gnathodids is reversed in the middle of the Tierra Blanca Member with Gnathodids dominant from that point upward. Relative abundance of these two genera serves as a local indicator of the upper or lower Lake Valley, and in conjunction with other forms confirms zonations.

Pseudopolygnathus multistriata Mehl and Thomas, 1947 is common and distinctive to the faunas of the Andrecito and Alamogordo Members. It has also been reported from Texas (Hass, 1959), Oklahoma (Cooper, 1939), Illinois (Rexroad and Scott, 1964), Missouri (Mehl and Thomas, 1947), and Germany (Bischoff and Ziegler, 1956; Freyer, 1961), and thus offers widespread correlation possibilities.

Scaliognathus anchoralis Branson and Mehl, 1941a is the most distinctive element in the Lake Valley fauna and is found in the middle one-third of the Tierra Blanca Member. It also occurs in the Harz Mountains in Germany (Branson and Mehl, 1941b). It has been reported as a Kinderhook — Osage form in Missouri by Branson and Mehl (1941a), but in the Texas and New Mexico occurrences it is Osage in age possibly due to delayed migration. Its widespread geographical distribution and restricted range makes this form of particular value for correlative purposes.

Staurognathus cruciformis Branson and Mehl, 1941a occurs in the lower 3 to 5 feet of the Tierra Blanca Member. It may extend lower in the section; however, this has not been established because the Nunn Member is generally covered. *S. cruciformis* is considered Kinderhook and Osage in Missouri (Branson and Mehl, 1941a). Restriction of the form to the Lake Valley Formation (Osagean) may be due to delayed migration.

REFERENCES CITED

Bischoff, G., 1956, Oberdevonische Conodonten (toId) aus dem Rheinischen Scheifergiberge: Hess. Landesamt. Bodenf., Notiz., v. 84, p. 115-137, pls. 8-10.

——— 1957, Die conodonten — Stratigraphie des rhenoherzynischen Unterkarbons mit Berucksichtigung der Wocklumeria-Stufe und der Devon/Karbon-Grenze: Abh. hessich. Landesamtes f. Bodenforsch. zu Wiesbaden, v. 19, 64 p.

——— and Ziegler, W., 1956, Des Alter der "Urfer Schichten" im Marburger Hinterland nach Conodonten: Notizblatt. hessisch. Landesamtes f. Bodenforsch. zu Wiesbaden, v. 84, p. 138-169.

——— 1957, Die Conodontenchronologie des Mitteldevons und des tiefsten Oberdevons: Hess. Landesamt. Bodenf., Abh., v. 22, p. 1-136, 21 pls.

Branson, E. B., and Mehl, M. G., 1934, Conodont studies no. 4, Conodonts from the Bushberg sandstone and equivalent formations of Missouri: Missouri Univ. Studies, v. 8, no. 4, p. 265-300, pls. 22-24.

——— 1938, Conodonts from the lower Mississippian of Missouri: Missouri Univ. Studies, v. 13, no. 4, p. 128-148, pls. 33-34.

——— 1941a, New and little known Carboniferous conodont genera: Jour. Paleontology, v. 15, p. 97-106, pl. 19.

——— 1941b, A record of typical American conodont genera in various parts of Europe: Denison Univ., Bull. Sci. Lab., v. 35, p. 189-194, pl. 7.

Cooper, C. L., 1939, Conodonts from a Bushberg-Hannibal horizon in Oklahoma: Jour. Paleontology, v. 13, p. 379-422.

Flugel, H., and Ziegler, W., 1957, Dies Gleiderung des Oberdevons und Unterkarbons am Steinberg Westlich Graz mit Conodonten: Mitt. Naturwiss. Ver. Steiermark, v. 87, p. 25-60, pls. 1-5.

Freyer, G., 1961, Zur Taxionomie und Biostratigraphie der Conodonten aus dem Oberdevon des Vogtlandes unter besonderer Berucksichtigung des To V/VI: Freiberger Forschrungsh. C-95, 96 p., 6 pls.

Hass, W. H., 1959, Conodonts from the Chappel Limestone of Texas: U.S. Geol. Survey Prof. Paper 294-J, p. 365-399.

Laudon, L. R., and Bowsher, A. L., 1941, Mississippian formations of the Sacramento Mountains, New Mexico: Am. Assoc. Petroleum Geologists Bull., v. 25, p. 2107-2160.

Mehl, M. G., and Thomas, L. A., 1947, Conodonts from the Fern Glen of Missouri: Denison Univ., Bull. Sci. Lab., v. 40, p. 3-20.

Pray, L. C., 1961, Geology of the Sacramento Mountains escarpment, Otero County, New Mexico: N. Mex. Inst. Min. and Tech., State Bur. Mines and Min. Res. Bull. 35, 144 p.

Rexroad, C. B., and Scott, A. J., 1964, Conodont zones in the Rockford Limestone and the lower part of the New Providence Shale (Mississippian) in Indiana: Ind. Dept. Conservation Geol. Survey Bull. 30, 54 p., pls. 2-3.

Roundy, P. V., 1926, The microfauna in Mississippian formations of San Saba County, Texas: U.S. Geol. Survey Prof. Paper 146, 63 p., 4 pls.

A STRATIGRAPHIC SECTION OF THE SIERRA BLANCA VOLCANICS IN THE NOGAL PEAK AREA, LINCOLN COUNTY, NEW MEXICO

Tommy B. Thompson

University of New Mexico, Albuquerque, New Mexico

Sierra Blanca was once described as an intrusive complex, but recent workers now recognize its dominant volcanic character. Continuous exposures of volcanic rocks are present throughout much of the steep western slope of Sierra Blanca. This paper presents a stratigraphic section of these rocks. This section extends from the ridge north of Elder Canyon (fig. 1) to the top of Nogal Peak almost four miles to the east. Three thick laterally-continuous andesite flows that have continuity throughout much of the area were recognized and used for correlation purposes.

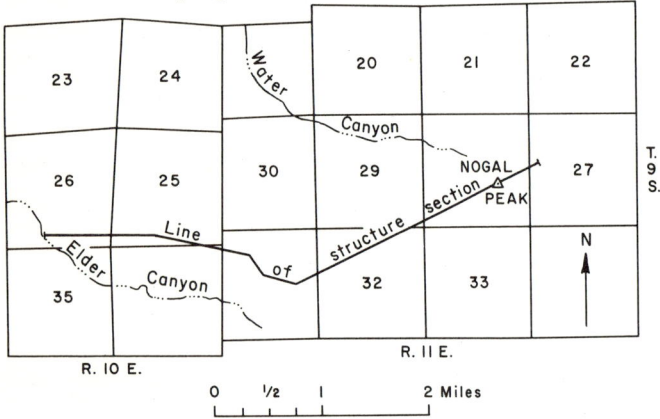

Figure 1. — Index map of the Nogal Peak area showing the location of the cross-section shown in figure 3.

The volcanic sequence (fig. 2) rests unconformably on the McRae (Cub Mountain of Bodine, 1956) Formation of Tertiary age, which, in this area, probably is more than 2,000 feet thick and includes interbedded conglomerate, sandstone, and shale (Griswold, 1959, p. 12). The basal unit of the volcanic sequence (unit 1) is a volcanic breccia consisting of rounded to angular hornblende andesite and andesite fragments in a matrix of reddish-brown to maroon hornblende andesite.

The succeeding volcanic rocks consist of dark-gray to purplish-gray andesite, hornblende andesite, and andesite breccia. Unit 18 is a thin bed of tuff. The tuff is entirely crystalline and none of the particles are greater than $1/4$ mm in maximum dimension. Angular hematite-coated plagioclase is the major constituent, and minor quantities of quartz and muscovite are present. Unit 30 is the lower of three massive andesite porphyry flows that form steep cliffs along the upper part of western Sierra Blanca. Units 32 and 34 directly overlie thin units of breccia and andesite flows and form massive cliffs. Unit 34 has been traced approximately 10 miles to the south along the western face of the mountain and is present on the east side of the drainage divide of Sierra Blanca. By tracing this unit to the head of Water Canyon it was possible to measure the entire stratigraphic section to the top of Nogal Peak.

The uppermost flow of the Nogal Peak section (unit 41) is a porphyritic hornblende andesite consisting of andesine (An_{43}) phenocrysts in a matrix of plagioclase and pyroxene with traces of magnetite, apatite, and cristobalite. Latitic flows have been noted by Weber on Church Mountain (Griswold, 1959, p. 13) approximately $4\frac{1}{2}$ miles northeast of Nogal Peak; however, the relationship between these two units is not known.

Some of the units studied are remarkably uniform in lateral extent (fig. 3); however, there are irregularities in thickness of the units as well as in depositional surfaces. The relief on the depositional surface for any particular eruption does not appear to be great. Commonly, a single volcanic eruption commenced with accumulation of breccia containing fragments as much as three or four feet in diameter. The size of these fragments decreases upward in the flow, and the upper and last part of the eruption is free of breccia. Evidence in the form of a zone of petrified trees indicate there was a local hiatus between two volcanic eruptions at a locality about 10 miles south of Nogal Peak. This zone is not present in the Nogal Peak section.

The actual measured thickness of the Sierra Blanca volcanic rocks exposed in the Nogal Peak area is 3,340 feet. The thickness of the volcanic pile was estimated to exceed 4,000 feet (Griswold, 1959, p. 13).

Flow centers have not been definitely located but several stocks in Sierra Blanca (see Kelley and Thompson, this guidebook) probably were the sources of the Sierra Blanca volcanic rocks.

REFERENCES CITED

Bodine, M. W., Jr., 1956, Geology of Capitan coal field, Lincoln County, New Mexico: N. Mex. Inst. Min. and Tech., State Bur. Mines and Mineral Res. Circular 35, 27 p.

Griswold, G. B., 1959, Mineral deposits of Lincoln County, New Mexico: N. Mex. Inst. Min. and Tech., State Bur. Mines and Mineral Res. Bull. 67, 117 p.

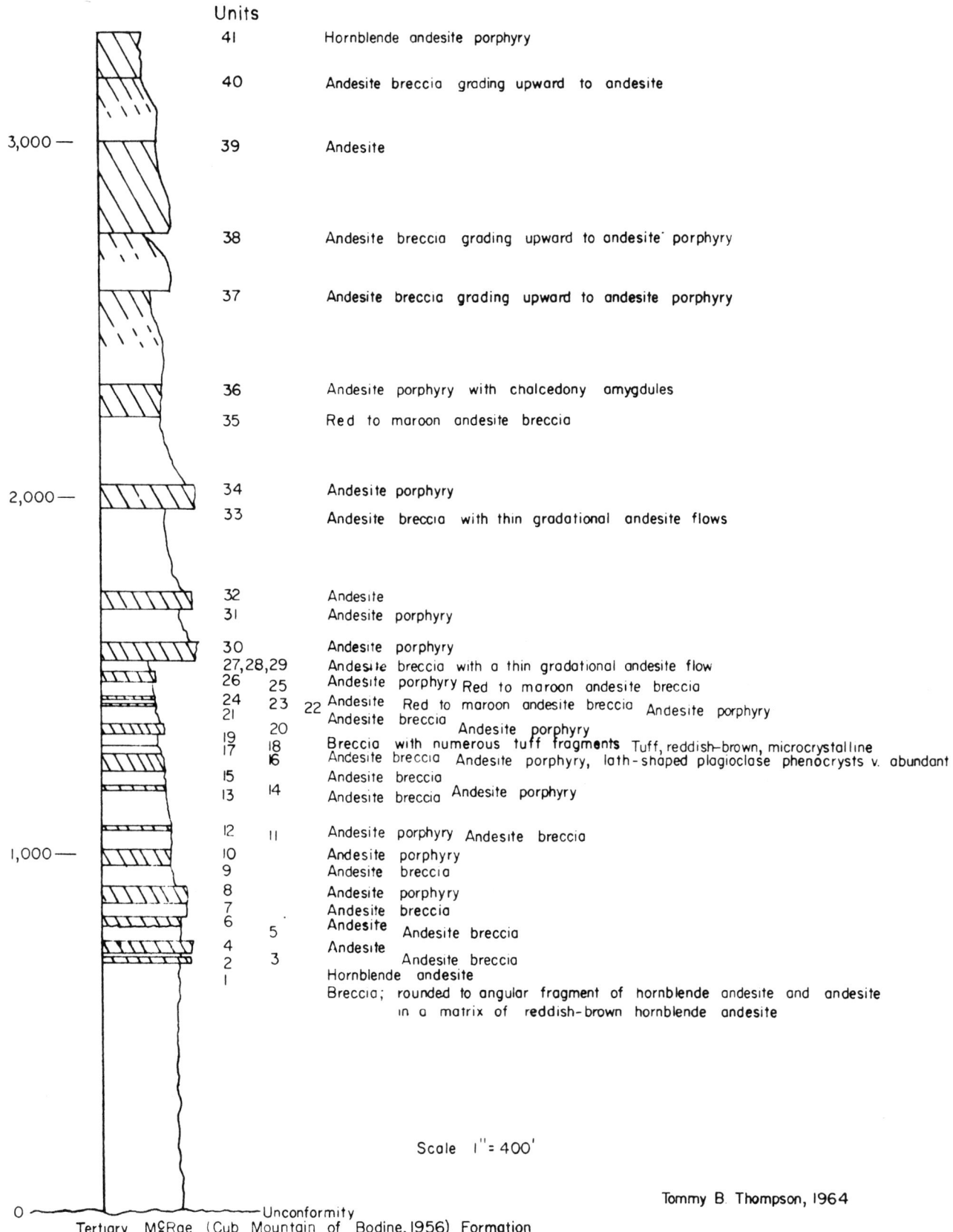

Figure 2. — Graphic section of the Sierra Blanca Volcanics in the Nogal Peak area, New Mexico.

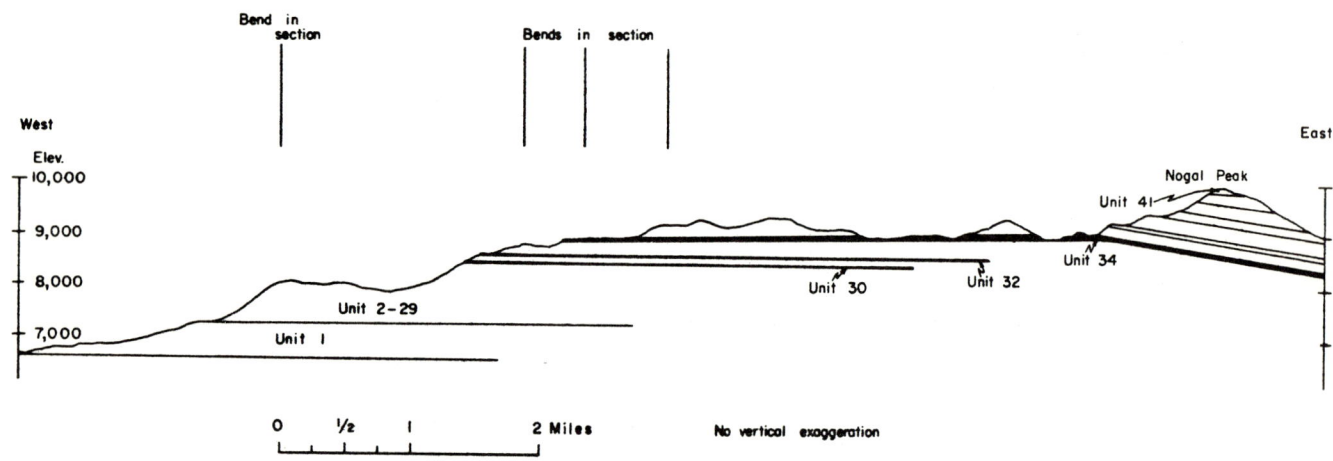

Figure 3. — Stratigraphic cross-section, Nogal Peak area, New Mexico. Units are the same as those in figure 2.

GLACIAL DEPOSITS ON SIERRA BLANCA PEAK, NEW MEXICO

Gerald M. Richmond
Denver, Colorado

Recently Gerald M. Richmond of the U.S. Geological Survey, Denver, Colorado published a short article concerning glacial deposits in New Mexico. The parts of that article which concern glacial deposits on Sierra Blanca Peak are given below. A few minor changes have been made in the excerpts with the permission of the author.

GERALD M. RICHMOND, 1962, CORRELATION OF SOME GLACIAL DEPOSITS IN NEW MEXICO: ART. 213 IN U.S. GEOLOGICAL SURVEY PROF. PAPER 450-E, P. E121-E125.

Clear evidence of Pleistocene glaciation in New Mexico is mostly confined to the higher parts of the Sangre de Cristo Mountains, and to the Sierra Blanca in the south-central part of the State. (See index map, fig. 1.) An ancient till, correlated with the Cerro Till of the San Juan Mountains, has also been reported from the Canjillon Divide area in the north-central part of the State, west of the Rio Grande (Ellis, 1935; Smith, 1936).

Glaciation in the Sangre de Cristo Mountains has been reported by Salisbury (1901) and Stone (1901), and subsequently by Ellis (1931). Ray (1940) was the first to recognize multiple glaciation in the region. He described moraines of five "substages" of the Wisconsin "glacial stage" in the vicinity of Wheeler Peak, northeast of Taos, and in the vicinity of Lake Peak, northeast

TABLE 1. — *Correlation of Wisconsin "substages" of Ray (1940) with moraines found by the writer*

(Figures are altitudes of end moraines, in feet)

		Wheeler Peak, Rio Hondo		Lake Peak, South Fork Rio Nambe		Sierra Blanca Peak	
		Richmond, 1962b	Ray (1940)	Richmond, 1962b	Ray (1940)	Richmond, 1962b and this article	Smith & Ray (1941)
RECENT	Neoglaciation	Gannett Peak Stade 12,000 (avg.)		Neoglaciation			
		Temple Lake Stade 11,850 (avg.)	W V	Temple Lake Stade 11,500			
LATE PLEISTOCENE	Pinedale Glaciation	Late stade 11,000	W IV / W III	Late stade 11,400	W IV	Late stade 11,300	Complex of Wisconsin moraines
		Middle stade 10,850		Middle stade 11,100		Middle stade 10,900	
		Early stade 10,200		Early stade 10,750	W III	Early stade 10,500	
	Bull Lake Glaciation	Late stade 9,700	W I	Late stade 10,500		Late stade 10,400	
		Early stade 9,400		Early stade 10,100	W II	Early stade 9,850	
MIDDLE PLEISTOCENE				Third pre-Bull Lake Glaciation 10,000			

of Santa Fe. He also showed that deposits described as moraines in the Moreno Valley (Ellis, 1931), are not of glacial origin. Smith and Ray (1941) further reported a complex of Wisconsin moraines on the northeast side of Sierra Blanca Peak below a cirque mentioned briefly by Antevs (1935).

In order to correlate Ray's "substages" with the glaciations of the Wind River Mountains of Wyoming (Blackwelder, 1915; Richmond, 1948, 1957a, 1962; Moss, 1951b; Holmes and Moss, 1955), the writer briefly re-examined the succession of glacial deposits along Rio Hondo on the slopes of Wheeler Peak, along Rio Nambe on the slopes of Lake Peak and on Sierra Blanca Peak (fig. 1). New topographic maps in two of these areas have made possible a more accurate means of plotting end moraines and of determining their altitudes than was available to Ray. Deposits of glaciations recognized by the writer are correlated with those described by Ray (1940) as shown in table 1.

CRITERIA OF CORRELATION

Deposits of three glaciations—from oldest to youngest, the Buffalo, Bull Lake, and Pinedale—were described in the Wind River Mountains of Wyoming by Blackwelder in 1915. Subsequent work has demonstrated 3 pre-Bull Lake glaciations (Richmond, 1962) included in deposits formerly called Buffalo, 2 stades of Bull Lake Glaciation (Richmond, 1948; Moss, 1951a; Holmes and Moss, 1955), 3 stades of Pinedale Glaciation (Richmond, 1948, 1962), and 2 stades (Temple Lake and Gannett Peak) of Neoglaciation (Hack, 1943; Moss 1951a, 1951b; Richmond, 1957b). Criteria for recognition of these glaciations and their subdivisions in the Wind River Mountains and elsewhere have been described in many papers (Blackwelder, 1915, 1931; Fryxell, 1951; Moss, 1951a; Holmes and Moss, 1955; Richmond, 1957a, 1962; Nelson, 1954).

The following characteristics of the deposits in the Wind River Mountains were used as the basis for correlation with the deposits in New Mexico described here.

First and second pre-Bull Lake Glaciations.—deeply weathered; red clayey soils; lack glacial topography; confined to interstream divides.

Third pre-Bull Lake Glaciation.—Weathering as above, but forming poorly preserved broad, mature moraines on canyon walls or floors.

Locally deposits of all three glaciations are superposed and separated by thick red clayey soils.

Bull Lake Glaciation.—Commonly two broad, mature moraines (early and late stages) in canyons; dissected by axial and tributary streams; mature zonal soils 3 to 4 feet thick. The two tills grade into separate outwash deposits, which, where superposed, are separated and overlain by mature zonal soils similar to those on the moraine deposits.

Pinedale Glaciation.—Commonly 3 well-preserved rough, bouldery moraines (early, middle, and late stades) in canyons upstream from moraines of the Bull Lake Glaciation. Immature zonal soils 1 to 2 feet thick. Outwash gravels underlie separate terraces or form compound fills. Locally thin azonal soil or dark alluvial silty-clay layer separates outwash of early and middle stades.

Neoglaciation. — Temple Lake Stade — small moraines or rock glaciers in cirques. Thin azonal soil, tundra or scrub spruce vegetation. Gannett Peak Stade—fresh moraines or rock glaciers above those of Temple Lake Stade; no soil; commonly barren, but locally with lichen on boulders and sparse pioneer vegetation; moraines lie in front of existing glaciers or in recently evacuated cirques.

SIERRA BLANCA

From the shallow cirque on the northeast side of Sierra Blanca Peak (altitude 12,003 feet), a bouldery lateral moraine extends along the north side of the canyon of the North Fork of the Rio Ruidoso to a terminal moraine 50 feet high at an altitude of 9,850 feet about a mile from the cirque headwall (fig. 1). The deposit

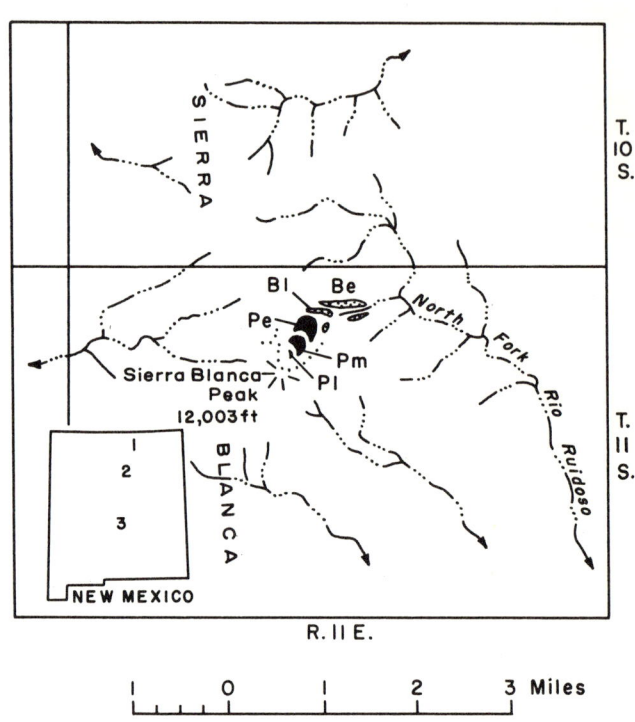

Figure 1. Moraines on Sierra Blanca Peak, Sierra Blanca, New Mexico. Be and Bl, early and late stades of Bull Lake Glaciation; Pe, Pm, and Pl, early, middle, and late Stades of Pinedale Glaciation. Index map: 1, Wheeler Peak; 2, Lake Peak; 3, Sierra Blanca. Adapted from Richmond, 1962b, figure 213.3.

is trenched about 30 to 40 feet by the creek, and bears a mature Brown Podzolic soil about 3 feet thick. The B horizon of the soil is strong-brown (7.5 YR 5/6) and contains noticeable illuviated clay, though it is not plastic. The boulders are mostly of granite porphyry, and many, both on and in the till, are deeply disintegrated. A second broad terminal moraine of similar character lies at an altitude of 10,400 feet. It also is about 50 feet high and is littered with boulders, some 10 to 12 feet in diameter. These two moraines are believed to represent the early and late stages of Bull Lake Glaciation. A small lake basin back of the upper moraine is filled with arkosic sand and gravel which extends upslope as an outwash plain into still another bouldery morainal ridge, about 30 feet high, which forms an arcuate loop on the steep slope leading into the cirque at an altitude of 10,500 feet. The moraine is grass covered except for a few spruce along its outer slope and lateral extensions. It is but little dissected, bears an immature Brown Podzolic soil about 10 inches thick, and is yellowish brown (10YR 5/4). A similar moraine, nearly 100 feet high, lies across the slope at an altitude of 10,900 feet, and a third, about 60 feet high, at 11,300 feet. These three moraines are believed to represent the early, middle, and late stages of Pinedale Glaciation.

The cirque floor is between 11,400 and 11,500 feet in altitude. Talus along the cliffed headwall is stable and covered by soil and grass or spruce, and spruce extends as scattered clumps to the top of the peak. No deposits having the characteristics of the Temple Lake or Gannett Peak Stades of Neoglaciation were seen, and no snowbanks were present on July 10, 1957.

A steep basinlike slope on the northwest side of the peak may have been occupied by ice during the Bull Lake Glaciation, but not in Pinedale time. The slope is steep and no moraines have been preserved.

REFERENCES

Antevs, Ernst, 1935, The occurrence of flint and extinct animals in pluvial deposits near Clovis, New Mexico, Pt. 2 of Age of Clovis Lake clays: Philadelphia Acad. Nat. Sci. Proc., p. 304-312.

Blackwelder, Eliot, 1915, Post-Cretaceous history of the mountains of central western Wyoming: Jour. Geology, v. 23, p. 97-117, 103-217, 307-340.

──────── 1931, Pleistocene glaciation in the Sierra Nevada and Basin Ranges: Geol. Soc. America Bull., v. 42, p. 865-922.

Ellis, R. W., 1931, The Red River lobe of the Moreno glacier: New Mexico Univ. Bull., v. 4, p. 1-26.

──────── 1935, Glaciation in New Mexico: New Mexico Univ. Bull., Geol. Ser., v. 5, p. 1-31.

Fryxell, F. M., 1951, Grand Teton National Park: U.S. Geol. Survey topographic map. (Text on back)

Hack, J. T., 1943, Antiquity of the Finley Site: Am. Antiquity, v. 8, no. 3, p. 235-241.

Holmes, G. W. and Moss, J. H., 1955, Pleistocene geology of the southwestern Wind River Mountains, Wyoming: Geol. Soc. America Bull., v. 66, p. 629-654.

Moss, J. H., 1951a, Early man in the Eden Valley: Pennsylvania Univ. Mus. Mon., v. 6, 124 p.

──────── 1951b, Late glacial advances in the southern Wind River Mountains, Wyoming: Am. Jour. Sci., v. 249, no. 12, p. 865-883.

Nelson, R. L., 1954, Glacial geology of the Frying Pan River drainage, Colorado: Jour. Geology, v. 62, p. 325-343.

Ray, L. L., 1940, Glacial chronology of the southern Rocky Mountains: Geol. Soc. America Bull., v. 51, p. 1851-1918.

Richmond, G. M., 1948, Modification of Blackwelder's sequence of Pleistocene chronology in the Wind River Mountains, Wyoming (abs.): Geol. Soc. America Bull., v. 59, p. 1400-1401.

──────── 1957a, Three pre-Wisconsin glacial stages in the Rocky Mountain region: Geol. Soc. America Bull., v. 68, p. 239-262.

──────── 1957b, Correlation of Quaternary deposits in the Rocky Mountain region, U.S.A.: Internat. Congress of INQUA, 5th, Madrid-Barcelona, 1957, Resumés des communications, p. 157.

──────── 1962a, Three pre-Bull Lake tills in the Wind River Mountains, Wyoming: Art. 159 in U.S. Geol. Survey Prof. Paper 450-D, p. D132-D136.

──────── 1962b, Correlation of some glacial deposits in New Mexico: Art. 213 in U.S. Geological Survey Prof. Paper 450-E, p. E121-E125.

Salisbury, R. D., 1901, Glacial work in the western Mountains in 1901: Jour. Geology, v. 9, p. 718-731.

Smith, H. T. U., 1936, Periglacial landslide topography of Canjillon Divide, Rio Arriba County, New Mexico: Jour. Geology, v. 44, p. 836-860.

Smith, H. T. U., and Ray, L. L., 1941, Southernmost glaciated peak in the United States: Science, v. 93, p. 209.

Stone, G. H., 1901, Note on the extinct glaciers of Arizona and New Mexico Science, v. 14, p. 798.

GEOLOGIC OUTLINE OF THE JICARILLA MOUNTAINS, LINCOLN COUNTY, NEW MEXICO

A. J. Budding
New Mexico Institute of Mining and Technology
Socorro, New Mexico

INTRODUCTION

The Jicarilla Mountains are an extension of the north-trending ranges of the Sacramento Mountains and Sierra Blanca which dominate the landscape of south-central New Mexico. Although the highest points in the Jicarillas are not as lofty as Nogal Peak and Sierra Blanca Peak to the south, they stand out as well-developed topographic prominences between the Tularosa Basin to the west and the high plains to the east.

The absence of good quality topographic maps of the Jicarilla Mountains is a disadvantage in making detailed geological investigations. Perhaps the best available in the form of planimetric maps are the semicontrolled mosaics, prepared from aerial photographs by the Soil Conservation Service of the U.S. Department of Agriculture. Four photo-maps, of the NW quarter, SW quarter, SE quarter, and NE quarter, each on an approximate scale of one inch equals one half mile, cover the area between lat 33°45' and 34°00' N. and between long 105°30' and 105°45' W., or what perhaps in the not too distant future will become known as the "Jicarilla 15 minute quadrangle." The Jicarilla Mountains, as used here, will include the area covered by the NW and SW quarter photo-maps.

STRATIGRAPHY

Sediments of Permian, Triassic, Cretaceous and Tertiary age form the bedrock in many parts of the Jicarilla Mountains. The following descriptions will serve to outline the lithologic character and thickness of these beds, and any other characteristics specific to the area.

Permian Rocks

Only the upper part of the Yeso Formation is present in the area. Best exposures are to be found along the right-of-way of old U.S. Highway 54, about 2½ miles northeast of Luna, where gypsiferous siltstones and fine- to medium-grained sandstones of pale-yellow to pale-orange color form the upper 50 feet of this formation.

Rocks belonging to this formation are also present in a narrow north-trending belt between the intrusives of Jack's Peak and the Jicarilla monzonite, but are difficult to recognize among the extensive talus and cliff debris that surrounds the peak. As a consequence of its lithologic characteristics, the Yeso Formation does not form spectacular outcrops, but is usually a slope former.

Investigations in the area show, that in the northern Jicarilla Mountains, the Glorieta Sandstone forms a recognizable unit between the underlying Yeso Formation and the overlying San Andres Formation. Further to the south, in the vicinity of Jicarilla and near Lone Mountain, where doming by intrusives has brought the Permian sequence close to the present erosion surface, intertonguing of Glorieta and San Andres lithologies obscures the contact between these two formations. Northeast of Luna, the Glorieta Sandstone is a 120-foot thick unit consisting mainly of medium-grained, well-sorted quartz sandstone of pink to gray color. Grain size is somewhat variable in individual beds, and in the coarser grained layers, cross-bedding can occasionally be observed.

The uppermost unit of unquestionable Permian age is the San Andres Formation. In the area under discussion the formation consists mostly of a chert-bearing dark-gray porous limestone, with sandstone interbeds near its base, and discontinuous gypsum layers near the top.

Due to its resistant nature to erosive forces, and its considerable thickness, exposures of the San Andres Formation are widespread. Much of the area south of Ancho, and north and south of the Jicarilla monzonite is underlain by this formation. The high plains north and east of Jack's Peak are on a low angle dip slope of San Andres limestone.

Thickness measurements of this important unit are complicated by a lack of relief in critical areas, the intertonguing nature of the underlying Glorieta Sandstone and the San Andres Formation, and the varying importance of gypsum beds in the upper part. Northeast of Luna, where the Glorieta Sandstone can be distinguished as a separate unit, the San Andres Formation is 510 feet thick. To the south, the formation thickens, and 615 feet is thought to be present near the Jicarilla intrusive. In this area, however, Glorieta Sandstone intertongues may increase the thickness considerably.

Overlying the San Andres Formation, and below the Triassic Dockum Group, is found a series of yellow and red sandstone, limestone and gypsum beds, which, in view of their stratigraphic position, are tentatively correlated with the Bernal Formation (Bachman, 1953). A similar unit has been recognized in adjoining quadrangles, and either a Permian or Triassic age has been assigned to these beds.

Outcrops of the Bernal(?) Formation are not plentiful, mainly due to the nonresistant nature of the beds to the forces of weathering and erosion. The soil, derived from this unit, has a fine-grained, sandy texture, and a bright-red color, which makes the San Andres-Bernal(?) contact clearly distinguishable, even if bedrock is not exposed. The red soil color is sufficiently different from the darker hues of red and brown, which characterize the soils of the Triassic Dockum Group sediments.

The lower 185 feet of the Bernal Formation is well

exposed along the road, about 0.2 mile east of Ancho. At this locality, which will be visited by the Field Conference, the formation consists mainly of yellow-brown to orange-red siltstones and fine-grained sandstones, with thin beds of limestone.

Total thickness of the Bernal is somewhat variable throughout the area, but usually is between 270 and 320 feet.

Triassic Rocks

Sediments of Upper Triassic age are represented by the Santa Rosa Sandstone and the Chinle Formation, which together make up the Dockum Group. The contact between these two units is gradational, and their total thickness, about 560 feet, is generally about equally divided between the two formations.

The boundary between the Bernal(?) Formation and the Santa Rosa Sandstone is apparently a surface of unconformity, but lack of continuous outcrops obscures the true relationship. The Santa Rosa Sandstone consists of reddish-brown, medium-grained, friable sandstones with interbedded mudstones. Coarser grained layers, where cross-bedding can frequently be observed, are seen to grade into thin lenses of conglomerate, with yellowish-brown and black chert pebbles. The occurrence of such pebbles in the soil in areas of few outcrops is frequently the only indication of the presence of the Santa Rosa Sandstone.

The Santa Rosa Sandstone grades upwards into the mudstones and siltstones of the Chinle Formation. Outcrops of this formation are generally poor, and only in places where the Dakota Sandstone forms a resistant cap of a mesa, can exposures be found on the lower slopes. Red to purple colors are typical of this formation, and also characterize the soil.

Cretaceous Rocks

During the Jurassic and lower Cretaceous, the region of the Jicarilla Mountains was one of erosion and nondeposition. During the Upper Cretaceous period, marine conditions returned and the sediments formed during that period can be subdivided into three groups, which, in comparison with rocks of similar stratigraphic position in other parts of New Mexico, have been named Dakota Sandstone, Mancos Shale, and Mesaverde Group.

The Dakota Sandstone overlies the Triassic Chinle Formation unconformably and due to its resistance to erosion, forms sandstone cliffs and mesa cappings of considerable extent. Several well-cemented quartz sandstone beds occur in the stratigraphic sequence, which also includes some sandy shales and carbonaceous shales. Thickness is variable, and in the Jicarilla Mountains from 120 to 200 feet of Dakota Sandstone is present. A complete section is exposed about two miles east of Ancho, and here the formation consists of massive, medium-grained quartz sandstones, with carbonized and silicified plant remains, and interbedded dark-gray shales.

The Dakota Sandstone is overlain conformably by the Mancos Shale, which underlies large tracts in the southern parts of the Jicarilla Mountains. The medium-gray, calcareous shales, which make up the bulk of this formation, show little resistance to erosion, and outcrops are almost wholly confined to arroyo bottoms. Total thickness of the Mancos Shale can only be computed, and it is estimated that about 410 feet of this formation is present.

Still higher in the stratigraphic section, conspicuous brown sandstone beds begin to occur, and the mixed sequence of sandstone and shales has been correlated with the Mesaverde Group. The base of this formation has been chosen at the first prominent sandstone ledge, which occurs about 410 feet above the Dakota-Mancos contact. The shales of the Mesaverde Group are bluish-gray, calcareous shales with septarian concretions; the sandstones are medium-grained, and buff to brown in color. Several sandstones of the Mesaverde Group are fossiliferous and contain gastropods, pelecypods, and occasionally ammonites. At least 415 feet of Mesaverde Group sediments are present, mostly in the southern part of the area.

Tertiary Rocks

Although the period following the deposition of the Upper Cretaceous Mesaverde Group was dominantly one of tectonism, igneous activity and erosion, remnants of Tertiary sediments are found in a few places.

The high plains, which extend east of the line Luna-Jack's Peak, are part of an old plateau surface, which is partly covered by consolidated gravels. The boulders in these gravels consist of limestone, chert and jasper, igneous rocks, sandstone, some mudstone, and quartzite. The presence of igneous rock fragments in the conglomerate indicates, that at the time of deposition, igneous activity had taken place in the Jicarilla Mountains area, and that certain intrusives had been laid bare by erosion. Many of the fragments of the sedimentary rocks can be directly related to the more resistant members of the pre-Tertiary sequence: limestone derived from the San Andres Formation, chert and jasper from the conglomerate beds of the Santa Rosa Sandstone, sandstone fragments derived from the Dockum Group sandstones, Dakota Sandstone and Mesaverde Group, etc.

Bretz and Horberg (1949) called attention to the fact, that the Ogallala Formation once extended west of the Llano Estacado, into the foothills of the Sacramento Mountains. They report gravel residuals, with pebble counts comparable to those obtained from the consolidated gravels of the Jicarilla Mountains, from eastern Lincoln County and neighboring De Baca County. In the Jicarilla Mountains, two observations tend to refute the idea that the consolidated gravels are a wholly locally derived product, of recent, say Quaternary age: in the first place, the physiographic position of the gravels, several hundreds of feet above the present arroyo bottoms; secondly, a rather high percentage of quartzite pebbles in the conglomerate, which cannot be of local derivation, but which must have come from northerly source areas, such as the Pedernal region.

The matrix of the conglomerate is fine-grained, sandy and calcareous. Usually, cementation is not complete, and it is only rarely, that ledges of conglomerate are exposed.

In view of Bretz and Horberg's extensive investigations (1949) of this formation between the Sacramento Mountains and the Pecos River, the consolidated gravels are considered to be the equivalents of the Pliocene Ogallala Formation. The gravels were deposited as a consequence of uplift of the Central New Mexico mountains, and laid down as a gravel apron east of these ranges, grading further east, in Texas, into the sandstones and shales of the Ogallala Formation. In the Jicarilla Mountains, thickness is variable but may be as much as 50 feet in places. As deposition of the consolidated gravels took place on an erosional surface, they overlie rocks ranging from San Andres Formation to Dakota Sandstone.

PETROLOGY

Igneous rocks of much diversity in composition and form occur in the Jicarilla Mountains. Sills, dikes, stocks, and possibly laccoliths and plugdomes are present; their composition is predominantly of an alkalic character, as far as preliminary petrological observations allow the drawing of such a conclusion.

Monzonite and Related Rock Types

The largest body of monzonitic composition crops out in the vicinity of the village of Jicarilla, and this rock type forms here a pluton of irregular shape, about 7 miles long in a northwest direction, and about four miles northeast. This intrusive, which will be referred to as the Jicarilla monzonite, extends east into the vicinity of Jack's Peak, outside the area presently under discussion.

Along its northern and southern boundaries, the monzonite is in contact with sediments of the San Andres-Glorieta sequence, while east of Jicarilla, Yeso Formation borders the intrusive. Crosscutting relationships between the monzonite and overlying sediments are found along the western boundary of the pluton, and here the contact cuts Bernal, Santa Rosa, and Chinle Formations. Within the monzonite proper, several outliers of San Andres limestone indicate that the present erosion surface is close to the roof of the pluton.

The common rock type is a leucocratic, gray to buff monzonite porphyry with varying amounts of quartz. Plagioclase (oligoclase) in the form of euhedral to subhedral crystals, as much as one inch in length, and anhedral quartz, much corroded and embayed, form phenocrysts. The dark mineral is either hornblende or biotite, but usually only outlines are preserved, and alteration has changed the original phenocrysts into a mixture of chlorite, epidote, calcite, rutile needles, and opaque constituents. The groundmass is fine-grained, and consists mostly of potash feldspar, and some quartz. Sericitization of the feldspars, particularly in the groundmass, is rather intense. Accessory minerals are apatite and zircon.

The pluton has created room for itself in a number of ways: by shouldering aside incompetent Yeso beds, possibly by stopping where the contact trangresses stratigraphic boundaries, and by uplifting and doming of the overlying San Andres and younger formations. This latter effect accounts for the predominant dip of the sediments away from the intrusive. Several satellite bodies of monzonite, not visibly connected with the main mass, but most likely derived from the same magma source, occur north of the main pluton. These smaller intrusives are roofed by San Andres limestone. A dominant joint direction in the monzonite trends WNW, with a dip to the northeast.

Dikes and sills of monzonitic composition, but of smaller dimensions than the Jicarilla monzonite, are abundant throughout the area, and are particularly numerous in the Cretaceous sequence northeast of White Oaks. Emplacement of these sills at higher levels of the crust is indicated by a very fine-grained groundmass, presence of flow banding, and vesicular character of some of the rocks.

Trachyte and Related Rocks

Along the southern edge of the area, and for the most part situated in the Capitan quadrangle to the south, stands the circular mountain mass of Patos Mountain. Extensive areas of talus surround the precipitous northern slopes, and the first recognizable sedimentary rocks exposed are of the Mesaverde Group.

The igneous rocks of Patos Mountain are predominantly trachytes. Potash feldspar is dominant, constituting more than 75 percent of the mineral components, mafics, either green hornblende or brown biotite, form less than 5 percent. The alignment of tabluar feldspar crystals gives the rock a trachytic texture. In the central part of the mass plagioclase crystals, of sodic andesine composition, are mantled by potash feldspar; the quartz content of these rocks is about 10 percent. Towards the northern boundary, plagioclase disappears as a rock constituent, the rock becomes very leucocratic, and the quartz content increases to 20 percent. Consequently, this rock would be most appropriately referred to as a felsite. Preliminary investigations of this interesting igneous complex tend to indicate, that its main composition is trachyandesitic to trachytic, with more quartz-rich differentiates occurring along its northern edge.

Lamprophyric Dike Rocks

Lamprophyric or basic dikes form a NNE-trending swarm cutting the Mancos Shale in the area northwest of Patos Mountain. Dikes of this nature have been reported from the White Oaks District by Lindgren, Graton, and Gordon (1910), where they are referred to as kensantite-minette. Other noteworthy occurrences of basic dikes are as crosscutting bodies in the Jicarilla monzonite, and as more irregular plugs in the Chinle Formation along the road between Ancho and Luna.

The dike rock is fine-grained, phanerocrystalline, and medium- to dark-gray in color. A thin section from a sample collected along the road two miles east of White Oaks, contains the following mineral constituents: plagioclase (labradorite), 40 percent; alkali feldspar, 35 percent; diopsidic augite, 10 percent; biotite, 10 percent; and accessory and opaque constituents 5 percent.

STRUCTURAL AND IGNEOUS EVOLUTION

After the numerous epeirogenic movements, which controlled the deposition of Paleozoic and Mesozoic sediments, the strongest factors responsible for shaping the structural complexities of the Jicarilla Mountains were the igneous events, which gave rise to the emplacement

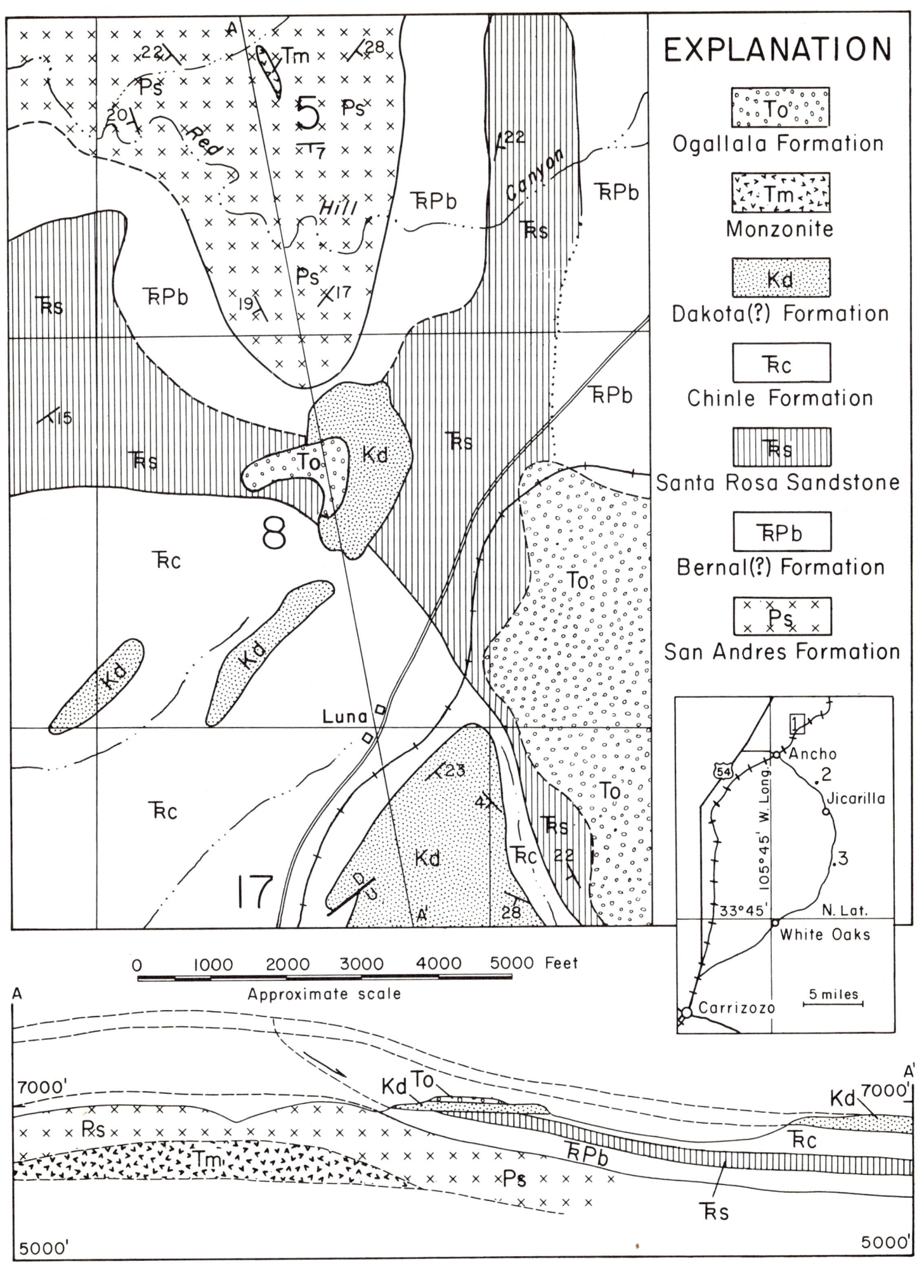

of the monzonitic intrusives. Rounded or irregular domes, and intervening narrow, doubly plunging synclines, or small structural basins, are the characteristic structures. Faulting is of minor importance; the only fault of any consequence occurs near White Oaks. It trends northerly and follows a broad valley for about one mile, then swings northeast and ends in the incompetent Triassic sequence southwest of the Jicarilla monzonite. This fault, of which the east and southeast side is downthrown, is cut by a monzonite sill in the Mesaverde Group, and by lamprophyric dikes.

The largest structural dome is underlain by the Jicarilla monzonite, and around its periphery, bedding dip is outward. Smaller domes frequently do not expose the underlying intrusive, but the San Andres Formation and younger rocks outline these structures quite well. Under such conditions, it is often striking to note, that domes exhibit steep flanks and relatively flat crests. The intervening synclinal structures, usually well outlined by the outcrop pattern of the resistant Dakota Sandstone, are irregular and branching, plunging synclines with flat bottoms and steep flanks. Examples of such synclines are found east of the railroad tracks between Ancho and Luna, and in a less accessible part of the area, about four miles southwest of Jicarilla.

Tectonic and igneous events followed the deposition of the Mesaverde Group, but detailed evidence of their sequence is lacking. Tectonic stresses, possibly related to the Laramide deformation, caused faulting in the vicinity of White Oaks before the emplacement of the monzonite stocks. This igneous activity occurred prior to the deposition of the Pliocene Ogallala Formation, and initially was of a monzonitic character. During this period, the great stocks of Jicarilla monzonite and satellitic bodies were emplaced. The following event was the intrusion of the lamprophyric dikes, and perhaps also the emplacement of the trachyte plug of Patos Mountain, both of which may represent differentiates of an alkaline olivine basalt magma, part of which, during the Quaternary, reached the surface as the Little Black Peak lava flow.

Igneous activity in the Jicarilla Mountains was accompanied or followed by extensive uplift. The newly formed domes were subject to erosion, and differences in resistance between the pre-Tertiary sediments resulted in the formation of gravitational gliding structures. Around the periphery of many of the domes, large sheets of Dakota Sandstone rest on an erosional surface, underlain by rocks of the Chinle, Santa Rosa and Bernal Formations. Several sheets of Dakota Sandstone are present north and south of the Jicarilla monzonite, and it is likely that these reached their present position as a result of gravitational gliding during the erosion process. One of the best examples of "decoiffement" may be seen about a half mile north of Luna (fig. 1). Details of this particular structure have been described in an article by the author (Budding, 1963). Outliers of the Ogallala gravels cover part of the structure, and a pre-Pliocene age is thus indicated for the gliding process.

Extensive erosion followed this period of uplift, and a clastic debris apron of Ogallala Formation gravels formed east of the Jicarilla Mountains. Later erosion removed most of this cover, but small outliers are still preserved.

MINERAL DEPOSITS

Mining activity in the Jicarilla Mountains has been extensive and diverse in character. At the present time, intermittent exploration work is carried on, and mining is at a standstill. Major areas of mining and minerals are summarized below. For more detailed descriptions, the reader is referred to Griswold (1959).

1) Jicarilla District, located near the hamlet of Jicarilla. Most of the gold, occurring in this area, was recovered from placer deposits, but some lode deposits exist. These vein deposits are presumably the primary source of the placer gold. Pyrite, arsenopyrite, quartz, small amounts of copper minerals, and gold occur as fracture fillings and disseminations in the monzonite. Placer gold has been mined from the sand and gravel fill of many arroyos of the district. It has been reported that most of the gold is contained in the lower few inches of the arroyo fill, and this fact, together with the scarcity of water at this elevation, made gold mining a marginal operation.
2) Many small magnetite-hematite deposits are scattered throughout the area. Their usual occurrence is at the contact of monzonite or related intrusive, and limestone of either the San Andres or Yeso Formations. Major production of the area has been from a series of mining claims west of Jack's Peak and known as the Jack Mines.
3) Gypsum is abundant in the upper part of the San Andres Formation. At Ancho, a plaster mill operated from 1912 to 1922, according to local residents. Gypsum was presumably obtained from outcrops across the Southern Pacific Railroad tracks.
4) During about the same period, a brick plant operated at Ancho. Raw material for this operation was obtained from a mine about 2 miles east of the town, where shale was mined from the Dakota Formation. The clay was shipped to Ancho and fired to an attractive red building brick, marked Ancho No. 1. The foundations of the brick plant, and several thousands of bricks still remain near the railroad siding at Ancho.

REFERENCES CITED

Bachman, G. O., 1953, Geology of a part of northwestern Mora County, New Mexico: U.S. Geol. Survey Oil and Gas Inv. Map OM 137.

Bretz, J. Harlan, and Horberg, Leland, 1949, The Ogallala formation west of the Llano Estacado: Jour. Geology, v. 57, p. 477-490.

Budding, A. J., 1963, Origin and age of superficial structures, Jicarilla Mountains, central New Mexico: Geol. Soc. America Bull., v. 74, p. 203-208.

Griswold, George B., 1959, Mineral deposits of Lincoln County, New Mexico; N. Mex. Inst. Min. and Tech., State Bureau Mines and Min. Res. Bull. 67.

Lindgren, Waldemar, Graton, Louis C., and Gordon, Charles H., 1910, The ore deposits of New Mexico: U.S. Geol. Survey Prof. Paper 68.

RESUME OF THE GEOLOGY OF THE GALLINAS MOUNTAINS

Ralph M. Perhac

University of Michigan*
Ann Arbor, Michigan

INTRODUCTION

Central New Mexico is characterized by a number of intrusive masses which have uplifted and domed the overlying sedimentary rocks. The Gallinas Mountains in northern Lincoln County (fig. 1) are one of the largest of these igneous centers and affords an excellent opportunity for investigating the nature of the intrusives and attendant structural deformation. Also the uplifted and tilted sedimentary rocks allow study of the Permian stratigraphy in that area and its relation to regional sedimentation.

The range consists of a granite core overlain by nearly 2,000 feet of clastic sedimentary rocks into which were intruded a variety of alkalic and subsilic hypabyssal rocks. Doming and faulting accompanied the igneous activity. Because of the limited sedimentary section and absence of fossils, dating of geologic events in the Gallinas Mountains is difficult. However, lithologic correlation and stratigraphic position can be used to date the sediments. Similarly, the igneous activity and structural deformation can be dated by comparison with other areas.

STRATIGRAPHY

Precambrian Rocks

A light-gray granite underlies the sedimentary rocks. This granite, which is exposed by faulting, in only three places in the mountains is massive, equigranular, and medium- to fine-grained. Its mineralogy is simple; quartz, microcline, and sodic oligoclase (Ab_{88}) are the essential constituents.

The granite can only be dated as pre-Abo because the Abo Formation is the oldest unit lying upon it (table 1). In the absence, however, of any known Paleozoic intrusive activity in New Mexico and by analogy with nearby areas, the granite is probably Precambrian. Similar granite is exposed at a number of places near the Gallinas Mountains. In the Pedernal Hills, 50 miles north of the range, a Precambrian granite is exposed, and there are small granite hills near Duran, Cedarville, and Corona. Although alluvium obscures the granite-Permian contacts, all of these hills are probably inliers from a pre-Abo landmass which existed in this part of the state throughout much of the Paleozoic (Thompson, 1942, p. 13).

Table 1. — Permian stratigraphy of the Gallinas Mountains, New Mexico.

Series	Formation	Approx. Thickness (feet)	Lithology
Upper Leonard	Glorieta	250	Quartzose sandstone
Lower Leonard	Yeso	1,500	Mostly fine-grained feldspathic sandstone with minor siltstone, shale, limestone, and dolomitic limestone
Wolfcamp	Abo	150	Arkosic conglomerate, plus ferruginous sandstone and siltstone

Paleozoic Rocks

Abo Formation

The Abo Formation is the oldest sedimentary unit exposed in the area. It lies unconformably on granite, and grades upward into the Yeso Formation. Because of this gradational contact, the thickness of the Abo is not easily measured. The Abo has a thickness of about 150 feet in this area if the disappearance of pebbles is used to mark the Abo-Yeso boundary.

The formation consists of a basal arkosic conglomerate member and an overlying member composed of red, feldspathic shale, sandstone and conglomerate. Although

---

*Present address: Production Research Division, Humble Oil and Refining Co., Houston, Texas

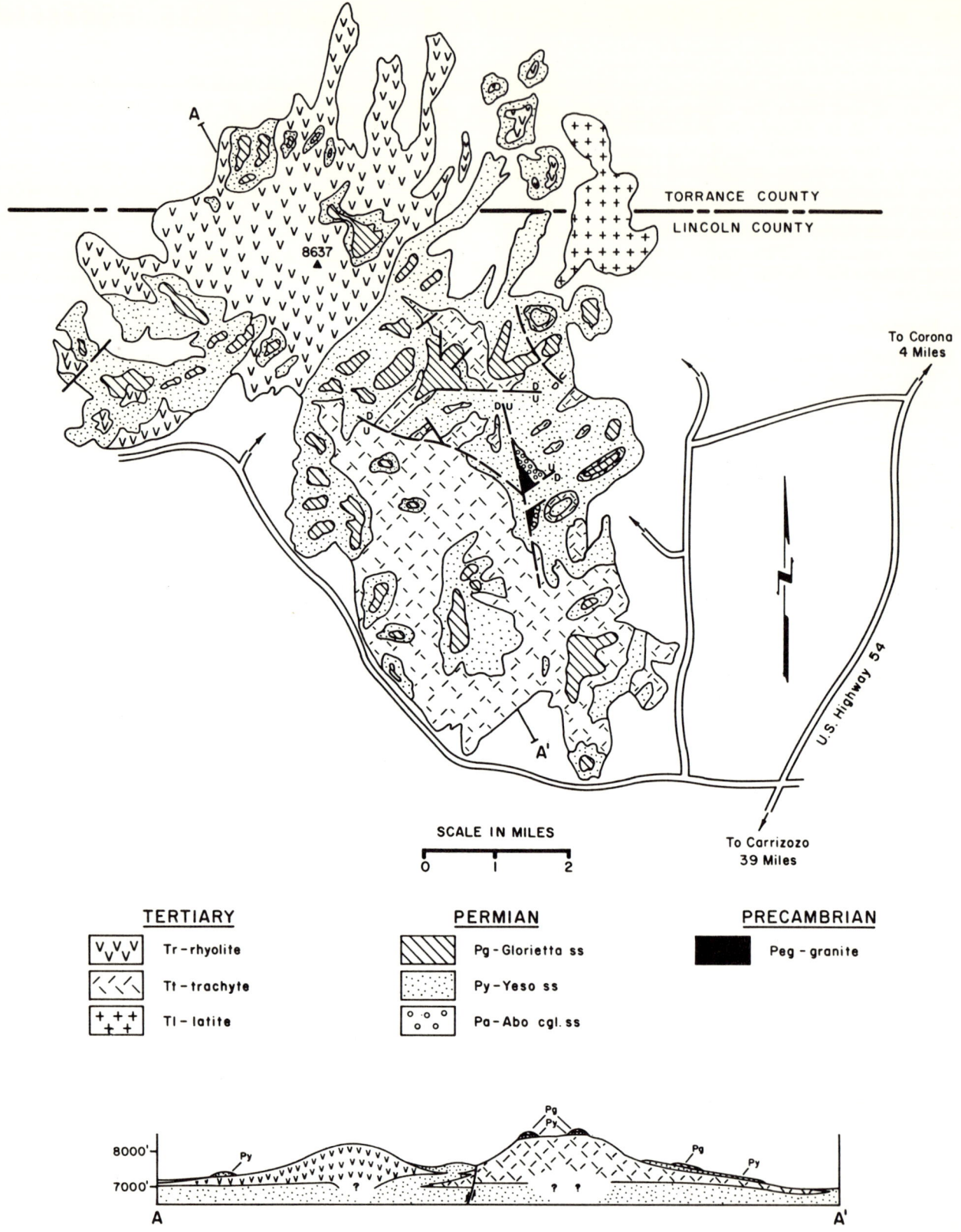

Figure 1. — Geologic map of the Gallinas Mountains, New Mexico.

only 20 to 40 feet thick, the arkose is the most distinctive member. It is granitic in composition and were it not for the few rounded schist and quartz pebbles, it could easily be mistaken, in the field, for a true granite. However, its clastic texture is apparent in thin section. Overlying the arkose is a member consisting of siltstone and shale with many interbedded lenses of conglomerate and coarse sandstone. This entire member is noticeably red and feldspathic. Schist and quartzite fragments are common also in this unit.

Yeso Formation

Conformably overlying the Abo is the Yeso Formation. This is both the thickest (about 1,500 feet) and most extensive sedimentary rock unit in the Gallinas Mountains. Although the Abo-Yeso contact is arbitrary, the upper Yeso boundary is clearly marked by the distinct Glorieta quartzose sandstone.

Within the Yeso Formation, fine-grained feldspathic sandstone is the most abundant lithologic type, comprising over 90 percent of the formation. The remainder is dolomitic limestone, shale, siltstone, and one gypsum bed (occurring only at the south end of the range). The fine-grained feldspathic sandstone is buff-colored. Individual grains, which are cemented by a clay-limonite matrix, are sub-rounded and generally well-sorted. Cross-bedding occurs at several places in the Yeso and the uppermost beds contain oscillation ripple marks.

Most specimens of Yeso sandstone contain over 75 percent quartz, about 10 to 15 percent feldspar, and 5 percent matrix. The remainder of the rock consists of chert and some accessory minerals. Composition differs throughout the formation, although compositional variations are not random. For example the upper Yeso is generally more quartzose and less feldspathic than the lower part, and the amount of clayey matrix diminshes upwards. Not only are mineralogical changes evident, but textural differences are also apparent. Grains are more rounded and better sorted higher in the section, and quartz overgrowths are more abundant in the upper beds.

Dolomitic limestone is the second most abundant lithologic type within the Yeso Formation. This carbonate rock occurs as small, thin discontinuous lenses which are rarely continuous for more than a few tens of feet, the one exception being a 3- to 6-foot thick bed about 40 feet below the Yeso-Glorieta contact. Dolomitic limestone occurs persistently throughout the Gallinas Mountains at this particular stratigraphic position, and individual lenses are commonly continuous for hundreds of feet.

Glorieta Sandstone

The distinctive Glorieta quartzose sandstone conformably overlies the Yeso Formation and is the youngest sedimentary unit present in the Gallinas Mountains. Its thickness is indeterminable because it is the highest stratum in this area. At least 250 feet are exposed in the Gallinas Mountains; in nearby areas, the Glorieta is nearly 300 feet thick.

In the Gallinas Mountains the Glorieta is a light-colored orthoquartzite containing as much as 97 percent quartz. Most specimens examined consist of quartz and minor amounts of feldspar and chert. The abundance of quartz overgrowths is a distinctive feature of this rock. These overgrowths have given the rock an interlocking texture which accounts for its extreme toughness. It is an excellent marker for stratigraphic and structural purposes because of its generally uniform characteristics.

The most striking difference between the Yeso and the overlying Glorieta Sandstone is the quartzitic nature of the Glorieta. Quartz grains in the sandstones of both formations exhibit solution and reprecipitation phenomena as shown by corrosion of, and deposition of overgrowths on individual quartz grains. The better sorting and lack of matrix in the beds of Glorieta Sandstone, however, enable the individual overgrowths on the grains to coalesce and to form the interlocking texture of orthoquartzite. The fact that the Glorieta is orthoquartzitic throughout much of New Mexico suggests that the quartz overgrowths are probably diagenetic rather than a local phenomena caused by igneous activity and deformation of the Gallinas Mountains.

Sedimentary Petrogenesis of the Paleozoic Rocks

The basal arkosic member of the Abo is clearly derived from a granite and it's texture and freshness of it's components indicate little transportation. Therefore, the lower member of the Abo is simply a grus into which some exotic material has been introduced. The irregular distribution of rock types, both laterally and vertically, in the upper part of the Abo indicates that it is a flood plain deposit. Siltstone is the most abundant rock in the upper Abo; however, lenses of sandstone and conglomerate, possibly representing paleo-stream channels, appear at different horizons. The proximity to source is indicated by the local abundance of conglomerate and fresh biotite schist fragments. Apparently a typical crystalline complex, consisting of granite and metamorphics, was the source area for the Abo.

A non-marine environment for most of the Yeso is suggested by the presence of red beds and by the lack of fossils and absence of extensive carbonate and evaporites so typical of the lagoonal and definite marine Yeso to the south. The presence of oscillation ripple marks and cross-bedding and the excellent sorting of grains suggest that the upper Yeso may be a beach sand. If so, then most of the Yeso is non-marine. An occurrence of non-marine Yeso in the Gallinas area is compatible, of course, with the regional northerly facies changes of the Permian sediments in New Mexico.

According to Needham (1942, p. 36), the Glorieta is a near-shore marine deposit laid down by an advancing sea prior San Andres time. The Gallinas stratigraphy supports this concept. With an overlying marine limestone and an underlying beach sand, a near-shore environment for the Glorieta is quite likely.

Therefore the lithology of the Paleozoic rocks in the Gallinas Mountains is suggestive of a transgressive sequence: basal arkose (lower member of the Abo) grading through feldspathic sandstone (upper member of the Abo and the Yeso Formations) into relatively pure quartz sandstones (Glorieta Sandstone). The transgressive nature of this sequence of rocks becomes even more suggestive when it is recalled that a marine limestone (San Andres Formation) probably overlay the Glorieta at one time in what is now the Gallinas Mountains.

(Erosion, however, has removed all San Andres from the mountains so that it now overlies the Glorieta only in adjacent areas.) Apparently throughout Abo and Yeso time, the Gallinas Mountains area became progressively closer to a shore line and by late Yeso time, the shore line was in the vicinity of the range. Admittedly, local shore line fluctuations may have occurred in late Yeso time. The persistent limestone in the upper Yeso may well be a deposit from such a local advance and retreat of the sea prior continuous marine innundation. Continuous marine deposition probably began during Glorieta time. In general, the Gallinas sedimentary geology supports the concept of a northerly advancing sea during early Permian time.

Tertiary Igneous Rocks

Nearly half the Gallinas Mountains is directly underlain by igneous rocks that occur in several laccoliths, dikes, sills, and one stock. Many textural, mineralogical, and chemical features suggest that the major intrusives are consanguinous and crystallized, at a relatively shallow depth, from a highly fluid subsilicic alkalic magma. This magma differentiated prior to emplacement, into trachyte, rhyolite and latite. Subsilicic alkalic stocks and hypabyssals are not restricted to the Gallinas Mountains; they are characteristic of many of the Lincoln County intrusives. The exact depth at which the Gallinas rocks solidified has not been determined; however, structural and stratigraphic studies suggest that the sedimentary cover did not exceed 1,500 to 2,000 feet.

Porphyritic Trachyte

A laccolith of alkalic porphyritic trachyte occurs in much of the southeastern part of the Gallinas Mountains. The magma was intruded conformably into the Yeso Formation, the upper contact generally being 50 to 75 feet below the upper Yeso carbonate member. Locally, apophyses from the laccolith invade the Yeso and Glorieta at different levels.

The trachyte is a light-gray rock with prominent phenocrysts (orthoclase and/or albite) set in an aphanitic groundmass. Essential minerals are albite, orthoclase, and hornblende or aegirine-augite. An average composition is: 68 percent orthoclase, 25 percent albite, 4 percent mafics, and 3 percent accessories. The presence of riebeckite is significant in that it reflects the alkalic nature of the magma. The alkalic character is also indicated by other accessory minerals, by abundant albite and albitization, and by chemical composition.

A characteristic feature of the rock is the albitized phenocrysts. The phenocrysts are albitized orthoclase and plagioclase (albite) with albitized orthoclase overgrowths. Much of the feldspar may thus be classed as alkalic feldspar which is a replacement perthitic intergrowth.

Within the trachyte are a few occurrences of a microsyenite phase. The two rocks are similar mineralogically except for more mafics (aegirine and aegirine-augite) in the syenite. The most striking difference, however, is the phaneritic texture of the syenite. Although the origin of this minor phase is obscure, it may be related to local viscosity differences within the trachyte magma.

Porphyritic Rhyolite

Underlying much of the northwestern part of the range is an alkalic porphyritic leuco-rhyolite. Like the trachyte, the rhyolite was intruded as a conformable sheet which thickens in its central part to form a laccolith. The rock is light-colored, extremely fine-grained, and porphyritic. Locally, miarolitic cavaties, lined with quartz or kaolinized feldspar, are present. The mineralogy is simple: orthoclase, albite, and quartz, plus accessories. Like the trachyte, deuteric and hydrothermal alteration are common. Most potash feldspar is albitized.

The rhyolite composition is quite variable. For example, albite ranges from 4 to 26 percent. A typical specimen contains about 70 percent orthoclase, 15 percent quartz, 10 percent albite, 2 percent mafics, and 3 percent accessories.

Other Igneous Rocks

Porphyritic latite occurs only at a small isolated mountain (Cougar Mountain) immediately north of the main Gallinas range. Although contact relations are obscure, the Yeso beds a few hundred yards west of the latite are horizontal and do not change attitude near the intrusive. Thus the intrusive appears to be a small stock. The rock is distinctive. Hornblende and large oligoclase phenocrysts are set in a light gray aphanitic ground mass consisting almost entirely of orthoclase, minor quartz, and accessories. The rock composition is: 50 percent oligoclase, 45 percent orthoclase, and 5 percent hornblende.

A small porphyritic andesite dike crops out near the center of the Gallinas Mountains. This dike is about 5 feet wide and probably not over a couple hundred feet long. It is the only andesite occurrence in the area.

A peculiar brecciated rock occurs at five places in the mountains. These bodies may be pipe-like as suggested by the fact that they are nearly circular plan view. The rock consists of a trachyte matrix into which are set angular rock fragments of shale, sandstone, limestone, andesite(?), granite, and mainly trachyte. Tentatively, these small bodies are classed as erruptive breccia pipes.

Age of the Intrusives

Unfortunately, the intrusives can be dated only as post-Glorieta. An early Tertiary age for the intrusives seems reasonable by comparisons with other areas and by relating the igneous activity to the structural deformation. One point in support of an early Tertiary age is the similarity between the central New Mexico intrusive belt in Lincoln County and the Tertiary petrographic provinces in Montana, Colorado (transverse porphyry belt), and Texas (Big Bend). The four areas all contain subsilicic and alkalic rocks. Hypabyssals (particularly laccoliths) are common. Mineral deposits are associated with the intrusives. Finally, all areas are along or near the eastern margin of the Rocky Mountain deformed belt. Because of these similarities, perhaps a distinct subsilicic and alkalic petrographic province may exist in central New Mexico.

CONTACT METAMORPHIC ROCKS

Contact metamorphism is rare. Even limestone in direct contact with igneous rock typically is not even recrystallized, let alone metasomatically altered. Exceptions do exist and at a few localities, limestone was converted to an iron-rich calcite-diopised-tremolite-quartz skarn. With the exception of one marble occurrence, rocks were not metamorphosed unless metasomatic introduction of at least silica and considerable iron (perhaps magnesia also) occurred. Thus the intrusion, ipso facto, did not alter the rocks, but rather, the contact metamorphism is related to a later stage of hydrothermal mineralization at which time the Gallinas iron-ore deposits were formed.

STRUCTURAL GEOLOGY

The most prominent structural feature of the Gallinas Mountains is the doming associated with the igneous intrusions. The range is, therefore, a faulted double domal uplift resulting from the intrusion of a rhyolite and trachyte laccolith. The doming, the shape of the igneous masses, and the conformability of the intrusive contacts with both overlying and underlying beds indicate that the intrusives are laccoliths. Both the trachyte and rhyolite masses occur as thin sills along the edges of the range and thicken noticeably toward the central part of the igneous masses. The periphery of the trachyte is about 30 feet thick whereas the center attains a thickness in excess of 500 feet. This shape is characteristics of a laccolith. Conformability is apparent. For example, the top of the igneous mass is nearly always at the same stratigraphic horizon, but at different elevations. At the center of each crystalline mass, both the contact and attitude of the beds are horizontal. Along the flanks of the dome, the beds and contacts dip gently (10 to 15 degrees) quaquaversally. Although the igneous rocks are essentially massive, a faint foliation was seen at a few places. In every instance, the attitude of the foliation parallels that of the overlying strata. Both the trachyte and rhyolite intrusives may be pictured, therefore, as laccoliths from which minor apophyses intruded the sedimentary rocks at different stratigraphic levels.

The brittle Yeso rocks were extensively faulted and shattered as a result of intrusion and attendant doming. Most faults, both major and minor, are high-angle normal faults with some (but indeterminate) strike-slip component. The faults have a rather distinct northwest and northeast strike pattern, the former being more prominant. This domal mountain range is somewhat elliptical and has a northwest major axis. Therefore, the fact that most of the faults strike northwest is not entirely unexpected. Whether the structural trends reflect pre-existing (Precambrian) basement trends or not is a moot question.

Like the igneous activity, the structural deformation can only be dated as post-Glorieta. In nearby areas, however, similar deformation has affected Dakota rocks, hence a post-Dakota age for the Gallinas uplift is likely. The real problem is to relate the diastrophism to one of the two disturbances capable of deforming Cretaceous strata in central New Mexico: the Late Cretaceous or early Tertiary Laramide orogeny, or the later Tertiary Basin and Range disturbance. Admittedly Basin and Range deformation has affected much of southern New Mexico, but the folding and extensive intrusive activity in the central New Mexico intrusive belt is more characteristic of Laramide diastrophism.

REFERENCES CITED

Needham, C. E., 1942, Permian system of central New Mexico, in Bates, R. L., and others, The oil and gas resources of New Mexico, 2nd ed.: N. Mex. Inst. Min. and Tech., State Bur. Mines and Min. Res. Bull. 18, p. 34-37.

Thompson, M. L., 1942, Pennsylvanian System in New Mexico: N. Mex. Inst. Min. and Tech., State Bur. Mines and Min. Res. Bull. 17.

GEOLOGY OF THE LITTLE BLACK PEAK QUADRANGLE SOCORRO AND LINCOLN, COUNTIES, NEW MEXICO

Clay T. Smith
New Mexico Institute of Mining and Technology
Socorro, New Mexico

INTRODUCTION

The Little Black Peak quadrangle lies 8 miles north of Carrizozo, New Mexico between parallels of long 105° 45' and 106° W., and between lat 33°45' and 34° N. (See plate 1). A network of ranch and mining roads branching from U.S. Highway 54, which passes north-south through the eastern quarter of the quadrangle, brings any point to within 2½-3 miles of motor transport. However, except for State Road 10, which traverses the northwest quarter of the quadrangle, and U.S. 54 the roads are unimproved and often impassable after rains or snow.

Scattered mesas and broad alluviated valleys averaging 6,000 feet above sea level dominate most of the area. The rugged topography of Lone Mountain and its surrounding peaks attains elevations of over 8,000 feet along the extreme eastern and southeastern edge of the quadrangle. In the southwest corner of the quadrangle a Recent lava flow, apparently derived from a small cinder cone called Little Black Peak, occupies more than 17 square miles and extends many miles to the south. Older flows from craters farther west locally modify the topography along the western margin of the quadrangle.

The geology of the eastern half of the quadrangle was published by Smith and Budding (1959) and most of the quadrangle is included in Griswold's (1959) bulletin on the Mineral Deposits of Lincoln County. Kelley (1949) describes a few of the iron deposits on the flanks of Lone Mountain, and Allen (1951) published a brief note on the Little Black Peak lava flow.

The major part of the quadrangle is typical of the semi-arid southwest; it receives less than 14 inches of precipitation annually and the vegetation is dominated by cactii, chamisa, rabbit brush, and subordinate grasses. On the higher elevations of Lone Mountain ponderosa pine, juniper, and pinon are common. Water is extremely scarce and where wells have developed meager ground-water supplies, the quality is very poor. The average mean temperature is between 55°F and 60°F, but the extremes may range from a few degrees below 0°F to 110°F.

GEOLOGY

The Little Black Peak quadrangle lies in a broad gentle trough between the Carrizozo anticline to the west and the complexly folded and intruded beds of the Jicarilla Mountains to the east. The structure is synclinal plunging gently to the south and southwest where it merges with the larger and more complex Tularosa Basin. The San Andres Limestone of Permian age is the oldest formation exposed with rocks of Triassic, Cretaceous, and Tertiary-Quaternary age overlying it. Small intrusive masses and numerous dikes of variable compositions are closely associated with the tightly folded beds of the Jicarilla Mountains on the eastern margin of the quadrangle. These are presumed to be Tertiary in age although some of the basaltic dikes may be younger and related to the recent lava flows (See pl. 1 in pocket).

Sedimentary Rocks

San Andres Formation

The San Andres Formation was first described by W. T. Lee (1909) for exposures in the San Andres Mountains of southern New Mexico. Needham and Bates (1943) remeasured the old type section giving more detail regarding the units. Kottlowski and others (1956) re-examined all the units in the San Andres Mountains and measured a slightly better exposed section of the San Andres Formation west of the original type locality. North and west of the Little Black Peak quadrangle a prominent mappable unit, the Glorieta Sandstone, occurs at the base of the San Andres Formation. The U.S. Geological Survey considers the Glorieta Sandstone a member of the San Andres whereas others (Keyes, 1915; Hager and Robitaille, 1919) describe it as a separate formation. In the Little Black Peak quadrangle a sandy facies at the base of the San Andres which may be equivalent to the Glorieta Sandstone is not a mappable unit.

The San Andres Formation is over 700 feet thick, although complete sections are not exposed within the quadrangle. A thickness of 765 feet was measured on the west slope of Lone Mountain, but folding near the contact makes this section somewhat incomplete. Another incomplete section measured in secs. 15 and 22, T. 5 S., R. 11 E., gave 595 feet of beds, a calculated thickness of 660 feet was determined on the south slope of Lone Mountain, but this too is an incomplete section. However, the formation appears to be thicker in this quadrangle than at the type locality to the southwest.

The San Andres Formation in the Little Black Peak quadrangle is divisible into three units — a lower sandy facies, a middle limestone facies, and an upper gypsum facies — although these are not readily mappable. Near the base soft buff-yellow friable quartz sandstone beds weathering reddish brown are interbedded with gray fine-grained massive limestone beds. In areas to the east the sandstone also intertongues with the underlying Yeso Formation. This sandy facies is the Glorieta Sandstone of the Chupadera Mesa region to the northwest. However, in the Little Black Peak area the sandstone beds are lenticular and discontinuous and grade upward into more massive limestone beds; no sharp boundary can be demarcated.

The middle limestone facies is composed of massive limestone beds ranging from blue to gray to dark gray in color interbedded in the lower part of the unit with medium-grained, well-sorted quartz sandstone beds and in the upper part with narrow gypsum stringers. Solution cavaties are common throughout, and locally the beds are fossiliferous. Several genera of gastropoda, fragments of crinoid stems, *Dictyoclostus* sp. ?, and possibly some coiled nautiloids are represented. Much of the limestone is fetid and occasionally contains sparse hydrocarbons.

The upper gypsum facies of the San Andres Formation is well-developed in the area and locally may comprise nearly 400 feet of the formation. Gypsum and light-gray limestone alternate in layers from 20 to 30 feet thick. The gypsum beds are massive, white and contain few impurities. The limestone beds have thin shaly partings and an occasional thin sandstone layer. Solution fretwork is common on exposed limestone surfaces and collapse structures resulting from removal of gypsum in solution are common. Most of the surface exposures of the upper part of the San Andres Formation are mantled with a soft, fine, silty gypsiferous layer, the residue from solution of both limestone and gypsum beds.

Fossils are lacking in the upper part of the San Andres Formation in the major part of the formational exposures and no diagnostic forms were identified in the Little Black Peak quadrangle, but the lithologic relationships and the stratigraphic position left no doubt regarding the age nor identity of the formation. Kottlowski and others (1956) report diagnostic ammonoids from the upper part of the formation in the San Andres Mountains which indicate a Leonardian age.

The contact between the San Andres Formation and the overlying Bernal Formation is a disconformity on which a karst topography developed. Large sink holes filled with layers of the overlying material as well as breccia of the upper gypsum facies of the San Andres Formation suggest that the development of some of the karst topography antedated the deposition of the Bernal Formation. Largo Canyon, the principal drainage channel in the western and northern part of the quadrangle, has been controlled by the coalescence of several large filled sink holes in the underlying San Andres limestone and gypsum. Resistant knobs of limestone are often surrounded by the Bernal beds representing the old highs from the Permian karst which have been exhumed by recent erosion. Relief on the surface ranged from a few tens of feet to perhaps a few hundred feet during deposition of the overlying Bernal Formation. Karst action, however, is not confined to late or immediate post-Permian time, but appears to have been almost continuously operative, since a few sink holes contain collapsed remnants of late Tertiary gravels.

Bernal Formation

The Bernal Formation was defined by Bachman (1953) from exposures near Bernal, Mora County, New Mexico. Originally the Bernal was considered to be an upper member of the San Andres Formation, but the marked disconformity at its base suggested formational status. Other writers (Allen and Kottlowski, 1958; Bates, 1942; Wilpolt and Wanek, 1951; and Griswold, 1959) have variously interpreted these beds as Chalk Bluff, Whitehorse Group, or upper San Andres Formation depending upon locality, thickness, and exposures. Outcrops are very limited in the quadrangle and contact relations are vague; field evidence would ally the Bernal more closely with the overlying Triassic beds than with the underlying Permian rocks. In the Little Black Peak quadrangle the formation is considered Permian and Triassic and transitional because of a lack of definitive evidence in either direction.

The Bernal Formation is predominately clastic and fine-grained; silt sizes predominate and claystone stringers can be found interbedded with the fine sandstones and siltstones. Because of the relief on the basal contact and apparent gradation into the overlying Santa Rosa Formation, the thickness varies from nearly 300 feet in the east-central portion of the quadrangle, to less than 200 feet on the south flank of Lone Mountain, and to only a few tens of feet in the southwest corner of the quadrangle.

The basal part of the Bernal is buff-colored, poorly-sorted, medium-grained sandstone which grades upward into siltstone. The main bulk of the formation is reddish-brown to yellowish-brown fine-grained sandstone and siltstone with interbedded claystone layers weathering to a bright orange-red soil. Most of the formation is very friable and weathers easily so that outcrops are rare. Locally, cross-bedding, and some channeling and scour-and-fill structures may be seen in the coarser sandstone layers. The upper part of the formation is siltstone and claystone and the contact is generally chosen on the basis of a soil color change, and the appearance of small chert pebbles and rounded grit in the soil indicating the presence of the overlying Santa Rosa conglomerates.

No fossils were found in the Bernal beds and precise determinations of the age are not possible. For reasons already cited the unit is considered as Permian and Triassic and transitional between the marine environment of the underlying San Andres limestone and the fluviatile non-marine deposits of the overlying Santa Rosa Sandstone.

Santa Rosa Sandstone

The Santa Rosa Sandstone was named by Darton in 1919 but publication was delayed (Darton, 1922). No type locality other than the ". . . prominent in mesas og Guadalupe Co. and along Pecos River at Santa Rosa" (Wilmarth, 1938) has ever been designated and the thickness is variously reported as 500 to 600 feet and 50 to 100 feet. Darton himself (1922) does not give a thickness for the unit. Affinities to the Shinarump Conglomerate of Arizona have been suggested for the Santa Rosa Sandstone and the stratigraphic positions are similar; however, direct equivalence cannot be proven and the vertebrate faunas are too sparse to allow detailed correlation. There is considerable question regarding its formational status because of the gradational nature of the upper contact with the overlying Triassic mudstones and siltstones of the Chinle Formation. However, in the Little Black Peak quadrangle it is a mappable unit.

The Santa Rosa Sandstone is principally a coarse- to medium-grained, cross-bedded, sandstone and pebble conglomerate. Thin-bedded claystone and siltstone partings less than 2 feet in thickness are interbedded with the sandstone layers. The beds are predominantly red to reddish brown on fresh surface and weather to dark reddish brown or buff. Locally near the top of the formation buff to white, coarse-grained, cross-bedded sandstone beds are prominent. Exposures in the lower part of the unit are fair because the pebble conglomerate often forms resistant cappings on cuestas and mesas. The upper part of the formation grades upward into the overlying Chinle siltstones and mudstones and the contact is rarely exposed. The variation of the upper contact, because of such gradation, results in considerable differences in measured thickness in the Santa Rosa Sandstone. Around Lone Mountain less than 150 feet has been measured, although 6 miles to the north in sec. 16, T. 5 S., R. 11 E., nearly 250 feet are assigned to the formation. There is no break in sedimentation between the underlying Santa Rosa Sandstone and the overlying Chinle Formation and the Santa Rosa is here considered a basal sandy phase of the Late Triassic sedimentation.

Chinle Formation

The Chinle Formation was first described by Gregory (1916) from exposures in the Chinle valley of northeastern Arizona. The name has since been extended over much of the Colorado Plateau region, westward into southern Nevada, and eastward into northern and central New Mexico. Similar Triassic red beds were described by Cummins (1890) as the Dockum Group in northwestern Texas, and these have since been extended northward into Kansas and Colorado and westward into New Mexico. Because of lithologic similarity, a lack of diagnostic fossils, and the writer's personal familiarity with the Arizona nomenclature, the term Chinle is preferred for the Little Black Peak quadrangle.

The Chinle Formation in the quadrangle is thin-bedded siltstone, mudstone, and claystone with thin sandstone and limestone-pebble conglomerate lenses. The rocks are purplish red to chocolate brown, weathering to reddish brown. The layers are soft and friable and outcrops are rare. The formation is characterized by reddish sandy soil alternating with darker reddish-purple clayey soil. It forms covered slopes beneath the mesa cappings of the overlying harder beds, and broad valleys with very little relief throughout the central part of the quadrangle. A few fragments of fossil wood have been found, but no other fossils have been reported. The Late Triassic age and assignment of these beds to the Chinle Formation in the Little Black Peak quadrangle is based upon lithologic similarity and stratigraphic position.

There is a marked disconformity at the top of the Chinle Formation, although the relief on this contact is only a few feet at the most. From 200 to over 400 feet of Chinle Formation is present in the Little Black Peak quadrangle, the variability probability being due in part to differences in selection of the lower contact with the Santa Rosa Sandstone. Triassic beds extend only a few tens of miles south of the latitude of the mapped area in this part of New Mexico so that some depositional variation near the edge of the basin might also be expected.

Dakota Formation

The Dakota Sandstone was first described by Meek and Hayden (1862) from exposures in Dakota County, Nebraska. Subsequent workers have extended the name to encompass almost all of the basal sandstones of the Upper Cretaceous rocks in the Rocky Mountains. The fluctuations in strand lines and marine environments which characterize the Upper Cretaceous rocks in New Mexico suggest that many of the basal sandstone units are not time-equivalent. In the Little Black Peak quadrangle the basal sandstone of the upper Cretaceous sequence is referred to as Dakota Formation with no implication regarding its specific age or relationship to the other Dakota units which have been described to the north, west, and south.

The Dakota Formation is confined to the southern and eastern parts of the quadrangle forming prominent cuestas and mesa cappings. The best exposed section is in a railroad cut about half a mile north of Coyote siding, where the upper contact is marked chiefly by the disappearance of the exposures to the south, and the lower contact is clearly defined at the north end of the cut.

The basal part of the formation is thick-bedded (2-4 feet) to massive, white quartz sandstone, medium-grained, and weathering buff to brown. Thin shaly partings and thin, even-bedded siltstone and sandstone comprise the central part of the formation. Interbedded sandstone and shale forms the upper part of the formation which grades upward into the overlying Mancos Shale. Some of the sandstone beds are coarse-grained and conglomeratic and many exhibit varying degrees of cross-bedding. Locally, thin coal seams are found in the shaly central portion of the formation. Complete sections of the Dakota Formation could be measured only in the southeast corner of the quadrangle. Here the thickness ranged from 144 feet south of Lone Mountain to 182 feet in the railroad cut north of Coyote siding. At least part of the variation probably is due to the placing of the upper contact which is conformable with the overlying Mancos Shale. The contact is arbitrarily selected at that point where shale predominates over sandstone; such a point is a function of exposures as well as lithology.

Mancos Shale

The Mancos Shale was named by Cross (1899) from exposures in Mancos valley in and around the town of Mancos, Colorado. Reeside (1924) pointed out that faunas of Greenhorn, Carlile, Niobrara, and Pierre age had been reported from the Mancos Shale. Obviously parts of the shale from some areas are not the same age as shale having similar lithologies in other regions. However, despite the variation in age, the drab, lead-gray shale containing sparse thin-bedded limestone and sandstone layers has the same uniform, monotonous lithology throughout most of New Mexico, Colorado, Arizona, Utah, and Wyoming.

A complete section of Mancos Shale is not exposed

in the Little Black Peak quadrangle, although 600 to 700 feet of beds are indicated. Exposures are poor; the shale weathers into a brownish-gray soil and is too soft to resist erosion. Some of the deeper recent arroyo banks and deep road cuts are the only places where the beds can be observed in reasonably fresh condition. The shale is sandy near the base and grades upward into dull-gray to black calcareous fissile layers less than a few inches thick. About 100 feet above the base fossils are abundant and *Ostrea lugubris, Camptonectes platessa, Inoceramus labiatus, Cardium pauperculum,* and *Helioceras pariense* have been identified. The Late Cretaceous age is clearly determined from the above forms.

Tertiary Volcanic Breccia

In the extreme southeast corner of the quadrangle the upper part of the ridge trending northward from Baxter Mountain is capped with volcanic sediments, agglomerate, tuff, and breccia, interbedded with mudstone, sandstone, and shale. These beds resemble in some ways the Cub Mountain Formation of Bodine, 1956, (Weber, personal communication, 1964) but the isolated nature of the outcrop and the abundance of volcanic debris makes correlation doubtful. There is no question but that the unit is some part of the Sierra Blanca volcanic pile, but no indication is available as to whether it is early or late in the sequence. The beds contain fragments of the Lone Mountain intrusive mass and lap onto the outcrop surface, so they are post-Lone Mountain; however, they are cut by monzonitic, latitic, and lamprophyric dikes and thus are earlier than the latest phases of the intrusive activity. A tentative late Tertiary age is herein assigned although this may represent anything from late Miocene to early Pleistocene.

The volcanic debris is irregular and lenticular and individual beds are difficult to trace. The basal unit in one area is flow breccia containing large inclusions (boulder size) of Mancos Shale in a fine-grained groundmass which is light gray on fresh surface and weathers to mottled red, green, or yellow; irregular and contorted flow structure is common. In other areas the basal unit is well-cemented quartz sandstone, so thoroughly lithified that it resembles quartzite on broken surface. The sandstone is fine- to medium-grained, gray to white on fresh surface, weathering to buff to brown. In places it is conglomeratic with fragments similar to those in the flow breccia. These basal units seldom exceed 30 feet in thickness, although where both are present the sandstone overlies the flow breccia and the two units combined may be as much as 50 feet thick.

The principal mass of the volcanic debris is agglomerate with thin mudstone and sandstone interbeds in the lower third of the layers. The lower 100 feet is a greenish-gray fine-grained matrix in which abundant inclusions of shale, limestone, sandstone, monzonite, and latite occur in a wide variety of shapes and sizes. Feldspar fragments and phenocrysts are abundant. The middle 150 feet is finer-grained agglomerate, light gray on fresh surface but weathering reddish brown. The groundmass is felsitic and the inclusions are usually less than 3 inches in diameter; most are angular to subrounded. Where rounding is pronounced the beds appear conglomeratic. The upper 100 or more feet is very coarse agglomerate with inclusions up to 2 feet in diameter. It is light gray on fresh surface weathering pale red, reddish orange, and grayish orange to brown. It is well-indurated forming conspicuous knobs and resistant cliffs near the top of the unit. The three agglomerate layers with the interbedded mudstone and sandstone exceed 375 feet in thickness and the entire Tertiary unit is estimated to be a minimum of 400 feet thick.

The Tertiary material rests upon Mancos Shale and the older beds with angular unconformity. The surface of deposition was very irregular (relief of more than 100 feet is common). Bedding within the unit is vague or contorted, but generally strikes north-south and dips westerly at 10 to 15°.

Quaternary Deposits

Deposits of gravels and alluvium containing fragments of most of the earlier rocks cover considerable areas in the western part of the Little Black Peak quadrangle. At least two stages of deposition of this type can be recognized and farther east a still earlier and more lithified deposit has been correlated with the Ogallala Formation (Budding, 1964).

Older gravels cap small mesas and form high level terraces along some of the larger stream valleys. There is some reason to believe that some of these gravels may be lag or deflation deposits from a former much more extensive gravel sheet correlative with the Ogallala Formation farther east. These beds contain cobbles and pebbles of quartzite, monzonite, sandstone, and limestone. The quartzite indicates sources far beyond the limits of the quadrangle.

More recent alluvium fills the valley floors and some of the sink holes. It commonly reflects the nearby rock outcrops since most of the material is locally derived. Drainages have very low gradients and most of the alluvium is thus very fine-grained; the arid climate also results in considerable amounts of wind-blown sand and silt accumulating as alluvium.

Igneous Rocks

Tertiary and Quaternary intrusive and extrusive rocks are abundant in the southern and eastern portions of the Little Black Peak quadrangle. Sills, dikes, small stocks, and flows are represented in a wide variety of compositions and textures. The lack of exposures and the paucity of contemporaneous sediments and cross-cutting relationships makes dating the different compositional types difficult. At least three and possibly four periods of igneous activity are delimited by the rocks exposed.

Intrusive Rocks

The intrusive rocks can be grouped into two major types, those with abundant megascopic quartz, and those with little or no visible quartz. The Lone Mountain stock is typical of those with little or no visible quartz although more basic types are known, and a sill in the Mancos Shale in secs. 23, 24, and 26, T. 6 S., R. 10 E., is characteristic of those with abundant megascopic quartz. Intrusive rock exposures are limited to the extreme eastern and southern parts of the quadrangle with the largest outcrop that of the Lone Mountain stock; a similar but smaller exposure occurs in secs. 2 and 11, T. 5 S., R. 11 E., east of Largo. Numerous dikes and sills are associated with the larger intrusive masses, but no direct connections can be demonstrated.

The great bulk of the intrusive rocks are of the Lone Mountain type and contain little or no visible quartz. The Lone Mountain stock has been described in some detail by Butler (1964) and compared to similar intrusives farther east.

"Lone Mountain is formed of Kalialaskite porphyry .... From one side of Lone Mountain to the other, the intrusive rock is remarkably uniform in appearance. The color of a fresh rock surface is a distinctive brownish gray. Feldspar phenocrysts compose about one-third of the rock and reach 5 mm in size. Little quartz is visible in the rock.

"The dark mineral content of most Lone Mountain specimens is about 5 percent, but the mineralogy of these dark minerals varies. In specimens obtained near the Ferro mine and in specimen A47, the dark minerals are hornblende, biotite, and magnetite. In the northeast half of the mountain, however, bright-green pyroxene (aegerine-augite) is the dominant dark mineral, and it is accompanied by some hornblende. No magnetite or biotite is visible in specimens from this side of the mountain.

"Lone Mountain intrusive rocks weather to a dull reddish brown. Because hornblende decomposes readily, some hornblende grains are partially altered to limonite. This alteration can even be observed on otherwise fresh rock surfaces." In thin section Butler (1964) observed that a few of the plagioclase phenocrysts have been broken and the pieces slightly rotated with respect to one another. He interprets this as evidence that the plagioclase crystallized early, before the magma was completely emplaced.

A second type of quartz-free intrusive occurs in the White Oaks mining district in the southeast corner of the quadrangle. Dark colored dike rocks of varying compositions cut the lighter colored dikes associated with the Lone Mountain stock. The dark dikes are composed of feldspar and a dark mineral, sometimes hornblende, sometimes biotite, and more commonly pyroxene. Graton (Lindgren and others, 1910) described these as lamprophyres principally kersantite or minette; Griswold (1959) in his detailed mapping in the White Oaks district used the term "mica trap." One late dike associated with mineralization in the western part of the White Oaks district would be a vogesite from megascopic examination. Budding (1964) reports compositions which would include all the typical lamprophyres, kersantite, minette, vogesite, spessartite, or possibly even camptonite, depending upon slight variations in mineral content.

Two small dikes of basaltic composition crop out south and west of Coyote siding. They are dense, greenish-black, olivine basalt, weathering dark yellowish brown. Megascopically, they are identical with the extrusive Little Black Peak basalt flow, although lacking the vesicular and scoriaceous surface. No evidence as to their age other than post-Cretaceous and post-rhyolite was obtained, and since earlier basalt flows than the Little Black Peak flow occur to the west, no direct correlation is possible.

The rocks containing visible quartz are granitic in composition, usually containing abundant hornblende or biotite. They are fine-grained, often aphanitic, gray to white on fresh surface and weathering to dark gray or brown. They are found mostly north and west of Lone Mountain cutting the sediments that enclose the main intrusive mass. They generally contain less than 25 percent quartz and may represent slightly more silicic differentiates of the same parent magma. Compositional and textural terms such as microgranite, rhyolite, and granodiorite have been used to describe different dikes or sills of this group which indicates the variations which have been observed. Within the mass of the Lone Mountain intrusive local areas containing visible quartz are recognized and one large enough to map is shown near the northeastern boundary.

The intrusive rocks of the Little Black Peak quadrangle are obviously closely related to one another and to similar intrusive masses farther east (Budding, 1964). Compositionally they fall near petrographic classification boundaries and thus the nomenclature is confused. Butler (1964) has followed Johannsen's classification (1939), although the rock names are somewhat misleading. The almost complete lack of plagioclase coupled with an average of less than 10 percent quartz in most samples allies the Lone Mountain rocks with the alkali-syenites. An applicable name to this type of material would be nordmarkite (Brogger, 1890). The paucity of dark minerals and a similar lack of plagioclase in those rocks containing from 25-30 percent visible quartz would place such rocks in the kalialaskite category of Johannsen (1939). Some definitions of granophyre would also describe these rocks, as could the term granite-porphyry. The abundance of alkalis and the deficiency of silica make this general province petrographically interesting.

Extrusive Rocks

The extrusive rocks of the Little Black Peak quadrangle are confined to the southwestern corner of the quadrangle and are exclusively basaltic. Two flow episodes apparently distinctly separated in time, but relatively recent, are recognized. An earlier series of basaltic flows emanate from Broken Back crater about four miles west of the quadrangle and crop out over portions of secs. 2, 3, and 10, T. 6 S., R. 9 E., and parts of secs. 27, 28, 33, 34, and 35, T. 5 S., R. 9 E. The Little Black Peak flow is younger, nearly overlapping some of the Broken Back flows in the SE¼ sec. 2, T. 6 S., R. 9 E., and extending some 44 miles southward into the Tularosa Basin. The difference in age is determined by the thin soil cover and weathered surface found on the Broken Back flows as compared to the lack of weathering and soil on the Little Black Peak flow.

The Little Black Peak flow is greenish-gray to black on fresh surface and weathers reddish brown to grayish black. The rock is extremely vesicular, particularly in the upper 2 feet. It is dense, fine grained to aphanitic, with lath-like phenocrysts of plagioclase and small green phenocrysts of olivine. In thin section a very crude trachytic texture is discernible particularly around the olivine phenocrysts. The principal minerals are calcic labradorite (An_{66}-An_{70}), titaniferous diopsidic augite, olivine (Fa_{20}-Fa_{23}), and magnetite. Alteration is very slight, hematite being the only identifiable secondary product. Reddish-brown rims on a few of the olivine crystals may be iddingsite, but the development is too fine grained for certainty in the determination.

A complete chemical analysis of a sample of the Little Black Peak flow was published by Allen (1951) and showed:

SiO_2	50.77%	Na_2O	3.50%
Al_2O_3	14.00	K_2O	1.51
Fe_2O_3	2.34	TiO_2	1.71
FeO	7.48	P_2O_5	0.34
MnO	0.16	H_2O - 110°+	1.72
MgO	6.96	H_2O - 110°−	0.07
CaO	9.08	CO_2	0.00

This is a typical alkali olivine basalt and as such the relatively low silica content coupled with the relatively high alkali suggests close affinities with monzonite in the White Oaks mining district in the southeast corner of the quadrangle, a partial analysis of which was reported by Lindgren and others (1910).

These flow rocks are very young, and the Little Black Peak flow may have been extruded within historic time (Allen, 1951). The Broken Back flows have been modified sufficiently by erosion and weathering so that although a post-Pleistocene age is suggested, they could be older.

Structure

The Little Black Peak quadrangle lies at the extreme northeastern end of the Tularosa Basin where a synclinal structure is more pronounced than the fault trough pattern characteristic of the Tularosa structure farther south. Most of the northern part of the quadrangle is a broad plain with a gentle homoclinal dip to the southeast. Along the eastern and southern margins of the quadrangle numerous folds are exposed. The folds are closely related to the Tertiary intrusive activity; in most cases they are domed structures apparently resulting from the intrusion of rounded plug-like bodies. A small syenitic mass is exposed in the northernmost dome in sec. 35, T. 4 S., R. 11 E., and in sec. 11, T. 5 S., R. 11 E., and the nordmarkite plug of Lone Mountain occupies several square miles in the southeast corner of the quadrangle. The domes are generally circular or elliptical in outline with the surrounding beds upturned sharply around the margins of the structure and nearly flat over the tops. The vertical nature of the deforming forces is best illustrated in secs. 16 and 28, T. 5 S., R. 11 E., where beds dipping from 30-40° change strike through more than 90° in distances of less than 1,000 feet; the result is a remarkable dome with square corners.

Tightly compressed synclines are found between the domes where the thin sedimentary cover has not been pushed upward by the doming action. The synclines plunge steeply in a westerly direction but their axes are determined by the intrusive centers which they border and thus have random directions. A larger syncline plunging to the southwest crops out west of Lone Mountain; the structure is outlined by the Dakota Formation and may represent broader and more open folding not associated with the Tertiary intrusives. The western limb of this syncline is concealed beneath the Little Black Peak basalt flow along the southern margin of the quadrangle, but kipukas of Dakota Formation farther south attest to the southwesterly continuation of the structure. In the extreme southwest corner of the quadrangle the northeasterly-plunging nose of the Carrizozo anticline is outlined by the San Andres-Bernal contact. Apparently the easterly limb of the anticline and the westerly limb of the aforementioned syncline coincide. The dips of the beds on the limbs of these folds seldom exceed 20°, and the broad open folding is in sharp contrast to the abrupt bending associated with the domes to the east.

Faulting is practically non-existent in the Little Black Peak quadrangle. Two types of faults are recognized: fractures of minor displacement (less than 50 feet) associated with the intrusive activity and commonly filled with later dikes or veins, and fractures associated with landslide or slump blocks practically confined to the Dakota Formation.

Faults of the first type are most prominent in the extreme southeast corner of the quadrangle in the White Oaks mining district. The area of the mines is extensively fractured but displacements are practically nil, and the introduction of the several dikes and sills seems to have simply resulted in a dilation of the country rocks without much relative shifting of adjacent blocks.

The landslide blocks are torreva type and the individual blocks have rotated downward and outward with respect to the original mesa position. Total displacements are difficult to assess because erosion has removed some of the intervening material. However, in secs. 25 and 26, T. 5 S., R. 10 E., a single block of Dakota lies 300 feet below and nearly one-half mile north of the present undisturbed mesa position. This particular mesa is surrounded by such blocks at various levels with a much smaller and slightly lower mesa half a mile to the southeast, also surrounded by similar torreva blocks. The terrain surrounding these mesas is not particularly steep and such extensive landsliding is puzzling. It is suggested that the mesas may be associated with a large sink hole in the underlying San Andres Formation which is concealed by the Chinle Formation and which provides the local steep slopes necessary for the development of the torreva blocks. Similar sliding may have affected the strip of Dakota Formation just east of the railroad in secs. 18, 19, and 20, T. 5 S., R. 11 E., but exposures are too poor to identify the fault planes.

ECONOMIC GEOLOGY

Ground Water

Ranching and mining have contributed to the economy of the Little Black Peak quadrangle, but the lack of adequate water both in quantity and quality, has severely handicapped development. Abandoned ranch houses abound, particularly in the northern and western parts of the quadrangle. Dry farming on a small scale has been unsuccessful and forage for cattle requires extremely large holdings to support a herd of economic size. Many wells have been drilled and abandoned because the underlying San Andres and Glorieta formations, which serve as aquifers, contain ground water so high in carbonate and sulfate that the water is unfit even for cattle or irrigation. Precipitation is insufficient for the average size tank and the amount of gypsum at the surface, particularly in the northern part of the quadrangle, increases the dissolved solids in the surface water nearly to tolerable limits. Locally, wells in the alluvium may often produce good water under favorable circumstances, but these are sporadic producers. To the east and south where the Santa Rosa Sandstone or the Dakota Formation may be tapped for ground-water supplies the quality is better, but recharge areas for these units are limited and supplies may be rapidly exhausted. In some areas of the arid southwest recent lava flows such as the Little Black Peak flow have proved to be excellent aquifers. However, the Broken Back and Little Black Peak flows do not seem to be sufficiently confined to provide such storage.

Mining

Mining in the Little Black Peak quadrangle is confined to the southeast part and is concentrated around the Lone Mountain nordmarkite stock. Gold, tungsten, and iron ores have been produced from this area which is included in the White Oaks mining district. Production has been sporadic and the records are poor (Griswold, 1959). Gold mining has yielded the bulk of the total value, although the iron ores have the greatest reserve.

The gold veins are discussed by Griswold (1959), although detailed information is lacking. Limited examination and exploration was done shortly after World War II, but the district has been abandoned for at least ten years. The veins are narrow and pockety and the grade averaged less than $12 per ton during the years of best production. The veins occur along the margins of monzonitic and syenitic dikes or in small fractures cutting the dikes. The intrusive masses cut the Mancos Shale and parts of the Tertiary sediments on the eastern slope of the ridge between Baxter and Lone Mountains. No pattern of intrusion or vein structure has been established because of the lack of outcrops, but, where measured or exposed in old mine workings, the veins generally strike north-south and are almost vertical. Several mines were productive and the reader is referred to Griswold (1959) for the most recent information.

Tungsten is present in the White Oaks district as huebnerite ($MnWO_4$) associated with the gold veins. During World War I over 100,000 pounds of concentrates were produced and a few thousand pounds have been produced intermittently since then. The most recent recorded production was 20 pounds in 1952 (Griswold, 1959). The old dumps probably contain some tungsten values since it was not considered an ore during the principal gold mining period.

Iron ore in the form of magnetite and hematite has been mined from several localities in and around the Lone Mountain stock. Kelley (1949) has described the major deposits and published detailed maps of some. Official records of production exist for only the Yellow Jacket and Ferro mines, although prospects and pits from which a few tons of ore have been extracted are found around the periphery of the stock.

Magnetite and hematite occur as pyrometasomatic and replacement deposits in the lower members of the San Andres Limestone. Some calcsilicate minerals have been developed but skarn zones so characteristic of typical pyrometasomatic deposits are lacking. The magnetite and hematite occur disseminated throughout the limestone and as layers and veins of completely replaced limestone. In the Ferro mine the ore was localized along the contact between the intrusive and the limestone. West of the Little Black Peak quadrangle similar magnetite and hematite deposits are being worked as replacements of limestone and sandstone beds as well as replacing some of the massive gypsum beds in the Yeso Formation. Such occurrences offer intriguing possibilities regarding the occurrence of additional ore in depth around the Lone Mountain stock. The stock has been intruded near the base of the San Andres Formation and drilling depths of less than 1,000 feet should prospect the contact zone with most of the upper part of the Yeso Formation, the zone that is particularly favorable in the deposits to the west.

A little gypsum from the upper part of the San Andres Formation has been burned locally for plaster and some of the gravels have been utilized for road metal. Parts of the Little Black Peak flow have been quarried for road metal and large parts of the cinder cones west of the quadrangle which mark the source for the Broken Back flows have been used for the same purpose.

GEOLOGIC HISTORY

Mapping to the south of the Little Black Peak quadrangle suggests that during the early part of the Paleozoic the quadrangle was part of the Pedernal positive area and was reduced to an area of low relief. Pennsylvanian seas inundated the area and about 1,750 feet of limestone, sandstone, and shale was deposited. Following the retreat of the Pennsylvanian seas the sandstone and siltstone of the terrestrial Abo formation was spread over the flood plain. Permian seas returned to the area, alternately advancing and dessicating, and sandstone, siltstone, limestone, and gypsum of the Yeso Formation was deposited. The Glorieta Sandstone and San Andres Limestone are repetitions of the alternate advance and dessication of the Permian marine invasions. After the final gypsum deposits of the upper San Andres beds were laid down the area remained above sea level for a considerable period of time. Fluviatile and lacustrine conditions are reflected by the Bernal Formation, and the Santa Rosa Sandstone is a broad sheet of river gravels and sands. The finer muds and silts of the Chinle Formation represent a continuation of such savannah-like conditions with considerably reduced elevations in the sedimentary provenance. From the end of Triassic time until Upper Cretaceous time the area was undergoing erosion although any crustal movements were epeirogenic as they had been throughout the Paleozoic. The Upper Cretaceous marks the last marine invasion of the area and the Dakota Formation and the Mancos Shale represent the beach and off-shore deposits of the Upper Cretaceous seas. Uplift at the end of the Cretaceous resulted in withdrawal of the sea but no orogeny assignable to the Laramide is recognizable.

The Tertiary marks the advent of igneous activity and the first events were the intrusions of the Lone Mountain and associated stocks. Their forcible introduction into the upper crust domed and warped the thin overlying sedimentary cover perhaps creating the fractures which were later filled with dikes and sills of similar material. However, following the intrusion of the stocks, certainly not later than Miocene and perhaps earlier, volcanic activity on a broad scale began south of the quadrangle. Debris was spread over a wide area and this cover was also intruded by the later dikes and sills. During the last stages of igneous activity, or perhaps earlier in the case of the magnetite and hematite deposits, mineralization occurred around the Lone Mountain stock. Associated with the mineralization were lamprophyric dikes. During or after these last stages of intrusive activity basaltic dikes were intruded which may have been the feeders or precursors of the later basaltic flows of Broken Back crater, and Little Black Peak. Spreading westward and southward from sources to the east and north a broad sheet of gravels was deposited over the eroded surface of the domed and warped beds. These gravels, correlated with the Ogallala Formation of the High Plains to the east, contain fragments of all the rock units except the Broken Back and Little Black Peak flows. This gravel sheet is presumably Pliocene in age and places an upper limit on the duration of the intrusive and mineralizing activity of the Lone Mountain area. Quiescent eruptions extruded the Broken Back and Little Black Peak flows, the latter so recently that it fills present-day topographic features. Erosion is continuing to sculpture the present surface.

Soon after the retreat of the Permian seas solution of gypsum and limestone in the San Andres Formation created a karst topography upon which the Bernal Formation was deposited. Such solution has continued to the present time and recent sink holes have developed in the San Andres Formation in the northern part of the quadrangle. The age of any particular depression is not readily determined, although the recent ones can be recognized by their topographic expression. The present course of Largo canyon, the principal drainage for the northern and western parts of the quadrangle is apparently controlled by the coalescence of a series of large sinks or depressions. This is also the course which the Little Black Peak flow followed through the quadrangle.

The entire area is characterized by a lack of orogenic movement and remarkable stability throughout a long period of geologic time. The folding present is due principally to vertical forces accompanying the intrusion of the stocks and the emplacement of the numerous dikes and sills has resulted only in dilation of the crust rather than crumpling or shortening. The prevalence of alkaline igneous rocks also points to a stable block as opposed to organic belts.

BIBLIOGRAPHY

Allen, J. E., 1951, The Carrizozo malpais: Roswell Geol. Soc., 5th Field Conf., Guidebook of the Carrizozo-Capitan-Chupadera Mesa region, Lincoln and Socorro Counties, New Mexico, 1951, p. 9-11.

———————— and Kottlowski, F. E., 1958, Roswell-Capitan-Ruidoso and Bottomless Lakes Park, New Mexico: N. Mex. Inst. Min. and Tech., State Bur. Mines and Min. Res., Scenic Trips to the geologic past, No. 3.

Bachman, G. O., 1953, Geology of a part of northwestern Mora County, New Mexico: U.S. Geol. Survey Oil and Gas Inv. Map OM 137.

Bates, R. L., 1942, The oil and gas resources of New Mexico: N. Mex. Inst. Min. and Tech., State Bur. Mines and Min. Res. Bull. 18.

Bodine, M. C., 1956, Geology of Capitan coal field, Lincoln County, New Mexico: N. Mex. Inst. Min. and Tech., State Bur. Mines and Min. Res. Circ. 35.

Brogger, W. C., 1890, Syenitpegmatitgange, in Die Mineralien der Syenitpegmatitgange der sudnorwegischen Augit- und Nephelinsyenite: Zeitschr. fur Kryst., v. 16, p. 54-56.

Budding, A. J., 1964, Geologic outline of the Jicarilla Mountains: New Mexico Geol. Soc., 15th Field Conf., Guidebook of the Ruidoso Country, [New Mexico], 1951.

Butler, Patrick, Jr., 1964, Magnetite from intrusives and associated contact deposits, Lincoln County, New Mexico: unpublished Master's thesis, N. Mex. Inst. of Min. and Tech.

Cross, W., 1899, Description of the Telluride quadrangle: U.S. Geol. Survey Geol. Atlas, Folio 57.

Cummins, W. F., 1890, The Permian of Texas and its overlying beds: Texas Geol. Survey, 1st Ann. Rept.

Darton, N. H., 1922, Geologic structure of parts of New Mexico: U.S. Geol. Survey Bull. 726E.

Gregory, H. E., 1916, The Navajo country; a geographic and hydrographic reconnaissance of parts of Arizona, New Mexico, and Utah: U.S. Geol. Survey Water-Supply Paper 380.

Griswold, George B., 1959, Mineral deposits of Lincoln County, New Mexico: N. Mex. Inst. of Min. and Tech., State Bur. of Mines and Min. Res. Bull. 67.

Hager, D. and Robitaille, A. E., 1919, Geological report on oil possibilities in eastern New Mexico: unpublished report.

Johannsen, A., 1939, A descriptive petrography of the igneous rocks: Chicago, University of Chicago Press, 1578 p.

Kelley, Vincent C., 1949, Geology and economics of New Mexico iron-ore deposits: Univ. N. Mex. Pub. in Geology, no. 2, 246 p.

Keyes, C. R., 1915, Conspectus of the geologic formations of New Mexico: Des Moines, 12 p.

Kottlowski, F. E., Flower, R. H., Thompson, M. S., and Foster, R. W., 1956, Stratigraphic studies of the San Andres Mountains, New Mexico: N. Mex. Inst. Min. and Tech., State Bur. Mines and Min. Res. Mem. 1.

Lee, W. T., 1909, The Manzano Group of the Rio Grande Valley, New Mexico: U.S. Geol. Survey Bull. 389.

Lindgren, W., Graton, L. C., and Gordon, C. H., 1910, The ore deposits of New Mexico: U.S. Geol. Survey Prof. Paper 68, 361 p.

Meek, F. B., and Hayden, F. V., 1862, Descriptions of new Cretaceous fossils from Nebraska Territory: Acad. Nat. Sci. Phila. Proc., v. 13, p. 419-420.

Needham, C. E., and Bates, R. L., 1943, Permian type sections in central New Mexico: Geol. Soc. America Bull., v. 54, p. 1653-1667.

Reeside, J. B., Jr., 1924, Upper Cretaceous and Tertiary formations of the western part of the San Juan Basin of Colorado and New Mexico: U.S. Geol. Survey Prof. Paper 134, 70 p.

Smith, Clay T., and Budding, A. J., 1959, Reconnaissance geologic map of Little Black Peak fifteen-minute quadrangle, east half, New Mexico: N. Mex. Inst. Min. and Tech., State Bur. Mines and Min. Res. Geol. map 11.

Wilmarth, M. G., 1938, Lexicon of geologic names of the United States: U.S. Geol. Survey Bull. 896.

Wilpolt, R. H., and Wanek, A. A., 1951, Geology of the region from Socorro and San Antonio east to Chupadera Mesa, Socorro County, New Mexico: U.S. Geol. Survey Oil and Gas Inv. Map OM 121.

GEOLOGY OF THE CARRIZOZO QUADRANGLE, NEW MEXICO

Robert H. Weber
New Mexico Bureau of Mines and Mineral Resources,
New Mexico Institute of Mining and Technology
Socorro, New Mexico

INTRODUCTION

The results of detailed geologic mapping of the Carrizozo 15-minute quadrangle, summarized herein, are pertinent to both major regional features and local aspects of physiography, stratigraphy, petrology, and structure that will be viewed during the course of the 15th Annual Field Conference. The setting of the area in relationship to nearby geographic features is shown in figure 1. The geology has been highly generalized in the geologic map and section (fig. 2).

The mapped area includes segments of the Sacramento section of the Basin and Range Province and a western lobe of the Great Plains Province. It is bounded on the east by the Tertiary volcanic pile and intrusive complex of the northern Sierra Blanca, and by the western flanks of a series of domical intrusive bodies that extend northward outside the quadrangle into the Jicarilla Mountains. Sloping westward from the foot of the mountainous tract into the floor of the northern end of the Tularosa Valley, a closed intermontane basin, is a broad bajada that occupies most of the central part of the area. The bajada surface is breached near its eastern edge by a discontinuous chain of hills (Chaves Mountain, Cub Mountain, Willow Hill, etc.) capped by small intrusive bodies. Southeastward- to eastward-dipping Upper Cretaceous sandstones and shales, the beveled surface of which underlies most of the bajada, crop out in the slopes of these hills and in a narrow cuesta and scattered low hills near the foot of the slope. Recent basaltic flows of the Carrizozo Malpais mantle the floor of the valley, covering the trace of Triassic redbeds and the uppermost part of the Permian sequence. Permian strata are contorted by solution collapse and folding where they emerge from beneath the western edge of the malpais, rising in elevation northwestward onto the summit of Chupadera Mesa.

Elevations range from a minimum of about 5,000 feet on the floor of the Tularosa Valley to a maximum of 9,500 feet on the northern shoulder of Nogal Peak on the crest of the Sierra Blanca. Nogal Peak, with an elevation of about 10,000 feet, is in turn overshadowed by the 12,003-foot eminence of Sierra Blanca Peak (Cerro Blanco) 8.5 miles to the south.

Geologic mapping in the northeastern quarter of the quadrangle was contributed by Frederick J. Kuellmer. The writer was assisted briefly in the field by John H. Schilling. John E. Allen aided at the plane table during measurement of the Cub Mountain Formation type section. Line illustrations were drafted by Bob Price. Teri Ray provided editorial assistance. The geology of the area has been summarized recently by Griswold (1959), to whom the reader is referred for fuller coverage of the surrounding region of Lincoln County.

STRATIGRAPHY

Exposed rock units include Permian Yeso and San Andres Formations; local equivalents of Upper Cretaceous Dakota Sandstone, Mancos Shale, and Mesaverde Group; early Tertiary Cub Mountain Formation, volcanics of the Sierra Blanca, and a suite of intrusive rocks; late Tertiary to Recent valley fill, colluvium, landslides, and talus; and Recent basalt flows. Triassic rocks are concealed by the Carrizozo Malpais. An oil test (Standard of Texas No. 1 Heard-Federal), just outside the northwest corner of the quadrangle in sec. 33, T. 6 S., R. 9 E., provides additional stratigraphic control that includes Precambrian basement rock, a com-

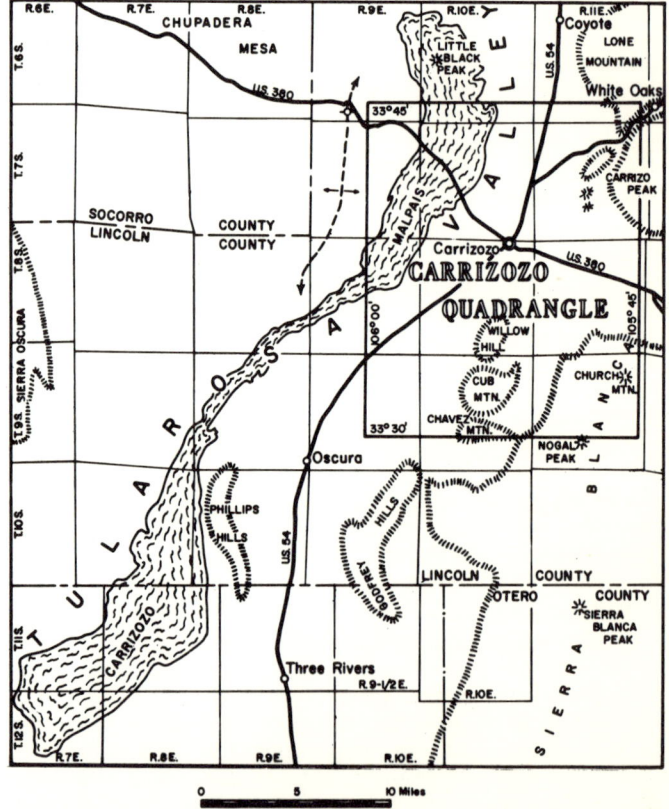

Figure 1. — Index map of Carrizozo quadrangle and vicinity, New Mexico.

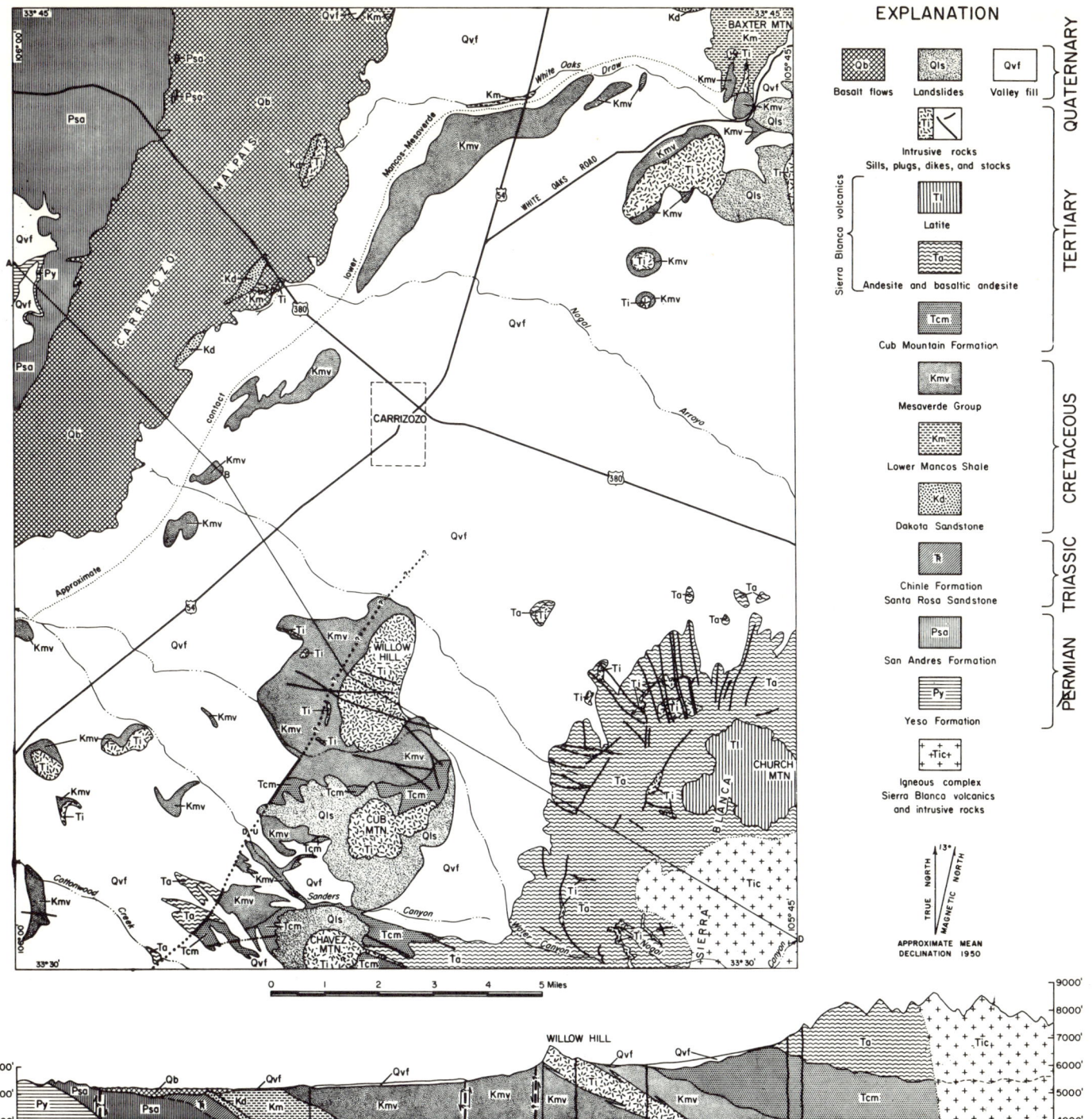

Figure 2. — Generalized geologic map and cross-section of the Carrizozo quadrangle, New Mexico.

plete section of the Pennsylvanian, and an abnormally thickened section of the Yeso Formation. Pre-Pennsylvanian Paleozoic rocks are lacking in this section, probably as a result of the combined effects of Devonian, Late Pennslyvanian, and Wolfcampian erosion, and nearness to the Pedernal landmass to the east (Kottlowski, 1963).

Precambrian Rocks

Although the southward projection of the Pedernal uplift lies only a short distance to the east (Foster and Stipp, 1961), there are no outcrops of Precambrian rocks within the Carrizozo quadrangle, nor in the immediate vicinity. The Heard test penetrated 310 feet of Precambrian gabbro with minor amounts of schist and gneiss underlying Pennsylvanian rocks below 7,740 feet. Core samples consist of a hypidiomorphic-granular aggregate of medium- to coarse-grained labradorite, augite, olivine rimmed with pyroxene and antigorite, and magnetite with local reaction rims of biotite.

The nearest outcrops of Precambrian rocks lie 30 miles west of the town of Carrizozo in the western slopes of the Sierra Oscura. Kottlowski (1953) described briefly the prevailing rock type near the northern end of the range as a muscovite leucogranite with intrusive relationships with small bodies of gray quartzite. Nearly equal proportions of quartz, potash feldspar (orthoclase and microcline), and oligoclase also permit designation as a sodic quartz monzonite. The high degree of variability in lithology of the Precambrian southward along the eastern front of the San Andres Mountains has been shown by Kottlowski and others (1956).

In the northern Sacramento Mountains near Bent, 34 miles south of Carrizozo, small outcrops of probable Precambrian rocks immediately underlie the Abo Formation. Granodiorite, quartzite, and possibly quartz diorite are represented, according to Foster (1959, p. 139) and Pray (1961, p. 25).

In the Gallinas Mountains, 40 miles north of Carrizozo, exposed basement rocks include aplitic granite and biotite gneiss, which are overlain by the Abo Formation (Kelley, 1949).

Pennsylvanian Rocks

The earliest Paleozoic rocks remaining in the Carrizozo area are of Pennsylvanian age. There are no outcrops of this sequence within the quadrangle, so the section cut in the Heard test provides the best available representation of the local stratigraphy. A maximum thickness of 1,745 feet and minimum thickness of 1,350 feet of Pennsylvanian rocks are represented, depending upon interpretation of the upper beds in this sequence as referable to the Pennsylvanian or to the early Wolfcampian Bursum Formation (Kottlowski, 1960, 1963).

As logged by R. W. Foster (in Griswold, 1959, p. 110), and including possible equivalents of the Bursum Formation, the total thickness is 1,700 feet in the interval between 6,040 and 7,740 feet. Dark gray shales and thin sandstones in the lower part are succeeded upward by gray to slightly reddish gray shales and claystones with interbeds of paler gray limestones and sandstones. The upper part contains large amounts of dark reddish gray to reddish brown mudstone interbedded with dark gray shale and claystone, arkosic sandstone, and limestone. Abundant arkosic beds in the Heard test have been cited by Kottlowski (1960, 1963) as indicating that the Pedernal landmass lay only a short distance to the east.

Pennsylvanian sequences in central New Mexico are commonly referred to the Magdalena Group, consisting of the Sandia Formation overlain by the Madera Formation. Faunal equivalents of the Morrow, Derry, Des Moines, Missouri, and Virgil Series have been recognized. The relatively thin section in the northern Sierra Oscura was subdivided by Thompson (1942) into 4 groups and 8 formations largely on the basis of fusilinid zones. Additional formational names have been applied to locally mappable lithologic units in the nearby San Andres and Sacramento Mountains (Kottlowski and others, 1956; Pray, 1961). Inasmuch as the problems of nomenclature, faunal ages, facies variations, and regional correlations have been discussed recently by Kottlowski (1960, 1963) a thorough review seems unwarranted in this paper.

Permian Rocks

Strata of Permian age crop out only in the extreme northwestern corner of the Carrizozo quadrangle, along the western edge of the Carrizozo Malpais, where they dip prevailingly eastward to southeastward beneath the basaltic flows. The exposed section includes only the uppermost part of the Yeso Formation and the lower part of the San Andres Formation. A complete section of the Yeso, underlying Abo Formation, and possible equivalents of the Bursum Formation were cut by the Standard of Texas No. 1 Heard-Federal oil test. The Bernal Formation may be present under the eastern part of the quadrangle.

Bursum(?) Formation

The possible equivalence in the Heard test of redbeds at the top of the Pennsylvanian section and the base of the Abo Formation to the Bursum Formation in the Sierra Oscura has been indicated by Kottlowski (1960, 1963) and Griswold and Foster (Griswold, 1959, p. 9, 110). Griswold assigned ". . . 230 feet of marine limestone interbedded with dark-red mudstone and arkosic conglomerate." in this interval to the Bursum. To the south, in the northern Sacramento Mountains, Bursum equivalents have been recognized by Otte (1959) under the term *Laborcita Formation*. Faunas of both Virgilian and Wolfcampian age have been identified from the Bursum and Laborcita Formations.

Abo Formation

The nearest outcrops of the Abo lie about 24 miles west of Carrizozo in the slopes extending eastward from the Sierra Oscura. Referring again to the Heard test, Foster (Griswold, 1959, p. 110) characterized the 1,560-foot Abo section (possibly including some Bursum), in the depth interval between 4,480 and 6,040 feet, as "Interbedded dark reddish-brown mudstone, claystone, and arkosic conglomerate. Mostly arkosic conglomerate in lower 700 feet." The 1,545-foot section in the Heard test assigned to the Abo by Kottlowski (1963, fig. 12) lies in a northward-trending prong of the Pennsylvanian Orogrande basin (Kottlowski's fig. 11), thinning rapidly eastward onto the Pedernal landmass.

Yeso Formation

Only the uppermost part of the Yeso is exposed along the contact of the overlying San Andres Formation at the northwestern edge of the quadrangle. A complete stratigraphic section was cut in the Heard test, but the Yeso was found to be anomalously thick as a result of folding and the presence of a thick salt sequence. Surface structure on the Carrizozo dome evidently is largely due to local thickening of the Yeso. How much of this is a product of close folding (of the type exposed in the Lincoln fold belt 30 miles ESE of Carrizozo), and how much may be a product of thickening by plastic flow of halite beds into the anticlinal axis is not clearly indicated.

As logged by Foster (Griswold, 1959, p. 110), the Yeso in the Heard test has a total thickness of 4,265 feet in the depth interval of 215 to 4,480 feet. The sequence consists of interbedded limestone, salt, gypsum, sandstone, and mudstone, of which salt beds comprise 900 feet. Deduction of the 900 feet of salt from the total thickness still leaves an abnormal thickness, as compared with the thickest nearby measured section of about 1,695 feet in T. 7 S., R. 7 E. (Wilpolt and Wanek, 1951).

Lacking a persistent Glorieta Sandstone horizon at the base of the San Andres Formation in the mapped area, the top of the Yeso Formation was arbitrarily established in outcrop at the base of a prominent (21 to 25 feet thick) gypsum bed that overlies yellowish orange to reddish brown friable siltsones and thin sandstones of typical Yeso lithology. The gypsum and overlying lenticular quartz sands and persistent silty dolomite are lithologically like those higher in the San Andres, and the contact is easily mappable in this area.

Marginal limits of the Yeso salt basin have not been determined inasmuch as the Heard test provides the only illustration of salt beds in this area. Solution effects probably would preclude outcrop of the halite. Surface drainage on the east side of the Carrizozo dome enters numerous solution cavities in gypsum and limestone beds along the west edge of the Carrizozo Malpais and, if circulation is deep enough in the upper Tularosa Valley, may be expected to have leached soluble salt beds. The high sodium chloride content of Malpais Spring, at the southern tip of the malpais, suggests active solution of salt deposits in groundwaters that received a major component of recharge from cavernous drainage in the Carrizozo area. Pray (1961) noted the presence of halite in the subsurface and a progressive northward increase in the abundance of redbeds and evaporites in the Yeso of the Sacramento Mountains.

There is no firm basis for dating the Yeso Formation in the Carrizozo quadrangle. Regional correlations indicate a Leonardian age (Pray, 1961).

San Andres Formation

Outcrops of the San Andres Formation are limited to the northwestern corner of the quadrangle, eastward from which it is buried beneath the Carrizozo Malpais. Only the lower part is exposed, permitting establishment of a mappable basal contact with the underlying Yeso Formation. The upper boundary is less certain. In the adjacent Little Black Peak quadrangle to the north, the San Andres is overlain by sandstone and shales referred to the Bernal Formation by Becker and others (Dane and Bachman, 1958) and Smith and Budding (1959). Absence of the Bernal west of Carrizozo, as shown by Kottlowski (1963, fig. 16, p. 70), suggests that post-Bernal Triassic beds directly overlie the San Andres in that area.

Basal beds consist of 21 to 25 feet of white to gray, mottled and banded gypsum with thin interbeds of gray dolomite and silty, gypsiferous limestone overlain by 21 to 39 feet of varicolored friable sandstone, then about 50 feet of yellowish gray silty dolomite and fossiliferous mottled limestone. Dolomites and limestones are interbedded with gypsum and lenticular quartz sandstones (possibly equivalent to the Glorieta Sandstone) upward in the section. Siliceous limestones and lenticular, brown-weathering chert zones are locally conspicuous.

Extensive collapse resulting from solution of gypsum and limestone has produced a chaotic variation in strikes and dips, with beds draped over the topography to an extent that makes the topographic map a fair approximation of a structural map. Dips range generally between 5 and 10 degrees, but locally steepen to as much as 65 degrees. The prevailing gentle eastward dip is apparent only in the profile of the general slope of ridge and hill crests. Recent damming of surface run-off in the Tularosa Valley by basalt flows of the Carrizozo Malpais has accelerated solution activity. Storm drainage from the western slopes pond against the edge of the basalt for a short time, then drains abruptly when the "plug is pulled" in tubular channelways in underlying gypsum beds. Recent collapse in the central part of the malpais has broken through 177 feet of basalt and underlying valley alluvium.

The partial section of the San Andres penetrated in the Heard test extended from the surface to a sample depth of 270 feet (215 feet, according to Foster in Griswold, 1959). To the north, Smith and Budding (1959) recorded an average thickness of 600 feet in the Little Black Peak quadrangle. A similar thickness of about 685 feet was reported by Allen and Jones (1951) in the Capitan quadrangle to the east.

Fossils are locally abundant in the carbonate beds and cherty zones, and include brachiopods, gastropods, bryozoa, pelecypods, echinoid spines, cephalopods, and corals. Specific identification has not been made of a small faunal collection from these beds, but it is expected that they are Leonardian inasmuch as they are from the lower part of the formation. Whether or not the upper beds include strata of Guadalupian age has not been determined.

Bernal Formation

Local sequences to the north and east of the Carrizozo quadrangle include post-San Andres redbeds that have been referred to the Triassic under the designation *Bernal Formation* (Allen and Jones, 1951; Smith and Budding, 1959) and to undifferentiated rocks of Guadalupian age that include equivalents of the Bernal, Grayburg, Queen, Seven Rivers, Yates, and Tansil Formations, or Whitehorse Group (Dane and Bachman 1958). Correlative beds do not crop out in the Carrizozo quadrangle. If present, they are buried beneath the Carrizozo Malpais. However, as shown by Kottlowski (1963, fig. 16, p. 70), the western edge of the Bernal probably lies along a north-south line passing through Carrizozo. In the Little Black Peak quadrangle, a few miles to the north, the Bernal consists variably of 200 to 300 feet of red to buff calcareous sandstone with silty partings and shale beds, overlain by redbeds of the Santa Rosa Formation (Smith and Budding, 1959).

Inasmuch as the Bernal was originally defined as representing the upper clastic member of the San Andres Formation in Mora County, and was believed to correlate with the Guadalupian Chalk Bluff Formation, (Bachman, 1953), it is similarly treated here as a part of the Permian System.

Triassic Rocks

Redbeds younger than the Bernal Formation and older than the Dakota Sandstone in the Capitan and Little Black Peak quadrangles have been correlated with the Santa Rosa Sandstone and Chinle Formation by Allen and Jones (1951) and Smith and Budding (1959). The trace of equivalent beds in the Carrizozo quadrangle probably extends southwestward under the eastern edge of the malpais, emerging a few miles to the southwest (in the southeastern corner of the Chihuahua Ranch quadrangle) in the western slope of Bull Gap Ridge. Triassic rocks pinch out southward in the vicinity of Mescalero. As a consequence, the Dakota(?) Sandstone rests directly on the San Andres Formation on the crest of the Sacramento Mountains (Pray and Allen, 1956).

Santa Rosa Sandstone

About 295 feet of light gray, buff, green, and red quartz sandstone, siltstone, and chert-pebble conglomerate have been correlated with the Santa Rosa sandstone in the Capitan quadrangle (Allen and Jones, 1951). The thickness averages 200 feet in the Little Black Peak quadrangle, where the Santa Rosa consists of red, micaceous, quartz sandstone with lenses of shale, siltstone, and quartz- and chert-pebble conglomerate in the upper part. In both areas, the Santa Rosa rests on the Bernal Formation, whereas west of Carrizozo it may rest directly on the San Andres Formation, as suggested by Kottlowski (1963).

Chinle Formation

Overlying the Santa Rosa sandstone in the Capitan quadrangle are 181 feet of red mudstone, siltstone, and claystone, with local limestone interbeds near the top. This sequence was correlated with the Chinle Formation by Allen and Jones (1951). A correlative sequence of redbeds, averaging 400 feet in thickness in the Little Black Peak quadrangle, consists of red to lavender quartz sandstone and mudstone (Smith and Budding, 1959). The uppermost part of the Chinle underlies the Dakota Sandstone in the kipuka near the eastern edge of the Carrizozo Malpais, 2.5 miles north of U.S. Highway 380, as indicated by patches of red soil. Exposures are otherwise lacking in this quadrangle.

Cretaceous Rocks

A thick succession of calcareous sandstones, shales, mudstones, and thin argillaceous limestones crops out discontinuosuly in a belt 7 to 8 miles wide extending southwestward across the central part of the quadrangle. Although a complete stratigraphic section is nowhere exposed, and broad covered intervals precluded detailed stratigraphic studies, equivalents of the Dakota Sandstone, Mancos Shale, and Mesaverde Group have been recognized. Undulations in attitude, displacement along both exposed and possible concealed faults, and thickening due to sill intrusion make thickness approximations of dubious value. The total thickness in the surrounding region is shown by Kottlowski (1963) to range from 1,460 to 1,850 feet, whereas Melhase (1927) estimated between 3,500 and 3,600 feet in the vicinity of Oscura. Faunal equivalents of the Greenhorn, Carlisle, and lower Niobrara were recognized by William A. Cobban (personal communication) during a very brief examination of a collection made during the course of the present study.

Dakota Sandstone

The basal unit of the Cretaceous sequence is a quartz sandstone whose lithologic features and stratigraphic position conform with those of the Dakota Sandstone of central New Mexico. Outcrops are scattered along a narrow arcuate belt extending from the south flank of Lone Mountain westward, then southwestward along the eastern margin of the Carrizozo Malpais. Several kipukas that project through the basalt flows strike northeasterly and dip 7 to 25 degrees southeasterly.

Basal contacts with the underlying Chinle Formation are not exposed but are probably close to the western edge of Dakota outcrops in the malpais. The lower beds are white, tan, pinkish buff, and yellow fine-grained to coarse-grained quartz sandstones. Small carbonized wood fragments are present locally. Fine bedding laminae, cross-laminations, and local ripple-marked surfaces become more prominent upwards. Weathered surfaces range from tan through dark brown to black, the darker hues resulting from a strong tendency toward the formation of desert varnish. Case-hardened surfaces are also common. Cementation by calcite varies from weak to very firm, with some tendency to increase upward. The upper contact is apparently gradational into the Mancos Shale, dark shales of the latter interfingering with sandstones of the Dakota.

The total thickness was not determined due to the lack of exposed contacts and complication by sill intrusions. Allen and Jones measured 134 feet of Dakota in the Capitan quadrangle, and Smith and Budding gave an average thickness of about 150 feet in the Little Black Peak quadrangle. Melhase reported 200 feet of Dakota in Bull Gap Ridge, where the upper part contains shaly coal and a coal bed.

Mancos Shale

Black to gray, fossiliferous, calcareous, pyritic shales, shaly to sandy limestone, and thin sandstones that overlie the Dakota Sandstone are correlated with the Mancos Shale on the basis of lithology and stratigraphic position. Outcrops are very sparse, of small lateral and vertical extent, and complicated by sill intrusions. Only the lower part is differentiated on the accompanying geologic map (fig. 2). Actually, however, dark gray calcareous shales containing abundant marine fossils intertongue with lenticular sandstones and gray to olive shales of the Mesaverde much higher in the section, extending southeastward high into the western slopes of Willow Hill. Under conditions of more continuous outcrop, some of these upper tongues probably could be differentiated on geologic maps of a mile-to-the-inch scale.

Incompetent shales of the Mancos were favorable hosts for sill intrusions. Local baking has so indurated them that they have been misinterpreted as limestones by some observers.

Faunal collections from highly fossiliferous beds in the Mancos have received only cursory examination. Pelecypods from the lower part are of Greenhorn aspect, whereas upper tongues contain forms indicative of the upper Carlisle (William A. Cobban, personal communication).

Mesaverde Group

Overlying and interfingering with tongues of the Mancos Shale is a thick sequence of marine and non-marine sandstones, shales, and thin coal beds that is the local equivalent of the Mesaverde Group. Outcrops are scattered across the central part of the quadrangle in narrow cuestas and isolated hills, many of which are capped by sills. The broad bajada that forms the eastern slope of the Tularosa Valley is largely underlain at very shallow depths by an erosion surface that bevels prevailingly eastward- to southeastward-dipping beds of the Mesaverde. The section in all probability is repeated by faults, downthrown to the west, creating an exaggerated apparent thickness.

Yellowish gray to buff, massive to thin-bedded, fine- to medium-grained, lenticular, calcareous sandstones are particularly prominent in outcrops. Thin-bedded gray to yellowish brown siltstones, sandstones, gray to olive clays and shales, carbonaceous shales, and coal beds are usually covered. Cross-lamination is prevalent, and ripple marks were noted at several places. Fossiliferous marine sandstones and shales interfinger with sandstones containing silicified driftwood fragments and coaly shales. Weathered surfaces are prevailingly buff to brown; liesegang banding is locally prominent.

Three, possibly four, coal beds have been prospected in the section exposed on the west side of Willow Hill and the northwestern foot of Cub Mountain. Two of these at Cub Mountain have been mined, but the workings are now caved and inaccessible. Wegemann (1914, p. 424) reported a bed in the Conner and Smith mine 4 feet 10 inches thick, including four shale partings. The upper coal seam as measured by Melhase (1927) is 2 feet 6 inches thick.

Faunal equivalents of the upper Carlisle and lower Niobrara were tentatively identified in collections from marine sandstones of the Mesaverde in the western slopes of Willow Hill (William A. Cobban, personal communication).

Tertiary Rocks

Overlying the Mesaverde Group is a thick sequence of continental redbeds, the Cub Mountain Formation, succeeded upward by the andesitic pile of the Sierra Blanca, and latite. Widespread injection of dikes, sills, domed plugs, and stocks of granite, alkali syenite, monzonite, andesite, diorite, basalt, gabbro, and lamprophyre accompanied and followed volcanism. Although inadequately dated, these rocks are probably largely early Tertiary in age. Silts, sands, gravels, and their indurated equivalents of the valley fill in the eastern slope of the Tularosa Valley may include beds of late Tertiary age.

Cub Mountain Formation

The term *Cub Mountain Formation* was used by the writer to designate a thick interval of continental redbeds that rest on the Mesaverde Group in the slopes of Cub Mountain, T. 9 S., R. 10 E. (unpublished manuscript). Correlative beds in the Capitan coal field subsequently were described by Bodine (1956) under this term. Bodine had not intended that his paper serve as the type definition, as a typographically omitted footnote would have explained. The term has, however, been adopted, although handicapped by the lack of a formal definition and described type section.

Outcrops extend from the northern slopes of Cub Mountain southward into the Three Rivers drainage area in the Sierra Blanca Peak quadrangle. The western limits are along a northeast-trending fault west of Cub and Chaves Mountains. Eastern limits are marked by depositional contacts with younger rocks east of the two peaks. Pervasive landslide and intrusive activity obscure the section in the slopes of Cub Mountain. The type section accordingly was measured in the arroyo banks of Sanders Canyon, between Cub and Chaves Mountains, where outcrops extend in a very narrow band from the SW¼SW¼ sec. 16 to the SW¼SW¼ sec. 24, T. 9 S., R. 10 E., a distance of over three miles. Basal contacts with the Mesaverde are generally obscure, and appear locally conformable (although probably at least disconformable). The contact was mapped at the base of the lowest impure arkosic sandstone, or the base of the lowest red or variegated clayey to silty bed, whichever feature provided the most useful datum locally. The upper contact was placed at the base of the lowest bed of the Sierra Blanca volcanic pile, which in this area is pinkish gray to grayish red ash and lapilli tuff.

The sequence consists of white to gray and yellowish buff to brown, massive to thin-bedded, fine- to coarse-grained, poorly sorted arkosic sandstone beds (many of which are cross-laminated and show pronounced channeling at the base), interbedded with red, maroon, purple, brown, greenish gray, and variegated montmorillonitic claystone, mudstone, siltstone, and fine-grained sandstone. Thin lenses of conglomerate contain pebbles of quartzite, silicified rhyolite and latite(?), and minor amounts of chert, granite, and silicified wood. Coarser-grained beds higher in the section are characteristically gray to grayish red graywackes containing abundant mafic minerals, fragments of andesite and mud pellets. These beds probably reflect active volcanism in the source area, and provide criteria for subdividing the Cub Mountain Formation into lower and upper members. Seams and veinlets of gypsum are prevalent in fine-grained beds throughout most of the section.

The total thickness of the Cub Mountain in the type section is about 2,400 feet. The long traverse in the measured section, variations in attitude, and several apparently minor faults make this figure subject to correction. Nevertheless, it probably lies within the range of lateral variations in thickness.

Correlation with the Eocene(?) Baca Formation of central New Mexico (Wilpolt and others, 1946; Tonking, 1957) is strongly suggested by similarities in stratigraphic postion, lithology, and inferred depositional environment. It must be recognized that such a correlation does not imply complete synchrony in time nor continuity in basins of deposition of the Baca and Cub Mountain. Stratigraphic age limits for the Baca are post-Mesaverde Group and pre-Datil Formation. By tenuous extrapolation, a single potassium-argon age determination on the Spears Member of the Datil in the Socorro area, 37 m. y. (latest Eocene), may be grossly applicable to the upper member of the Cub Mountain (Burke and others, 1963; Weber, 1963).

Sierra Blanca Volcanics

Directly overlying the Cub Mountain Formation is a sequence of andesitic volcanic rocks that form the bulk of the northern Sierra Blanca. Small outcrops are also scattered along the western (downthrown) side of the fault extending northeastward near the western foot of Chaves and Cub Mountains. Local masses of younger latite are presented in and adjacent to Church Mountain and in Gaylord Peak in the Sierra Blanca. Similar latites are prominent to the south in the Godfrey Hills (Sierra Blanca Peak quadrangle), where they overlie andesitic rocks like those in the Sierra Blanca.

The basal contact with the Cub Mountain is poorly exposed, but lithologically distinguished by the abrupt appearance of pinkish gray to grayish red ash and lapilli tuff. The section above the contact is obviously of volcanic origin, whereas below are water-laid clastic sediments of the Cub Mountain. Andesite and basaltic andesite flow breccias, flows, tuff breccias, and lapilli tuffs of light to dark gray, bluish gray, purplish gray, and pink to red color, related intrusives, and minor volcanic conglomerate have a residual aggregate thickness of 3,500 feet or more in the higher parts of the Sierra Blanca. An unknown additional thickness has been stripped from the crest of the range by subsequent erosion. Textures range from aphanitic to highly porphyritic with random to flow-aligned phenocrysts of plagioclase and augite. Vesicular and amygdaloidal phases are prominent locally. Pervasive propylitic alteration of variable intensity is indicated by widespread development of epidote, chlorite, and calcite, accompanied by greenish alteration colors and local bleaching.

Light to dark gray, reddish gray, and brown porphyritic aphanites of latitic composition are responsible for the topographic prominence of Church Mountain. Similar rocks make up the main mass of Gaylord Peak. Possible correlatives in the foothills at the northern end of the Sierra Blanca have been highly altered to quartz, epidote, and chlorite. Sparse to abundant phenocrysts of saussuritized andesine, sanidine, clinopyroxene, and biotite set in a cryptocrystalline to fine-grained groundmass are distinguishing features of these rocks. Contact relationships with the adjacent andesites are obscured by extensive talus and colluvium. Textural and structural features that include massive phases of considerable thickness, local low- to high-angular planar flow banding, welded tuffs, breccias, and an exposed thickness of over 1,400 feet suggest emplacement as a volcanic dome with associated intrusive elements.

Correlation of the Sierra Blanca volcanics with the better known volcanic assemblages that extend from the Socorro area westward across the Datil-Mogollon volcanic field is handicapped by 50 miles of separation. Lithologic similarities of the volcanic rocks and analogies in stratigraphic relationships of the Baca to the Datil volcanics, and of the Cub Mountain to the Sierra Blanca volcanics, led the writer to suggest a possible correlation of the latter with andesites in the lower part of the Datil Formation in Socorro County (Weber, 1963, p. 138). Depending upon the validity of so speculative a correlation, a frame of age reference that bounds the andesites of the Socorro area by potassium-argon ages of 37 m. y. for underlying latite of the Spears Member and 32 m. y. for overlying rhyolite of the Hell's Mesa Member (Burke and others, 1963; Weber and Bassett, 1963) may be grossly relevant to the age of the Sierra Blanca volcanics. Although the andesites and latites of the "lower volcanic group" in the Magdalena and San Mateo areas have been considered to be pre-Datil (Weber, 1963), later field observations strongly suggest that they may be assignable to the basal part of the Datil Formation.

Intrusive Rocks

An extensive series of small stocks, domed plugs, sills, and dikes cut all previously described rock units but are most prevalent in and adjacent to the Sierra Blanca. A wide range in composition is represented, from alkali syenite through monzonite to gabbro, and minor ultrabasic types. Soda- and potash-rich varieties are prominent, whereas oversaturated quartz-bearing rocks are relatively sparse within the limits of the quadrangle. The larger intrusive masses are prevailingly syenitic to monzonitic in composition. Characteristic mineral assemblages include sodic orthoclase, anorthoclase, albite, hornblende, augite, aegerite-augite, aegerite, biotite, analcime, nepheline, leucite, and sodalite, with calcic plagioclase in the normal monzonitic to gabbroic rocks. Late magmatic and deuteric soda and potash enrichment are prevalent in the alkalic varieties. Zeolites, especially thomsonite, are widely distributed late magmatic to hydrothermal minerals.

Both simple and compound dikes cut all rocks indiscriminately, except for thicker sills, locally forming swarms that are only partly indicated on figure 2. Sills were emplaced preferentially in incompetent shaly zones in the Mancos, Mesaverde, and Cub Mountain. They are also common in the Sierra Blanca volcanics, where controls of emplacement are less clear. Plugs and stocks also show little evident structural control, although their tendency toward alignment along northerly trends may have structural significance. The igneous complex in the southeastern corner of the quadrangle consists of a zone of Sierra Blanca volcanics so riddled by stocks, sills, and dikes as to preclude differentiation at the map scale. The largest stock in this complex is a normal hornblende-biotite monzonite that extends southward from Nogal Canyon into Bonito Canyon (syenodiorite of Griswold and Missaghi, 1964).

A belt of topographically prominent alkali syenite sills with associated feeder intrusives extends through Chaves and Cub Mountains and Willow Hill. Chaves Mountain is capped by a sill of porphyritic analcite syenite connected with a feeder dike on the east. Phenocrysts of orthoclase, and clusters of smaller crystals of augite rimmed successively by aegerite-augite and aegerite, are set in a felted matrix of highly altered albite(?). Analcite is abundant as an intergranular component. The core of Cub Mountain consists of a pluglike mass of similar composition with the addition of some nepheline. Mottled zones of pronounced orthoclasation are conspicuous on the crest of the peak. Sill offshoots contain more abundant intergranular nepheline. The Willow Hill sill, which reaches a thickness of 800 feet, differs in being largely homogenous, fine-grained leucosyenite containing sparse small glomerocrysts of albite and small amounts of aegerite-augite and biotite, set in a matrix of altered orthoclase. The regularity of jointing paralleling the sill walls results in a pseudo-bedded appearance.

Several large domed plugs lie just outside the northeast corner of the quadrangle. These have been considered by some observers to be laccoliths, but evidence is lacking that they are floored intrusives. Doming of peripheral sedimentary wall rocks is strikingly shown on aerial photographs of Lone Mountain and clearly indicated on the map by Smith and Budding (1959). Modes of this rock by Butler (1964) range from quartz syenite to granite. Carrizo Mountain has a similar topographic expression, but marginal relationships are obscured by landslides and alluvial fans. Modes indicate a biotite-hornblende-quartz syenite porphyry with local trachytic texture (Butler, 1964). Trachytic texture is a conspicuous feature of many of the syenite sills and dikes of the Carrizozo quadrangle, a number of which have a foliated appearance.

Dark-colored lamprophyric intrusives are associated with some of the syenites in the southern part of the quadrangle. Among the recognized varieties are biotite-rich kersantite, augite-rich spessartite or camptonite, and monchiquite. Possible extrusive equivalents may be represented in analcite-basanite breccias at the western foot of the Sierra Blanca.

Age relationships within the intrusive suite are obscure due to the scarcity of cross-cutting contacts. Compound dikes of diverse composition indicate considerable overlap by hazy contacts and local reversals of sequence of intrusion. Gradational boundaries between leucocratic and melanocratic syenites also suggest essential synchronicity. Alkali syenite sills, which appear to be relatively late, are cut locally by dikes of gabbroic composition.

Major intrusives of the Carrizozo area are tentatively considered to be early Tertiary in age, although positive criteria for dating are lacking. They are to a large extent younger than the Sierra Blanca andesites, but intrusive contacts with the latite of Church Mountain were not seen. Genetic relationships with alkalic intrusives of the Cornudas Mountains on the Texas-New Mexico line to the south (Warner and others, 1959) are suggested by strong petrologic similarities.

Quaternary Rocks

Three classes of rock units of Quarternary age have been differentiated on figure 2: valley fill, landslides, and basalt. Colluvium and talus have been omitted.

Valley Fill

Several locally differentiable units, the oldest of which may be late Tertiary in age, are included within the broad category of valley fill. Much of the bajada on the east side of the Tularosa Valley is underlain by a poorly exposed sequence of weakly cemented clayey muds, silts, and sands. These beds are overlain locally by a thin, coarse, caliche-cemented gravel composed largely of fragments of intrusive rocks like those in Chaves and Cub Mountains and Willow Hill. Younger unconsolidated sandy to clayey gravels thinly veneer most of the bajada surface, merging westward with Recent sandy to clayey alluvium that abuts the eastern edge of the Carrizozo Malpais. These younger beds extend upslope into a series of coalescent alluvial fans with apices at the mouths of the principal canyons along the mountain front. Mud-flow scallops are conspicuous on the higher parts of some of the fans.

Landslides

Scalloped slopes surrounding Cub and Chaves Mountains are landslide features. A narrow band along the western foot of Willow Hill and similar, though less conspicuous, features in the higher elevations of the Sierra Blanca have not been differentiated on figure 2. Incompetent clays and shales in the Mesaverde and Cub Mountain sequences are particularly prone to yield to gravitational slumping where exposed in steep slopes under the load of thick sills and sandstones.

Basalt Flows

The floor of the northern Tularosa Valley is mantled by a sheet of basaltic lavas, commonly known as the Carrizozo Malpais, that extends southwestward for a distance of about 44 miles, and ranges in width from half a mile to more than five miles. An areal extent of about 127 square miles and a volume of close to one cubic mile have been calculated by Allen (1951). The flows issued from a vent marked by a cluster of small cinder cones near the northern end of the malpais. Little Black Peak, the most prominent of these, is visible to the north from U.S. Highway 380 where it crosses the malpais.

The surface of the lava field is marked by ropy corrugations, pressure ridges, low tumuli, and collapse features typical of pahoehoe flows. Two major flow units totaling 162 feet in thickness are exposed in the walls of a sinkhole that collapsed through the lavas two miles south of the highway. The basal flow there consists of gray, massive, fine-grained olivine basalt 60 feet thick, with a thin vesicular to scoriaceous zone at the top. The upper flow is lithologically similar, has a local thickness of 102 feet, and bears a thicker vesicular zone at the top. Underlying the basal flow is valley-floor alluvium composed of pinkish gray, silty limestone gravels with an exposed thickness of 15 feet.

Lithologic characteristics include sparse to abundant small olivine phenocrysts set in a fine-grained intergranular to subophitic matrix of andesine-labradorite laths, augite, and olivine in the midsections of the flows, grading to glassy phases at the upper surface. A chemical analysis of the upper flow is as follows:

SiO_2	50.77%	Na_2O	3.50%
Al_2O_3	14.00	K_2O	1.51
Fe_2O_3	2.34	TiO_2	1.71
FeO	7.48	P_2O_5	0.34
MnO	0.16	H_2O-	1.72
MgO	6.96	H_2O+	0.07
CaO	9.08	CO_2	0.00

Three explosive episodes are indicated by cinder cones at the vent. The latest of these is Little Black Peak, which rises to a height of 85 feet with slopes of 25 degrees, and contains an intact crater 32 feet deep. Another older cone with a smaller crater lies at the north-northwestern foot of Little Black Peak. The earliest visible cone apparently had the largest crater; it is represented only by remnants of the northern rim that lie a little farther out to the north and northeast.

The freshness of surficial flow features, lack of erosional dissection, and intact conditions of the latest cone all point to Recent origin of these flows. Absolute age criteria have not been obtained, but an estimate of 1,000 to 1,500 years seems reasonable.

Older basaltic lavas that issued from vents marked by two cones at Broken Back Crater, 8 miles to the west-northwest, probably underlie the northwestern edge of the Carrizozo Malpais.

STRUCTURE

The Carrizozo quadrangle occupies the western limb of a broad north-northeastward-trending syncline approximately 40 miles long and 25 to 30 miles wide. Consequently, all rocks older than the valley fill dip prevailingly southeastward to eastward. Relatively minor cross folds, solution collapse structures, and intrusion domes are superimposed upon the larger structure.

Only one major fault is clearly indicated, and that trends northeast along the western foot of Chaves and Cub Mountains. It may continue farther northeastward along the western foot of Willow Hill, but its trace is concealed by landslides and alluvium. The downthrown side is on the west. Other parallel faults are suspected in the area to the west where extensive cover and lack of marker beds in Cretaceous rocks precluded positive recognition. Another northeastward-trending fault is inferred to lie just under the western edge of the malpais because beds of the San Andres exposed to the west are flexed sharply downward toward the east.

Trends of dike swarms offer additional structural implications, the significance of which is not clear. Although the trends range through all quadrants, there is a progressive clockwise rotation of dike sets when traced from west to east around the northern end of the Sierra Blanca. The radial pattern tempts speculation that the dike trends may be related to magmatic pressures active during emplacement of stocks in the Sierra Blanca.

Additional structural implications may be drawn from the northerly trend of major intrusive masses along the axis of the Sierra Blanca syncline. The west-northwesterly alignment of basaltic vents at Little Black Peak and Broken Back Crater with the prominent monzonite dike and flexure of the Jones Camp iron deposit also seems more than fortuitous. Paralleling this trend is a major transverse fault that crosses the Sierra Oscura and disappears under alluvium 16 miles west of Carrizozo (Dane and Bachman, 1961).

Structural features comparable with those of the Lincoln fold system east of the Sierra Blanca have not been recognized in the Carrizozo area, although folds in the subsurface Yeso in the Heard test may be related. Craddock (1960) ascribed the Lincoln folds and faults to eastward gravitational gliding (decollement), triggered by plutonic doming to the west.

All observed structures are of post-Mesaverde Group age. The Cub Mountain Formation may be a product of Laramide events in this area during which broad, open folding created sediment-source highlands and a depositional basin. The extent to which this basin coincided with the present limits of the Sierra Blanca syncline is unknown. Subsequent volcanism and igneous intrusion possibly were accompanied by increased downwarping of the synclinal trough, with attendant readjustment by faulting. Local doming was a product of igneous intrusion. High-angle basin-and-range block faulting then outlined major ranges and intervening basins such as the Tularosa Valley. According to Pray (1961, p. 124), uplift of the Sacramento Mountain block ". . . probably began in late Cenozoic time and appears to be still in progress." Inasmuch as the Sierra Blanca lie along a north-northeastward extension of the Sacramento Mountain block, Pray's interpretation may be expected to be applicable to the Carrizozo area.

MINERAL DEPOSITS

Griswold (1959) has provided thorough coverage of the mineral resources of the Carrizozo quadrangle and surrounding area of Lincoln County; therefore, only passing metion of these features will be made herein.

Except for small amounts of coal from the Mesaverde Group in the Willow Hill field, mineral production has been negligible, although districts with a significant history of mineral production (White Oaks, Nogal, Bonito) lie just outside the eastern and southern boundaries of the quadrangle. Narrow fissure veins containing calcite, siderite, iron oxides, barite, and quartz, with small amounts of oxidized iron, copper, lead, and zinc sulfide minerals have been explored to shallow depths in a number of prospects along the western margin of the Sierra Blanca (Schelerville district). Most of these veins are in or adjacent to sheared syenite and diorite dikes of westerly trend that cut andesitic volcanic rocks. Pyrite, molybdenite, and minor amounts of chalcopyrite are locally conspicuous in altered parts of the monzonite stock in Nogal Canyon. The geology of that area, and results of a geochemical survey, have been described by Griswold and Missaghi (1964).

Cuttings of the salt section in the Yeso Formation from the Heard test have been examined for potash minerals, but the known results have been negative. Gypsum beds in outcrops of the San Andres Formation show little promise for commercial exploitation when compared with known, and currently productive, deposits elsewhere in New Mexico.

REFERENCES CITED

Allen, J. E., 1951, The Carrizozo Malpais: Roswell Geol. Soc., 5th Field Conf., Guidebook of the Carrizozo-Capitan-Chupadera Mesa Region, Lincoln and Socorro Counties, New Mexico, 1951, p. 9-11.

────── and Jones, S. M., 1951, Preliminary stratigraphic section, Capitan quadrangle, New Mexico: Roswell Geol. Soc., 5th Field Conf., Guidebook of the Carrizozo-Capitan-Chupadera Mesa Region, Lincoln and Socorro Counties, New Mexico, 1951.

Bachman, G. O., 1953, Geology of a part of northwestern Mora County, New Mexico: U.S. Geol. Survey Oil and Gas Inv. Map OM 137.

Bodine, M. W., Jr., 1956, Geology of Capitan coal field, Lincoln County, New Mexico: N. Mex. Inst. Min. and Tech., State Bur. Mines and Min. Res. Circ. 35, 27 p.

Burke, W. H., Kenny, G. S., Otto, J. B., and Walker, R.D., 1963, Potassium-argon dates, Socorro and Sierra Counties, New Mexico: N. Mex. Geol. Soc., 14th Field Conf., Guidebook of the Socorro Region, p. 224.

Butler, P. A., Jr., 1964, Magnetite from intrusives and associated contact deposits, Lincoln County, New Mexico: N. Mex. Inst. Min. and Tech. unpub. Master's Thesis.

Craddock, Campbell, 1960, The origin of the Lincoln County fold system, southeastern New Mexico, in Structure of the earth's crust and deformation of rocks: Internat. Geol. Cong., 21st, Copenhagen, 1960, Rept. pt. 18, p. 33-34.

Dane, C. H., and Bachman, G. O., 1958, Preliminary geologic map of the southeastern part of New Mexico: U.S. Geol. Survey Misc. Geol. Inv., Map I-256.

────── 1961, Preliminary geologic map of the southwestern part of New Mexico: U.S. Geol. Survey Misc. Geol. Inv. Map I-344.

Foster, R. W., 1959, Precambrian rocks of the Sacramento Mountains and vicinity: Soc. Econ. Paleontologists and Mineralogists and Roswell Geol. Soc., Joint Field Conf., Guidebook of the Sacramento Mountains of Otero County, New Mexico, 1959, p. 137-149.

────── and Stipp, T. F., 1961, Preliminary geologic and relief map of the Precambrian rocks of New Mexico: N. Mex. Inst. Min. and Tech., State Bur. Mines and Min. Res. Circ. 57, 37 p.

Griswold, G B., 1959, Mineral deposits of Lincoln County, New Mexico: N. Mex. Inst. Min. and Tech., State Bur. Mines and Min. Res. Bull. 67, 117 p.

────── and Missaghi, Fazlollah, 1964, Geology and geochemical survey of a molybdenum deposit near Nogal Peak, Lincoln County, New Mexico: N. Mex. Inst. Min. and Tech., State Bur. Mines and Min. Res. Circ. 67, 24 p.

Kelley, V. C., 1949, Geology and economics of New Mexico iron-ore deposits: Univ. N. Mex. Pub. in Geology no. 2, 246 p.

Kottlowski, F. E., 1953, Geology and ore deposits of a part of the Hansonburg mining district, Socorro County, New Mexico: N. Mex. Inst. Min. and Tech., State Bur. Mines and Min. Res. Circ. 23, 9 p.

────── 1960, Summary of Pennsylvanian sections in southwestern New Mexico and southeastern Arizona: N. Mex. Inst. Min. and Tech., State Bur. Mines and Min. Res. Bull. 66, 187 p.

────── 1963, Paleozoic and Mesozoic strata of southwestern and south-central New Mexico: N. Mex. Inst. Min. and Tech., State Bur. Mines and Min. Res. Bull. 79, 100 p.

──────, Flower, R. H., Thompson, M. L. and Foster, R. W., 1956, Stratigraphic studies of the San Andres Mountains, New Mexico: N. Mex. Inst. Min. and Tech., State Bur. Mines and Min. Res. Mem. 1, 132 p.

Melhase, John, 1927, Report on the Sierra Blanca coal field, Lincoln and Otero Counties, New Mexico: Unpub. private report.

Otte, Carel, Jr., 1959, Late Pennsylvanian and early Permian stratigraphy of the northern Sacramento Mountains, Otero County, New Mexico: N. Mex. Inst. Min. and Tech., State Bur. Mines and Min. Res. Bull. 50, 111 p.

Pray, L. C., 1961, Geology of the Sacramento Mountains escarpment, Otero County, New Mexico: N. Mex. Inst. Min. and Tech., State Bur. Mines and Min. Res. Bull. 35, 144 p.

────── and Allen, J. E., 1956, Outlier of Dakota(?) strata, southeastern New Mexico: Am. Assoc. Petrol. Geol. Bull., v. 40, p. 2735-2740.

Smith, C. T., and Budding, A. J., 1959, Reconnaissance geologic map of the Little Black Peak quadrangle, east half: N. Mex. Inst. Min. and Tech., State Bur. Mines and Min. Res. Geol. Map 11.

Thompson, M. L., 1942, Pennsylvanian System in New Mexico: N. Mex. Inst. Min. and Tech., State Bur. Mines and Min. Res. Bull. 17, 92 p.

Tonking, W. H., 1957, Geology of Puertecito quadrangle, Socorro County, New Mexico: N. Mex. Inst. Min. and Tech., State Bur. Mines and Min. Res. Bull. 41, 67 p.

Warner, L. A. Holser, W. T., Wilmarth, V. R., and Cameron, E. N., 1959, Occurrence of nonpegmatite beryllium in the United States: U.S. Geol. Survey Prof. Paper 318, 198 p.

Weber, R. H., 1963, Cenozoic volcanic rocks of Socorro County: N. Mex. Geol. Soc., 14th Field Conf., Guidebook of the Socorro Region, 1963, p. 132-143.

────── and Bassett, W. A., 1963, K-Ar ages of volcanic and intrusive rocks in Socorro, Catron, and Grant Counties, New Mexico: N. Mex. Geol. Soc., 14th Field Conf., Guidebook of the Socorro Region, 1963, p. 220-223.

Wegemann, C. H., 1914, Geology and coal resources of the Sierra Blanca coal field, Lincoln and Otero Counties, New Mexico: U.S. Geol. Survey Bull. 541, p. 419-452.

Wilpolt, R. H., McAlpin, A. J., Bates, R. L., and Vorbes, Georges, 1946, Geologic map and stratigraphic sections of Paleozoic rocks of Joyita Hills, Los Pinos Mountains, and north Chupadera Mesa, Valencia, Torrance, and Socorro Counties, New Mexico: U.S. Geol. Survey Oil and Gas Inv. Map OM 61.

Wilpolt, R. H., and Wanek, A. A., 1951, Geology of the region from Socorro and San Antonio east to Chupadera Mesa, Socorro County, New Mexico: U.S. Geol. Survey Oil and Gas Inv. Map OM 121.

TECTONICS AND GENERAL GEOLOGY OF THE RUIDOSO-CARRIZOZO REGION, CENTRAL NEW MEXICO

Vincent C. Kelley and Tommy B. Thompson
University of New Mexico
Albuquerque, New Mexico

INTRODUCTION

The Ruidoso-Carrizozo region, as considered in this paper and in the accompanying tectonic map (in pocket), is about 75 miles wide and 100 miles long. It extends from near Corona on the north to near Tularosa on the south and from the edges of the Jornado del Muerto and the San Andres Range on the west to the eastern end of the Capitan Mountains on the east. It includes several prominent large mountain masses such as Gallinas, Jicarilla, Capitan, and Sierra Blanca and the edges of the great Sacramento and San Andres Ranges. The region also includes great table land areas such as Chupadera Mesa and a part of the High Plains along its western edge. All the Claunch to Carrizozo lowlands and the northern one-third or so of the Tularosa Valley are included.

Approximately the eastern one-third of the area drains to the Pecos Valley, and the western two-thirds is all interior drainage into the Carrizozo, Tularosa, or Jornado del Muerto basins.

Altitudes of the area lie mostly between 5,000 and 7,000 feet. The lowest part is in the Tularosa Valley, where it is about 4,200 feet; the highest altitude is 12,003 at Sierra Blanca Peak. It is perhaps of special note that the greatest relief in New Mexico is on the western escarpment of Sierra Blanca where it stands 7,800 feet above Tularosa Valley. This compares with some 7,100 feet off the Santa Fe Range; some 6,800 feet off Wheeler Peak near Taos; some 5,700 feet off the Sandia Mountains; and some 5,500 feet off Mount Taylor.

The tectonic map which forms the basis for the text was constructed especially for the Fifteenth Field Conference from numerous geologic maps and some additional field work by the authors. The map has many generalized areas owing to the small scale and to lack of adequate geologic maps or stratigraphic and structural control in places. Structure in the central part of Chupadera Mesa was virtually impossible to check owing to its inclusion in the White Sands Proving Grounds. At the scale of the map and with the 200-foot contour interval it is difficult to show accurately the dips of contour spacings at attitudes in excess of 15° (See "Contour Spacings" inset on the tectonic map).

GENERAL GEOLOGY

Within the area rocks of nearly every system are present. Precambrian crystalline cores are exposed in the bold escarpments of the Oscura and San Andres Ranges with carbonate and clastic strata of Cambrian to Permian age in succession above. In the eastern part of the area several small Precambrian inliers, overlain by Permian strata, are scattered from the Gallinas Mountains on the north to the Sacramento Mountains on the south. The most extensive strata are the San Andres and Yeso Formations of Permian-Guadalupe age, and together they surface at least 75 percent of the area, mostly in very low-dipping attitudes. Cretaceous Dakota, Mancos, and Mesaverde beds underlie some 750 square miles, or nearly 10 percent of the map area, and occupy an oval-shaped area between Ruidoso and Carrizozo. A lesser area of Late Cretaceous Paleocene McRae (Cub Mountain)[1] continental sediments and middle Tertiary bedded volcanic breccias and flows occupies the base and high ridges of Sierra Blanca. All the Cretaceous and Tertiary beds are preserved along a downwarp that has been referred to as the Sierra Blanca basin (Darton, 1938, p. 215).

Numerous stocks, laccoliths, plugs, and sills of various compositions and textures are scattered throughout the area. Many of the sills are diabasic, but the stocks and laccoliths are commonly syenitic to monzonitic. Saturated to undersaturated types are prevalent, but a few, such as Capitan and the northern Gallinas laccolith, are oversaturated. Dikes are numerous and occur in profuse swarms of composite and multiple associations, especially around the large Sierra Blanca stocks. Most of these are 20 feet or less in width and range in length from a fraction of a mile to as much as four miles. The Jones dike on Chupadera Mesa is as much as 575 feet wide and is about 10 miles in length.

STRUCTURAL ELEMENTS

The structure of the Ruidoso-Carrizozo area consists of a diverse assemblage of basins, sags, slopes, uplifts, intrusive domes, laccoliths, stocks, faults, and lesser folds. The dominant structural element of the area is the broad Mescalero arch composed of the Pecos slope on the east

---

[1] There is little, if any, doubt that the so-called Cub Mountain of Bodine is the McRae Formation (Kelley and Silver, 1952, p. 115-120). The beds at Sierra Blanca are slightly more than 60 miles from the McRae exposures in the Jornado del Muerto. The general lithologies and stratigraphic successions are remarkably alike. The workers (Bodine, 1956, p. 8) who were responsible for the extra name in the Sierra Blanca country mention the similarity of the formation to the Baca and correlation with the McRae, whereas the situation is about the reverse. The Baca is different in many respects, whereas the McRae is practically identical. The responsibility of applying a new name to a sequence already named is with the proposer, and in this case it does not appear that the workers checked the McRae sections or the descriptions by Bushnell (1953, p. 22-45). The McRae was properly named in 1952; the name Cub Mountain was used in print in 1956 without adequately defining a type locality or giving a measured section with tops and bottoms. Since it still has not been properly introduced and as yet does not have formal status, the term McRae is used here for the sequence in the Sierra Blanca and Capitan areas that, with little doubt, were deposited in continuity with the McRae beds in what is termed here the McRae basin.

and declivities into the Claunch sag and Sierra Blanca basin on the west. This arch roughly follows the buried Permian Pedernal topography. Considerable modification of the arch occurs along the Lincoln County porphyry belt which also more or less follows the same course.

West of the arch the Claunch sag, Sierra Blanca basin, and Tularosa basin form a fairly continuous downwarp between the arch on the east and the Chupadera, Oscura, and San Andres line of uplifts on the west.

Faults consist of three principal types, 1) the large ones upon which the Oscura, San Andres, and Sacramento blocks are uplifted, 2) the lesser faults modifying these blocks or occurring singly or in groups near some of the igneous intrusions, and 3) those such as the Ruidoso fault zone, which somehow appear to be related to the Sierra Blanca basin. Crustal folds are not numerous, but small superficial folds in the incompetent Yeso Formation are very abundant.

The individual elements that make up the structure of the area are described and discussed below.

Claunch Sag

The Claunch sag is a southward continuation of the Estancia basin to the north of the area. The sag is about 50 miles long and 10 to 22 miles wide. On the west the sag is bounded by the Chupadera platform and the Carrizozo anticline. The eastern boundary is irregularly formed by the Gallinas, Tecolote, Jicarilla, and Lone laccolithic domes (fig. 1A). The greatest width is midway, where an eastern reentrant occurs against the small Tecolote domes (See tectonic map in pocket). The narrowest part of the sag is at the southern end, where there is a constriction between the Carrizozo anticline and the Lone dome. The Claunch sag plunges southward throughout its length into the Sierra Blanca basin at an average rate of about 50 feet per mile. The boundary on the west is taken as a low escarpment formed by the long Chupadera fault. Throw on the fault appears to reach about 350 feet in the central part. Several southwesterly plunging narrow anticlines modify the central part of the sag as shown on the tectonic map.

Tularosa Basin

The Tularosa basin is a northerly-trending depression 10 to 35 miles wide and about 130 miles long. It lies between two prominent uplifts, the westward-tilted San Andres uplift on the west and the eastward-tilted Sacramento uplift on the east. Fault scarps are especially evident along the bases of the middle parts of both uplifts.

Only the northern end of the basin is of direct concern here. In this part the basin turns from northerly to northeasterly and appears to merge with and plunge into the Sierra Blanca basin. The Tularosa basin, the Claunch sag, and the Estancia basin constitute a long regional depression despite modification by the Carrizozo anticline and the Sierra Blanca basin. In the northern end, fault boundaries to the depression either give way to downflexing or are covered by overlapping sediments. The relations are discussed further under adjoining elements and under Tectonic History and Regional Relations.

Sierra Blanca Basin

The Sierra Blanca basin is a north-northeasterly trending asymmetrical depression about 36 miles long and up to 24 miles wide. The area, as outlined by the Dakota Sandstone, is approximately 750 square miles. It lies adjacent to the Mescalero arch on the east and the Oscura uplift on the west. It is probably bounded on the southwest by a low nose or arch that may connect the Sacramento and Oscura uplifts in the subsurface beneath the Tularosa basin valley fill. On the north the basin is terminated irregularly by Lone dome and the White Oaks and Capitan faults and in part by the Mescalero arch. The northern portion of the basin has been modified locally by the Carrizo and Patos laccoliths. In a general way this basin forms a link in the regional Claunch-Tularosa depression, but the northeastern part presently froms an embayment into the Lincoln County porphyry belt.

The Sacramento uplift to the south merges with the basin through the northward-plunging Black Mountain and Cienegita anticlines. Structural relief of these folds approaches 5,000 feet.

The eastern limb of the basin gradually slopes away from the Mescalero arch to the Ruidoso fault zone, which has a throw of 1,200 to 1,400 feet. To the west of the fault zone a syncline and the Cienegita anticline are crossed prior to the final descent into the basin. The Sierra Blanca basin is the deepest depression within the area of the tectonic map. The westerly limb of the basin in T. 10 S. has an inclination of approximately 1°.

Jornado del Muerto Basin

The Jornado del Muerto basin is a long depression west of the San Andres, Oscura, and Chupadera uplifts. In the latitude of the San Andres uplift it is a broad downwarp (Darton, 1922, p. 235). Against the Oscura uplift it is bounded by a large normal fault, and west of the Chupadera platform in the extreme northern end it again appears to be a synclinal downwarp (Torres syncline). Along its length it is somewhat arcuate following the combined curved configuration of the San Andres and Oscura uplifts.

Mescalero Arch

The Mescalero arch extends from the Sacramento uplift, where the crest is in the escarpment, northeasterly to the central flank of the Capitan intrusive. North of the intrusive the arch is shifted to the west and passes through the Jicarilla intrusives and northward toward Tecolote and Corona where the crest is irregular owing to igneous intrusions and crossing of north-northeast trending folds and faults. The eastern limb of the arch consists of a gentle, more or less even, regional dip of 0.5 degree toward the Pecos Valley. Even from the crest of the Sacramento uplift to the Pecos Valley the overall regional dip of the Pecos (Sacramento) slope is only about one degree. The western limb of the arch descends or is faulted down into the Tularosa basin, into the Sier-

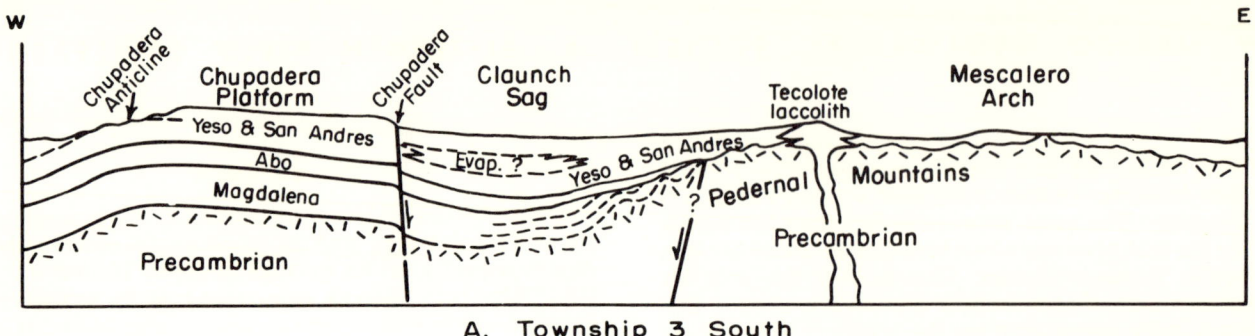
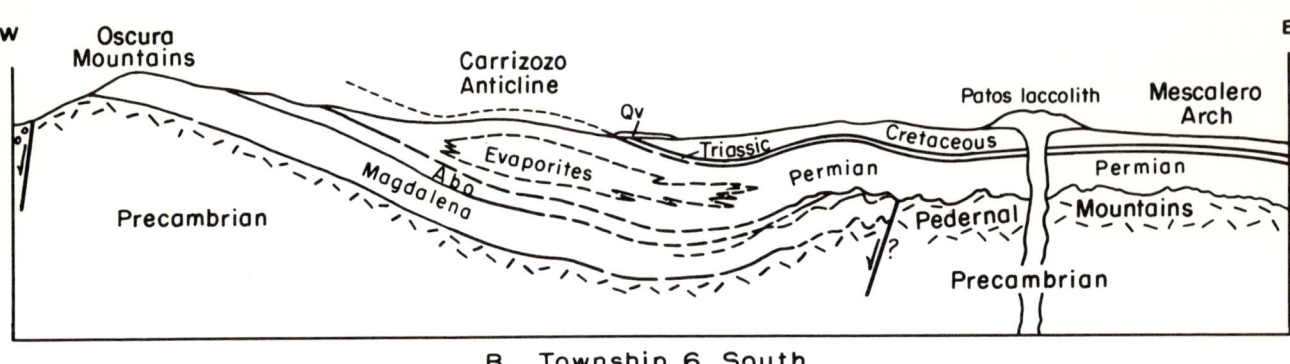
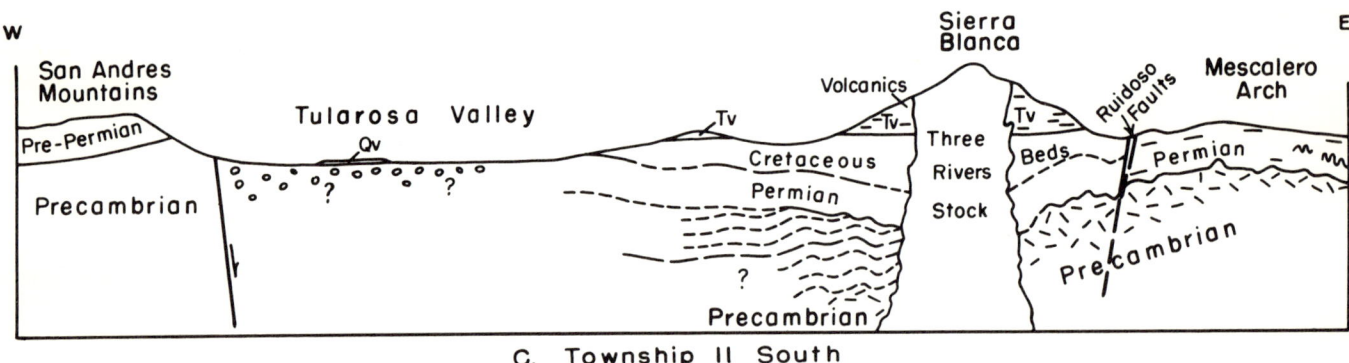
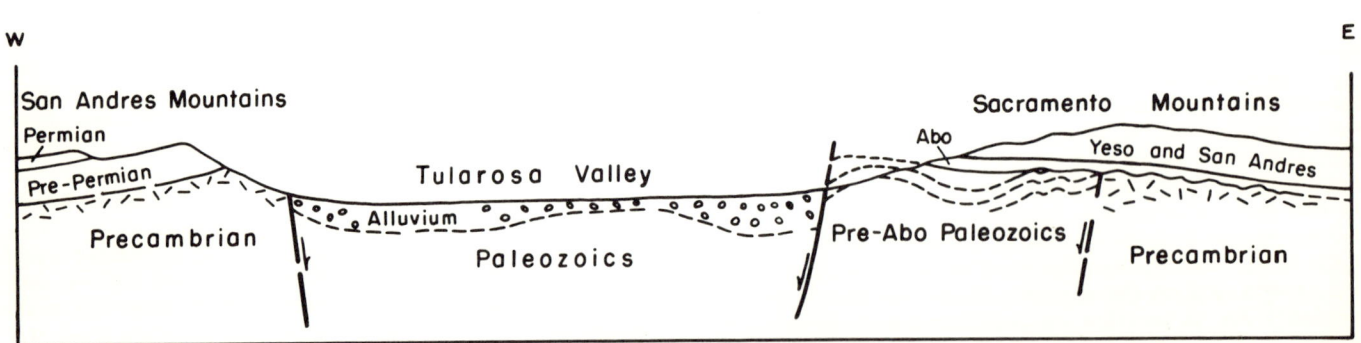

Figure 1. — Diagrammatic structure sections of the Ruidoso-Carrizozo region.

ra Blanca basin, and into the Claunch sag (fig. 1C). It is steeper than the eastern limb nearly everywhere and very irregular. The crest appears to be offset left across the Capitan intrusive and elsewhere lost in complications of irregular intrusive domes. The axis of the arch on the northern side of the Capitan intrusive is about 1,400 feet structurally lower than on the southern side. Some of the possible reasons for this are discussed under Tectonic History and Regional Relations. Where the arch is uninterrupted by modifying structures it is smooth and broad. Such places are found northwest of the Capitan intrusive, east of Capitan and Ruidoso, and north of the Gallinas uplift.

Northeast of the Sacramento uplift the crest is at about 9,000 feet on top of the Permian strata. It descends northward to about 7,500 feet south of the Capitan intrusive. Northwest of the Capitan Mountains, the crest is at about 6,300 feet at the same datum. It rises again toward Corona where, although considerably modified by the Corona syncline and other structures, it is about 7,000 feet.

Chupadera Platform

The structural Chupadera platform is the north-south table land known as Chupadera Mesa. It is the source of Darton's term (1922, Bull. 726E) Chupadera (formation) which surfaces so large a part of the region.

The Chupadera platform extends from an arbitrary northwesterly-trending boundary with the Oscura uplift, near the Yeso-San Andres contact, northward to the southwestern corner of Estancia Valley. The bench is about 45 miles long and 10 to 15 miles wide. It is bounded on the west by the crest of the Chupadera anticline. This is the Oscura anticline of Darton (1922, Bull. 726E, p. 235), and the extension of the name northward along the bench reflected his belief that fault blocks like the Oscura were broken anticlines. It appears, however, that the anticline dies out straight southward against the homocline of the Oscura block, as shown on the tectonic map, instead of curving southwestward to the Oscura fault and the plunging drag of the uplift as Wilpolt and Wanek (1951) showed.

Its eastern boundary is the heretofore unmapped Chupadera fault scarp. The Chupadera fault extends from U.S. 380 northward around a nose from the Jones dike to almost the southern end of the Estancia Valley, a distance of nearly 50 miles. The throw may be as much as 350 feet in the central part.

The Chupadera platform probably has an over-all low dip of one degree or less toward the east or southeast. In the central part it appears to be essentially flat, and there is some suggestion that the eastern edge next to the Chupadera fault may be higher locally than to the west. The area is largely inaccessible within the White Sands Proving Grounds. Numerous superficial folds in the incompetent Permian beds occur throughout the central and southern parts. Many of these folds are probably due to solution collapse and some, like the anticline over the long Jones dike, may be due to igneous intrusions. Many additional small folds might have been shown in the area if photographs had been available at the time of preparation of the map.

Oscura Uplift

The Oscura uplift is an eastward tilted fault block about 27 miles long and as much as 14 miles wide. It dips eastwardly on an overage of 10 to 15 degrees (fig. 1B). The bold western escarpment at its middle maximum development is about half a mile high. It very much resembles the Sandia Mountains with its bold Precambrian granite escarpment surmounted by a relatively thin rimrock of Pennsylvanian beds. From a structural point of view it has affinities with the Sandia and Caballo uplifts in possessing a north-plunging nose at its northern termination without a similar termination at the southern end.

Maximum throw on the frontal fault may be as much as 7,000 feet, but this is distributed, in part, in at least one step fault. In the southern part of the uplift the frontal fault swings southeasterly and parallels the hinged Mockingbird Gap graben. In the southern part of the Oscura uplift several hinged faults within the range parallel the north-northwesterly frontal fault. These faults slice the southern end of the uplift into narrow blocks, and throws are both up and down to the east on individual faults. These faults, together with those in Mockingbird Gap and in the northern, northeasterly-trending part of the San Andres uplift, form a remarkable set that appears to be mechanically related in some manner to the swing in the San Andres-Oscura uplift line and the change in the direction of tilt of the uplifts. The Yates fault is different in trend and in some aspects of throw from the faults to the south. It is pivotal, having nearly 2,400 feet of throw in the central part near the small syncline in the southern block. These features are discussed further under Tectonic History and Regional Relations.

San Andres Uplift

The San Andres uplift is nearly 80 miles long and only about 12 miles wide in its widest exposed part. It is a westerly-tilted block having generally low dips that extend beneath the valley fill of the Jornado del Muerto downwarp to the west. Precambrian rocks form the lower part of the eastern escarpment through most of its length, and in many places several thousand feet of Paleozoic rocks from Cambrian to Pennsylvanian surmount the basement up to the main skyline crest.

Local fan scarps follow the base of the uplift on the Tularosa side, attesting to the dominantly fault-block origin. Most of the southern part of the uplift is remarkably free of faults; but in the northern part they become rather numerous, especially from Rhodes Pass northward. The highest part of the uplift is Salinas Peak (altitude 9,040 feet), a prominent landmark in the region, which is held up by a large porphyry laccolith emplaced in the Pennsylvanian series.

The northern 26 miles of the uplift is crossed by a group of faults characterized by staggered offsets and pivotal movements. The tilt of the uplift decreases until at the northern end the Precambrian is exposed all the way around to the western side as in the eastward-tilted Mockingbird Gap graben and the Oscura uplift.

The Mockingbird Gap graben is about 7 miles wide. Its northwesterly-trending boundaries are covered by panfans that connect with both the Tularosa and Jornado valley fill. The structural boundaries of the graben are buried by this alluvium and, owing to the prominence of the double pass, it appears that a zone of closely spaced faults may have marked the marginal zones of subsidence. The graben itself appears to represent a sort of torque axial zone of the wide band of crossing faults between Salinas Peak and the southern end of the Oscura uplift, all of which may be a part of the mechanics of twisting the San Andres-Oscura chain from a westerly to easterly tilt. Only a small corner of the San Andres uplift is shown on the map; therefore, for these details one must consult the Geologic Map of Southwestern New Mexico (Dane and Bachman, 1961).

Sacramento Uplift

The Sacramento Uplift is a great cuesta with a bold western fault escarpment. Its over-all inclination eastward to the Pecos Valley is scarcely more than one degree. However, numerous gentle open folds, both crustal and superficial, modify the general structural slope. The western escarpment is modified by prominent folds which are, for the most part, pre-Permian and of greater structural relief than the younger folds (fig. 1D). The fault nature of the escarpment is clearly indicated by fan scarps and bedrock step faults along or near the rather even or regular base of the uplift. Pray (1961, p. 124-125) has described and mapped these faults and internal structures in some detail and has concluded that throw on the Sacramento frontal fault or fault zone into the Tularosa basin is at least 7,000 feet in the central 15 miles of the uplift.

The tectonic map joins Pray's map on the north, and the northward plunge of the uplift which begins near High Rolls, about four miles south of the tectonic map, is shown east of Tularosa. It plunges in several noses and chutes into the Sierra Blanca basin in the western part and on to the Mescalero arch south and southeast of Ruidoso. The maximum crestal altitude of the top of the known Permian beds in the Sacramento uplift is probably near 10,000 feet, and the plunge to the bottom of the Sierra Blanca basin is on the order of 6,500-7,000 feet in a distance of 35 to 40 miles. The eastern nose of the broad northward Sacramento plunge becomes the Mescalero arch, but the descent to this arch is very gradual and in 10 to 15 miles is scarcely 1,000 feet.

Lincoln County Porphyry Belt

Within the area of the tectonic map is exposed perhaps the greatest concentration of Tertiary intrusive centers in New Mexico. Between Corona on the north and Ruidoso on the south there are at least 9 stock and laccolith centers that range from about 5 to 25 square miles in outcrop area; and one, the Capitan intrusive, covers about 110 square miles. In addition, there are a number of smaller centers and countless dikes and sills.

The principal centers are as follows:

Name	Composition	Area	Form
Gallinas:			
North	Trachyte	16	Laccolith
South	Rhyolite	11	Laccolith
Tecolote	Syenite-diorite	5	Laccolith
Jicarilla	Monzonite(?)	25	Laccolith & stock(?)
Lone-Baxter	Syenite(?)	6	Stock & laccolith
Carrizo	Microgranite(?)	11	Laccolith
Patos	Monzonite(?)	7	Laccolith
Capitan	Microgranite	110	Stock & laccolith
Three Rivers	Monzonite to granite	24	Stock
Bonita Lake	Monzonite to granite	12	Stock

The Gallinas intrusives have been mapped by Kelley (1949, fig. 33) and Perhac (1961). They are dominantly two large laccoliths intruded into the Yeso Formation. The floor is locally exposed in the southern laccolith where Precambrian is found to underlie the intruded Yeso beds. In most places, however, the exposed sedimentary contact is the roof, and Glorieta and San Andres caps of the laccoliths are found on high ridges and peaks. The central part of the northern laccoliths appears to be about 1,600 feet thick. The thickest part of the southern laccolith may be no more than 800 feet. The emplacement of the laccoliths appears to have domed the general area for several miles around.

The Tecolote intrusions are a small cluster of elliptically shaped laccoliths of diverse trends. The largest one, under Tecolote Peak, is deroofed along a length of about three miles and has a principal width of about one mile. It is at least 400 feet thick. The lesser laccoliths trend northeasterly and easterly and either adjoin or lie a short distance to the south of the main laccolith. The laccoliths that immediately adjoin the main mass on the south and east are multiple, in part consisting of an earlier, lower diorite laccolith that has been intruded and superposed by the later-prevalent monzonite porphyry. Several doubly-plunging anticlines and noses in the Permian country rock near the igneous exposures suggest the presence of other small, buried laccoliths. A few small dikes and sills are present. Rawson (1957) has mapped and studied the intrusions and associated structures in detail.

The Jicarilla intrusive appears to be a major exposure of a cluster of centers lying north of the White Oaks fault. The main Jicarilla intrusive may be mostly a stock, but some of its irregular protuberances and nearby satellitic exposures may be laccoliths. Likewise, the domes and noses in Permian beds to the west in the vicinity of Ancho may be due to subsurface laccoliths that have not been deroofed. Some of these may be tongue-like or "half" laccoliths that branch in the subsurface from the main stock.

The Lone-Baxter intrusion has laccolithic and stocklike like aspects. Beds are considerably disturbed next to the main contact (Kelley, 1949, p. 154), and the Baxter Mountain salient near White Oaks appears to crosscut the Permian and Mesozoic contacts.

The Carrizo and Patos intrusions are similar and circular in outline. They are boldly exposed in steep sides. The floor of the Patos laccolith appears to dip slightly to the southeast, whereas the Carrizo intrusive has a nearly level contact with the surrounding Cretaceous rocks suggestive of a laccolith. Neither of these laccoliths is known to have a sedimentary cap.

The Capitan intrusive is about 22 miles long and 4 to 6 miles wide. It is anomalous among the other large intrusive centers in size, shape, and trend. The smooth-topped range is cut in two about one-third the length from the western end by a deep wind gap. In general, Permian strata are turned up, often steeply along its sides. Where exposed there may be considerable irregularity of the contact due to offshoots of the intrusion and local incorporation of beds. Outcrops bow around the ends, and at the western end in particular the intrusive extends beneath the Permian strata in sill-like tongues. The smooth skyline of the mountain is remarkable, and this fact led the senior author to the discovery in 1943 of outlier caps of Permian sandstone and limestone on the western top. Similar caps very likely top the smooth crest in the eastern part of the mountains. The Capitan intrusive appears to have been emplaced along a fault or north-facing monocline, inasmuch as the general structural level north of the intrusive is considerably lower than to the south.

The Three Rivers stock is the largest intrusive in the Sierra Blanca basin and forms Sierra Blanca Peak. It is roughly circular and has a tongue that extends from the main body northward 2 miles near the head of Bonita Canyon. The rock type ranges from monzonite to granite. The stock intrudes andesite flows and volcanic breccias of the Sierra Blanca Volcanics and may well have been a locus of the volcanic extrusion vents. Numerous dikes and sills are injected into the surrounding volcanics from the stock. Dikes of intermediate composition also crosscut the stock.

The Bonita Lake stock is an irregular body in the Sierra Blanca basin that forms Mon Jeau Peak and occupies the surrounding area of Bonita Lake. The rock type varies from monzonite to granite and has been intensely altered and sheared locally. Numerous dikes occupy shear zones within the stock.

Dikes

The area of the tectonic map contains a multitude of dikes. The intensity of occurrence ranges considerably, and the scale of the map and the current detail of mapping result in only the more prominent ones being shown. The greatest concentration of dikes occurs in the Sierra Blanca basin, which includes those of the well-known Capitan swarm. The dikes rang in composition but are predominantly mafic (See Elston and Snider, this guidebook).

The dominant pattern of the dikes is radial from Sierra Blanca basin and the large stocks therein. In the Three Rivers area there are some dikes that appear to be approximately concentric with the basin. In the southern part of the basin the dikes appear to parallel fold axes.

The total volume of dikes in this basin has caused a considerable extension. Jones (1951) has estimated an east-west extension of at least one mile within the Mesaverde belt of the southern part of the Capitan quadrangle.

The dikes crosscut sediments, volcanics, and, to a much lesser extent, stocks, making at least some of them the youngest rocks in the basin.

Several large dikes occur in the Chupadera platform area. The largest of these, the Jones dike, has been mapped in detail (Kelley, 1949). It trends west-northwesterly across the southern part of the bench. At Jones Camp the dike reaches a maximum width of 575 feet. The intrusion was multiple and/or composite. A central dike or part of the intrusion is hornblende monzonite about 225 feet wide. On both sides are marginal facies or perhaps separate dikes, each about 125 feet wide. The leucocratic, fine-grained marginal dikes are highly banded parallel to the steep dike walls and are intruded locally by the central dike. Numerous diabase sheets that were fed locally along the margin of the dike cut across upturned Yeso beds and spread as tonguelike sills in the Yeso to as much as a thousand feet or so from the dike. The sills are as much as 75 feet thick and occur in several horizons of the Yeso. Near the dike the Yeso is turned up at angles ranging from 50° to vertical, but the full zone of upturning is commonly 1,500 to 2,500 feet wide on either side, which fact suggests a larger, wider intrusive at depth.

Another large west-trending dike was mapped and described by Wells in 1931 (Bates, 1942, p. 291). This dike of monzonite porphyry cuts across the Chupadera anticline in T. 4 S. and is about 5½ miles long and up to 400 feet in width.

West of Gran Quivira about 15 miles along the northwestern edge of the Chupadera platform is a system of small hornblende diorite or syenodiorite dikes. These are up to 6 miles long and 500 feet wide. They have arched the Permian beds along their trends, and Bates and others (1947, p. 41-42) concluded that the dikes may have fed overlying laccoliths and sills.

White Oaks Fault

The White Oaks fault is a curving fracture some 20 miles in length that bounds the Jicarilla-Lone cluster of intrusives on the south. It is downthrown on the south to a maximum of several hundred feet near White Oaks. The development of the fault and the upthrow of the northern side appear to be partly a result of the Jicarilla intrusions and partly due to later subsidence of the Sierra Blanca basin.

Capitan Fault

The Capitan fault trends westward from the southwestern side of the Capitan intrusive. It is downthrown on the south as much as 1,300 feet northeast of the town of Capitan but decreases to the west, where it probably turns southward between McRae beds downfaulted against Mesaverde beds. To the east, the fault appears to drop Permian beds against the Capitan intrusive for several miles. No similar faults are known to bound other parts of the intrusive, and it appears probable that the Capitan fault is related to the subsidence of the Sierra Blanca basin at a time after the emplacement of the Capitan intrusive.

Ruidoso Fault Zone

The Ruidoso fault zone is a north-northeasterly trending fault zone between Sierra Blanca basin and the Mescalero arch, and it extends 25 miles from south of Ruidoso to the Capitan fault. The Capitan fault appears to be the northern boundary of the fault zone, and it is significant to note the eastward bow of the Mescalero arch, due possibly to basinward collapse along the fault zone. Along the Magado Creek fault in the central part of the zone the throw is as much as 1,400 feet, whereas to the south the zone dies out into flexures from the Sacramento uplift and into southeasterly-trending faults. In the vicinity of Ruidoso a north-northeasterly plunging syncline appears to have been formed by drag along the fault zone.

Lincoln and Related Folds

Small folds related to the incompetency of the Yeso Formation are widespread in the region and, in general, are almost coincidental with the Yeso distribution or presence at shallow depth. Although generally related to incompetency of the Yeso, their origin is diverse and due to such causes as surficial gravity effects, intrusion, solution collapse, and compressive and gravity tectonics. Especially noteworthy areas of these folds occur south and east of Corona (Fischer and Hackman, 1964), in the Claunch sag west of Tecolote, on Chupadera Mesa, around the Capitan Mountains, and in the area of the Hondo drainage. The Corona ones appear to be in part tectonic and in part collapse folds. Those on Chupadera platform are in part tectonic, in part collapse, and in part intrusive in origin.

The folds in the Hondo drainage region have been termed the Lincoln fold system (Craddock, 1960). These folds appear to be most highly developed, and are certainly best exposed, in the triangle defined by Lincoln, Arabella, and Hondo. Most of the folds are disharmonically or incompetently confined to the Yeso. Many, however, are large, and involve the Glorieta and San Andres as well. These are exemplified by the McDaniel and Tinnie anticlines, which are a few hundred to two thousand feet wide and as much as 12 miles long. Craddock in 1960 and elsewhere in this guidebook describes and illustrates these folds in detail.

In general, the fold axes are arcuate or aligned convexly to the east, about the Hondo drainage, in part, and about the eastern end of the Capitan intrusive. Most of these folds are probably tectonic or gravity tectonic in origin, but the timing and motivating causes are still problematical.

Carrizozo Anticline

The Carrizozo anticline is an elliptically shaped, doubly-plunging fold. It trends north-northeasterly and is about 17 miles long and 9 miles wide. It lies athwart the Tularosa basin-Claunch sag trend between the southern end of the Chupadera platform and the Sierra Blanca basin. The fold is broad and rather flat-topped. Closure appears to be limited by a short western limb to about 400 feet. The eastern limb is steeper than the western limb, especially along the easternmost outcrops near the Carrizozo lava flow. The fold was tested for petroleum by the Standard of Texas No. 1 J. F. Heard-Federal in 1951 to a depth of 8,050 feet. The hole was spudded in San Andres, bottomed the limestone at about 150 feet, and after drilling a Yeso section with many salt beds for about 4,300 feet, went through a more or less normal upper Paleozoic section to Precambrian gneiss.

It is said that the surface sections of Yeso thicken toward the area of the Carrizozo anticline; and, if so, the drilled thickness could indicate the presence of an evaporite basin. The lithologic logs of the well show a ratio of evaporite to clastics in the central 2,000 feet of the Yeso of about 1:1. This may be a rather low ratio for development of a salt anticline or roll. The diagrammatic relations depicted in figure 1B are intended to illustrate either a salt anticline or a primary thickness of evaporites. In either case the anticline might be nonexistent or only a terrace below the Yeso. There is also some possibility that the apparently thick section is due to folding or a low-angle fault which may have duplicated the section.

TECTONIC HISTORY AND REGIONAL RELATIONS

The Ruidoso-Carrizozo region is situated across an east-west lower Paleozoic wedge-edge belt and a north-south Pennsylvanian mountain belt. During lower Paleozoic time the borderland of the ancient Sonoran geosyncline extended from east to west through the area. A sedimentary platform (New Mexico-Texas arch, Eardley, 1962, pls. 2-6) to the north was repeatedly elevated epeirogenically along east-west hingelines that downwarped the region to the south. This caused stripping or restricted deposition to the north and preservation or increased deposition to the south. The present wedge belts of the several lower Paleozoic systems extend from the northern end of the San Andres Mountains (Tps. 9-11 S.), probably east-northeastward, beneath what is now the Sierra Blanca basin, toward Capitan.

The above postulations are for the most part based on projections of relations that may be observed in the San Andres, Oscura, and other ranges to the west. It is not possible to directly deduce the lower Paleozoic relations in the Ruidoso-Carrizozo region owing to incomplete exposures and borderland disturbances that began in Devonian and continued through Mississippian time. Beginning perhaps sometime in the Mississippian the earlier east-west lines of hinging appear to have given way to warping and truncation (Kelley and Silver, 1952, p. 88, 133) along northerly lines. By late Pennsylvanian time, and continuing through Early Permian time, the north-trending Pedernal mountains developed in full prominence along with other similar uplifts in northern New Mexico and southern Colorado. In New Mexico these have been referred to collectively as Pedernal ridge (Darton, 1922, p. 202; 1928, p. 279), Pedernal land mass (Thompson, 1942, p. 12), or Pedernal axis (Read and Wood, 1947, p. 226).

The evidence for the existence of such mountains in the Ruidoso-Carrizozo region lies in the existence of a marked unconformity at the bases of the Abo and Yeso in the area, in the conglomerate lithologies in the Pennsylvanian and Permian formations, and rapid thickness and facies changes. Continental detrital tongues in the Late Pennsylvanian (Virgilian) Holder Formation, abundant conglomerates in the Laborcita (Bursum) and Abo Formation, and local unconformities within and between these formations indicate considerable uplift and erosion to the east of the northern Sacramento escarpment (Otte, 1959, p. 92-93). Pray (1961, p. 92) also concluded that the lower Wolfcampian beds of the northern part of the uplift grade upward and eastward toward a source area into nonmarine red bed facies. Otte (1959, p. 61-62), together with Pray, found also that the abrupt thickening of the Abo, in the northern part of the Sacramento Mountains, from 500 to 1,400 feet was largely related to a sharp north- or northeast-trending eroded flex of Wolfcampian age wherein the Abo overlapped onto the highland to the east. It is difficult to determine from map and facies alone in so small an area the trend of the positive or source area. However, when viewed with the regional relations in the subsurface as well as at the surface it appears that the western escarpment of the Sacramento Mountains contains the lower western edge of the Pedernal mountains (fig. 1D). On the basis of regional exposures of the Precambrian from the Pedernal Hills in Torrance County to the Sacramento uplift, the western edge of the buried Pedernal mountains would project northward in the subsurface in Rs. 10 and 11 E. Pre-Abo folds similar to those in the Sacramento uplift with Precambrian possibly upfaulted on the east could be expected in the subsurface (fig. 1).

From Bent in Tularosa Canyon on the south to the vicinity of the Gallinas Mountains on the north several inliers of Precambrian have been found protruding nearly always through Yeso beds. In these places it is common for the Precambrian to protrude abruptly as "peaks" or "monadnocks" in middle or upper Yeso even though lower Yeso beds or Abo beds may be exposed nearby. Even in such exposures as close to each other as Red Cloud Canyon in the Gallinas Mountains and Chameleon Hill north of Corona there is considerable stratigraphic difference of position in the covering Yeso. If the Pedernal was an old age of peneplain surface, then once erosion had reached the general level of the Precambrian, the exposures would have been much more expansive than they are. It appears, therefore, that the Pedernal surface was not a peneplain but rather a mature or late-mature topography (fig. 1). As such, older strata (Permian or Pennsylvanian) may be expected in subsurface valleys or in channels or "straits" if the topography was flooded by transgressing Yeso waters. It appears that all the Pedernal topography was completely buried by the Yeso deposits with remarkably little coarse Precambrian clastics having contaminated the characteristically "clean" Yeso deposits.

The thick section of Yeso drilled in the Standard No. 1 Heard well on the Carrizozo anticline suggests that a subsiding Yeso evaporite basin existed west of the Pedernal mountains, possibly along most of the present extent of the Tularosa-Claunch sag.

During Late Permian time the region probably became emergent in the form of wide, low plains. By either very late Permian or Early Triassic time the emergence appears to have assumed the form of a westward-trending arch from near Tularosa to near Reserve in the western part of the state. Triassic and Jurassic red beds formed extensively to the north in a broad continental basin that was eventually lowered, accompanying sedimentation, by as much as two or three thousand feet. In the eastern part of the state the arch appears to have been crossed by Triassic sediments to form a connection with the Mexican geosyncline. The original Triassic and Jurassic southern sedimentary edges were eroded and removed by continued and expanded Jurassic and Early Cretaceous arching which culminated in the Dakota Formation truncating all previous Mesozoic deposits down to and through the Triassic.

Subsidence in the region continued at an accelerated rate through Late Cretaceous time. The east-west arch was obliterated or possibly retained only as a broad eastwardly-convex headland from the Cordilleran geanticline into west-central New Mexico. In Montanan time the region was dominated by floodplain conditions as represented by the Mesaverde beds. However, as indicated by Kelley and Silver (1952, p. 137) and Bushnell (1955, p. 86-87), Laramide disturbances began in this region in late Montanan time, and these caused shift from paludal-type floodplain environment of the Mesaverde to the drier depositional conditions represented by the thick McRae deposits. The similarity of the "Cub Mountain" to the more expansive and much better known outcrops of the McRae strongly suggests that the McRae basin extended across most of the region from the Rio Grande eastward to at least the Mescalero arch. The deposits of this basin are made up principally of Cretaceous and Triassic debris, but locally they derived material from sharply rising uplifts that contributed debris from rocks as old as Precambrian (Kelley and McCleary, 1960, p. 1419-1420). Furthermore, minor contemporaneous volcanism contributed at various times and places to the basin. The McRae beds reflect early Laramide deformation in their lithology, but except locally along the Caballo-Fra Cristobal uplifts to the west, they are not strongly involved in deformation that is typical of the late Paleocene of Eocene in the Rockies. Thus, the Ruidoso-Carrizozo region probably was out of the Laramide Rockies orogenic belt.

The thick Sierra Blanca Volcanics lie with considerable unconformity on beds from Mesaverde to McRae in age (fig. 2). The age of the Sierra Blanca Volcanics is not known for certain, but general relationships to the older McRae beds, on the one hand, and the intrusive stocks and regional geomorphology, on the other hand, make it fairly certain that they are not likely to be younger than Oligocene nor older than Eocene. The sequence is at least 3,340 feet thick as shown by Thompson elsewhere in this guidebook. The areal extent of the original eruptions was undoubtedly several times that of the present exposures. The base of the sequence is

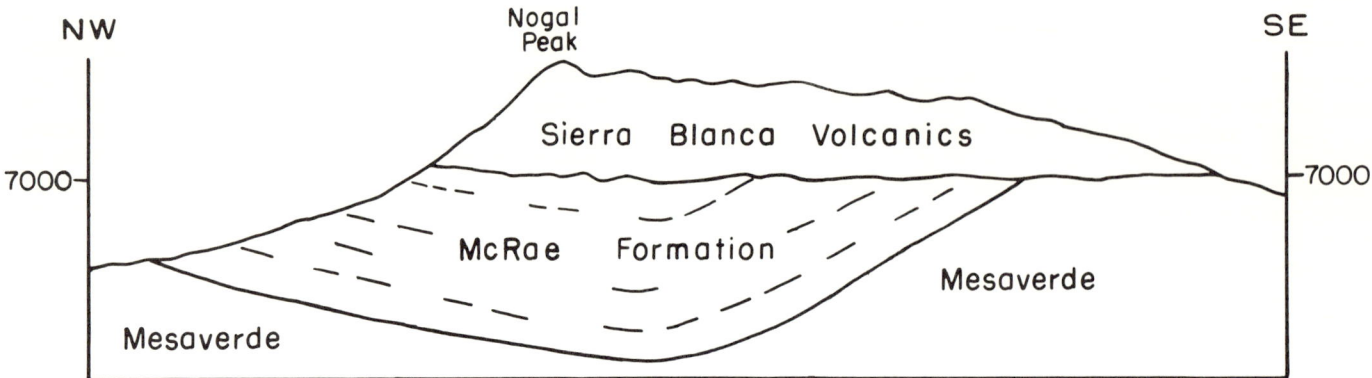

Figure 2. — Diagrammatic section through the Sierra Blanca basin showing the unconformity at the base of the Sierra Blanca Volcanics.

an irregular erosional surface having relief of a few hundred feet. The sequence is in general nearly horizontal and does not appear to have been involved in the basin as defined by the downwarping of McRae, Mesaverde, and older rocks. Except for the erosional irregularities, the general attitude of the contact with the underlying beds is rather uniform and reflects little if anything of the northeasterly-trending axis of the Sierra Blanca basin. Along the southern and southwestern margin of the volcanic pile the beds are tilted northward, apparently in continuation with the northerly plunge of the Sacramento uplift.

Beneath the nearly horizontal volcanic pile the Sierra Blanca basin axis trends northeasterly. The basin is slightly asymmetrical with the southeastern limb being steeper. The basin rims were bevelled before the volcanic eruptions, which probably issued through centers now masked and occupied by the large stocks.

If the volcanics are Eocene or Oligocene, then the principal subsidence of the Sierra Blanca basin could be late Laramide. It may be noted from the tectonic map that the Sierra Blanca basin indents or appears to deflect the Mescalero arch south of the Capitan intrusive and that similar north-northeasterly trending fold axes near Corona and Tecolote also appear to interrupt the arch trend. This relationship suggests that the Mescalero arch is older than the Sierra Blanca basin and therefore also Laramide. The regional extent of the arch and the Tularosa-Claunch sag, together with the rather obvious areal modification of both of these features by the Carrizozo anticline and the Sierra Blanca basin, serve to indicate their relative ages.

The Mescalero arch roughly follows the axis of the buried Pedernal mountains, and the Tularosa-Claunch sag appears to follow a mid-Permian Yeso downwarped evaporite basin (figs. 1A, B). Therefore, the Mescalero arch, the Tularosa-Claunch sag, and a gentle arch that probably followed the trend of the Chupadera-San Andres line of uplifts may have all formed as long, north-south, broad, open folds in Eocene (post-McRae) time. The Early Tertiary Chupadera arch was undoubtedly less prominent than the present structural platform and probably had not been modified by the Chupadera fault.

A second sag with broad and very gentle flanks may have coincided with the present Jornado del Muerto syncline.

As indicated above, the north-south arches and sags were probably followed in Eocene time by the north-northeasterly trending echelon folds including the Sierra Blanca basin, the Tecolote-Corona folds, and possibly also the Carrizozo anticline. The cause of the northeasterly-crossing structures is puzzling, but in the broader picture it is to be noted that they are parallel to, and undoubtedly part of, the turn to the northeast of the northern parts of the San Andres uplift and the Jornado del Muerto basin as well as the Rio Grande depression between the northern end of the Fra Cristobal and San Pasqual uplifts.

Volcanic eruption and intrusion of the "porphyries" probably followed the northeasterly folding. Although the porphyries may be of two or more distinctly different ages, the similarities in composition, texture, and tectonic setting appear to favor penecontemporaneous intrusion of the entire belt. If this is correct, then the key to the relative ages lies in the intrusion of the Sierra Blanca Volcanics by the stocks. Since the volcanics lie essentially unfolded above the Sierra Blanca basin, since the stocks intrude the volcanics, and since the laccoliths of the belt are correlatives of the stocks, then the intrusive centers in general are likely to be late Eocene or Oligocene. The numerous dikes in the Sierra Blanca region and, by analogy, the Jones and other large dikes, are probably also of about the same age. Some of the intrusives of the Tecolote and Jicarilla areas are shaped and aligned in a north-northeasterly direction, thereby suggesting some control by the earlier folds.

The tilted fault-block uplifts were the last of the major tectonic elements to form. The uplifting may have begun in late Miocene and continued to the present. The fault scarps of the Sacramento and San Andres uplifts appear to have followed the trends of the east and west flanks of the Laramide Tularosa sag, which in turn is thought to be controlled by a north-south sag of Yeso time. The Oscura fault probably developed along the western flank of the broad, gentle Laramide Chupadera arch. The uplifts appear to have formed out of the older arches by accelerated rise and eventual faulting of sections of the old arch flanks. By this interpretation the Tularosa basin would be a sag whose limbs were flexed up and broken by high-angle faults. The Tularosa basin would not be due to "keystone" grabening of a collapsed arch as first proposed by Herrick (1904, p. 175).

Faults such as White Oaks, Capitan, and the Ruidoso zone are probably also late Tertiary in age, although perhaps in general somewhat older than the large Basin and Range faults. The evidence for the late age of faults such as the Ruidoso and Capitan lies in the downfaulting of the sediments along the southwestern boundary of the Capitan intrusive. Under "Lincoln County Porphyry Belt," the White Oaks fault was described as being mechanically related to the emplacement of the Jicarilla cluster of intrusions, thereby implying a late Laramide timing like the intrusions. The Capitan fault might have a similar relationship to the forcible rise of the large Capitan masses. The Ruidoso fault zone, on the other hand, might be older and a part of the subsidence mechanism of the Sierra Blanca basin. However, owing to the fact that the Ruidoso zone terminates at the Capitan fault rather than being offset by it, the younger interpretation for the zone is preferred by the authors at this time. The Chupadera fault is probably late Tertiary, and its position may have been determined by an evaporite-clastic ratio change. The beds of higher evaporite content in the Claunch sag to the east may have slumped along the fault owing to either flowage or solution.

At present it is assumed that the Ruidoso, Capitan, and White Oaks faults, even if they did originate early, suffered some movement in post-intrusive time and contributed to further lowering of the Sierra Blanca basin area. But movement on these faults was not accompanied by additional downbending of the basin flanks in the Sierra Blanca Mountains. Dropping on the Ruidoso and Capitan faults was, however, accompanied by additional downwarping in the Capitan area, and this operation may have shifted the Mescalero axis eastward in the Bonito drainage area. This is discussed below in connection with the cause of the convexity of the Lincoln fold belt.

The regional relationships resulting from this study throw some light on the problem of the Lincoln folds described by Craddock in this guidebook and elsewhere (1960). As indicated above, the sharp folds in the Yeso and San Andres display arcuate patterns partly about an axis roughly defined by the Hondo drainage and partly around the eastern end of the Capitan intrusive. The latter folds were either formed by longitudinal eastward push by the intrusive or, if of earlier age, simply deflected convexly eastward by the intrusion. The arcuate disposition of the folds across the Hondo drainage is more puzzling. There appears to be little doubt that most of the folds are shallow and bottom in the incompetent Yeso Formation. The folds in the Yeso are generally closed and more or less upright except that they are slightly asymmetrical to the west in places (Craddock, 1960, p. 37). Craddock has concluded that the folds are principally due to gravity detachment and movement in the direction of the regional dip. Of this there is little doubt; but our work reveals no "early" Sierra Blanca intrusions that created the eastward tilt, but rather that the tilt preceded the intrusions. The "focus" of the Lincoln fold arc (Craddock, 1960, p. 42) in the Sierra Blanca intrusives is fortuitous, and there is no eastward crustal bowing that appears directly attributable to the intrusives. Instead, the arcuate arrangement of the Lincoln folds is nearly concentric with respect to the northeastern edge of the Sierra Blanca basin. The basin succeeded the Mescalero arch and appears to have moved it eastward, south of the Capitan intrusive, possibly both before and after the intrusion. It is possible that this "rolling" eastward of the Mescalero axis by encroachment of the basin may have added sufficient tectonic overpressure to the gravity stresses in the Lincoln-Hondo area to cause the convex bending of the folds.

One of the principal yet unnoted structural anomalies in the region is marked difference in position and structural altitude north and south of the Capitan intrusive. The left "offset" or shift in the axis of the Mescalero arch is about 9 miles, and the crest of the Mescalero arch south of the intrusive is about 1,600 feet higher than the Pecos slope directly to the north of the intrusive. It is also to be noted that the "shift" involves more than just the area near the intrusive, for the northerly-trending 6,200-foot structural contour along the southeastern border of the map is some 12 to 18 miles east of the same contour to the north of the intrusive. It is possible that the higher structure on the south is somehow related as a counterpart to the large downwarping of the Sierra Blanca basin. We have suggested above that the downwarping of the northern end of the basin "rolled" back the arch and caused its eastward shift. However, if the basin caused the general rise and shift of contours to the east, then the contours should shift westward again along the regional slope of the Sacramento uplift; and this does not seem to be the case. Therefore, it appears that the Capitan intrusive merely followed an easterly-trending fault or downflex to the north. This cannot be the Capitan fault, which is of opposite throw, unless pivotal movement is inferred. The strong structural anomaly across the Capitan intrusive lends greater importance to the regional alignment described below as the Capitan lineament.

The twist in the structure at Mockingbird Gap has been described above. The origin has long been puzzling to geologists who have observed it. It is to be noted on a geologic map of New Mexico that there is a large deflection of the San Andres uplift to the northeast north of Rhodes Pass. Similar or parallel deflections affect the Jornado and Tularosa basins, the northern Sacramento or Mescalero arch, and the course of the Rio Grande from the northern end of the Fra Cristobal Range to about 20 miles south of Socorro. Thus, the deflection of the San Andres uplift is part of a zone some 30 miles wide in a northeasterly direction that extends northwesterly from near the northern end of the Sacramento uplift to the Rio Grande, a distance of about 80 miles. The zone of deflection may be due to a large, plastic, right shift in the subcrust.

Although the Mockingbird Gap could be related to the mechanics of the large deflection, it appears more likely that it is the result of longitudinal growth of two oppositely inclined flexes and tilt blocks to a junction zone where the pivotal faults and general structural twist would develop. The "deflections" described above, if indeed they are deformational rather than the mere "following" of some older basement trend, probably formed prior to the late Tertiary uplifts which gave rise to the Mockingbird Gap structures.

Through the middle of the region there is a rather remarkable alignment of igneous features that has regional extensions considerably beyond the area. This alignment includes the Jones dike, the basaltic craters of the Carrizozo lava flows, the blunt northern end of the Carrizozo anticline, and the great Capitan intrusive with its included downflex. To the east, on more or less the same line, are long dikes east of Roswell and still farther in Texas, the Matador arch. This alignment, which may be referred to as the Capitan lineament, appears to have some coincidence and parallelism with the lower Paleozoic hinge zone. This zone of depositional trends was also evident throughout Triassic, Jurassic, and Early Cretaceous times when it served generally and broadly as the divide between the Mexican geosyncline to the south and the continental depositional basins to the north. The lineament is certainly old, perhaps even Precambrian, and has played an important role in the Ruidoso-Carrizozo region. The alignment of intrusives along the Capitan lineament suggests that the ancient hinge was in part a fracture zone. The strong structural decline to the north across the Capitan intrusive suggests this also. If this is an older feature, there may be stratigraphic and paleogeographic changes to the north of the intrusive that would be important to oil exploration.

The westerly-trending hinge has apparently been dormant or "crossed" at times by strong and persistent northerly trends. Such trends apparently started in Mississippian time along the Rio Grande to the west in the form of an arch. The Ruidoso-Carrizozo region did not experience the northerly-trending disturbances until Late Pennsylvanian time, when the Pedernal mountains developed from Colorado to the Mexican border. This great orogenic development set up north-trending folds and uplifts that, although deeply eroded or buried in succeeding times, still exerted a strong control upon the Tertiary and present tectonic features.

The following is a summary list of the order of tectonic and related geologic events which have affected the Ruidoso-Carrizozo region:

1. Periodic southward tilting into the Sonoran geosyncline. *Cambrian to Mississippian.*
2. Epeirogenic uplift and erosion. *Late Mississippian.*
3. a. Rise and folding of the north-trending Pedernal mountains. *Late Pennsylvanian.*
   b. Deep erosion and thick marginal continental deposition. *Late Pennsylvanian and Early Permian.*
4. Subsidence and complete burial of the mountain topography accompanied by some sagging on either side of the Pedernal uplift. *Middle Permian.*
5. Widespread stripping with probable return of the east-west arch. *Late Permian.*
6. Broadening and general rise of the arch across southern New Mexico. *Triassic.*
7. a. Overlapping from the north upon the southern source highlands. *Triassic and Jurassic.*
   b. Uplift and northward stripping followed by overlapping of Entrada beds. *Middle Jurassic.*
8. Broad uplift of the east-west arch followed by widespread southward truncation of beds down to Permian accompanied by overstepping of Lower Cretaceous beds. *Early Cretaceous.*
9. Deep burial by Cretaceous Mesaverde floodplain deposits of regional expanse. *Montanan.*
10. Some disturbance and formation of the Tertiary McRae basin across south-central New Mexico. Local uplifts and volcanism as forerunners of Laramide orogeny. *Laramian and Paleocene.*
11. Warping along lines of the old Pedernal mountains with development of broad, open alternating anticlines and synclines which were from east to west: Mescalero arch, Claunch-Tularosa sag, Chupadera-San Andres arch, and the Jornado del Muerto sag. *Eocene(?).*
12. Deep-seated plastic shift causing northeastward deflection in the Tularosa sag, Mescalero arch, San Andres arch, and Jornado del Muerto sag. Formation of the Sierra Blanca basin, Carrizozo anticline, and the Corona folds. Erosional truncation. *Eocene(?).*
13. Eruption of the Sierra Blanca Volcanics. *Late Eocene(?).*
14. Intrusion of stocks, laccoliths, and dikes. Some associated faulting. *Late Eocene or Oligocene(?).*
15. a. Some growth of the Mescalero arch and other arches and sags to the west.
    b. Dropping of the Sierra Blanca basin on the Ruidoso and Capitan faults.
    c. Increased tilt of Pecos slope and Sacramento cuesta. Probable time of maximum development of Lincoln-type folds.
    d. Monoclinal flexing begins uplift of Sacramento, San Andres, and Oscura uplifts.
    Miocene.
16. a. Monoclinal flexes develop into Basin and Range faults and the major uplifts rise with reference to the basins.
    b. Wide pedimentation extends into the area from the east.
    c. Deep erosion of the fault scarps and the Sierra Blanca volcanic pile.
    d. Deposition of alluvial fill in the Tularosa basin.
    Pliocene.
17. a. Continued uplift of fault blocks; fan scarps.
    b. Minor glaciation on Sierra Blanca Peak.
    c. Accumulation of White Sands.
    d. Eruption of the Carrizozo basalt flows.
    Quaternary.

REFERENCES CITED

Bates, R. L., and others, 1942, The oil and gas resources of New Mexico: New Mex. Bur. Mines and Min. Res. Bull. 18, 320 p.

——————1947, Geology of the Gran Quivira quadrangle, New Mexico: New Mex. Bur. Mines and Min. Res. Bull. 26, 57 p.

Bushnell, H. P., 1953, Geology of the McRae Canyon area, Sierra County, New Mexico; Univ. New Mex. Master's Thesis, 106 p.
────── 1955, Mesozoic stratigraphy of south-central New Mexico, in Guidebook of south-central New Mexico: New Mex. Geol. Soc. Sixth Field Conf. Guidebook, p. 81-87.
Craddock, Campbell, 1960, The origin of the Lincoln fold system, southeastern New Mexico, in Structure of the earth's crust and deformation of rocks: Internat. Geol. Cong., 21st, Norden, Rept., pt. 18, p. 34-44.
Dane, C. H., and Bachman, G. O., 1961, Preliminary geologic map of the southwestern part of New Mexico: U.S. Geol. Survey Misc. Geol. Inv. Map I-344.
Darton, N. H., 1922, Geologic structure of parts of New Mexico: U.S. Geol. Survey Bull. 726-E, 275 p.
────── 1928, "Red beds" and associated formations in New Mexico, with an outline of the geology of the state: U.S. Geol. Survey Bull. 794, 356 p.
Eardley, A. J., 1962, Structural geology of North America: New York, Harper & Row, 743 p.
Fischer, W. A., and Hackman, R. J., 1964, Geologic map and sections of the Torrance Station 4 NE quadrangle, Lincoln County, New Mexico: U.S. Geol. Survey Misc. Geol. Inv. Map I-400.
Griswold, G. B., 1959, Mineral deposits of Lincoln County, New Mexico: New Mex. Bur. Mines and Min. Res. Bull. 67, 117 p.
Herrick, C. L., 1904, Lake Otero, an ancient salt lake basin in southeastern New Mexico: Am. Geol., v. 34, p. 174-189.
Jones, S. M., 1951, Regional tectonics of the Lincoln-White Oaks-Chupadera Mesa area, in Capitan-Carrizozo-Chupadera Mesa region, Field trip no. 5, Roswell Geological Society.
Kelley, V. C., 1949, Geology and economics of New Mexico iron-ore deposits: Univ. New Mex. Pub. in Geol. no. 2, 246 p.
────── 1952, Origin and pyrometasomatic zoning of the Capitan iron deposits, Lincoln County, New Mexico: Econ. Geology, v. 47, p. 64-83.
────── 1955, Regional tectonics of the Colorado Plateau and relationship to the origin and distribution of uranium: Univ. New Mex. Pub. in Geol. no. 5, 120 p.
────── and McCleary, J. T., 1960, Laramide orogeny in south-central New Mexico: Am. Assoc. Petroleum Geologists Bull., v. 44, p. 1419-1420.
────── and Silver, Caswell, 1952, Geology of the Caballos Mountains, with special reference to regional stratigraphy and structure and to mineral resources including oil and gas: Univ. New Mex. Pub. in Geol. no. 4, 286 p.
Meinzer, O. E., and Hare, R. F., 1915, Geology and water resources of Tularosa Basin, New Mexico: U.S. Geol. Survey Water-Supply Paper 343, 317 p.
Otte, Carel, Jr., 1959, Late Pennsylvanian and early Permian stratigraphy of the northern Sacramento Mountains, Otero County, New Mexico: New Mex. Bur. Mines and Min. Res. Bull. 50, 111 p.
Perhac, R. M., 1961, Geology and mineral deposits of the Gallinas Mountains, New Mexico: Univ. Michigan dissertation.
Pray, L. C., 1961, Geology of the Sacramento Mountains escarpment, Otero County, New Mexico: New Mex. Bur. Mines and Min. Res. Bull. 35, 144 p.
Rawson, D. E., 1957, The geology of the Tecolote Hills area, Lincoln County, New Mexico: Univ. New Mexico Master's Thesis, 77 p.
Read, C. B., and Wood G. H., Distribution and correlation of Pennsylvanian rocks in late Paleozoic sedimentary basins of northern New Mexico: Jour. Geology, v. 55, p. 220-236.
Thompson, M. L., 1942, Pennsylvanian system in New Mexico: New Mex. Bur. Mines and Min. Res. Bull. 17, 92 p.
Wilpolt, R. H., and Wanek, A. A., 1951, Geology of the region from Socorro and San Antonio east to Chupadera Mesa, Socorro County, New Mexico: U.S. Geol. Survey Oil & Gas Inv. Map OM 121, Sheet 1.

THE LINCOLN FOLD SYSTEM*

Campbell Craddock

University of Minnesota
Minneapolis, Minnesota

INTRODUCTION

In the walls of the valley of the Rio Bonito at Lincoln, New Mexico, the Yeso formation contains large folds that provide a startling contrast with the low dips of the formation prevalent in the surrounding region, and in the overlying San Andres Limestone. Field work revealed that these Permian formations show similar crumpling over an area of at least 3,500 square miles (fig. 1). The incompetent Yeso is generally folded where well exposed, but the San Andres Limestone is flat lying over most of the region and only locally buckled into sharp narrow folds. Previous investigations have dealt with these folds incidentally or have been confined to a few anticlines or localities. During this study a number of unmapped folds have been discovered. This paper summarizes the distribution and probable origin of all these folds, designated here the Lincoln fold system. An index map (fig. 2) shows the location of areas portrayed on the more detailed tectonic maps (figs. 3-7).

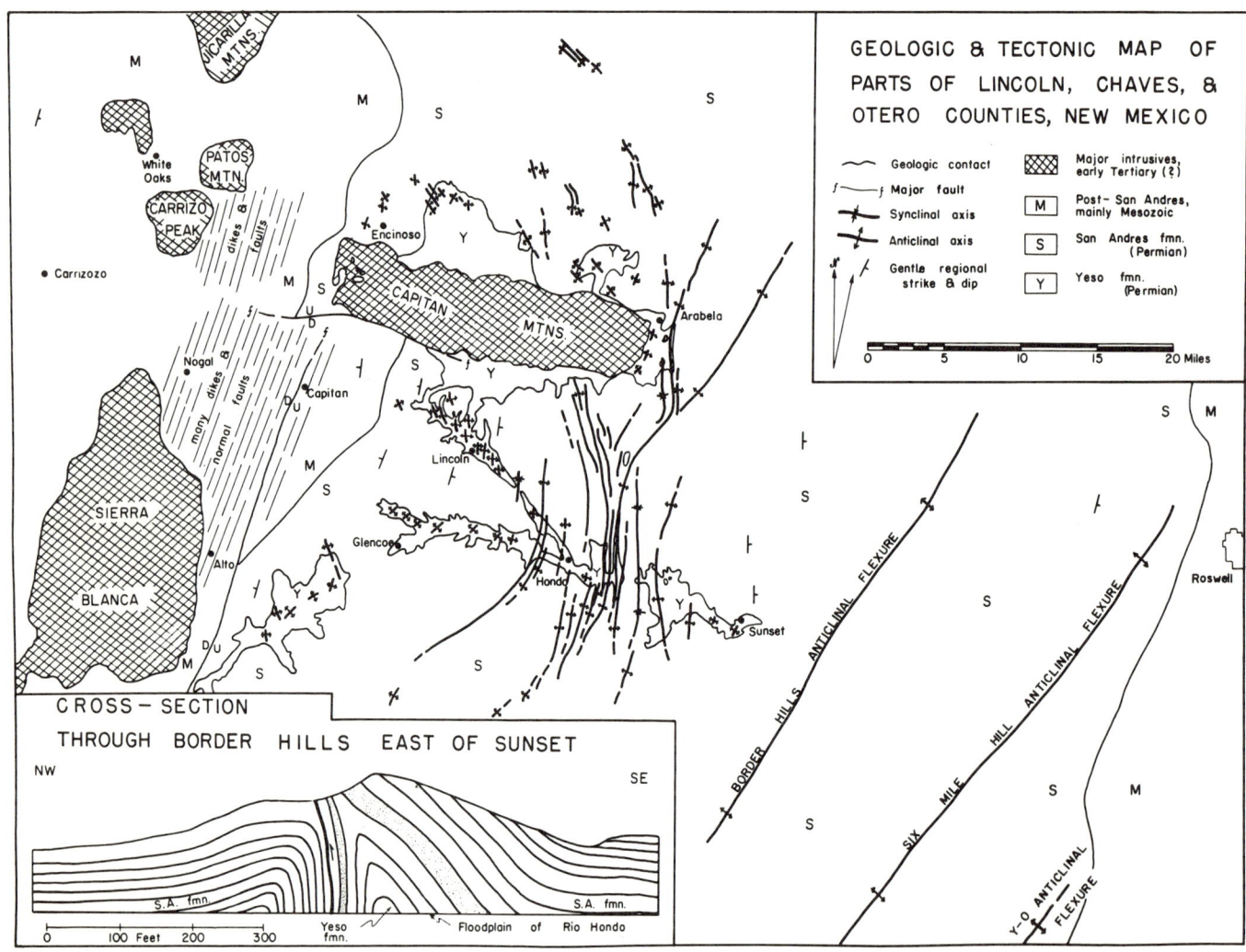

Figure 1. — Regional geologic and tectonic map.

*This article is an enlargement of a paper published in the Report of the International Geological Congress, 21st Session, Report, part 18, p. 34-44, Copenhagen, 1960.

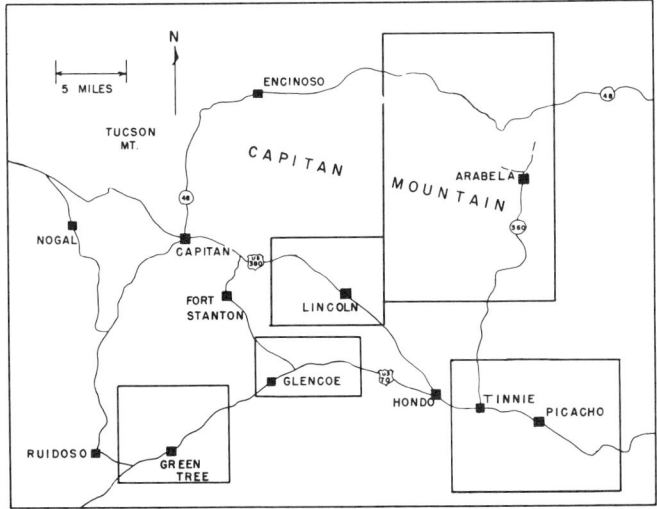

Figure 2. — Index map showing location of detailed tectonic maps.

The deformed region includes parts of Lincoln, Chaves, and Otero Counties and lies between the Great Plains to the east and the Cordilleran mountain system, expressed to the west in a series of north-south fault-block ranges. Over most of the map area the surface formations are Permian strata that dip almost 1° to the east or east-southeast. West of Lincoln these beds form a broad arch and descend westward with dips of 5 to 15° into a structural basin of middle Tertiary age with an igneous complex underlying its mountainous axis. South and southeast of Sierra Blanca is the Sacramento-Guadalupe Range, a gently eastward and northeastward dipping homocline separated from the desert basins to the west by major normal faults. Southeast of the map area is the important petroleum province, the Permian basin of west Texas and New Mexico. Throughout most of the west half of the map area lower Permian formations rest on a Precambrian basement, which indicates the existence of a south-trending rib of land in late Pennsylvanian and early Permian time. Lower Paleozoic formations occur east, south, and west of this buried landmass.

The writer learned of the Lincoln folds in 1954 and has worked on them intermittently since then. Preliminary reconnaissance on aerial photographs was followed by field study during the summers of 1957-59. Thanks are due Professor John Eliot Allen of Portland State College, Dr. Robert H. Weber of the New Mexico Bureau of Mines and Mineral Resources, and Mr. Walter A. Mourant of the U.S. Geological Survey for providing unpublished information from their work in various parts of the area and for help and encouragement during the field work. The writer expresses his gratitude to Harvey Meyer, Howard Stensrud, Neil Muncaster, John Anderson, and Jack O'Brien for assistance in the field. Mr. Mark D. Wilson has been both generous and helpful in sharing his broad experience in the regional geology of the area. This work was made possible by grants from the Graduate School of the University of Minnesota.

STRATIGRAPHY

Over most or all of the map area the Yeso Formation is separated from the basement by less than a few hundred feet of lower Permian red beds and locally some Pennsylvanian strata (Dunn, 1954). One of the Picacho wells, six miles southwest of Sunset, penetrated about 300 feet of pre-Yeso clastic rocks above the basement; farther north the Yeso lies directly on the Precambrian (Lloyd, 1949).

The Yeso is the oldest formation exposed in the map area and generally consists of 1,200 to 1,800 feet of siltstone, limestone, shale, mudstone, and evaporites (Pray, 1954). The lower Yeso does not crop out here, but where it is exposed to the southwest along the Sacramento escarpment red beds and evaporites are the predominant rocks. An incomplete section measured in the Bonito valley just east of Lincoln canyon (fig. 8) included 480 feet of Yeso, 65 percent siltstone and mudstone, 25 percent limestone, and 10 percent gypsum. The limestones form 14 to 35 foot units interbedded in the siltstone and their resistance to weathering causes the magnificient fold exposures at this locality. Above the uppermost limestone and below the base of the San Andres is a unit of red siltstone and gypsum of widely varying thickness. Seven sections measured through this interval ranged from 30 to 224 feet in thickness, and had a mean thickness of 100 feet. Single beds of gypsum as much as 40 feet thick occur in some of these sections, but evaporites are absent in others.

The San Andres Limestone consists of the Glorieta Sandstone Member and an overlying limestone member. The Glorieta, equivalent to the Hondo Sandstone Member of Lang (1937, p. 850), was measured east of state road 368 miles south of Arabela. At this locality it is 131 feet thick, and includes 60 feet of limestone and 71 feet of sandstone and siltstone. The upper unit is a 38-foot bed of massive, cross-bedded, fine-grained, yellow to buff sandstone which makes a distinctive key bed throughout the area. The overlying limestone member consists of rather uniform 3 to 24 inch beds of finely crystalline, medium to dark gray limestone and dolomitic limestone; beds of gypsum as much as 16 feet thick occur locally. The total thickness of the San Andres is about 1,000 feet.

No evidence of an unconformity between the Yeso and San Andres could be found in the field. At first glance the exposures near Lincoln (fig. 9) seem to exhibit such evidence but the contact was observed closely at 37 localities over the area and the two formations were found to be parallel and conformable in all cases.

Post-San Andres formations are preserved in the east near Roswell and in the west in the Sierra Blanca basin. These formations include the Chalk Bluff Formation of Permian age — 500 feet of siltstone, gypsum, sandstone, and limestone; the Dockum Group of Triassic age — 375 feet of variegated shale and coarse clastics; the Dakota Sandstone of upper Cretaceous age — 135 feet, the Mancos Shale, of upper Cretaceous age — minimum, 390 feet, and the Mesaverde Formation of upper Cretaceous age — minimum, 630 feet; Cub Mountain Formation of Bodine, 1956 — 2,200 feet of conglomerate, sandstone, siltstone, and variegated shales; and pediment surfaces of Pliocene(?) age veneered with ig-

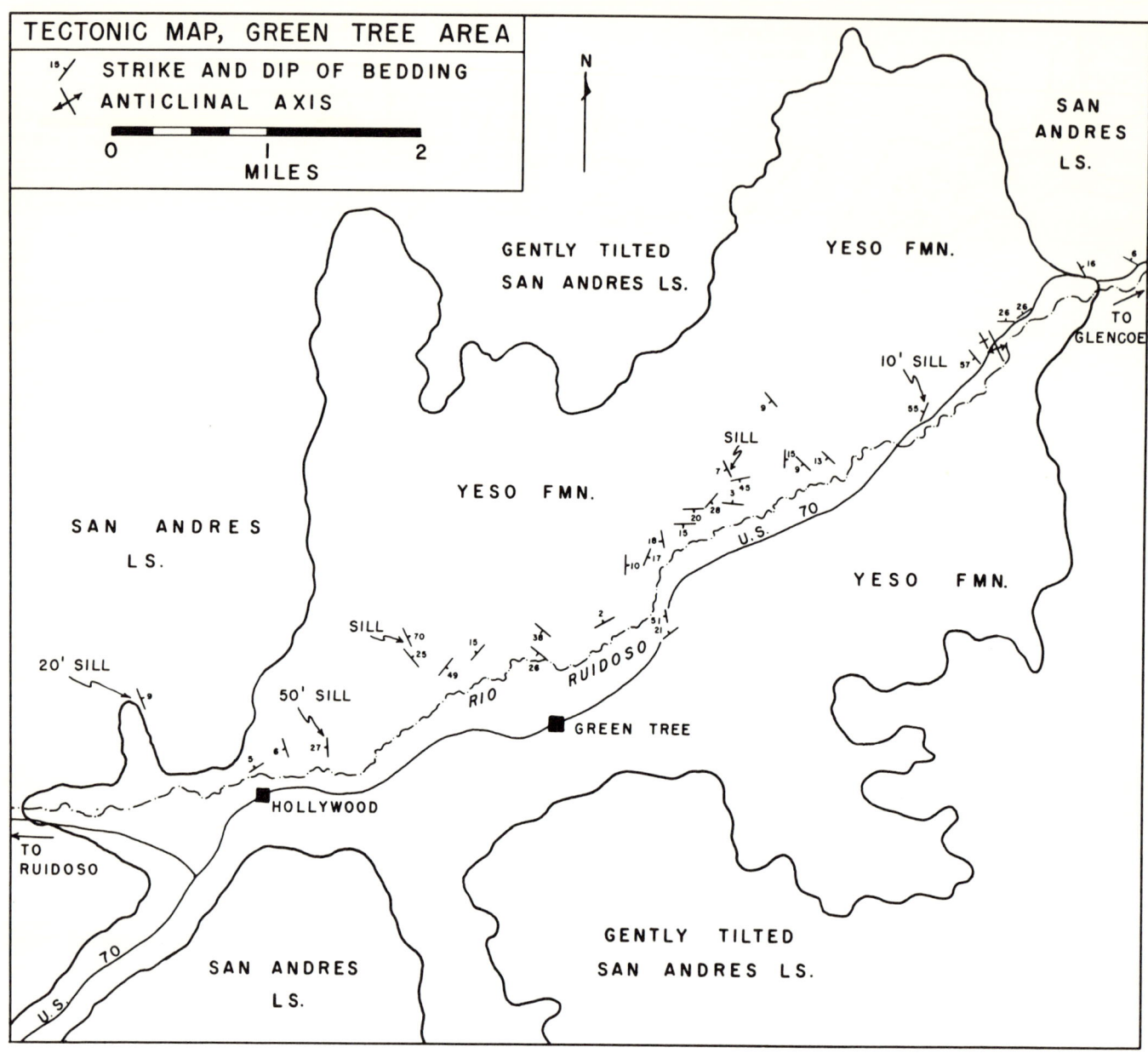

Figure 3. — Tectonic map, Green Tree area.

neous and limestone pebbles. The Cub Mountain Formation might be Upper Cretaceous (Bodine, 1953, p. 14; Kottlowski, and others, 1956) although reportedly it is separated from the Mesaverde by a substantial disconformity. Hence the section consists of a competent igneous and metamorphic basement, a 2,000-foot layer of incompetent fine-grained clastics and evaporite, a 1,000-foot plate of competent carbonate beds, and a cover of as much as 4,200 feet of younger formations — the lower 875 feet of which is mainly incompetent fine-grained clastics and evaporites.

CENOZOIC IGNEOUS ROCKS

The north-northeast trending axis of the Sierra Blanca basin is occupied by an igneous complex the detailed history of which has yet to be established. Geologists who have examined the area (Lindgren, 1910; Semmes, 1920; Knapp, 1933; Patton, 1951; Kelley, 1952; Bodine, 1953; Allen and Ferebee, manuscript) seem to agree however, that a widespread intrusive phase was followed by generally later volcanic activity which has continued into Recent time. Igneous rock fragments have not been reported in the Cub Mountain Formation, but it is crosscut by some of the intrusives in the main Sierra Blanca mass. On this basis the beginning of intrusive activity has commonly been dated as early Tertiary. It could have been late Cretaceous if the Cub Mountain should prove to be that old, or it might have been as late as middle Tertiary.

The intrusives of the early phase were emplaced as

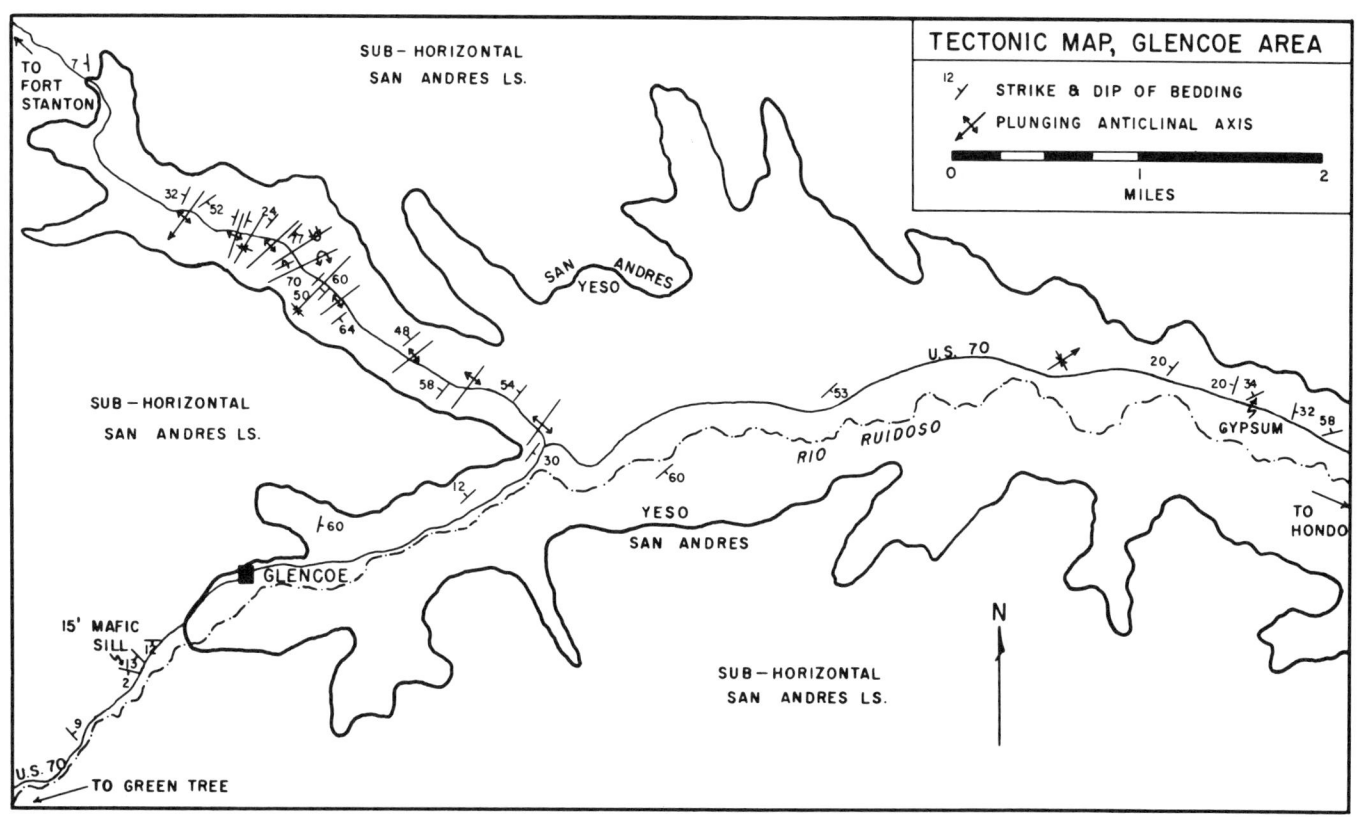

Figure 4. — Tectonic map, Glencoe area.

dikes, sills, stocks, and laccoliths, probably prior to the formation of the present structural depression. These rocks are of intermediate to felsic composition, and many are porphyritic; rocks reported from these intrusives include monzonite, diorite, syenite, and alaskite.

The main extrusives are a series of intermediate to felsic tuffs and agglomerates overlain by andesitic flows (Bodine, 1953, p. 16). The older volcanics are cut in many places by basic dikes, but few of these intrusives penetrate the upper flows. Bodine (1953) and Allen and Ferebee (manuscript) give conflicting interpretations of the relative ages for the dike swarm and the faults. This may be due to dike emplacement during both the intrusive and extrusive phases. Or it may imply that volcanism, subsidence, faulting, and dike emplacement all proceeded contemporaneously during the second igneous phase, or its early stages.

The area east of the Sierra Blanca basin contains scattered intrusives, similar in composition and probably in age to those in the main complex. The largest intrusive forms the Capitan Mountains, and is an unroofed pluton 4 to 5 miles wide and 21 miles long. It has been described by various writers as being composed of aplite, rhyolite, microgranite, and alaskite. The writer believes it is younger than the first intrusives in the main Sierra Blanca complex though it may be contemporaneous with some of the more felsic plutons. Eastward from Sierra Blanca to Arabela and almost to Sunset intermediate sills, described as andesite by Semmes (1920, p. 427) occur in the upper Yeso and the lower San Andres. At least some of these sills are older than the Capitan Mountains pluton, on the basis of truncation of the sills by the pluton south of Arabela.

DESCRIPTION OF THE FOLDS
The Yeso Folds

The Yeso Formation is exposed only in the valleys of the principal streams and along the margins of major plutonic bodies, especially the Capitan Mountains. Almost everywhere it crops out, the Yeso is moderately to strongly folded. Many details in the field attest to its mobility during deformation, particularly in the uppermost siltstone and gypsum unit. Three steeply-dipping clastic dikes 3, 5, and 15 feet in width were observed in the upper Yeso and the Glorieta Sandstone and consist of a siltstone matrix and subangular blocks of older sedimentary units. Since the first two occupy small faults and the last a fracture parallel to the crest of an anticline, it is probable they were injected from below during the folding and faulting. West of Lincoln many faults trend about N. 30° E. and offset the base of the San Andres 15 to 20 feet; the uppermost beds of the Yeso have flowed around the subsiding block and are nearly vertical. In the valleys northwest of Lincoln are some small, sharp east-west folds (fig. 7) which are probably younger than the larger main folds. The faults may be related to the formation of the Sierra Blanca basin and the east-west folds to the emplacement of the Capitan Mountains pluton; this suggests the Yeso may have been mobile over a considerable time span and not merely during the main folding.

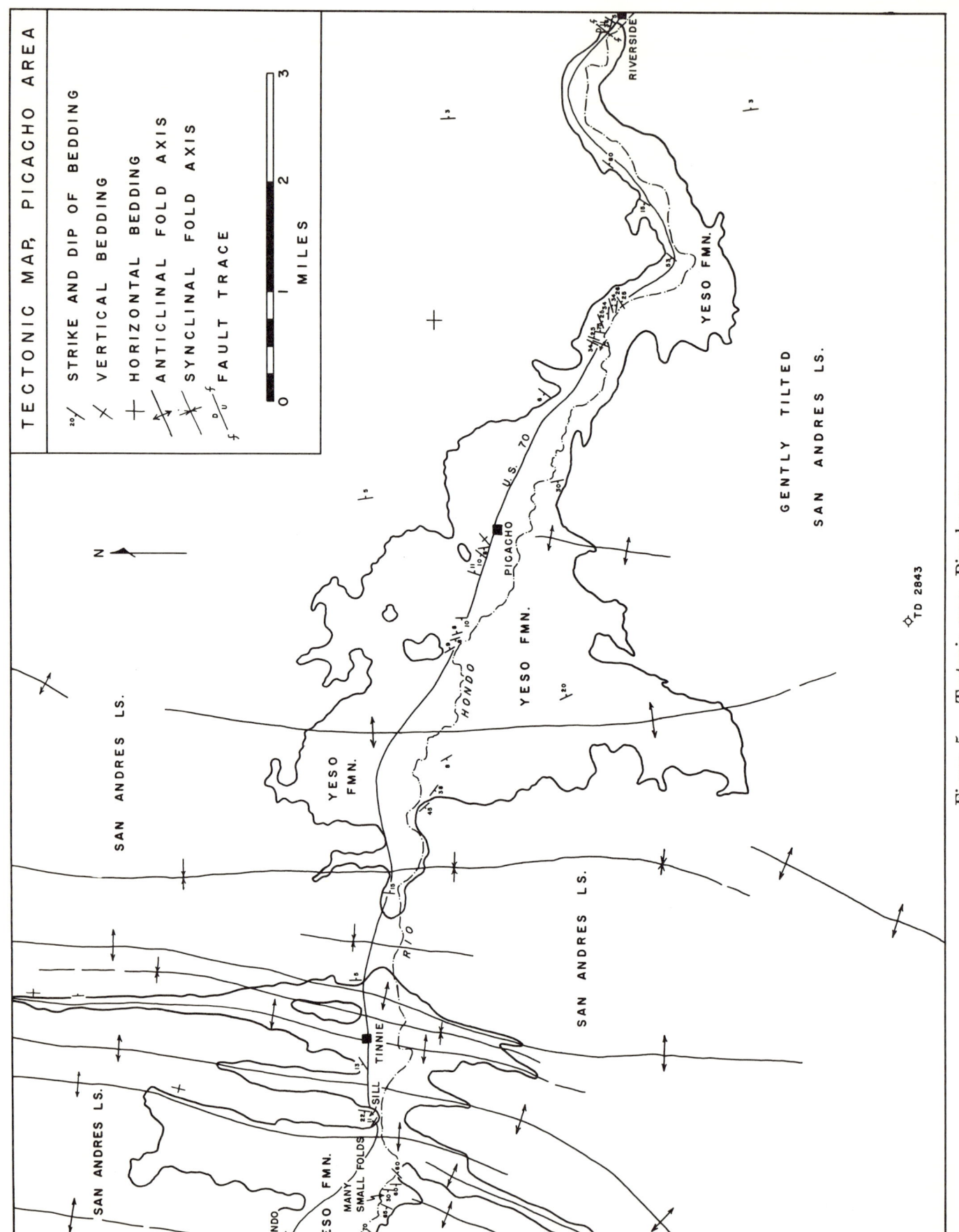

Figure 5.— Tectonic map, Picacho area.

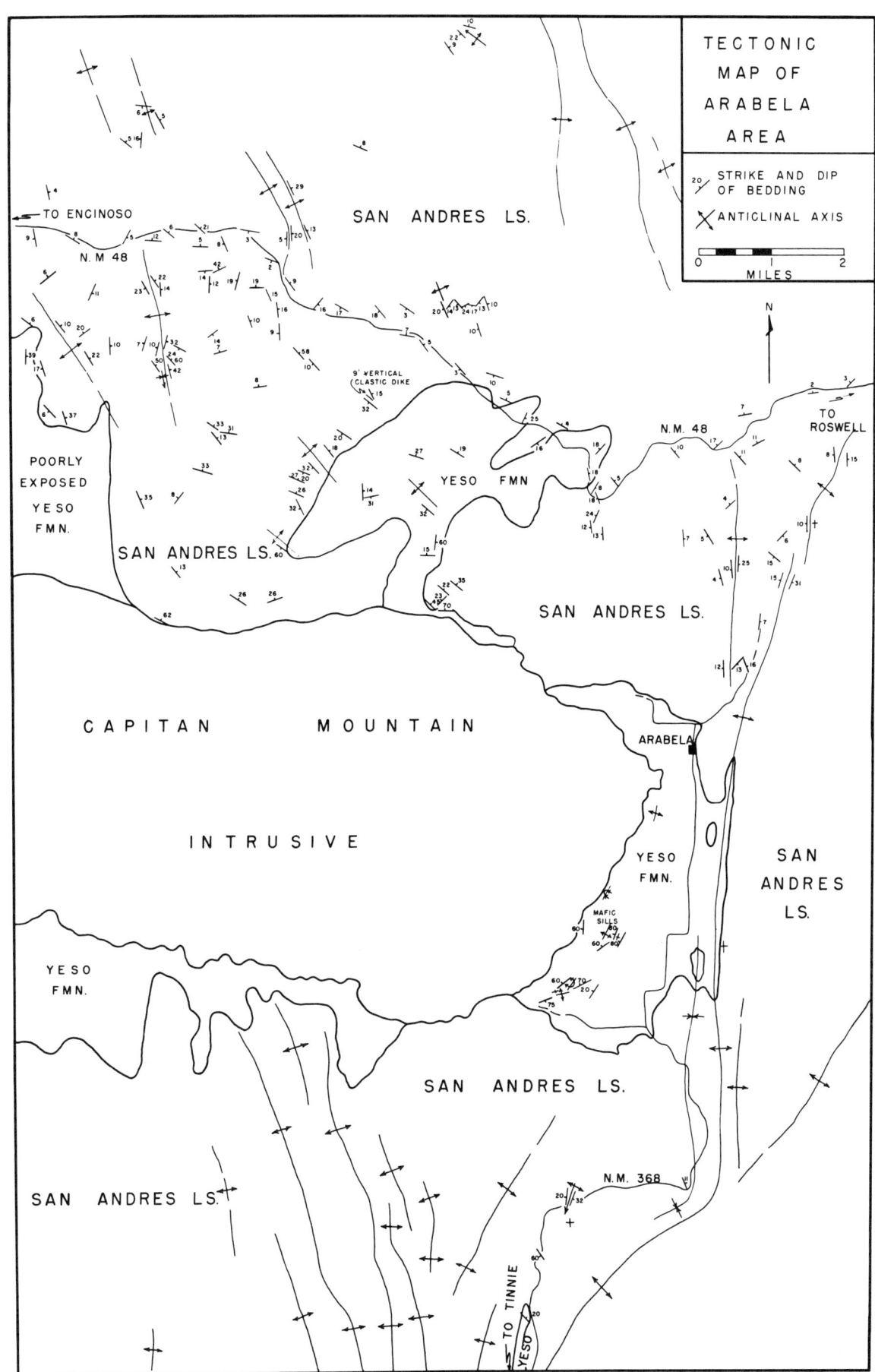

Figure 6. — Tectonic map, Arabela area.

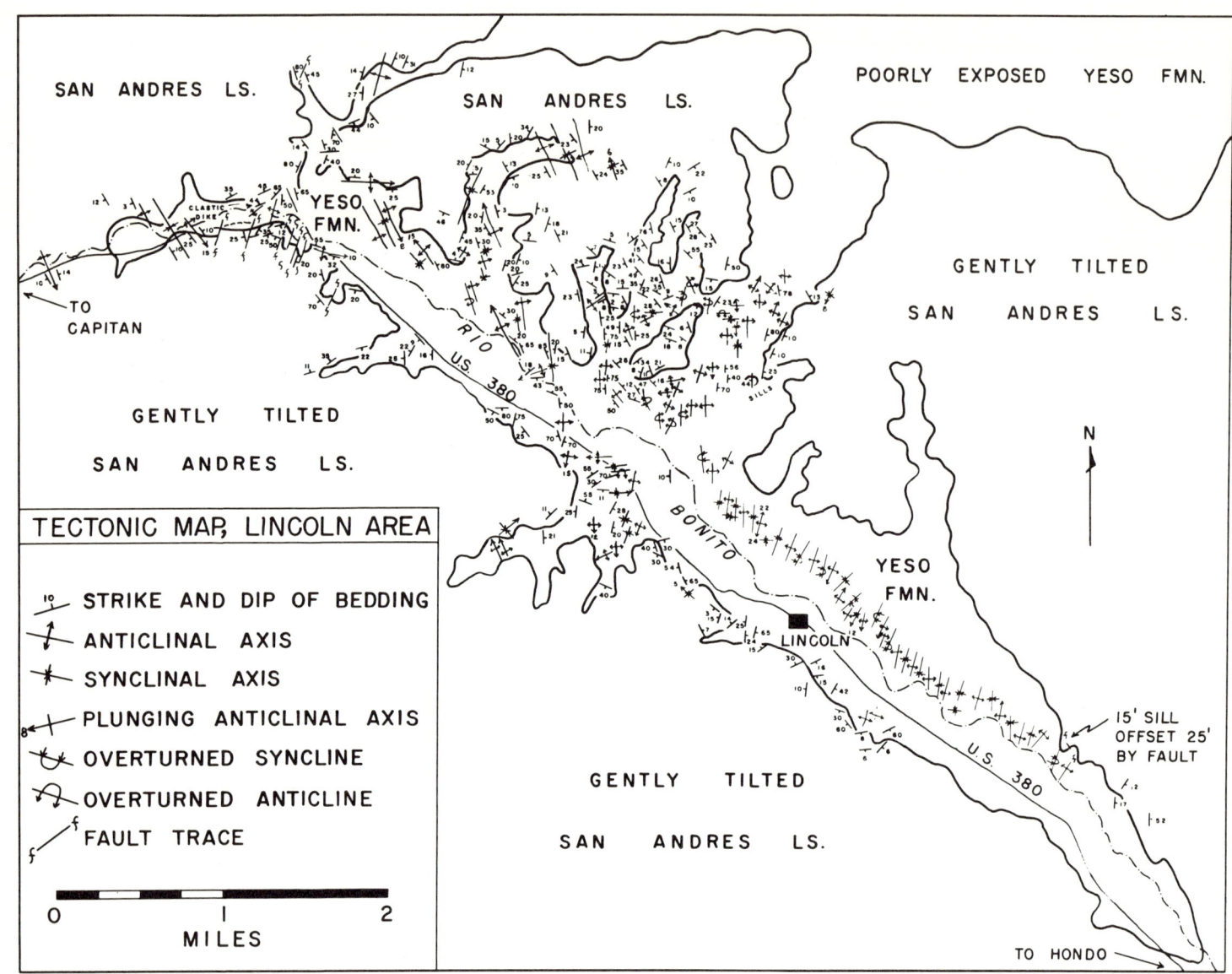

Figure 7. — Tectonic map, Lincoln area.

Despite local complications the overall pattern of the Yeso folds is quite regular and broadly symmetrical; axial planes are close to vertical in most folds, and the geometry is broadly that of parallel folding. The Yeso folds die out upward against the Glorieta in many places within a short vertical distance from very steep dips, a fact also noted by Semmes (1920, p. 429-430). This dying out is accomplished in the uppermost siltstone and gypsum unit, the thickness of which changes markedly in short distances. These folds are generally not faulted and tend to die out longitudinally; one well-exposed anticline measures 50 feet across and 150 feet long on a key bed and plunges 25° at both ends. The 22 folds shown in figure 9 have wave lengths varying from 325 to 1,200 feet, and all but three are between 510 and 1,000 feet; the mean is 713 feet. The apparent shortening of a key limestone bed in figure 9 is 5,600 feet or 25 percent.

Currie, Patnode, and Trump (1962) have analyzed the problem of the buckling of a competent layer embedded in a yielding homogeneous medium. For the case in which the thickness of the adjacent medium is less than the predicted fold wave length they find that

$$L = \pi \sqrt[4]{\frac{2 J T^3}{3} \times \frac{E}{E_o}}$$

where L = predicted initial wave length, J = thickness of one enclosing layer, T = thickness of the buckling competent layer, E = Young's modulus of the competent layer, and E_o = Young's modulus of the enclosing layer. If the Yeso folds at Lincoln are considered to be caused by buckling and attendant lateral shortening, the mean initial wave length was about 950 feet. The uppermost siltstone unit in the Yeso represents the enclosing layer so J equals 100 feet. On the assumption that the remainder of the measured Yeso section comprises two-thirds of the competent layer, T equals 570 feet.

Predicted initial wave lengths were calculated for

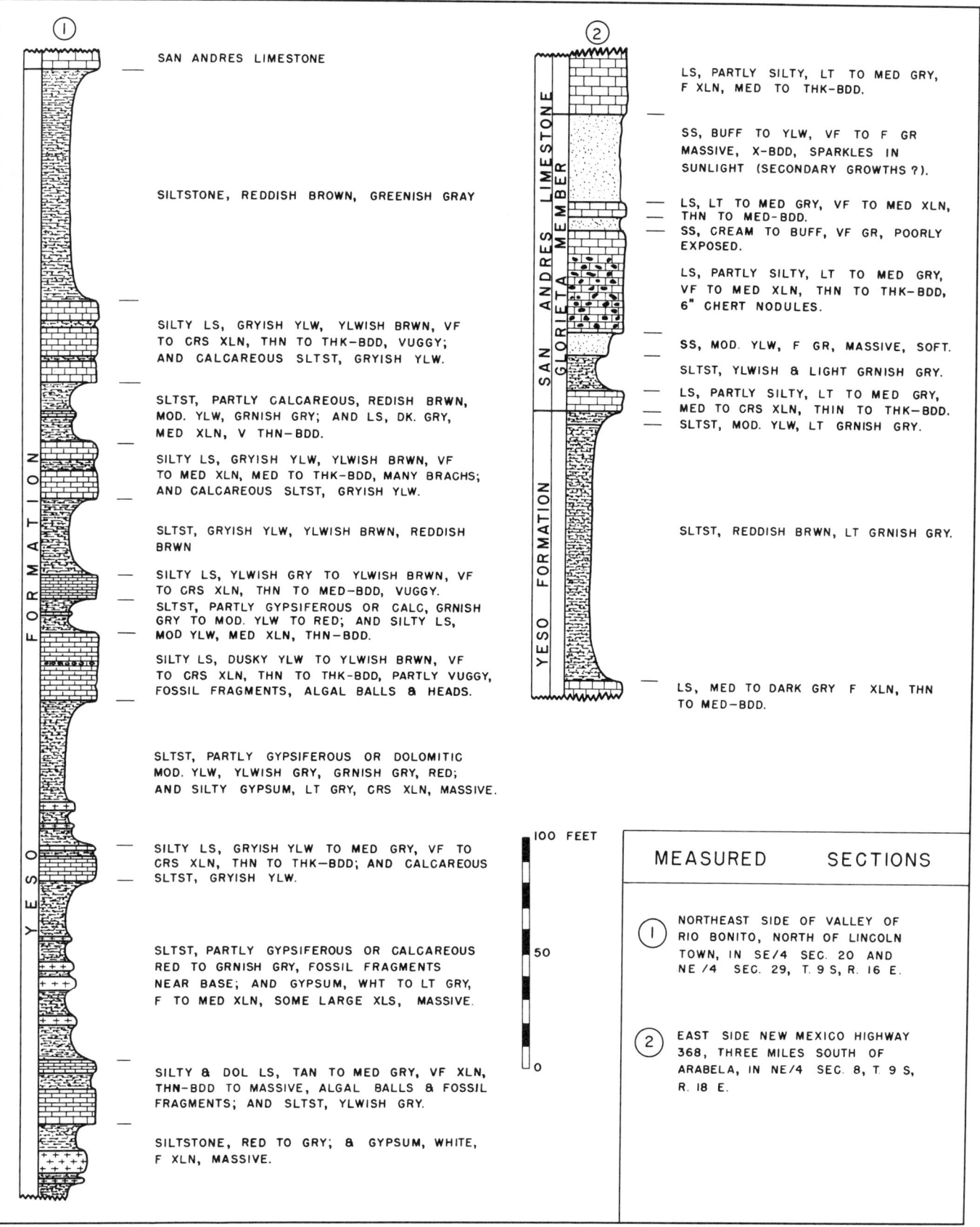

Figure 8. — Measured sections of Permian rocks.

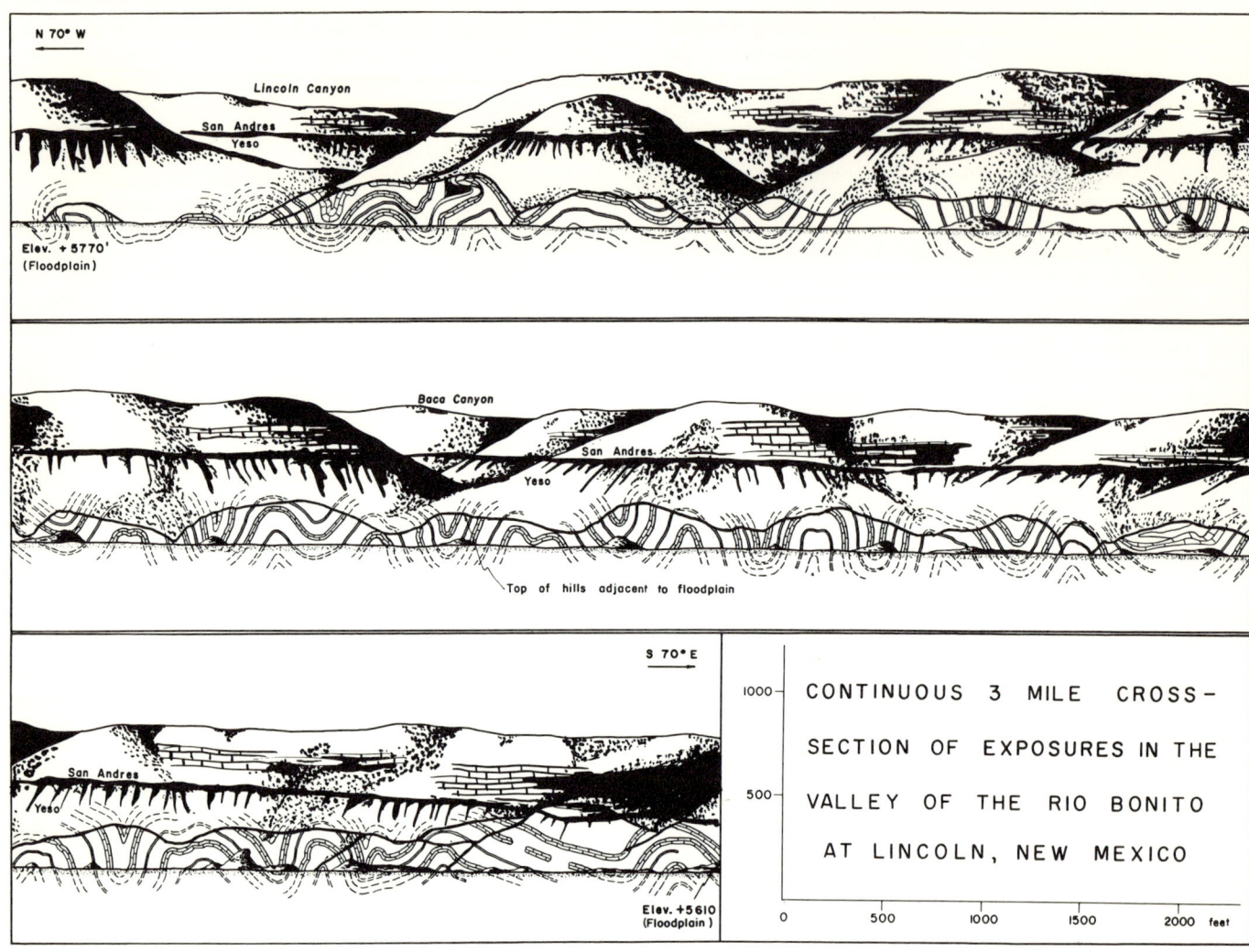

Figure 9. — View to NNE near Lincoln showing strongly folded Yeso formation and conformable overlying San Andres limestone.

various ratios between the elasticity of the layer and that of the enclosing medium. Values of E/E_o equal to 10, 5, 3, and 1 yield values of L equal to 1,865, 1,565, 1,380, and 1,048 feet respectively. Since a good approach to the actual initial wave length is obtained only as the ratio E/E_o approaches unity, it is awkward to account for these folds by a buckling process dependent on contrasting elasticity of the layers. This suggests that a more passive mechanism of folding may have been operative and that the apparent lateral shortening in these folded beds may exceed the true shortening.

The San Andres folds

Over most of the area the San Andres limestone is a gently warped plate though locally its basal beds are downfolded into the Yeso siltstone with dips as high as 70°. This prevailing gentle homoclinal structure is interrupted by sharp, narrow, long, and in many cases isolated buckles which tend to lift the Yeso-San Andres contact above its normal elevation. These also seem to be parallel folds and in some places show vertical or slightly overturned dips. The wave lengths of these folds are larger than in the less competent Yeso Formation; even in the zone of close folding east of Hondo successive anticlines rarely come within 1,200 feet, and in most places are at least 1,800 feet apart. Some of these folds are symmetrical, but many are not; some change their direction or asymmetry along strike as noted by Fiedler and Nye (1933, p. 78-81). An 11.3 mile section eastward across the main sheaf of folds from a point four miles west of Hondo reveals an apparent shortening of the Glorieta by 2.0 miles or 15 percent.

Although an independent origin is possible, the Border Hills, Six Mile Hill, and Y-O anticlinal flexures are here considered a part of the Lincoln fold system. These structures are narrow, sharp, locally faulted anticlines whose surface expression is almost confined to rocks of the San Andres limestone. Because distinctive units are rare in this thick carbonate section, it is difficult to determine if vertical displacement of the gently tilted strata on opposite sides of these flexures has occurred. However, if the Yeso-San Andres contact near Sunset is projected eastward five miles to the Border

Hills (fig. 1) using dips observable in the San Andres, the elevation of the contact is about the same below the flat-lying beds just northwest and just southeast of the flexure in this cross-section. This suggests that these structures are anticlinal buckles resulting from horizontal displacement of the San Andres strata; in this interpretation the observed reverse faults are a result but not a primary cause of the folding.

The general trends of all important axes in the Lincoln fold system have been plotted on figure 1. A sweeping arcuate pattern on the west passing eastward into more uniform, linear anticlines is evident. Some shallow dry holes near the projected trend of the northernmost folds on figure 1 suggest that this arc may continue farther northwest. Similar features extend southward; Renick (1926, p. 124-127) describes strongly folded Yeso beds beneath gently tilted San Andres 38 miles south of Glencoe.

AGE OF THE FOLDS

During the writer's early field studies near Lincoln it seemed probable that the Yeso folding represented a local Permian disturbance. However the discovery of conformable contacts between the Yeso and the San Andres, the local downfolding of the basal San Andres into the Yeso, and the large scale buckling of the limestone plate along axes parallel to those in the Yeso indicates a post-San Andres age. Merritt (1920) reports he has traced the Border Hills flexure into upper Permian red beds, which would argue for a post-Permian deformation.

The incomplete record of the Mesozoic in this area suggests that it was rather stable during that time, and that it was not until the emplacement of the early Tertiary intrusives that significant deformation occurred. One of these intrusives, the Capitan Mountains pluton, occurs in the folded area and provides important evidence on the chronology. Three lines of evidence suggest this pluton post-dates the main folding. First, the arcuate pattern of the folds, though possibly offset and locally deflected, continues obliquely across the Capitan Mountains; it is hard to conceive of this pattern developing after the emplacement of the pluton. Secondly, Kelley (1952, p. 69) reports clastic dikes in the lower San Andres on the west end of the Capitan Mountains in such a position that they could hardly have formed after the igneous intrusion. These clastic dikes may be the same age as those described above as essentially contemporaneous with the folding; if so, the Capitan Mountains pluton seems to post-date the folding. Finally, the complex cross-cutting and folding relations near Arabela indicate that the original folding and the intermediate sills in the folds are older than the pluton. The intense fracturing in the sills and the tightness of the folding suggest, but do not prove, that the sills preceded the pre-pluton folding.

Several localities near Arabela reveal small faults in the folded sills, but these may have been formed when the Capitan Mountains pluton was emplaced. However, southeast of Lincoln a 15-foot sill at the Yeso-San Andres contact is offset about 25 feet along a fault transverse to the fold axes. If this fault is related to the deformation that caused the folding, then this sill antedates the folding. This conclusion is consistent with the occurrence of sills in strongly folded Yeso beds elsewhere in the area, away from the Capitan Mountains; sills dipping 44°, 55°, and 70° have been observed. Thus, it is probable that the folding post-dates these earliest intermediate intrusions.

Northeast of Alto a major fault, the Cub Mountain Formation, and a flexure in the San Andres Formation all pass beneath a gently eastward-sloping gravel-covered surface having an elevation of about 7,000 feet. Between Hondo and Sunset another surface at about 5,800 feet altitude seems to bevel the folded San Andres formation (Fiedler and Nye, 1933, p. 13-14, pl. 5B). Bretz and Horberg (1949, p. 488) suggest that gravel of the Ogallala Formation of Pliocene age now capping the plains east of Roswell once covered most of the Sacramento-Guadalupe Range; Horberg (1949, p. 464-466) considers surfaces as high as 8,000 feet in the Guadalupe Range as remnants of this once continuous Ogallala surface. King (1942, p. 633), however interprets these high surfaces as portions of a pre-Cretaceous plain, and Kelly (1952, p. 70-71) considers similar surfaces near Capitan to be Pleistocene in age.

Although details of these surfaces have not been worked out, the surfaces west of Sunset and near Alto capped with limestone and igneous pebbles — may well be remnants of a Pliocene pediment surface sloping eastward to the Ogallala Formation of the Great Plains. This places an upper time limit on the major subsidence of the Sierra Blanca basin and the folding, and reinforces the conclusion that the folding probably occurred in early Tertiary time.

IMPROBABLE HYPOTHESES OF ORIGIN

The following explanations for the fold system or for specific parts of it have been offered in the literature or suggested to the writer:
1) Intra-Permian deformation,
2) Movements on basement faults,
3) Lateral pressure from the emplacement of the Capitan Mountains pluton,
4) Drag effects during the formation of the arch west of Lincoln,
5) Tilting of the Sacramento Mountain block,
6) Volume changes during the recrystallization of evaporites,
7) Surface subsidence due to subsurface evaporite solution,
8) Landsliding or other local mass wasting processes,
9) Injection of sills.

Although some of these mechanisms may have played a local role, each is considered improbable as a general explanation of the Lincoln fold system for one or more of the following reasons: 1) the early Tertiary age of the folding, 2) the shape of the folds in cross-section, 3) the regional extent of the fold system, 4) the map pattern of the folds in relation to other geologic features, and 5) the lithologic composition and physical properties of the folded formations.

PROBABLE ORIGIN OF THE FOLDS

Before discussing the probable origin of these folds it is desirable to reconstruct the geologic conditions prevailing early in the Tertiary, the inferred time of folding.

The tectonic history of this area during the Mesozoic is incompletely known, but the widespread intrusive activity in the Tertiary terminated a period of relative crustal stability. The strata may have had a slight southeastward inclination inherited from their position on the northwest shelf of a depositional basin during Permian time. The San Andres carbonate plate was buried beneath at least 4,200 feet of younger beds and possibly more.

Folding of the Permian rocks is probably related to these plutonic intrusions. If the age is correctly established by the evidence discussed, the folding followed the injection of the early intermediate sills but preceded the emplacement of the acidic pluton of the Capitan Mountains. Folding followed the sill injection by enough time to allow solidification and faulting of some of the sills. Thus the great monzonite and diorite intrusions may not have directly caused the folding, but rather may have triggered it in some manner. Gravitational gliding of sheets of Cretaceous Dakota Sandstone resulting from doming due to Tertiary intrusions has been reported near Capitan by Allen and Ferebee (manuscript) and in the Jicarilla Mountains by Budding (1963).

The intrusions are also linked to the Lincoln deformation by the map pattern of the fold system. Whenever folds are exposed in both the Yeso and the San Andres, the trends are parallel and hence must be genetically related. The fold system forms a sweeping arc which measures at least 15 miles across, excluding the isolated anticlines to the southeast, and at least 50 miles in length. The focus of this arc lies near the main intrusive complex of Sierra Blanca.

Where significantly exposed, the Yeso is generally crumpled into a series of mainly parallel folds; in many localities these folds die out upward abruptly against the flat base of the San Andres. Attempts to project these folds downward are beset with the space difficulty inevitable for all parallel folds, and their shape seems to require a plane of "dying out" a few hundred feet below the deepest present exposures. The San Andres folds, on the other hand, are unusual in being sharp, generally upward-directed buckles which in some cases are separated by broad, flat areas.

A puzzling discrepancy exists in the amount of apparent lateral shortening from folding between the value computed from the San Andres limestone and that from the Yeso formation. An apparent shortening of about two miles was measured on the Glorieta member of the San Andres across the conspicuous family of folds near Hondo. With allowance for numerous minor warpings and the three anticlinal flexures to the southeast the maximum apparent shortening across a width of 50 miles is about 3 miles or 6 percent. However, in the well exposed transverse section of just over 3 miles at Lincoln the Yeso folds show an apparent shortening of 5,600 feet or about 25 percent. Thus in this short distance the apparent shortening in the Yeso equals one-third of the total calculated for the San Andres across the entire area. The universally folded character of the Yeso where exposed in the area suggests it is deformed throughout the area of San Andres folding. At the very least the Yeso deformation extends 25 miles transverse to the fold axes. Applying the 25 percent apparent shortening measured at Lincoln yields a minimum apparent shortening of 8 miles in the Yeso, clearly greater than the amount calculated from the San Andres.

The most satisfactory explanation for the known relations involves a decollement or slippage along a surface in the lower Yeso formation, as first discussed by Allen and Ferebee (manuscript) based chiefly upon observations in the vicinity of Capitan. Gravitational movement occurred when the area was tilted slightly by the early intrusions in the Sierra Blanca complex. This movement was directly southeasterly down the then-present regional dip; the modern more easterly dip probably results from later northeasterly tilting, most of which is late Cenozoic in age (King, 1948, p. 120-121). The present average eastward dip between Lincoln and Roswell is about 1°, and the surface slope is slightly less. Formational dip at the time of folding was probably about the same although somewhat higher eastward dips may have existed near Capitan before the collapse of the Sierra Blanca basin. Since the coarsely crystalline plutonic rocks on Sierra Blanca require a roof and since the present structural basin there is considered to post-date the intrusions, surface slopes at the time of folding may have been considerable.

The Yeso folds are thus interpreted as a mainly passive response to instability created by gravitational shifting the entire sequence above a bedding surface in the lower Yeso. The eastward movement of the San Andres limestone plate near Lincoln is limited to about 3 miles, and the actual slippage along the basal surface in the lower Yeso may be less. If the Yeso folds are considered passive, the true lateral shortening may be less than the value obtained by "unfolding" the folds. Such a mechanism also implies some attenuation of the units in the Yeso to permit the folds to form. Detailed sections were measured in a limestone and the overlying siltstone in a 2½-mile traverse across the folds at Lincoln. Sixteen limestone sections ranged between 24.6 and 35.3 feet, and 8 reliable siltstone sections between 14.4 and 23.0 feet. If the original thickness is assumed constant and equal to the maximum measured thickness for each unit, then attenuation has locally reduced the thickness of the limestone by 30 percent and the siltstone by 37 percent.

Bucher's (1956) scale model experiments on the role of gravity in deformation indicate that the proposed mechanism of folding is possible. Interbedding layers of stiff stitching wax and grease in a compression box were imparted a slight slope by pressure against the left end of the box. (See Bucher's Plates 1 and 3.) The true shortening, as measured on the lowest wax layer which bent only at the left end, was about 10 percent. As the entire sequence shifted to the right under gravity to eliminate the slope, a set of folds strikingly similar to the Lincoln fold system was formed. The middle wax layer was undeformed in the left half of the box but to the right buckled into long wave length folds analogous to those in the San Andres. The apparent shortening in the layer was roughly equal to the true lateral shifting. The underlying and overlying grease layers were deformed across the width of the box into shorter wave length folds analogous to those in the Yeso formation. The apparent shortening of these grease layers averages 31 percent, greatly in excess of the actual value. This writer considers the Lincoln fold system to have formed in a similar manner, except that the initial tilt probably resulted

132

more from arching due to intrusions rather than lateral pressure.

The main folds in the San Andres in the Hondo-Picacho-Arabela area may be compared to folds in two other regions. The Jura Mountains in France and Switzerland is the type area for decollement folding; lateral shortening there over most of the belt is 6-10 km or 25 percent (Umbgrove, 1948, p. 1055) but may increase to 17.5 km at the east end (Collet, 1927, p. 139). Reeves (1946) described an arc of faulted folds in the Cretaceous rocks of the plains surrounding the igneous Bearpaw Mountains in northern Montana; his interpretation has been confirmed by new subsurface data reported by Shouldice (1963). Lateral shortening there is as much as 3 miles and the plainsward dip is approximately 3°. The deformation in all three regions has been attributed by some to gravitational shifting, and the folds in each case have these characteristics:
1) Their geometry suggests the presence of a basal shear plane,
2) Sharp anticlinal folds are separated in some cases by broad, flat areas,
3) Many folds are slightly asymmetric and tend to change the direction of inclination of the axial surface along their axes,
4) The fold system has a broad arcuate pattern.

Faults are abundant in the Bearpaw folds, common in the Jura folds, but rare in these San Andres folds.

The writer has not studied the Border Hills, Six Mile Hill, and Y-O flexures in detail, but they are probably genetically a part of the Lincoln fold system. A case can be made for considering them the result of movements of basement blocks on the basis of 1) their straightness, 2) the presence of steep strike faults in the surface formations, and 3) the existence of monoclines elsewhere in the region. On the other hand, evidence relating them to the Lincoln fold system includes 1) their regular spacing, 2) their general parallelism with each other and with the folds in the Hondo-Arabela area, 3) the variable nature of their asymmetry and faults along the strike, and 4) the probable lack of vertical displacement of the flat-lying beds on opposite sides of these flexures. It is possible that minor basement faulting may have localized these flexures, but their geometry seems to require significant lateral shortening rather than monoclinal flexing.

REFERENCES CITED

Allen, John Eliot and Ferebee, D. M., Tertiary decollement in Capitan quadrangle — an alternate hypothesis: (manuscript).
Bodine, Marc W., Jr., 1953, Geology of the Capitan coal field, Lincoln County, New Mexico: Master's thesis, Columbia University, 23 p.
Bretz, J. Harlen and Horberg, Leland, 1949, The Ogallala formation west of the Llano Estacado: Jour. Geology, v. 57, p. 477-489.
Bucher, Walter H., 1956, Role of gravity in orogenesis: Geol. Soc. America Bull., v. 67, p. 1295-1318.
Budding, A. J., 1963, Origin and age of superficial structures, Jicarilla Mountains, central New Mexico: Geol. Soc. America Bull., v. 74, p. 203-208.
Collet, Leon W., 1927, The structure of the Alps: London, Edward Arnold & Co., 290 p.
Currie, J. B., Patnode, H. W., and Trump, R. P., 1962, Development of folds in sedimentary strata: Geol. Soc. America Bull., v. 73, p. 655-674.
Dunn, David A., 1954, Resume of oil and gas exploration of the Sacramento Mountain area: N. M. Geol. Soc., 5th Field Conf. Guidebook, Southeastern New Mexico, p. 159-160.
Fiedler, Albert G., and Nye, S. Spencer, 1933, Geology and ground-water resources of the Roswell artesian basin, New Mexico: U.S. Geol. Survey Water-Supply Paper 639, p. 367.
Horberg, Leland, 1949, Geomorphic history of the Carlsbad Caverns area, New Mexico: Jour. Geology, v. 57, p. 464-476.
Kelly, V. C., 1952, Origin and pyrometasomatic zoning of the Capitan iron deposit, Lincoln county, New Mexico: Econ. Geology, v. 47, p. 64-83.
King, Philip B., 1942, Permian of west Texas and southeastern New Mexico: Am. Assoc. Petroleum Geologists Bull., v. 26, p. 535-763.
King, Philip B., 1948, Geology of the southern Guadalupe mountains, Texas: U.S. Geol. Survey Prof. Paper 215, 179 p.
Knapp, Vernon, 1933, The structural relations of the Capitan and eastern border of the Sierra Blanca Mountain groups in Lincoln County, New Mexico: Master's Thesis, Univ. of Colorado.
Kottlowski, Frank E. and others, 1956, Stratigraphic studies of the San Andres Mountains, New Mexico: N. Mex. Inst. Min. and Tech., State Bur. Mines and Min. Res. Mem. 1, 125 p.
Lang, Walter B., 1937, The Permian formations of the Pecos valley of New Mexico and Texas: Am. Assoc. Petroleum Geologists Bull., v. 21, p. 833-898.
Lindgren, Waldemar, 1910, The ore deposits of New Mexico: U.S. Geol. Survey Prof. Paper 68, 348 p.
Lloyd, E. Russell, 1949, Pre-San Andres stratigraphy and oil producing zones in southeastern New Mexico: N. Mex. Inst. Min. and Tech., State Bur. Mines and Min. Res. Bull. 29, 71 p.
Merritt, J. W., 1920, Structures of western Chaves County, New Mexico: Am. Assoc. Petroleum Geologists Bull., v. 4, p. 53-57.
Patton, Leroy T., 1951, Igneous rocks of the Capitan quadrangle, New Mexico, and vicinity: Amer. Mineralogist, v. 36, p. 713-716.
Pray, Lloyd C., 1954, Outline of the stratigraphy and structure of the Sacramento Mountain escarpment: Geol. Soc. Guidebook, Fifth Field Conf., Southeastern New Mexico, p. 92-106.
Reeves, Frank, 1946, Origin and mechanics of thrust faults adjacent to the Bearpaw Mountains, Montana: Geol. Soc. America Bull., v. 57, p. 1033-1047.
Renick, B. Coleman, 1926, Report of geology and ground-water resources of the drainage basin of the Rio Penasco above Hope, New Mexico: in Seventh biennial report of the State Engineer of New Mexico, p. 123.
Semmes, Douglas R., 1920, Notes on the Tertiary intrusives of the lower Pecos valley, New Mexico: Am. Jour. Sci., 4th Ser., v. 50, p. 415-430.
Shouldice, J. R., 1963, Gravity slide faulting on Bowes Dome, Bearpaw Mountain area, Montana: Am. Assoc. Petroleum Geologists Bull., v. 47, p. 1943-1951.
Umbgrove, J. H. F., 1948, Origin of the Jura Mountains: Kon. Ned. Akad. Wet. Proc., v. 51, p. 1049-1062.

THE LINCOLN FOLDS, LINCOLN, NEW MEXICO

Edward J. Foley

Consultant, Alpine, Texas

INTRODUCTION

In this paper only those folds on the north side of the Rio Bonito, in the immediate vicinity of Lincoln, New Mexico are discussed. They occur in an area of about 15 square miles and are believed by the writer to have originated as massive landslides or slump. His interpretation is based on several days of field work at Lincoln in 1951, and on six years of general familiarity with the geology of this entire region. During the field work he was accompanied by Mr. D. G. Garrott of the Humble Oil and Refining Company.

The town of Lincoln is situated in southeastern Lincoln County, New Mexico. It lies near the bottom of a deep canyon at an elevation of about 5,700 feet. The top of the surrounding plateau just above Lincoln lies at about 6,400 feet. The Capitan Mountains, six miles to the north, reach 10,230 feet, and Sierra Blanca, 6 miles to the southwest, attains an altitude of 12,003 feet.

Average rainfall around Lincoln is about 15 inches a year. However, the present climate and vegetative cover have no direct relationship to the problem of the origin of the Lincoln folds.

Upstream from their confluence at Hondo, the Rio Bonito and the Rio Ruidoso flow through the Permian Yeso Formation, which is composed of soft sandstone, siltstone, shale, gypsum and thin limestone beds. Overlying the Yeso is the weak Glorieta Sandstone. The rims of the canyons consist of the resistant San Andres Limestone, also Permian in age. Thus, a situation exists in which soft, fissile strata are overlain by thick competent beds. Oversteepened slopes in the soft materials are likely to be developed under such circumstances. The processes of erosion that result in such slopes also encourage landslides as well as mass slump as succeeding events.

DESCRIPTION OF THE DEFORMED AREA

In writing of the folds at Lincoln, Talmage stated (1935, p. 153-154), "In the vicinity of the best exposures, the folds seem patternless; some are inclined toward the east, others toward the west, and some pitch steeply to the south, others to the north. In one case, a strongly asymmetric fold is overturned to the east, and its western limb is broken by three small faults overthrust to the west." One of the folds is shown in figure 1. It is doubtful that adjoining folds are connected as shown by Craddock (1960, fig. 2, and p. 39). The rocks in this deformed area show many slightly open fractures, a condition typical of slides. Such openings are not likely to exist in folds of deep-seated origin. Small notches mark the traces of the apparent upper structural boundaries with undisturbed strata assigned to the uppermost part of the Yeso, Glorieta, and San Andres Formations. The mountain face just north of Lincoln Canyon is probably the slightly eroded main scarp of an old slide. This also applies to some of the other steep slopes in the area. These notches and slipping surface scarps may be seen to advantage on air photos (figs. 2, 3, 4). Scarps in concentric semicircles, depressions on the dip slopes of these, and hummocky topography in general may also be observed. All of these are quite characteristic of landslides. The slipping surface above the old highway slide opposite Salazar Canyon is obvious on the air photos. These slip surfaces, of course, may be considered as faults, though they are superficial, not deep seated.

Figure 1. — One of the small folds in deformed area on bank of Rio Bonito near Lincoln.

PREVIOUS EXPLANATIONS

The folds at Lincoln have been variously explained as crumpling between the massive San Andres Limestone and the igneous rock (Semmes, 1920), as drag folds (Talmage, 1935), as landslides (Panhandle Geological Society, 1939), as disharmonic folding, and as having resulted from forceful intrusion of sills related to the nearby Capitan Mountains pluton. The most recent work published on the area is "The Origin of the Lincoln Fold System, Southeastern New Mexico" (Craddock, 1960). This last paper also describes other roughly similar folds in the same general region which have been well known for many years, including the Y-O, Six Mile Hill, Border Hills, Picacho and Tinnie folds. All of them are complex and difficult to explain but, unlike the Lincoln folds, where only the Yeso Formation is deformed, they all have one thing in common — the San Andres Limestone is also involved in the folding. Craddock's explanation of these other folds and their origin appears to be valid. But, in the writer's opinion, the same explanation cannot be applied to the folds at Lincoln, nor should the words "Lincoln Folds" have been included in the title of Craddock's paper.

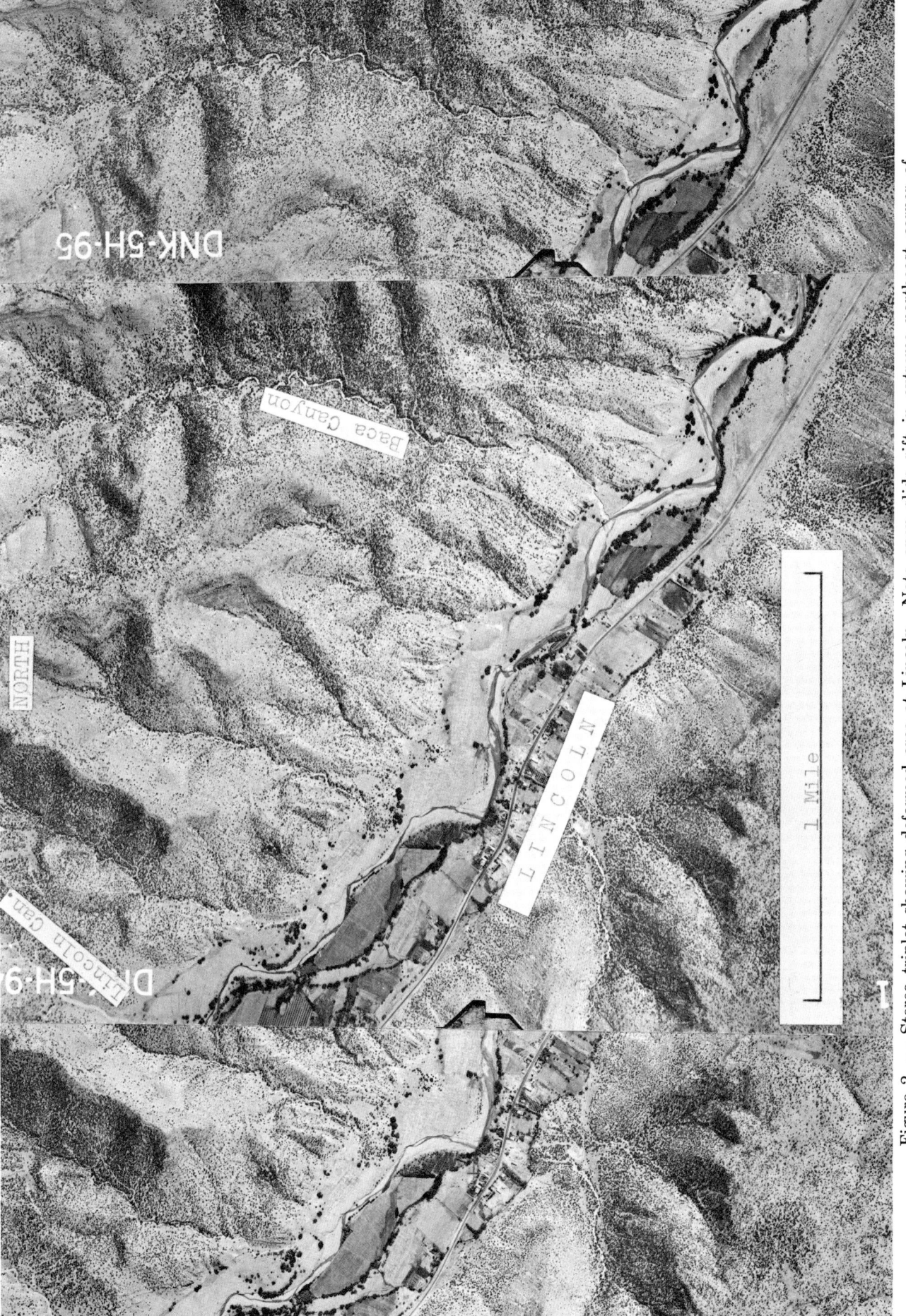

Figure 2. — Stereo triplet showing deformed area at Lincoln. Note open slide rift in extreme northeast corner of photo near head of Baca Canyon. Several small anticlines near floodplain. P.M.A. photo, 1951.

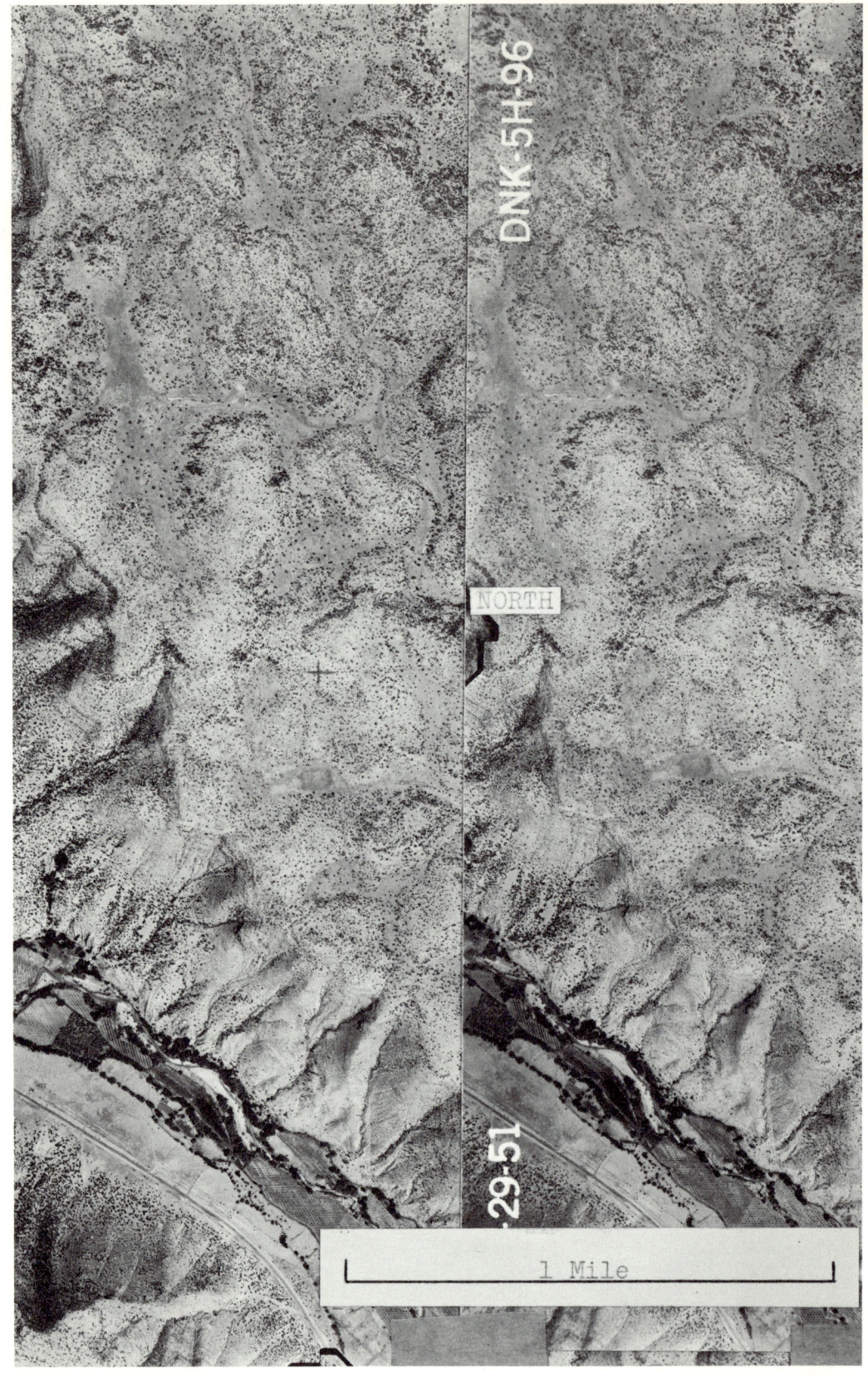

Figure 3. — Stereo pair showing southeast end of deformed area. Note perched slide masses on canyon wall at extreme southeastern end. Divergent strikes just above river.

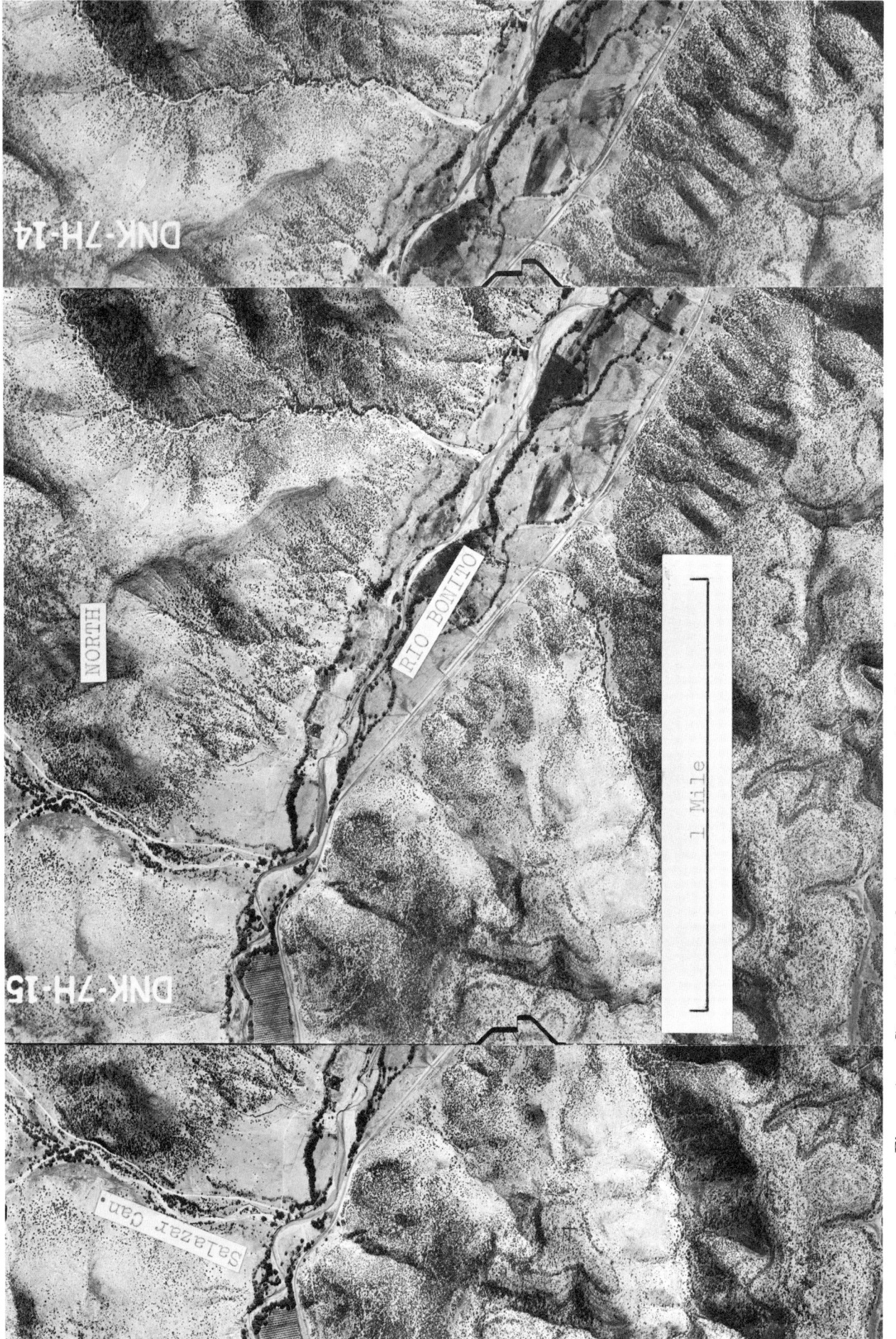

Figure 4. — Stereo triplet showing northwest end of deformed area. There is about a one mile gap between this view and Figure 2. Note huge slide mass opposite mouth of Salazar Canyon. This was caused by Rio Bonito and later reactivated by highway excavation. There are other perched slide masses along canyon walls, such as on east side of Salazar Canyon just below the fork.

One very important reference is a Highway Department sign opposite the mouth of Salazar Canyon, a few miles northwest of Lincoln. It warns against the slide area on the highway there!

ORIGIN OF THE FOLDS

The deformation at Lincoln probably is the result of massive slumping. In late Pleistocene and early Recent time there was a great deal more precipitation in the area around Lincoln than there is at present. At least one glacier existed in the nearby Sierra Blanca, and doubtless the rest of that range and the Capitan Mountains had a more or less permanent snow cap. Melted water from this ice and snow formed torrential streams, whose violence and carrying power is shown by river gravel that contains boulders as large as two feet in diameter. Although the main glacial cirque on Sierra Blanca drained into the north fork of the Rio Ruidoso, most of the northeastern part of the range drained into Rio Bonito. Salazar Canyon, above Lincoln, carried nearly all the runoff from the southern side of the western part of the Capitan Mountains. However, it is possible that Baca and Lincoln Canyons, respectively just east and west of Lincoln, may have carried some of this Capitan Mountain runoff earlier in our present erosion cycle. Canyons were steep sided, and cliffs were more than 800 feet high. The canyons were then considerably deeper than they are at present, as some aggradation has since taken place. Undercutting of these high cliffs is certain to have been a common occurrence, and the obvious result was collapse.

Heavy precipitation in times past also provided lubrication on slip surfaces. Now that the climate has changed and there is a great deal less rainfall, these valley walls are more or less stable except where they are excavated by man, as in highway construction. In recent years the highway itself was moving slightly on the slide mass just opposite the mouth of Salazar Canyon, and the pavement required continual repair because of humps and roughness. Huge limestone blocks, jumbled beds with open fractures, anomalous attitudes, landslide notches and tilted terraces are common elsewhere along the sides of the Rio Bonito and Rio Ruidoso. There is nothing at all anomalous about the presence of slumped and landslide masses in this area, and these have been recorded in a number of publications. (Roswell Geological Society, 1951, p. 2; 1953, p. 3, 4; Allen and Kottlowski 1958, p. 13, 15-17, 38-40.)

Mention has been made of the slip surfaces bounding landslide masses. Such surfaces are typically steep in their upper part and are curved, concave upward, with a cliffward dip at the toe. If, however, they merge with bedding planes the mass could be considered as a block slide. The lowest portion of these slip surfaces at Lincoln nicely fits Craddock's (1960, p. 42) requirement of a plane of "dying out," for it lies at a depth near the former level of the canyon floor; that is, before the later aggradation.

The strikes of the deformed beds near Lincoln are often divergent, although most are more or less perpendicular to the main valley. This is probably due to slumping from the cliffs on the tributary streams just above their mouths. The ancient Rio Bonito, as it undercut its bordering cliffs, doubtless flowed slightly northward of its present course.

A large open rift near the head of Baca Canyon is shown near the northeast corner of figure 2. It represents the initial movement on an old slide which never did progress more than about 30 feet down the canyon wall. This rift is about 500 feet long. It also may be seen in figure 2. Nearby is another incipient slide with an open rift about 100 feet long, 10 feet wide and 5 feet deep.

There are three sink holes on the plateau near the head of Baca Canyon, and these suggest that solution of underlying material may have contributed slightly to the origin of the slides. Incidentally, the steeper dips on the limestone plateau near the very head of Baca Canyon are so close to the Capitan Mountain pluton that they are undoubtedly associated with the uplift caused by its intrusion.

The deformation in the beds bordering Rio Bonito at Lincoln does not extend to the southern side of the canyon. If these steeply dipping beds are resistant enough to crop out on the north side of the canyon, they would do so on the south side if they had been continuous. Also it might be said that the Yeso formation is more or less of the same competency, vertically and laterally. Why then, in a small area, should some of it be folded and some of it not folded? The south boundary of the deformed zone is not a fault, not a fold, and not an intrusion. It is a stream bed. As stated in an early guidebook (Panhandle Geologic Society, 1939), the folding is probably due to solution and slumping rather than compression. Gravitational slumping, relatively unaided by solution, probably is the major cause of the deformation.

Bucher's (1956) laboratory experiments on "disharmonious folding" have been compared to the folding at Lincoln (Craddock 1960, p. 42). His box of wax and grease layers had pressure applied at one end, thereby causing thickening which produced a slope, and subsequent disharmonious folding in the soft grease. The location of the Lincoln folds is only a very few miles east of the crest of the buried ridge that was the Pedernal Positive Element (Roswell Geological Society, 1952, p. 31; Kottlowski, 1963, p. 110). The very gentle slope of the limestone plateau in this area is related to the presence of this buried ridge, not to compressive folding. The nearness of the Pedernal ridge, plus the very gentle slope of the formations at Lincoln, seem to preclude application of Bucher's experiments to this particular problem, although they may explain the folds farther east.

The age of all the folds has been given as late Tertiary. Doubtless this is right for all of the folds except for the ones at Lincoln. Craddock's conclusion (Craddock, 1960, p. 42) is that the most satisfactory explanation of the origin of the folds involves a decollement, or slippage in the lower Yeso and that this produced disharmonic folding. The writer agrees that this could be true of all the other folds in the region, except those in the Lincoln fold belt.

CONCLUSION

The Lincoln folds, that is, those in the immediate vicinity of Lincoln, have an origin that appears complicated, but is in reality very simple. They are the result of landslides that took place in late Pleistocene or early Recent time. The movement involved can be classified as slump, or block guide, with some rockslide and rockfall, and combinations of all four. The remarkable and complex deformation was caused by the pressure resulting from millions of tons of rock sliding against the bottoms or opposite walls of the canyons.

REFERENCES CITED

Allen, John E., and Kottlowski, Frank E., 1958, Roswell-Capitan-Ruidoso and Bottomless Lakes Park, New Mexico: N. Mex. Inst. Min. Tech., State Bur. Mines and Min. Res., Scenic Trips to the geologic past, No. 3.

Bucher, Walter H., 1956, Role of gravity in orogenesis: Geol. Soc. America Bull. v. 67, p. 1295-1318.

Craddock, Campbell, 1960, The origin of the Lincoln fold system, southeastern New Mexico: Internat. Geol. Cong., 21st, Copenhagen 1960, Rept., part 18, p. 34-44.

Kottlowski, Frank A., 1963, Pennsylvanian rocks of Socorro County, New Mexico: N. Mex. Geol. Soc. 14th Field Conf., Guidebook of the Socorro Region, p. 102-111, 2 figs.

Panhandle Geological Society, 1939, Guidebook for spring field trip, Sacramento Mountains, White Sands, Sierra Blanca region.

Roswell Geological Society, 1951, Guidebook of the Capitan-Carrizozo-Chupadera Mesa region.

────────── 1952, 7th Field trip, Guidebook, The Pedernal positive element and the Estancia Basin, 39 p.

Semmes, Douglas R., 1920, Notes on the Tertiary intrusives of the lower Pecos Valley, New Mexico: Am. Jour. Sci. 4th Ser. v. 50, p. 415-430.

Talmage, Sterling B., 1935, Folding of Chupadera beds near Lincoln, New Mexico (abs): Pan. Am. Geologist 64, p. 153-154.

DIFFERENTIATION AND ALKALI METASOMATISM IN DIKE SWARM COMPLEX AND RELATED IGNEOUS ROCKS NEAR CAPITAN, LINCOLN COUNTY, NEW MEXICO

Wolfgang E. Elston and Henry I. Snider
University of New Mexico, Albuquerque, New Mexico

INTRODUCTION

The prominent dike swarm between the villages of Capitan and Nogal has attracted the attention of almost every geologist who has travelled through the area. It extends from the vicinity of Sierra Blanca some 40 miles to the north-northeast, into the Jicarilla Mountain area. The longest individual dikes are tens of feet wide and about 3 miles long, but the majority are much smaller. Their best development is around Indian Divide and the area immediately to the southwest.

Air photos of the outcrop belts of the Mancos Shale, Mesaverde Group and Cub Mountain Formation show hundreds of low NNE-trending ridges, marked by prominent tree lines. On the ground, each ridge turns out to be a composite dike, made up of many individual dikes with complex cross-cutting relationships. The ridges are covered by innumerable dark boulders formed by spheroidal weathering of various types of diabase. Outcrops are poor except in cuts along U.S. Highway 380 and the abandoned railroad between Carrizozo and Capitan.

The dikes show features of more than local interest. The older dikes are various types of diabase; the younger dikes include both quartz-bearing rhyolite and nepheline-bearing phonolite. The plagioclases of altered diabase dikes generally show replacement of labradorite by oligoclase, a feature more commonly associated with the marine spilitic volcanic rocks of eugeosynclines than with dikes in a continental environment. Secondary potassium feldspar occurs in some of the dikes but seems to be more common in the nearby Carrizo Mountain stock. There, late magmatic or post-magmatic orthoclase progressively replaces plagioclase phenocrysts near the roof of the intrusion.

The only previous publication on the dikes (Patton, 1951) is confined to a brief description of olivine-free diabases. It lacks an discussion of field occurrences. This article is based on field work done by Elston for the New Mexico Bureau of Mines and Mineral Resources in 1956, followed by examination of 123 thin sections by Elston in 1957-58 and by Snider in 1962-63.

DIKE ROCKS

The dikes consist of seven rock types, which are, in order of age: (1) labradorite-olivine diabase porphyry, (2) olivine diabase porphyry, (3) diabase, (4) hornblende-biotite diabase, (5) rhyolite, (6) latite (grading into trachyte), and (7) phonolite. For brevity, these rocks are referred to as Types 1 through 7 throughout this paper.

The diabases, especially Types 3 and 4, are the most abundant; rhyolite is locally abundant but absent in some places; latite is rare and phonolite is confined to a few occurrences.

The most important properties of the dike rocks are summarized in table 1 and photomicrographs of typical examples are shown in figure 1. Detailed studies to determine exact composition of the minerals have not been made, and would be difficult because of alteration.

Field Relationships

As shown in figure 2, the dikes are irregular in shape. They are intrusive-magmatic rather than metasomatic, judging by the disruption of invaded rocks, sharp contacts, fine-grained chilled borders, and flow-lineation of crystals. Rhyolite has a distinct tendency to form sills in incompetent shale beds; other rock types tend to form dikes controlled by fractures.

Most relative ages could be established by cross-cutting relationships, but even where two dikes were parallel the younger could usually be recognized by its fine-grained chilled border. Also, irregular apophyses, a few inches long, of the younger dike locally invade the older dike.

The relationship of Type 2 to Type 1 is based on a single weathered outcrop (figure 2A). Microscopically, the Type 2 olivine diabase porphyry is finer-grained at the contact than a foot away from it, indicating chilling against pre-existing Type 1 rock. These age relationships are important because Type 2 is the most mafic rock in the complex. As for the remaining age relationships, detailed examination of composite dikes in 21 road and railroad cuts failed to show any exceptions to the order of intrusion given here. Away from artificial cuts only a few outcrops show conclusive cross-cutting relationships, and these also follow the same sequence. In none of the composite dikes examined were all seven rock types seen; the sequence was pieced together from several occurrences. The sketches in figure 2 show all rock types except Type 7 phonolite, but a phonolite dike cuts a Type 6 latite dike 0.1 mile east of the roadcut shown in figure 2C.

Differentiation Trends

The dikes do not follow a simple differentiation trend from mafic to felsic or mafic to alkalic. If the field relationships have been interpreted correctly, labradorite-olivine diabase porphyry (Type 1) is older than the more mafic olivine diabase porphyry (Type 2). Possibly, Type 1 is representative of the parent magma and Type 2 has been enriched in early-formed crystals.

Further differentiation would follow a clearly alkalic trend ending in phonolite (Type 7) if it were not for

Table 1.—Description of dike rocks of Capitan area.

	(1) Labradorite-olivine diabase porphyry	(2) Olivine diabase porphyry	(3) Diabase	(4) Hornblende-biotite[1] diabase	(5) Rhyolite	(6) Latite	(7) Rhonolite
Andesine-labradorite	60-70	40-50	50-65	55-75			
Albite-oligoclase					pr.	40-60	5-15
Potassium feldspar					65-85	20-50	60-90
Quartz					15-20		
Nepheline							5-10
Olivine	3-8	10-25	1-8	tr.-2			
Augite	15-30	15-30	15-30	12-35		8-30	pr.-8
Orthopyroxene		tr.	tr.				
Hornblende				⎫ 2-15			
Biotite				⎭ 2-8		tr.-5	tr.3
Opaque minerals	5-10	5-10	8-15	2-8	0.5	tr.-3	
Accessory minerals			Apatite tr., zircon tr.	Apatite tr.-2		Apatite tr.2	

(7) Rhonolite	Texture	Trachytic, with sparse phenocrysts of oligoclase and orthoclase.
	Alteration	Calcite pseudomorphous after phenocrysts of a ferromagnesian mineral (pyroxene?). Secondary cancrinite and sodalite may be present in traces around nepheline.
(6) Latite	Texture	Phenocrysts (sparse in some specimens) augite up to 3.0 mm long, sparse oligoclase. Groundmass felted intergrowth of K-spar and albite.
	Alteration	Secondary quartz and calcite in cavities, green biotite flakes probably from alteration of augite; kaolinite, sericite, chlorite, zeolite (scolecite ?) present in some specimens.
(5) Rhyolite	Texture	Fine-grained (0.125 mm) flow-banded granular aggregate of quartz and K-spar, sparse phenocrysts of embayed quartz, altered albite.
	Alteration	Potassium feldspar partly unmixed to perthite, sericitized. Some xls. rimmed with albite. Sparse albite phenocrysts, seriticized. Secondary calcite abundant.
(4) Hornblende-biotite diabase	Texture	Diabasic, plagioclase phenocrysts sparse, less than 2.5 mm long.
	Alteration	Generally fresher than diabase, but andesine-labradorite commonly replaced by oligoclase. Biotite formed by reaction from hornblende, secondary orthoclase, chlorite, serpentine, zeolite present.
(3) Diabase	Texture	Fine-grained, felty groundmass, phenocrysts less than 2 mm long, less abundant than in other diabase types.
	Alteration	Intensely altered. Plagioclase sericitized, olivine replaced by calcite and chlorite; augite by secondary green biotite, more rarely by chlorite with magnetite rims. Zeolite present in some specimens, also trace of secondary orthoclase.
(2) Olivine diabase porphyry	Texture	Diabasic; phenocrysts 2.5 mm long, make up 50-60% of rock, are less conspicuous in outcrops than in labradorite-olivine diabase porphyry.
	Alteration	Tends to be deeply weathered. In fresh specimens, olivine has magnetite rims, is partly serpentinized.
(1) Labradorite-olivine diabase porphyry	Texture	Diabasic; conspicous phenocrysts, mainly labradorite laths 5.0 mm long, make up 30-40% of rock.
	Alteration	Olivine partly replaced by calcite and serpentine, some crystals have magnetite centers.

[1] Most magmatic hornblende is "basaltic" hornblende (lamprobolite); magmatic biotite is reddish-brown, deuteric biotite is green.

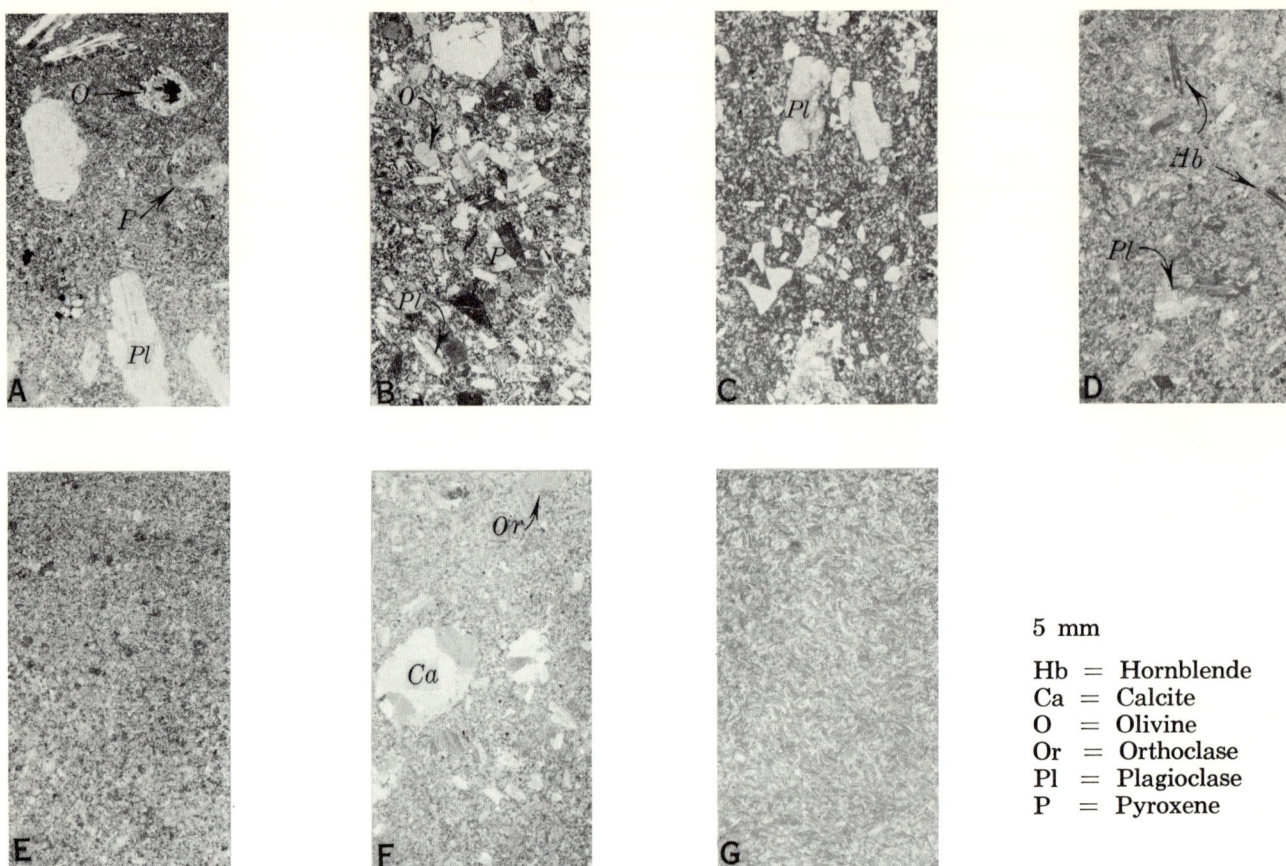

Figure 1. — Photomicrographs (crossed nicols) or rock types from a dike-swarm complex in Capitan quadrangle. Specimens from road cuts on U.S. Highway 380 west of Indian Divide.
A, labradorite-olivine diabase porphyry (Type 1); B, olivine diabase porphyry (Type 2); C, diabase (Type 3); D, hornblende diabase (Type 4); E, rhyolite (Type 5); F, latite (Type 6); and G, phonolite (Type 7).

the appearance of rhyolite (Type 5). As explained below in connection with the Carrizo Mountain intrusion, the rhyolite seems to be related to the larger granitoid stocks and laccoliths of the area; possibly it is not genetically related to the other dike rocks.

Alteration and Alkali Metosomatism

Deuteric and post-magmatic alteration is common in all types of dikes, particularly the diabase of Type 3. Olivine is altered to serpentine, calcite, penninite, magnetite, and goethite; pyroxene to chlorite, biotite, and calcite; and plagioclase is saussuritized to sericite, clays, calcite, zeolites, and opal.

The sodium content of plagioclase increases progressively with the degree of alteration. Throughout narrow Type 3 diabase dikes labradorite has generally been replaced by cloudy oligoclase. The centers of Type 3 diabase dikes more than 10 feet wide contain unaltered labradorite with extinction angles of about 30° on albite twins cut normal to (010). The margins of the same dike contain partially kaolinized or saussuritized oligoclase (extinction angles 0-18°). Secondary orthoclase commonly appears in the matrix of rocks as plagioclase becomes more sodic. Figure 3 shows the progressive changes in plagioclase of a Type 3 diabase dike, 24 feet wide. The samples were collected in a road cut on U.S. Highway 380, 7.0 miles west of the western village limit of Capitan. Going from the center of the dike towards the border, labradorite crystals first become cloudy and skeletonized, then are enveloped by ovoidal overgrowths of clear oligoclase. The sodium content increases gradually.

Most of the calcium displaced by the increasing amount of sodium in plagioclase goes into secondary calcite. Calcite is common not only in the matrix of altered rocks but also in small veinlets and in the wall-rock around dikes. Directly next to the dike that yielded the specimens for figure 3, sandstone of the Cub Mountain Formation has a calcite matrix. Only a trace of calcite is present in sandstone 6 feet away from the contact.

The kind of alteration and sodium metasomatism of plagioclase characteristic of Type 3 diabase dikes occurs in other types of diabase also, but to a lesser degree. In some dikes the chilled borders are relatively unaltered and contain calcic plagioclase. Table 2 summarizes the data. Since, at this stage of investigation, it is not known whether the rocks contain plagioclase or high- or low-temperature optical properties, extinction angles but no Ab:An ratios are given.

NEW MEXICO GEOLOGICAL SOCIETY • FIFTEENTH FIELD CONFERENCE

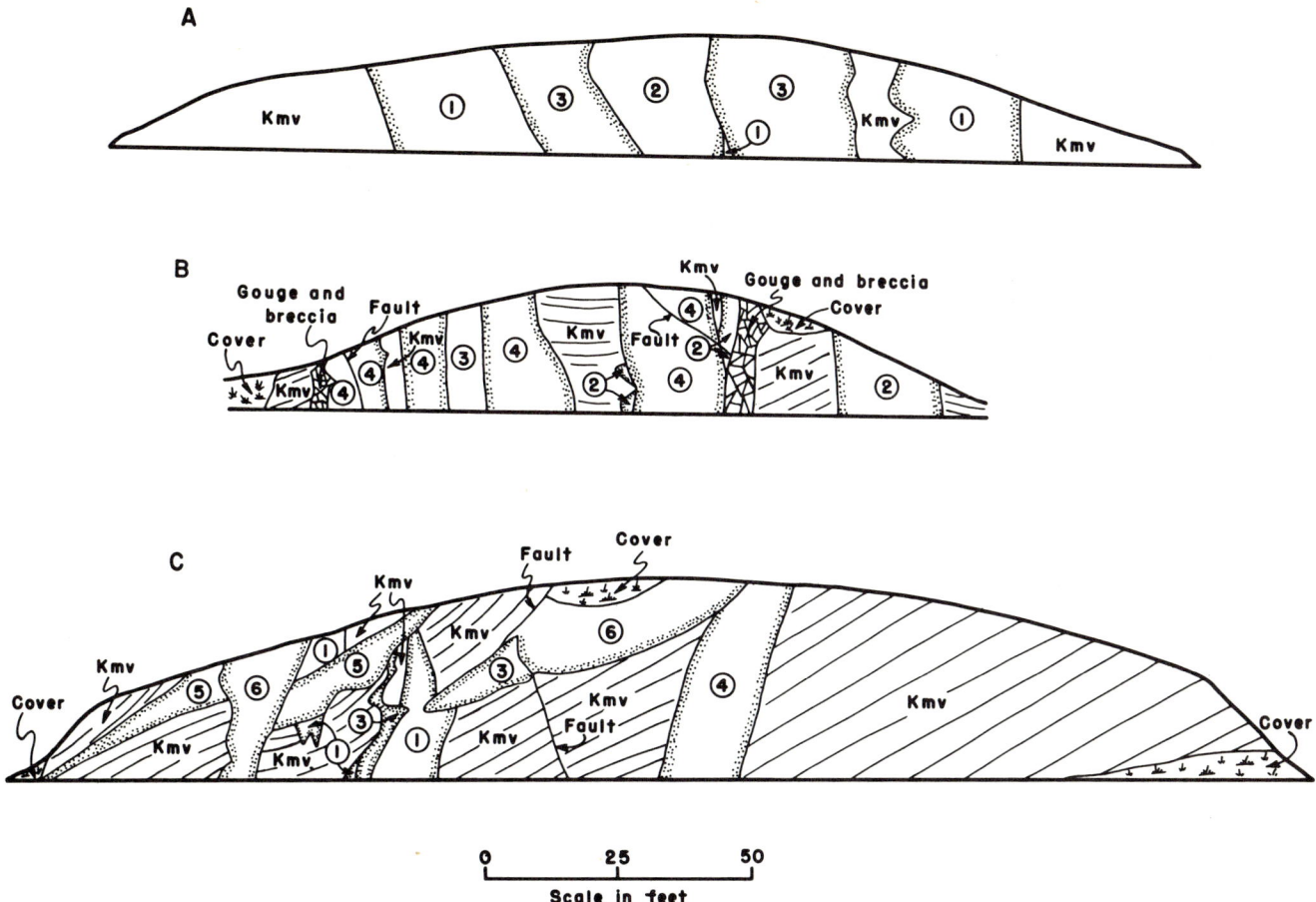

Figure 2. Sketches of road cuts along U.S. Highway 380, illustrating field relations of different rock types in dike swarm. ① Labradorite-olivine diabase porphyry. ② Olivine diabase porphyry. ③ Diabase. ④ Hornblende-biotite diabase. ⑤ Rhyolite. ⑥ Latite, Kmv-Mesaverde Formation. Stippling indicates chilled border. Locations west of western village limit of Capitan: A-3.4 miles, B-3.7 miles, C-6.6 miles.

NOTES ON CARRIZO MOUNTAIN

In addition to the detailed work on the dike swarm along Highway 380, a few reconnaissance traverses were run in 1956 across Carrizo Mountain to the north and the volcanic complex of the Sierra Blanca to the south. While the work was insufficient for definite conclusions, some interesting relationship became apparent.

Work on Carrizo Mountain showed that the top of the Mesaverde Formation does not dip under it and that it is not an "extrusive plug dome," as stated earlier (Anonymous, 1951). Instead, it is a steepsided intrusive body. At least, the Mesaverde beds that dip westward off Tucson Mountain toward the east side of Carrizo Mountain sharply reverse their dip within a few hundred feet of the igneous contact, and appear to be arched by the Carrizo Mountain intrusion. While diabase and rhyolite sills are common in westward-dipping Mesaverde beds, none were seen in the arched beds near Carrizo Mountain. It is possible that the sills do not reverse dip but continue beneath Carrizo Mountain, joining sills dipping inward from the west and forming flat cone sheets. If so, the sides of the cones would dip less than 30°, or half as much as in the famous Scottish cone sheets.

Patton (1951) gave the impression that the larger intrusive masses of the Capitan quadrangle, which make up the bulk of Capitan, Patos, Vera Cruz, and Carrizo Mountains are all varieties of alaskite (alaskite, kalialaskite, orthosite). Carrizo Mountain, however, is a differentiated body. A specimen of the border facies collected in Johnnie Canyon at the intrusive contact, about 2,200 feet below the summit, is fine-grained spherulitic rhyolite with vertical flow bands. It contains no phenocrysts. The groundmass consists of parallel potassium feldspar laths 0.1 mm long and about 20 percent quartz in the interstices. Opaque minerals make up 3 to 5 percent of the rocks and biotite 2 percent (figure 4D). The interior of the intrusion consists of a granite rock too dark to be called an alaskite. A specimen collected 0.6

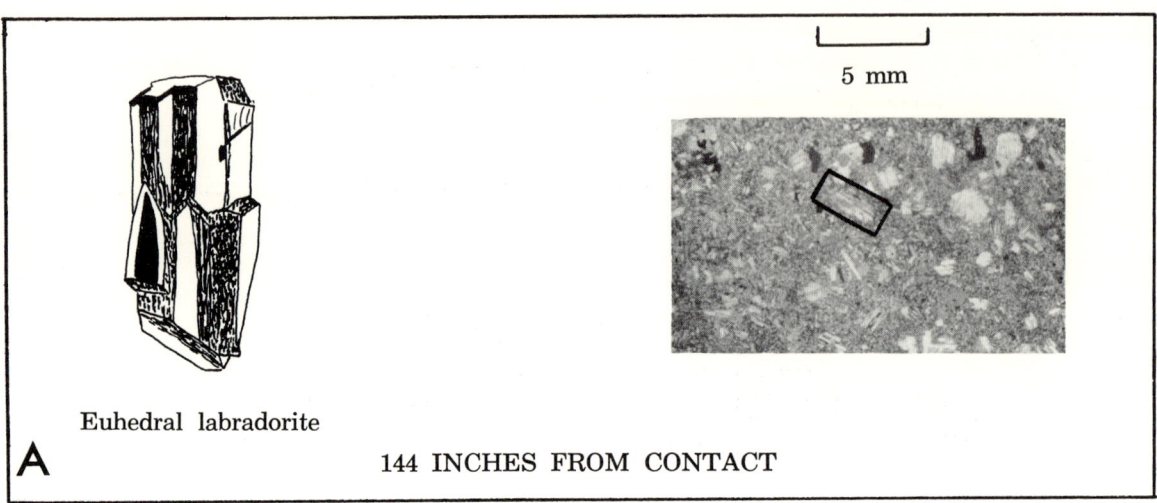
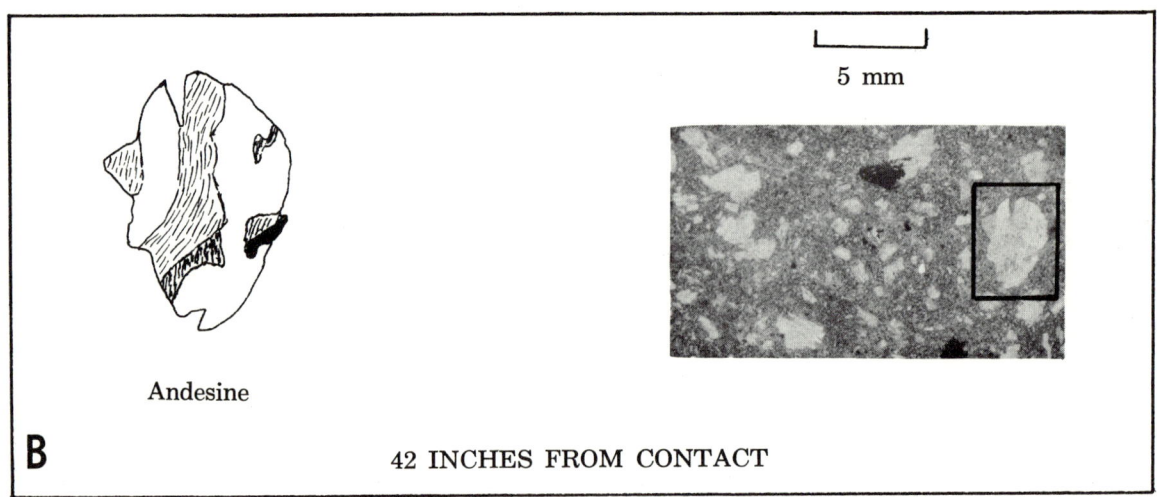
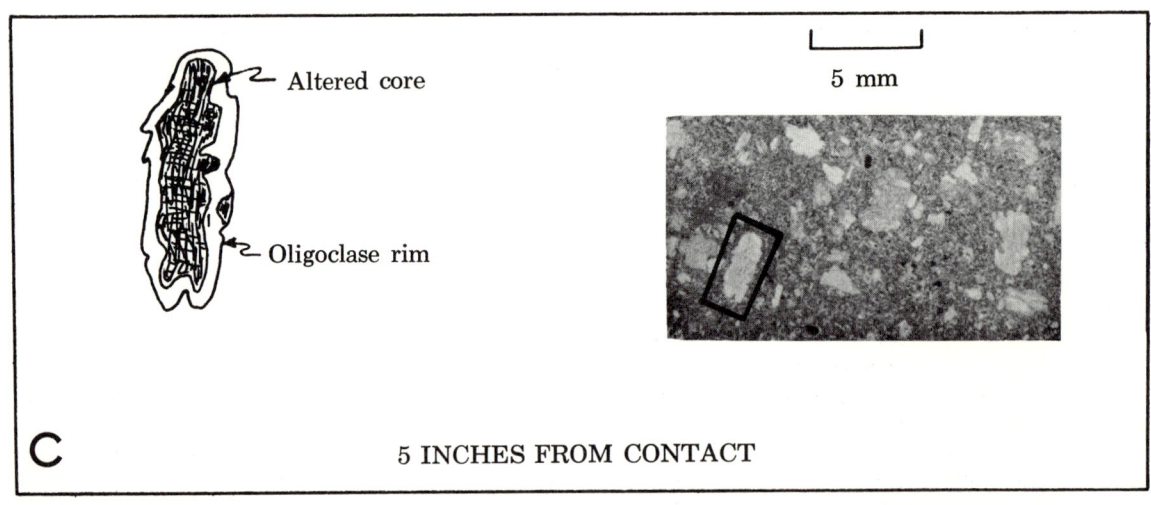

Figure 3. — Photomicrographs (crossed nicols) and drawings illustrating progressive sodium metasomatism of plagioclase in a diabase dike in Capitan quadrangle. (the crystal in the drawing is outlined on the photo to right). A, euhedral labradorite from Type 3 diabase similar to fig. 1C; B, partially rounded and altered plagioclase (andesine) showing faint curved twin planes; C, highly altered and rounded plagioclase phenocryst with clear oligoclase rim around saussuritized core.

Table 2. — Variation of extinction angles of plagioclase in diabase dikes with distance from border of dike.

Rock type number	Location on U.S. Highway 380, in miles west of western limit of Capitan	Distance from border of dike, inches	Maximum extinction angle of albite twins in plagioclase phenocrysts cut normal to (010)	Secondary orthoclase, percent
2	4.5	72	37	
		0	22	20
3	3.4	48	27	
		0	0	tr.
3	3.4	24	35	
		0	0-3	
3	7.0	12	20	
		144	32	
4	4.2	30	10	
		1	6	
4	4.2	60[a]	9	
		8[b]	30	
4	4.5	72	24	4
		3	19	10
		0[b]	21	5-8

[a]Altered rock.
[b]Fine-grained chilled rock with partly glassy matrix.

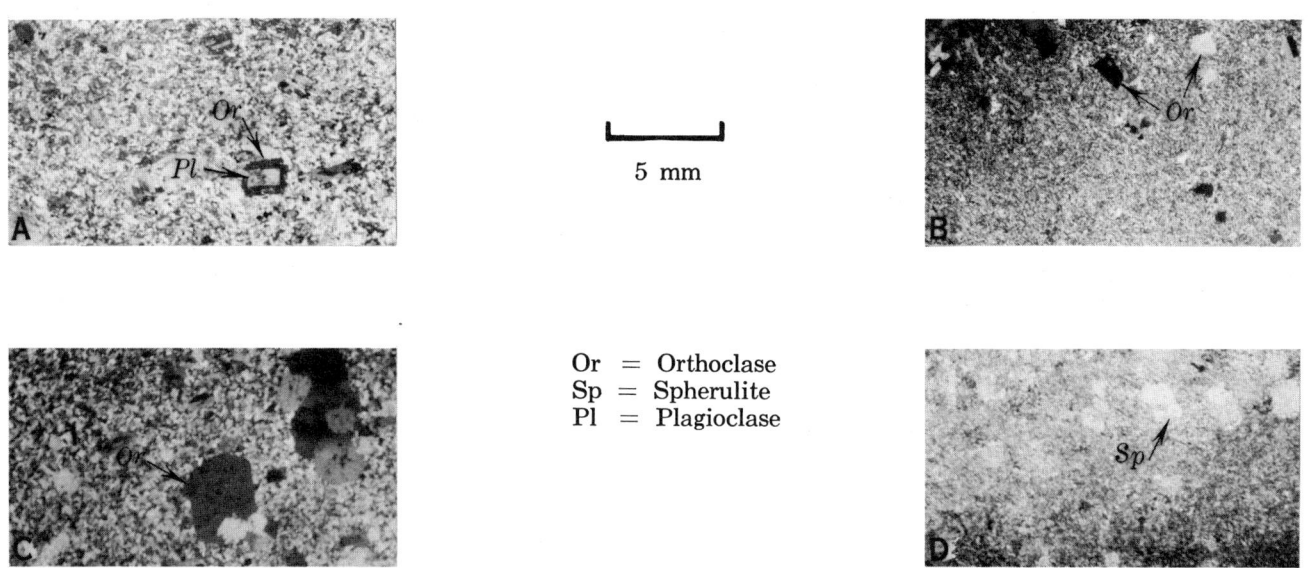

Or = Orthoclase
Sp = Spherulite
Pl = Plagioclase

Figure 4. — Photomicrographs (crossed nicols) of rocks from Carrizo Mountain in Capitan quadrangle. A, granite from central part of mass, 0.6 miles from contact in Johnnie Canyon, about 1,800 feet below summit; B, alaskite from SW¼ sec. 17, T. 7 S., R. 13 E., about 800 feet below summit; C, rhyolite from summit of Carrizo Mountain. Note orthoclase crystals; D, spherulitic rhyolite from contact of intrusion, Johnnie Canyon, SW¼ sec. 21, T. 7 S., R. 13 S., about 2,200 feet below summit.

miles west of the eastern contact in Johnnie Canyon and about 1,800 feet below the summit has abundant phenocrysts of oligoclase-andesine rimmed and partly replaced by orthoclase, set in a granitoid matrix of quartz and slightly perthitic orthoclase crystals about 0.2 mm in diameter. Opaque minerals and biotite phenocrysts make up about 13 percent of the rock (figure 4A). Higher up in the intrusion, orthoclase progressively replaces plagioclase phenocrysts. Rocks 800 feet below the summit (figure 4B) have abundant phenocrysts, or porphyroblasts, of orthoclase containing only ragged cores of plagioclase. They have less than 10 percent of dark minerals (partly chloritized biotite and opaque minerals) and could properly be called kalialaskite. At the summit (elevation 9,656 feet) the rocks again belong to the fine-grained border facies, showing that the top of the mountain is not far below the top of the original top of the intrusion. Unlike the border facies lower down, however, the rock at the summit lacks spherulites but contains abundant orthoclase phenocrysts or porphyroblasts, about 3 mm in diameter. Sparse quartz crystals are also present.

The evidence suggests that the larger orthoclase crystals near the roof of the intrusion were formed by metasomatic replacement of earlier minerals. Where plagioclase phenocrysts are present they are progressively replaced by orthoclase. The presence of orthoclase crystals in chilled border facies at the summit, and their absence lower down, suggest a post-magmatic origin.

The rhyolitic border facies of the Carrizo Mountain intrusion suggests an affinity with the rhyolitic (Type 5) phase of the dike swarm complex. Rhyolite sills and plugs are, in fact, most abundant in the country directly east of Carrizo Mountain. Further evidence can be found just north of the O-Bar-O ranch headquarters. There, a tongue of the Carrizo Mountain intrusion cuts across diabase dikes and is in turn cut by a phonolite dike. The age of the Carrizo Mountain intrusion relative to rocks in the dike swarm appears to be the same as that of the rhyolite.

NOTES ON THE VOLCANIC COMPLEX OF THE SIERRA BLANCA

A reconnaissance traverse from the village of Nogal to the head of Nogal Canyon, and from there to the top of Nogal Peak, showed the country rock to be pyroxene andesite flows and flow breccias for the entire distance. Their thickness must be in the thousands of feet. Diabase and rhyolite dikes, the continuation of the dike swarm studied along Highway 380, intrude the andesite. A body of brecciated quartz-bearing biotite syenite, intrusive into the andesite, was traversed for about a mile, beginning 6.0 miles from Nogal. Alteration is intense in this area. Thin sections of syenite show relict phenocrysts of andesine largely replaced by orthoclase, reminiscent of the rocks from Carrizo Mountain. Quartz makes up less than 5 percent of the rock. Prior to potassium metasomatism the rock was probably a quartz-bearing monzonite or quartz-poor granite.

Another type of alkali metasomatism is indicated by a specimen collected on the south side of Nogal Canyon, 3.3 miles from the fork of State Highway 37 and the Nogal Canyon road. About 80 percent of the rock is feathery albite-oligoclase in sheaves and spherulitic aggregates 2 to 7 mm in diameter; the rest is quartz, orthoclase, magnetite, calcite, and leucoxene. It appears to be an adinole, a rock formed by "a type of metasomatism brought about by the agency of liquid solutions of magmatic origin . . . , which involves an accession of soda or sodic compounds" (Harker, 1950, p. 128-130, especially figure 56). Most adinoles form by the albitization of argillaceous sediments next to albitized mafic igneous intrusions; the field relations of this occurrence are not yet known. It is mentioned merely because it illustrates the pervasive nature of alkali metasomatism in this region.

Traverses up Bonito Canyon and to the top of Monjeau Mountain showed field relations similar to those in Nogal Canyon. A quartz-bearing monzonite that underlies Bonito Lake and Monjeau Mountain again shows plagioclase crystals mantled and partially replaced by orthoclase. Augite phenocrysts are partially replaced by biotite. A dike of diabase porphyry cuts the monzonite on the west side of Bonito Lake, in a cut by the side of the Bonito Canyon Road, 5.1 miles from its junction with State Highway 48. The rock is highly altered and consists of phenocrysts of sericitized oligoclase-andesine up to 5 mm long and chloritized ferromagnesian minerals, in a fine-grained altered matrix. It somewhat resembles altered Type 1 labradorite-olivine diabase porphyry. The monzonite is either older than the dike swarm and therefore older than the Carrizo Mountain intrusion, or there is a second generation of diabase younger than the dikes studied along Highway 380. According to R. H. Weber (personal communication), post-phonolite diabase porphyry dikes are common in the Carrizozo area; and T. B. Thompson (personal communication) found numerous mafic dikes cutting across monzonitic intrusions in the Sierra Blanca. It appears that the rocks whose age relations were worked out in the Indian Divide-Carrizo Mountain area are only part of a more complex regional sequence.

SUMMARY AND CONCLUSIONS

The most probable sequence of magmatic events in the Carrizo Mountain-Indian Divide-Nogal region is as follows:
(1) Eruption of thousands of feet of pyroxene andesite flows and flow breccias in the southern part of the area.
(2) Intrusion of a NNE-trending dike swarm, extending from the vicinity of Sierra Blanca Peak some 40 miles into the Jicarilla Mountain area. The dikes fall into at least seven types, which are in order of age:

Type 1 — Labradorite-olivine diabase porphyry
Type 2 — Olivine diabase porphyry
Type 3 — Diabase
Type 4 — Hornblende-biotite diabase
Type 5 — Rhyolite
Type 6 — Latite grading into trachyte
Type 7 — Phonolite

(3) Intrusion of felsic stocks and laccoliths, probably contemporaneous with Type 5 rhyolite dikes.

Additional magmatic events may have occurred in surrounding areas. The age of the igneous rocks has not been determined, other than that they are younger than the Cub Mountain Formation (late Cretaceous to early Tertiary) and older than the late Tertiary high-level terrace deposits south of Indian Divide.

Magmatic differentiation resulted in a strong concentration of sodium and potassium in the late magmatic and post-magmatic stages. Evidence for this is seen in the following phenomena:

(1) Development of phonolite as the last phase of the dike-swarm complex.
(2) Replacement of labradorite by oligoclase dikes.
(3) Development of minor secondary orthoclase and biotite in some diabase dikes.
(4) Replacement of andesine phenocrysts by orthoclase in the upper part of the granitoid Carrizo Mountain intrusion and development of orthoclase porphyroblasts in the chilled border facies at the roof of the same intrusion.
(5) Replacement of andesine by orthoclase in the felsic intrusive rocks of the Nogal Canyon-Bonito Canyon region.
(6) Possible occurrence of adinole, a contact metasomatic rock produced by the introduction of sodium, in Nogal Canyon.

REFERENCES CITED

Anonymous, 1951, Road log—Lincoln to Carrizozo via White Oaks: Roswell Geol. Soc. 5th Field Conf., Guidebook of the Capitan-Carrizozo-Chupadera Region, p. 2-6.

Harker, Alfred, 1950, Metamorphism, 3rd ed., London, Methuen and Co., Ltd., 362 p.

Patton, L. T., 1951, Igneous rocks of the Capitan quadrangle, New Mexico, and vicinity: Am. Mineralogist, v. 36, p. 713-716.

MINERAL RESOURCES OF LINCOLN COUNTY

George B. Griswold

State Bureau of Mines and Mineral Resources
New Mexico Institute of Mining & Technology
Socorro, New Mexico

The history of mining in Lincoln County dates back as far as 1865 when gold placers were discovered in Dry Gulch near Nogal. Significant mining was carried on from 1880 to 1906, with $4 million worth of gold, coal, iron, silver, copper, and lead produced. Mining since 1906 has produced only $1.4 million, mainly from magnetite-hematite ores. Figure 1 is a mining district map of the County.

Lincoln County, however, has received new attention by exploration companies in the last few years. Interest has been centered on the iron deposits, on occurrences of molybdenum on Nogal and Sierra Blanca peaks, on silver veins along Bonito Creek, and coal in the Mesaverde Formation along the rims of the Sierra Blanca basinal structure. No new discoveries have been announced thus far.

IRON

There are about 24 known deposits of magnetite-hematite ore in Lincoln County, extending from the Gallinas Mountains in the north to the Capitan Mountains in the south. The deposits are all of the pyrometasomatic type, and are associated with the contacts of Early Tertiary stocks and dikes. The deposits have been described by Kelley (1949), Soulé (1947, 1949), Sheridan (1947), and Griswold (1959). The iron-ore reserves of Lincoln County have been estimated to contain 3,000,000 tons of 45-55 per cent grade (Kelley, 1949). The bulk of this is in one deposit—the Capitan, located about five miles north of the community of Capitan. This deposit is interesting because of the ore control exerted by a collapse structure in the San Andres Formation on the south flank of the Capitan Mountains alaskite intrusion.

Typically, the iron deposits of Lincoln County are within a few hundred feet of the igneous-sedimentary contact. With the exception of the Capitan deposit, the ore bodies are small, being in the less-than-100,000-ton class. The most favorable sediments for replacement are limestone beds of the San Andres and Yeso formations. The primary ore minerals are magnetite and some hematite. Most deposits have been subjected to oxidation, forming irregular masses of hematite-limonite within the original magnetite-rich zones. This conversion has yielded some deposits unsuitable for magnetic concentration.

GOLD

The most famous mining camp in central New Mexico is White Oaks, on the southern slopes of Lone Mountain about ten miles north-northeast of Carrizozo. The mines are about a mile west of the nearly deserted village of White Oaks. The mining heyday for White Oaks was from 1879 to 1904; the gold production during that period amounted to 143,000 ounces valued at $2,860,000. Although periodic attempts have been made to revive the district, little mining has been done since 1934.

The writer has made a cursory examination of the mines (Griswold, 1959), but the geology of the district is largely unmapped. Lone Mountain consists of monzonite intruded into Paleozoic and Mesozoic sedimentary rocks. The mines are in an area where the Mesaverde Formation and Mancos Shale are much invaded by wide north- and northeast-trending dikes of monzonite and mica trap rock. Zones of intense brecciation of the Cretaceous sediments are present. The Cretaceous is everywhere, much altered by the igneous intrusions. Tertiary agglomerate and tuff are reported on the upper ridges of the area (Smith and Budding, 1959). In spite of the complicated structural setting, the gold veins themselves are simple. For the most part, they are in steeply dipping north-striking fractures seldom more than a few inches wide. The gold occurs free as thin plates, wire, and tiny blebs accompanied by iron and manganese oxides, minor amounts of quartz, and gypsum. Frequently the pay zone is composed of several parallel veinlets. Where the veins cut the monzonite, little wall rock alteration is evident. The three most productive mines were deep: Old Abe, 1,500 feet; North Homestake, 1,400 feet; and South Homestake, 660 feet. Little water was found in any of the mines, and oxidation extends to the bottom levels. Judging from the stoped areas of the deep mines, the ore shoots were several times more persistent downward than along strike.

Three other somewhat isolated mines have produced lode gold in Lincoln County: Vera Cruz, located just north of U.S. 380 approximately ten miles east of Carrizozo; Helen Rae-American, three miles southwest of Nogal; and Parsons, in Tanbark Canyon, a side canyon off Bonito Creek, three miles west of Bonito Lake. The Vera Cruz and Parsons mines are in highly altered breccia pipes, whereas the Helen Rae-American is a north-striking fissure vein. The Helen Rae-American had the most productive history, including the small placer gold deposits in Dry Gulch below the vein outcrop.

The Jicarilla Mountains east of Ancho have yielded some placer gold. The placer deposits are restricted to narrow gullies and arroyos that drain the core of the mountain group which is underlain by monzonite porphyry. A few lode mines were worked in the area, but most of the gold came from the placers. Certain arroyos are reported to contain as much as $3.00 per cubic yard in gold, but the almost complete absence of water in the district has prevented large-scale mining.

COAL

The Sierra Blanca coal field is estimated to contain 1,644 million tons of bituminous coal (Read and others, 1950). Of this immense reserve, only a fraction can be

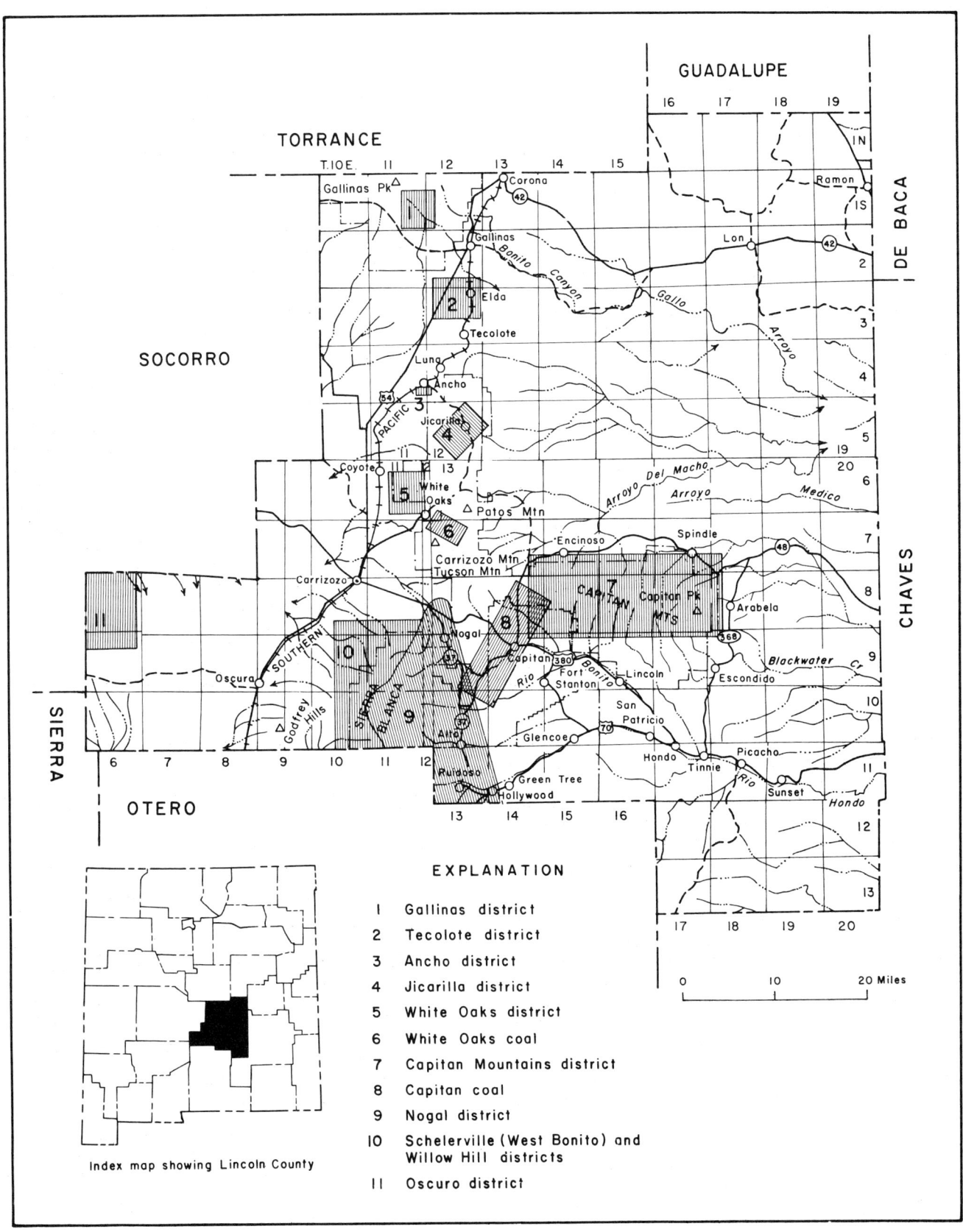

Figure 1. — Map of mining districts in Lincoln County, New Mexico.

considered exploitable because of depth of burial, structure, and thinness of the coal beds. Coal occurs at several horizons in the Mesaverde Formation but thicknesses exceeding 30 inches are rare. Coal mining has been conducted in two principal areas: near Capitan and just east of White Oaks. The total past production from Lincoln County is about 600,000 tons.

In recent years, the Sierra Blanca field has been examined as a possible source for providing low-cost fuel for steam electric power. Such a use would demand a large reserve of easily strippable coal. Thus far, searches for a large reserve have not been successful because of the complicated structure in the White Oaks and Capitan areas and the extreme depths in other parts of the field.

MOLYBDENUM

Molybdenite was accidentally discovered during the early period of gold-silver prospecting in Nogal and Bonito creeks in the Sierra Blanca. The presence of molybdenite did not cause concern to the early miners and was soon forgotten. In 1957, the Climax Molybdenum Co. (now American Metals Climax, Inc) drilled four diamond drill holes on a molybdenite prospect, known as the Rialto, on the east slope of Nogal Peak. Results of this drilling were discouraging and no further work was done. During the summer of 1963, interest rose again in the area when a large copper company staked many claims over a new molybdenite discovery on the northern slopes of Sierra Blanca Peak, about four miles south of the Rialto prospect. As of this writing, another mining company is reported ready to re-examine the Rialto deposit.

The Rialto deposit is contained within a syenodiorite stock that invaded early Tertiary basaltic andesite (Griswold and Missaghi, 1964). The stock is roughly circular in outcrop shape and has an average diameter of one mile. The surrounding volcanic rocks are bleached and pyritized as much as 1,000 feet outward from the stock contact. Hydrothermal alteration associated with the deposition of molybdenite is evident in the southern part of the stock. The molybdenite occurs both as true disseminations and as flakes in quartz-pyrite veinlets. Minor amounts of chalcopyrite accompanied the deposition of molybdenite. The meager amount of exploratory work done thus far on the deposit prevents an accurate estimate of the ore tonnage or grade. An interesting feature of the area is that the old Parsons gold mine is located on the south end of the stock. This mine worked low-grade gold ore contained within an intensely altered breccia pipe. Geochemical sampling by the writer (Griswold and Missaghi, 1964) has revealed anomalous amounts of molybdenum in the breccia.

LEAD-ZINC-COPPER-SILVER-GOLD

The Sierra Blanca contains numerous complex ore veins. The primary ore minerals are galena, sphalerite, chalcopyrite, argentite, and auriferous pyrite. The oxidized parts of the veins contain locally rich silver ore shoots of native and halide silver. The East Utah Mining Company is now actively exploring several such veins along upper Bonito Creek. The veins are simple fissure structures, frequently related to pre-ore andesite and latite porphyry dikes that cut the basaltic andesite volcanics. Although these veins are in the same vicinity as the previously discussed molybdenite occurrences, there is no direct genetic relationship.

FLUORSPAR-BASTNAESITE

The Gallinas Mountains west of Corona contain numerous but small fluorspar deposits. Some deposits carry as much as one per cent bastnaesite, a rare-earth carbonate mineral. Kelley (1949) and Kelley and others (1946) described the geology of the area, and Rothrock and others (1946) described the individual deposits. The core of the Gallinas Mountains is Tertiary syenite and monzonite that have intruded Abo, Yeso, and Glorieta formations. The intrusions occur mostly as sills, laccoliths, and dikes. The fluorspar and bastnaesite deposits are related to both pipe-shaped breccia zones and fault zones. The breccia type probably accounts for the largest tonnage of fluorspar-bastnaesite reserves. The breccias are composed of fragments of Permian sediments that have been much altered and partly replaced by fluorspar, barite, calcite, and quartz. The bastnaesite occurs as tiny, brownish yellow tabular crystals, and because of the similarity to both brownish calcite and barite crystals, the mineral is difficult to recognize in the field. Galena, sphalerite, bornite, chalcocite, and pyrite are present in some deposits.

The mineral assemblage of the deposits is suggestive of a carbonatite, but because the deposits are located in a carbonate-rich host, it is difficult to establish just how much carbonate was introduced during mineralization.

SELECTED REFERENCES

Anderson, E. C., 1957, The metal resources of New Mexico and their economic features through 1954: N. Mex. Inst. Min. and Tech., State Bur. Mines and Mineral Res. Bull. 39.

Bodine, M. C., 1956, Geology of Capitan coal field, Lincoln County, New Mexico: N. Mex. Inst. Min. and Tech., State Bur. Mines and Mineral Res. Circ. 35.

Campbell, M. R., 1907, Coal in the vicinity of Fort Stanton Reservation, Lincoln County, New Mexico: U.S. Geol. Survey Bull. 316, p. 431-434.

Griswold, G. B., 1959, Mineral deposits of Lincoln County, New Mexico: N. Mex. Inst. Min. and Tech., State Bur. Mines and Mineral Res. Bull. 67.

Griswold, G. B., and Missaghi, Fazlollah, 1964, Geology and geochemical survey of a molybedenum deposit near Nogal Peak, Lincoln County, New Mexico: N. Mex. Inst. Min. and Tech., State Bur. Mines and Mineral Res. Circ. 67.

Jones, F. A., 1904, New Mexico mines and minerals: Santa Fe, New Mexican Printing Co.

Kelley, V. C., 1945, Tertiary iron ore in Triassic collapse breccia (abs): Geol. Soc. America Bull., v. 56, p. 1172-1173.

——— 1946, Stratigraphy and structure of the Gallinas Mountains, New Mexico (abs): Geol. Soc. America Bull., v. 57, p. 1254.

———, 1949, Geology and economics of New Mexico iron-ore deposits: Univ. N. Mex. Publ. in geol., pub. 2.

——— Rothrock, H. E., and Smalley, R. G., 1946, Geology and mineral deposits of the Gallinas district, Lincoln County, New Mexico: U.S. Geol. Survey Strategic Minerals Inv. Prelim. Map 3-211.

Lindgren, Waldemar, Graton, L. C., and Gordon, C. H., 1910, The ore deposits of New Mexico: U.S. Geol. Survey Prof. Paper 68, p. 175-184.

Perhac, R. M., and Heinrich, E. W., 1959, Fluorite-bastnaesite deposits of the Gallinas Mountains, New Mexico, and bastnaesite paragenesis: Econ. Geology, v. 59, p. 226-239.

Read, C. B., Duffner, R. T., Wood, G. H., and Zapp, A. D., 1950, Coal resources of New Mexico: U.S. Geol. Survey Circ. 89.

Rothrock, H. E., Johnson, C. H., and Hahn, A. D., 1946, Fluorspar resources of New Mexico: N. Mex. Inst. Min. and Tech., State Bur. Mines and Mineral Res. Bull. 21.

Sheridan, M. J., 1947, Lincoln County iron deposits, New Mexico: U.S. Bur. Mines Rpt. Inv. 3988.

Smith, C. T., and Budding, A. J., 1959, Little Black Peak Quadrangle, east half: N. Mex. Inst. Min. and Tech., State Bur. Mines and Mineral Res. Geol. Map Series, no. 11.

Soulé, J. H., 1946, Exploration of Gallinas fluorspar deposits, Lincoln County, New Mexico: U.S. Bur. Mines Rpt. Inv. 3854.

——————— 1947, Capitan iron deposits, Lincoln County, New Mexico: U.S. Bur. Mines Rpt. Inv. 4022.

——————— 1949, Investigation of Capitan iron deposits, Lincoln County, New Mexico: U.S. Bur. Mines Rpt. Inv. 4514.

Talmage, S. B., and Wootton, T. P., 1937, The non-metallic resources of New Mexico and their economic features (exclusive of fuels): N. Mex. Inst. Min. and Tech., State Bur. Mines and Mineral Res. Bull. 12.

Walker, G. W., and Osterwald, F. W., 1956, Uraniferous magnetite-hematite deposit at the Prince mine, Lincoln County, New Mexico: Econ. Geology, v. 51, p. 231-222.

Wegemann, C. H., 1914, Geology and coal resources of the Sierra Blanca coal field, Lincoln and Otero Counties, New Mexico: U.S. Geol. Survey Bull. 541, p. 419-452.

x x x

NOTES ON THE MINERAL DEPOSITS OF THE GALLINAS MOUNTAINS, NEW MEXICO

Ralph M. Perhac

University of Michigan*
Ann Arbor, Michigan

INTRODUCTION

Many small mineral deposits occur in the eastern part of the Gallinas Mountains in the Red Cloud district. The deposits may be divided into two types — iron deposits and fluorite-copper deposits. Inasmuch as the iron ores occur only in limestone at an intrusive contact, they are geologically distinct from the other mineral occurrences. The fluorite and copper deposits, however, are not distinctly different from one another; they differ only in the tenor of fluorite and copper minerals. The small amounts of gold, silver, lead, and bastnaesite that were mined were recovered from the fluorite-copper deposits.

Although the presence of mineral deposits in the Gallinas Mountains was known as early as 1885, it was the increased mineral demand during World War II that spurred prospecting which resulted in the discovery of most of the deposits. About 10,000 tons of iron were mined in 1942 and 1943, and nearly 4,000 tons of copper ores were produced up to 1949. Between 1942 and 1955, fluorite was shipped from at least three mines in the district. And one mine, the Red Cloud fluorite mine, yielded bastnaesite between 1953 and 1955. Total fluorspar production probably was less than 2,000 tons, from which about 60 tons of bastnaesite concentrate were recovered (Griswold, 1959). Altogether 29 mines and prospects are located in the district. Except for assessment work, all are now idle.

The general geology of the Gallinas Mountains is discussed in another paper in this guidebook. Details of the bastnaesite mineralization are given in a previously published paper (Perhac and Heinrich, 1964).

FLUORITE-COPPER DEPOSITS

Except for two minor occurrences, all fluorite-copper deposits are in Yeso (Permian) sandstones and siltstones overlying a trachyte laccolith. During intrusion of the laccolith, the overlying sedimentary rocks were domed and extensively faulted (high-angle normal faults). Because of the brittle nature of the Yeso, brecciation is common along the faults. Individual breccia zones may be as much as 30 feet wide and range in length from a few feet to over 1,500 feet. It is along the faults and in the breccia zones that the epigenetic mineralization occurred. The large amount of open space and the many cross fractures (commonly joints) served as excellent channelways for the mineralizing fluids. As the ore fluid rose, it precipitated minerals in the open spaces associated with the faulting and accompanying brecciation.

*Present address: Production Research Division, Humble Oil & Refining Co., Houston, Texas

Ore minerals occur not only in breccia zones paralleling faults, but also in pipe-like shattered zones at the intersection of two or more major faults.

Open-space filling is, by far, the common mode of occurrence for the mineralization. Only in a few areas of intense mineralization has the sandstone actually been replaced. Typical ore specimens thus consist of either a highly brecciated rock criss-crossed by small veinlets or a porous mass of fluorite and copper minerals from the breccia zone. True fissure veins, without associated wallrock brecciation, are relatively rare.

The mineralogy of the deposits is summarized in table 1. Fluorite is the most abundant mineral, even in those deposits worked primarily for copper. Barite or quartz are generally the next most abundant minerals. Pyrite, although minor, is ubiquitous. Every deposit contains these four primary minerals. In addition the cerium fluo-carbonate, bastnaesite, was identified in all but three deposits. Some deposits are mineralogically simple, containing virtually only four hypogene minerals: fluorite, quartz, barite, and pyrite. In contrast, the Rio Tinto deposit contains at least nine hypogene minerals plus a variety of supergene species. Many deposits contain at least traces of the copper sulfides bornite and chalcocite. At some, oxidation was so complete that no trace of the sulfide is apparent, the presence of copper being shown by azurite, malachite, and particularly chrysocolla. Galena and its alteration products (cerussite, anglesite, and pyromorphite) occur in some deposits.

Most of the fluorite-copper deposits show evidence of at least two periods of hypogene mineralization. During the first period mineralizing fluids deposited quartz, barite, sulfide minerals, fluorite, bastnaesite, and perhaps calcite. They probably were deposited in this general order as indicated by such features as quartz-lined fractures, fluorite deposits on etched barite crystals, and bastnaesite crystals along fluorite cleavage and fracture planes. Following the initial phase of mineralization, the deposits were refractured as shown by the number of early-formed minerals that are fractured and bent or microfaulted. During the second phase, mainly barite, fluorite, and locally abundant calcite were precipitated. In addition, at a few deposits, minor late silica occurs as chalcedony lining tiny cavaties in the ore. Supergene alteration was the final step in the formation of the deposits.

Several facts indicate that these are low temperature mineral deposits. Fracture filling was the main type of deposition. Abundant open spaces, comb structure, crustification, and the presence of many short and irregular veinlets all attest to low temperature and pressure. (The sedimentary cover probably did not exceed 1,500 feet at the time of mineralization.) The lack of wallrock altera-

Table 1: Mineralogy of the Fluorite-Copper Deposits in the Red Cloud District, New Mexico

	1	2	3	4	5	6	7	8	9	10	11	12	13	14	15	16	17
Fluorite	X	x	x	x	X	x	x	X	x	X	x	x	x	x	x	x	x
Quartz	M	tr	m	m	m	m	tr	m	M	m	m	tr	m	m	x	m	m
Barite	x	x	tr	m	M	M	M	M	m	M	m	m	m	m	m	M	m
Bastnaesite	m			tr	tr	tr	m	tr	tr	tr	tr	tr	tr	tr	tr	tr	tr
Calcite	tr	tr	tr	tr							tr	M	tr	m		m	tr
Chalcedony													tr		tr		
Pyrite	tr	tr	tr	m	tr	tr	m	tr	tr	tr	tr	tr	tr	tr	tr	tr	tr
Galena		m	tr			tr							tr	m		m	
Bornite		tr	tr		tr								tr				
Chalcocite		m	M	tr									tr	tr			
Limonite	tr	tr	tr	tr	tr	tr	tr	tr	tr	tr	tr	tr	tr	tr	tr	tr	tr
Hematite	tr	tr	tr	tr	tr	tr	tr	tr	tr	tr	tr	tr	tr	tr	tr	tr	tr
Pyromorphite		tr	tr									tr		tr		tr	
Cerussite		?												m		tr	
Anglesite			tr											tr			tr
Chrysocolla		m	m		tr							tr	tr	tr		tr	
Malachite		tr	tr		tr							tr	tr	tr		tr	
Azurite		tr	tr									tr	tr	tr			

X = greater than 50%
x = 25 - 50%
M = 10 - 25%
m = 5 - 10%
tr = less than 5%

Prospects
1. Red Cloud Fluorite
2. Red Cloud Copper and Deadwood
3. Little Wonder
4. Last Chance
5. Eagle Nest
6. Bottleneck
7. Congress
8. Conqueror No. 4 and Hilltop
9. Summit
10. Hoosier Girl North
11. Hoosier Girl South
12. Eureka
13. Rio Tinto
14. All American
15. Sky High
16. Pride No. 2
17. M and E No. 13

tion and the presence of chalcedony also suggest a relatively low temperature for the ore-forming fluid. Finally, a fluid inclusion geothermometric study on bastnaesite indicates a formational temperature of 175 to 185°C. On the basis, therefore, of texture, structure, mineralogy, and temperature of formation, the Gallinas Mountains fluorite-copper deposits are considered epithermal.

IRON DEPOSITS

Five iron deposits occur in the Gallinas Mountains. They are typical limestone replacement lodes and all are in Yeso limestone (or its metasomatized equivalent) that is in contact with the underlying trachyte laccolith. It is evident, from the irregular shape of the mineralized zones and the exclusion of all rock types except limestone (gypsum at one deposit) as a host, that the iron minerals are replacement deposits. Fracture control, nevertheless, is evident, and the greatest ore concentrations typically are present along northwest or northeast fractures. In general, the ore fluids probably rose along the steep fractures and replaced limestone while migrating along bedding planes away from the fractures.

The mineralogy of the lodes is simple. Magnetite, hematite, and limonite are, for all practical purposes, the only minerals present. However, trace amounts of pyrite also were noted. The calcite that is commonly mixed with the iron minerals is undoubtedly derived from the host. This also applies to the gypsum mixed with the ore at the Red Cliff mine. Quartz is present in small amounts. Locally, tremolite and diopside, derived from a skarn, are dispersed throughout the mineralized rock.

The first step in the formation of the deposits was the introduction of SiO_2 from either minor silification of the Yeso sandstone near the ore zone, or crystallization of minor quartz in the limestone. At those deposits at which skarns occur some SiO_2 was utilized in the formation of lime silicate minerals. Iron was introduced following the addition of SiO_2. At the skarn deposits, some iron was first used for the formation of tremolite-diopside; the presence of dolomite in parts of the Yeso prevented extensive magnesia metasomatism. The skarn stage preceded precipitation of ore minerals. After satisfying all possible requirements of the silicates, the remaining iron in the mineralizing fluids was depostied as magnetite and hematite. The final phase in the formation of the ore deposits was surficial alteration. This is indicated by hydration of the iron minerals to the ubiquitous limonite, and possibly some oxidation of magnetite to hematite.

The temperature at which the iron deposits formed is not easily determined because no critical minerals or assemblages have been found. A priori, one would suspect a relatively high temperature. Two features, however, suggest that the temperature may have been considerably lower than that at which many other contact metasomatic deposits formed. First, the lime silicate assemblage (calcite-tremolite-quartz-diopside) could form at 250-300°C. This assemblage may be characteristic of albite-spidote hornfles facies rather than the higher temperature hornblende hornfles facies. The lower temperature is based on such considerations as: 1) disequilibrium as indicated by four phases in a three component system, 2) low CO_2 partial pressure, and 3) presence of chlorite-muscovite (critical for albite-epidote facies) matrix in sandstones near the deposits. Thus a temperature of 250-300°C (Turner, 1958) is possible for the metamorphism, hence a somewhat lower temperature for the ore deposition. Second, the presence of unreplaced gypsum in the ore indicates that the ore fluid temperature was less than that at which gypsum dehydrates to anhydrite (about 200°C considering pressure coefficients of transformation). Admittedly, original gypsum may have changed during mineralization and then hydrated back during surficial alteration. However, the gypsum lacks relict anhydrite and also lacks textures indicating original dehydration plus later hydration (Goldman, 1952). Thus the iron minerals may have formed at about 200°C.

In suggesting a low temperature for mineralization, certain assumptions are made: 1) temperatures assigned to the albite-epidote facies approach the correct order of magnitude, 2) an open system prevailed, 3) sufficient permeability existed to allow escape of CO_2 thereby resulting in low CO_2 pressure, and 4) gypsum was not dehydrated. If these conditions were met, then the Gallinas iron deposits probably formed in the temperature range of 200-250°C.

REFERENCES CITED

Goldman, M. I., 1952, Deformation, metamorphism, and mineralization in gypsum-anhydrite cap rock, Sulphur salt dome, Louisiana: Geol. Soc. America Mem. 50, 169 p.

Griswold, G. B., 1959, Mineral deposits of Lincoln County, New Mexico: N. M. Inst. Min. Tech., State Bur Mines and Min. Res., Bull. 67, 117 p.

Perhac, R. M. and Heinrich, E. W., 1964, Fluorite-bastnaesite deposits of the Gallinas Mountains, New Mexico and bastnaesite paragenesis: Econ. Geol., v. 59, p. 226-239.

Turner, F. J., 1958, Mineral assemblages of individual metamorphic facies in Fyfe, W. S., Turner, F. J. and Verhoogen, J., Metamorphic reactions and metamorphic facies: Geol Soc. America Mem. 73, p. 199-239.

OIL AND GAS TESTS IN LINCOLN COUNTY, NEW MEXICO

Kay C. Havenor
Consulting Geologist, Roswell, New Mexico

INTRODUCTION

The conference area, relative to petroleum exploration, remains unexplored. The area extends from T. 1 S. through T. 13 S., and from R. 8 E. through R. 19 E. and contains approximately 5,100 square miles. Eighteen dry exploratory tests have been drilled in the area. Three were drilled in the same section, and two in another section. The tests give an effective ratio of less than one test per 350 square miles which is not a firm basis to draw many conclusions on as to the future petroleum potential of the majority of Lincoln County. Of the eighteen tests probably as many as eight were geologically or geophysically located.

The primary objective of all these tests has been the shallow beds ranging in age from Cretaceous through Permian. The average depth of test drilled was 1,620 feet (excluding one 8,050 foot test on the west side of Area 3). The average depth of test covers a minimum depth of 400 feet, and a maximum of 3,429 feet. Of twelve tests considered, 5 probably bottomed in the Yeso, 4 in the Abo, and 3 in igneous rocks underlying the Abo. One test bottomed in the Cretaceous, and one in the Precambrian after penetrating a Pennsylvanian section.

Exploration activity in the Lincoln County area began with the drilling of the National Exploration No. 1 Picacho in November, 1919, and has continued until recently when the Bryce Dugger No. 1 Federal was plugged and abandoned in March 1963. The majority of drilling was done during the early 1950's.

Exploratory drilling in the conference area has been the natural outcome of several factors. The very productive San Andres Formation in Eddy and Lea Counties, to the southeast, can be seen in outcrop throughout much of the area. Similarly, the Dakota Sandstone which is productive to the north can be seen in scattered portions of the area. The presence of the petroliferous San Andres in conjunction with mappable surface structures would naturally give rise to exploratory drilling. Of most significance to the exploration history of this area is probably the long and often reported occurrences of oil slicks, and rainbow shows of oil in water tanks, and in wells of some parts of the area. In addition, a few small dead oil seeps have been reported.

Encouraged by structure, seeps, shows of oil in water wells, or only the close proximity to a main road, the tests were drilled. Several tests encountered shows of oil, and completion was attempted, but no commercial production has yet been found.

EXPLORATION AREAS

Lincoln County can be divided into three exploration areas for the purposes of this report (See figures 1, and 2).

Area 1 is primarily the dip slope of the Sacramento-Sierra Blanca-Jicarilla Mountains. Area 2 contains the intrusive complex of the Northern Sacramento, and Jicarilla Mountains and the Sierra Blanca. Area 3 is in the northern Tularosa Basin and extends north to the Chupadera Mesa and Gran Quivira area, and is predominately Permian sedimentary rocks covered in some areas by Quaternary basalt flows.

Area 1, the dip slope of the Sacramento-Sierra Blanca-Jicarilla Mountains, appears to be the least structurally deformed of the three divisions considered. It also contains 10 of the eighteen exploratory tests drilled in the conference area. Seven of the tests in Area 1 are well enough distributed in a north-south direction to provide a reasonable strike relationship of a very regional nature.

Three tests have penetrated igneous rocks in the Permian sedimentary rocks. In addition, three of the ten tests have penetrated probable Precambrian rocks, and have indicated the sedimentary section is a minimum of 1,600 feet thick, and a present known maximum thickness of 2,315 feet. Because of the large portion of red beds found in the Abo, and the evaporitic and associated facies of the Yeso, the prospective thickness of the sedimentary section present is probably much less than one-half the section penetrated.

The earliest test drilled in the area was the National Exploration No. 1 Picacho. This test was spudded approximately 900 feet below the Glorieta outcrop, and penetrated 1,630 feet of sedimentary section before reaching a total depth at 2,191 feet in igneous rock. No shows of oil or gas were reported. The test, drilled in 1919, is in the NE¼ sec. 21, T. 11 S., R. 18 E.

The most recent test, the Elliott Production No. 1-10 Federal, in sec. 10, T. 5 S., R. 16 E., was plugged and abandoned in April 1962. This test was drilled on the basis of a gravity high. The well spudded in the San Andres. The Yeso and Abo were thinner than was anticipated, and contained a high percentage of red beds and evaporitic rocks. At 2,240 feet this test encountered "Granite Wash" underlying rocks of the Abo Formation, and encountered Precambrian granitic (quartz diorite) rocks at a depth of 2,570 feet. At a total depth of 3,429 feet the test was still in igneous rock.

The fact that three of the ten tests drilled in Area 1 have penetrated igneous sills in the Permian is very suggestive of the presence of more complex structural conditions than may be realized. This combined with the very large Capitan Mountain Tertiary intrusive which nearly divides Area 1, may indicate much more igneous activity than is exposed. This is not, however, implying the area be condemned because of possible igneous activity. Despite the fact that small amplitude structures do exist in Area 1 and some sedimentary section is pre-

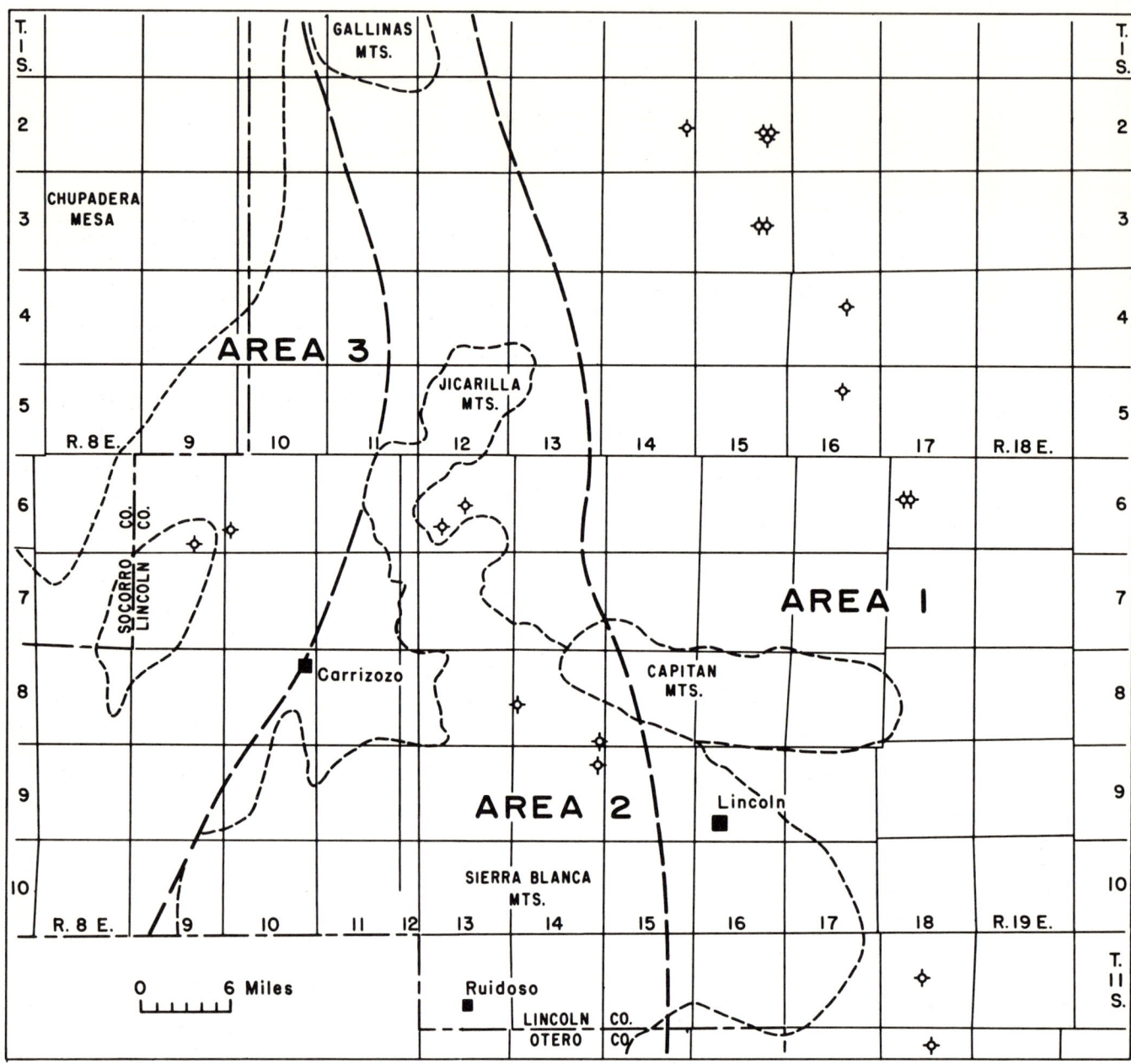

Figure 1. — Map showing oil and gas tests and exploration areas in Lincoln County, New Mexico.

sent, the thinness of the sedimentary section, the lack of source and resevoir beds below the generally dissected San Andres, and the absence of good shows of oil and gas, do not offer much encouragement for additional petroleum exploratory drilling throughout most of Area 1.

Area 2 contains outcrops of Tertiary intrusives; the Cretaceous Mesaverde Formation, Mancos Shale, and Dakota Sandstone; the Triassic Dockum Group; and the Permian Artesia Group, San Andres Limestone, Glorieta Sandstone, and Yeso Formation. The area is highly intruded, possibly one-fifth or more of the outcrop is Tertiary intrusives. Some mineralization has taken place around the contacts of these intrusives. The area is faulted and fractured; the majority of faults are normal, and down-thrown to the west. The structural grain, as determined by dike trends, faults, and intrusion zones, seems to be oriented north-northeast (approximately N. 15° E.).

Five test wells have been drilled in this part of the area. The first test chronologically was the Ray N. Sipple No. 1 H. E. Kelt, located in the SE¼NW¼ sec. 29, T. 6 S., R. 13 E. This well was spudded January, 1949 in the Cretaceous Mancos Shale. It penetrated the Greenhorn Limestone at 30 feet, the Dakota Sandstone at 300 feet, the Dockum Group at 515 feet, and bottomed at 1,027 feet in red shale. Two miles

OIL AND GAS TESTS, LINCOLN COUNTY, NEW MEXICO

Operator	Well	Farm	Location	Total Depth	Spudded	Completed	Status
Basabe & Rupe	1	Gyberg	1,980' FNL & FEL 24-2S-14E	1,320' sh	10- 1-52	12-10-52	P&A
B & B Oil Co.	1	Garger-Fed	1,980' FNL & FWL 23-2S-15E	570' ls	3- 1-55	10-12-55	Temp Abn
Malcolm & Morrow	1	C. C. Franks	871' FSL & 1,820' FWL 23-2S-15E	2,120' ls	9-22-53	5-12-54	Temp Abn
Malcolm & Morrow	1	C. C. Franks	2,013' FSL & 680' FWL 23-2S-15E	2,140' ls	8-13-52	9- 8-53	Temp Abn
Johnson & Spencer	1	Johnson	690' FNL & 660' FWL 23-3S-15E	900' ls	5-14-56	6- 5-56	Wtr Well
Johnson	1	Johnson-Fed	660' FNL & FWL 23-3S-15E	600' sh	1-12-56	2-15-56	Temp Abn
Albuquerque Expl.	1	Federal	660' FNL & 2,188' FWL 15-4S-16E	1,962' sh	10-10-53	2-29-56	P&A
Elliott Prod. Co.	1-10	Federal	660' FSL & 1,980' FWL 10-5S-16E	3,429' ign	3-16-62	4-23-62	P&A
Standard of Texas	1	Heard	1,980' FNL & FWL 33-6S-9E	8,050' ign	6-16-50	4-18-51	P&A
Bryce Dugger	1	Federal	1,655' FNL & 506' FWL 30-6S-10E	1,500' sh	1-25-63	3-12-63	P&A
Mark Vaughn	1	Chrenshaw	330' FNL & FEL 21-6S-13E	400'	6- 5-58	8- 5-59	P&A
Ray N. Sipple	1	Kelt	1,980' FNL & 2,310' FWL 29-6S-13E	1,027' sh	1- 6-49	6- 6-49	P&A
K. G. Miller	1	Miller	660' FNL & 1,980' FWL 20-6S-18E	782' ls	7-22-54	11-10-54	P&A
Western Ranchers	1	Beecher	1,650' FNL & 377' FWL 19-8S-14E	1,342' ls	2-15-59	2- 5-59	P&A
L. Capco	1	Spencer	330' FSL & FEL 36-8S-14E	2,181' ign	11-19-58	8- 5-59	P&A
L. Capco	1	Pearson	2,156' FSL & 1,660' FWL 12-9S-14E	1,005' ls	1-18-59	8- 5-59	P&A
National Expl.	1	Picacho	NE corner 21-11S-18E	2,191' ign	11-27-19	?	D&A
Stanolind	1	Picacho	660' FNL & 760' FWL 10-12S-18E	2,843' ign	1- 1-45	7-23-45	D&A

southwest, another test the Mark Vaughn No. 1 Chrenshaw, was drilled in 1959. It is located in the NE¼-NE¼NE¼ sec. 21, T. 6 S., R. 13 E. The test spudded in Cretaceous Mancos Shale, reached a total depth of 400 feet, and probably bottomed in the Dakota. A questionable report of a slight show of oil which may have been from the Dakota was indicated at 335 feet.

In 1959 three tests were drilled within a five mile radius of the town of Capitan. The Western Ranchers Oil Co., No. 1 Beecher, located in the NW¼SW¼-NW¼ sec. 19, T. 8 S., R. 14 E., reached a total depth of 1,342 feet. Tops reported were as follows: alluvium at surface, Santa Rosa Sandstone at 60 feet, Artesia at 440 feet, San Andres at 680 feet. The test is close to a major fault in an area dominated by Mesaverde outcrops and is possible that the Santa Rosa reported at 60 feet may be the Dakota Sandstone. The site has not been examined by the writer. No shows of oil or gas were reported.

The two remaining tests in Area 2 were drilled by the El Capoco Corp. The No. 1 Spencer, located in the SE¼SE¼SE¼ sec. 36, T. 8 S., R. 14 E., spudded in November 1958 in the Santa Rosa. It penetrated the San Andres at 560 feet, the Glorieta at 1,255 feet, the Abo(?) at 1,575 feet, and rhyolite at 2,120 feet. Total depth was 2,181 feet. Slight shows of oil were found at 600-630 feet, and 690-710 feet, but completion was not attempted. The No. 1 Pearson, in the NW¼NE¼SW¼ sec. 12, T. 9 S., R. 14 E., reached a total depth of 1,005 feet. It also spudded in the Santa Rosa. The well encountered fresh water at 200 feet, and flowed an estimated 60 barrels of fresh water per day. A completion was attempted from 806-834 feet by acidizing with 2,000 gallons, but the interval was swabbed dry with only a rainbow show of oil. The San Andres possibly was found at approximately 650(?) feet.

Area 3 consists of folded Permian sediments that are capped in part by Quaternary basalt flows or alluvium.

Two tests have been drilled in Area 3. The first is in the SE¼NW¼ sec. 33, T. 6 S., R. 9 E., and is the Standard Oil Company of Texas No. 1 J. F. Heard. The test was spudded June 1950 in Quaternary basalt overlying San Andres. Total depth reached was 8,050 feet. The sedimentary section penetrated included rocks from the Permian San Andres down through the Pennsylvanian Atoka. Of significance to regional interpretations, the Standard Oil Company of Texas test penetrated a Bursum to upper Virgil age "Pow Wow" type conglomerate from approximately 4,800 feet to 6,050 feet. Of additional interest is the occurrence of a salt section in the Upper Permian rocks. The absence of salt in outcrop probably is due to solution, and the structural closure mapped around this test may have been caused, in part, by the differential solution of salt and the resulting slump of overlying rocks.

The most recent test is the Bryce Dugger No. 1 Federal, in the SW¼NW¼ sec. 30, T. 6 S., R. 10 E., and was drilled on the western edge of the Carrizozo "malpais" Quaternary basalt flows. Total depth of the well was 1,500 feet. The top of the Glorieta was reported at 975 feet, and the Yeso at 1,145 feet. A show of oil was found in percussion cores of the San Andres from approximately 476-492 feet. An attempt was made to complete the well in the San Andres but the attempt failed primarily due to a lack of porosity. This writer's understanding is that Mr. Dugger intends to attempt drilling another test located slightly down dip in search of porosity.

CONCLUSIONS

Numerous shows of oil have, over the years, been reported from various stratigraphic units in the area including the Dakota, San Andres, Glorieta, and the Yeso. However, the majority of oil shows reported are from the San Andres. The writer has observed the San Andres and correlative carbonates in this area and as far west as central Arizona. Much of the formation has a fetid to petroliferous odor, and often contains porosity. It is difficult to imagine that in this vast expanse there would be no coincidence of hydrocarbons, reservoir rock, and trap. The old saying may be very applicable to San Andres exploration in this area, "Where there's smoke . . ."

From the writer's observations, the most likely possibility for potential accumulation other than San Andres would be in the Pennsylvanian rocks. Exposures in the Sacramento and Oscura Mountains suggest that reservoir quality rocks are present in the area. The problem here, of course, is finding an adequate thickness of Pennsylvanian rocks off the structurally high Pedernal landmass. Exploration in this region would of necessity be confined to Area 3, which is nearly entirely outside of Lincoln County.

With our present economic climate and state of knowledge, the "Frontier" area of Lincoln County will probably not see active exploration by the major oil companies, or the large independents. Exploration and investigation will have to be continued by individual geologists with imagination, and the drilling and "oil finding" will be done by men like the Bryce Duggers.

As we all know, one well per 350 square miles is not sufficient density to condemn any county. One good commercial well would surely change the entire picture. Perhaps when the density of wells approaches 1 per 50 square miles, we might then have some basis for critical evaluation.

WATER SUPPLIES NEAR CARRIZOZO, NEW MEXICO

James B. Cooper

U.S. Geological Survey, Albuquerque, New Mexico*

INTRODUCTION

The problem of a potable water supply has plagued the town of Carrizozo since the days of early settlement and has limited population growth and economic development of Carrizozo and also of adjacent areas within the northern part of the Tularosa Basin.

Perennial streams and permanent bodies of surface water are absent in the Carrizozo area. Most of the ground water in the area is saline and contains sulfate and chloride ions that give the water an objectionable taste; however, the water generally is suitable for stock and for irrigation uses. Gypsum, derived chiefly from the rocks of Permian age that ring the basin, is a common component of the formations that are aquifers near Carrizozo and is the chief source of the saline constituents in the ground water.

OCCURRENCE OF GROUND WATER

Ground water is relatively abundant near Carrizozo and occurs at shallow depths within the alluvium of Quaternary age. This alluvium covers older rocks of the basin floor between the mountains to the east and the Malpais (lava flow) to the west. Wells drilled into the alluvium to depths of 100 to 200 feet in this area yield as much as 400 gpm (gallons per minute). The underlying rocks of the Mesaverde Group of Late Cretaceous age contain sandstone beds that also are aquifers. Southwest of Carrizozo and near Nogal impermeable strata in the eastward-dipping rocks of Cretaceous age, and intrusive rocks of Tertiary age, commonly form ground-water barriers that raise the ground-water levels, and in places the water flows at the surface as springs.

Ground water in the alluvium is under water-table conditions. In rocks of Cretaceous age in the Carrizozo area the ground water is under different degrees of artesian pressure, although in much of the area the pressure is negligible. The shallower Cretaceous aquifers probably are in hydraulic connection with the alluvium. The water table slopes from the mountains toward the valley. Near the mountains the depth of water is about 100 feet. Away from the mountains, as the altitude of the land surface decreases, the depth to water is shallower. The ground water generally moves westward and northwestward towards the Malpais and thence generally southwestward beneath the lava, which occupies a topographic low near the middle of the basin.

The ground-water reservoir in the alluvium near Carrizozo is recharged by precipitation and by runoff from the mountains. About 40,000 acre-feet (13 billion gallons) of runoff water per year is available for recharge, but most of this runoff does not reach the aquifer because of evaporation and transpiration. Recharge to the Cretaceous aquifers is by precipitation on their outcrops, downward leakage from the alluvium, and from precipitation on the malpais where these rocks overlie sandstone. Annual precipitation on that part of the lava west of Carrizozo is about 20,000 acre-feet (6.5 billion gallons). Because of almost no runoff from the lava and the absence of vegetation, most of the precipitation is available for recharge.

HISTORY OF DEVELOPMENT

The first recorded attempt to obtain water of good quality at Carrizozo was made by the El Paso and Northeastern Railroad Co. (later to become part of the El Paso and Southwestern Railway Co. system). In 1901 a well was drilled in the railroad yards at Carrizozo to a depth of 895 feet. The well tapped Cretaceous sandstones, which yielded about 50 gpm from a pumping level of 400 feet below land surface. The non-pumping water level in the well was 90 feet below the surface. By 1906 the railway company had constructed two, and possibly three, additional wells at this location, the deepest of which was 1,125 feet. The water obtained from these wells is reported to have been softer and to have contained less sulfate and chloride than water from shallower aquifers; however, the presence of several hundred parts per million of sodium carbonate and sodium sulfate made it undesirable for drinking. The water was used by the railway company in locomotive boilers for several years.

In addition to the wells at Carrizozo the railway company drilled several other deep wells along its route from El Paso to Tucumcari during or shortly after construction of the railroad. Most of the wells yielded water of very poor quality. Water from the wells at Carrizozo was of better quality than that obtained from wells between Carrizozo and Santa Rosa, although the water was not ideal for boiler use. In a discussion of the water supply for this stretch of the railroad Campbell (1910, p. 164) states, "After the most thorough practicable treatment the well waters were still so bad that they caused violent foaming, low steam pressure, hard scaling, rapid destruction of boiler tubes, high coal consumption, extraordinary engine failures and repairs, small engine mileage, low train tonnage, excessive overtime, and a demoralized train service."

Mr. Campbell was directed by the railway company to find, if possible, a supply of good water. His efforts were successful, and by February 20, 1908 the Bonito pipeline was constructed and began supplying surface water of good quality to stations from Carrizozo north through Vaughn to Pastura, N. Mex.

The new source of water supply for the railroad, which was also made available in limited quantities to the inhabitants of settlements along the railroad, replaced the supply obtained from wells, and caused most of the wells to be abandoned and ultimately destroyed.

The source of the surface water was the South Fork of Rio Bonito, about 15 miles southeast of Carrizozo, on the eastern slope of Sierra Blanca. The stream was

*Publication authorized by the Director, U.S. Geological Survey

diverted by a small concrete dam into a pipeline that carried the water to storage in a natural basin about two miles southeast of the village of Nogal. The lake thus formed was first called Nogal Reservoir and later Nogal Lake. Nogal Lake was originally half a mile in diameter at the surface, a quarter of a mile in diameter on the bottom, had a depth of 36 feet, and had a storage capacity of 422 million gallons. The sides of the basin were puddled by working 300 to 400 cattle around the shore line until most of the leakage was eliminated. Campbell (1910, p. 176) states that the total puddling required two seasons and utilized 11,150 cow days.

From Nogal Lake the pipeline dropped abruptly to the alluvial plain, reached the railroad 12 miles north of Carrizozo at the station of Coyote, and extended from there northward. A branch line carried water to Carrizozo. The water-supply system included 116 miles of wood-stave pipe of diameters ranging from 16 down to 3½ inches, and 19 miles of iron pipe of 12-inch diameter. Service reservoirs of 2½ million gallons capacity were installed at Carrizozo, Coyote, Luna, and Corona and pumping plants were operated at Coyote and Luna.

By 1930-31 Nogal Lake had developed excessive leakage at high stages and its effective storage was reduced to about 163 million gallons. At this time the Southern Pacific Co., which had assumed operation of the railroad lines, constructed a dam across Rio Bonito below the junction of Bonito Creek and the South Fork of Rio Bonito to provide supplemental storage for the pipeline water system. The dam is constructed of rock with a concrete apron on the upstream face. It is 480 feet long on the crest and has a maximum height of 111 feet. The lake, called Bonito Lake, had an initial capacity of 400 million gallons. Since construction of Bonito Lake, only occasional use has been made of the water stored in Nogal Lake.

The conversion by the early 1950's to diesel locomotives made the operation of the water-supply system unnecessary by the railway companies. In 1955 the El Paso and Rock Island Railway Co., as owner, and the Southern Pacific Co., as lessee, made application to the State Engineer of New Mexico to make transfers of water rights from Bonito Lake. Permission was granted in July of 1955 for the transfer of about 1,450 acre-feet per year (470 million gallons) to the United States of America for the use of Holloman Development Center, and a like amount to the City of Alamogordo. The Town of Carrizozo was transferred rights to about 120 acre-feet per year (39 million gallons) and the Nogal Water Users Association received rights to 1.45 acre-feet per year (470 thousand gallons). Reserved to the railway companies were about 58 acre-feet per year (19 million gallons) to supply existing and long-standing water committments by the Southern Pacific Co. to water users associations, towns, villages, and communities northeast of Carrizozo to Pastura, N. Mex., by tank-car deliveries until such time as these water users could build their own water system.

In 1957, following the transfer of these water rights, a new iron pipeline was constructed by the U.S. Air Force for Holloman Air Development Center, from Bonito Lake along a route northwestward through Carrizozo and thence southwestward generally following U.S. Highway 54 to Alamogordo—a distance of about 80 miles. At Alamogordo the lake water is mixed with ground water of inferior quality (water that contains between 250 and 500 ppm of either sulfate or chloride ions and less than 750 ppm of the two together) to supply a larger quantity of water yet maintain a quality acceptable for most uses. The City of Alamogordo and Holloman Air Development Center share equally the water obtained through the pipeline from Bonito Lake. In addition to water from the lake, a private well near Carrizozo has been used on occasion to supplement flow in the pipeline.

PRESENT GROUND-WATER DEVELOPMENT

About 100 wells are in operation near Carrizozo. The wells range in depth from about 50 to 300 feet. The principal use of water is for public supply and for domestic and stock purposes. About a dozen wells are used for irrigation of crops. Use of water by industry is negligible. Stock and domestic wells are pumped at rates of only a few gpm. Irrigation and public-supply wells are pumped at rates of 60 to 500 gpm. The largest water withdrawal is at a locality about a mile south of Carrizozo, where two municipal wells and one private well tap a thick section of alluvium that yields 400 gpm or more to each well. All of the wells are finished in alluvium at depths of 140 feet. The water is hard and is high in sulfate ions; however, it is of better quality than ground water found at other locations within the area.

POTENTIAL GROUND-WATER DEVELOPMENT

On the basis of presently available information, about 20,000 acre-feet (6.5 billion gallons) per year of water could be obtained from wells in the Carrizozo area. Most of this water would be of inferior quality. As water-treatment processes become more refined and less costly, and as the population growth demands better economic development of thinly-settled areas, water now unused because of its quality may become a valuable resource.

SELECTED REFERENCES

Campbell, J. L., 1910, The water supply of the El Paso and Southwestern Railway from Carrizozo to Santa Rosa, N. Mex.: Am. Soc.-Civil Eng. Trans., Vol. 70, p. 164-189.

Cooper, J. B., 1959, Ground water in the vicinity of Carrizozo, Lincoln County, N. Mex.: U.S. Geol. Survey open-file rept., 45 p., 1 pl., 2 figs. (typewritten).

Dinwiddie, G. A., 1963, Municipal and community water supplies in southeastern N. Mex.: N. Mex. State Engineer Technical Rept. 29A, 140 p., 38 figs.

Hendrickson, G. E., 1949, Ground-water resources of the Carrizozo area, N. Mex.: U.S. Geol. Survey open-file rept., 14 p., 1 fig. (typewritten).

Meinzer, O. E. and Hare, R. F., 1915, Geology and water resources of Tularosa Basin, N. Mex.: U.S. Geol. Survey Water-Supply Paper 343, 317 p., 19 pls.

CHEMISTRY OF WATER OF A SECTION OF THE EASTERN FLANK OF THE SACRAMENTO MOUNTAINS, LINCOLN AND OTERO COUNTIES, NEW MEXICO

F. R. Hall

New Mexico Institute of Mining and Technology*
Socorro, New Mexico

INTRODUCTION

The area described in this report is in Lincoln and Otero Counties, New Mexico, and lies between Tps. 8 and 12 S. and Rs. 11 and 19 E. (fig. 1). Approximately 1,400 square miles are included within these boundaries and they roughly coincide with the topographic boundary of the western part of the Rio Hondo drainage basin.

The part of the eastern flank of the Sacramento Mountains chosen for this study is of interest because ground water occurs in several major rock types where the chemistry of water has not been too affected by human activities, and because the area is a source of a substantial amount of recharge to the Roswell artesian basin.

This paper is based on work performed as part of a research project on chemistry of water of the Roswell basin at the New Mexico Institute of Mining and Technology. Particular thanks are due to those colleagues and graduate students with whom various aspects of the study were discussed. The author is deeply indebted to members of the U.S. Geological Survey at Albuquerque and Roswell for supplying chemical analyses not available in publications and for participating in many discussions of the problems involved in the study. Walter A. Mourant of the Geological Survey, who has worked extensively in the area, was especially helpful to the author.

TOPOGRAPHY AND DRAINAGE

The major topographic features of the area are the Sacramento Mountains, on the west, dominated by the Sierra Blanca, the Capitan Mountains along the northern boundary, and a broad upland area gently sloping to the east and incised by streams. The range in elevation above mean sea level is from about 10,000 feet in the mountains to about 4,700 feet at the eastern boundary.

Rio Hondo, the master stream draining the area, is formed by the junction of the Rio Bonito and Rio Ruidoso which have headwaters in the Sacramento Mountains (fig. 1). Relatively minor amounts of water are contributed by the Capitan Mountains. The stream beds are generally lower than the water table, and the streams have nearly perennial flow except toward the east where the Rio Hondo begins to lose water downstream from Picacho (Mourant, 1963, p. 10). The general flow distribution is modified, however, by diversions for irrigation and water-supply pipelines and locally where the water table is below the stream bed. The flow data in the following description of the major streams are from the records of the U.S. Geological Survey (Mourant, 1963, p. 7-12; Reiland and Haynes, 1963).

Rio Bonito

The source of the Rio Bonito is high in the Sacramento Mountains on the northern slope of the Sierra Blanca. The stream flows into Bonito Lake (sec. 12, T. 10 S., R. 12 E.), an artificial impoundment, where water is diverted to the Bonito Creek pipeline. Below the dam, the Rio Bonito gains some water but has no major tributaries. Salado and Magado Creeks contribute only minor amounts of water. The Rio Bonito at the gage just above the junction with the Rio Ruidoso (fig. 1) has an average annual flow of about 10 cfs (cubic feet per second) after having lost water to diversions at Bonito Lake and for irrigation of about 1,700 acres. The contributing area is 306 square miles. Selected flow-duration data show the following pattern:

Percent of time	Flow is equal to or greater than, cfs
51.2	0.1 (Approximate median flow)
39.1	1.0
33.4	2.0
15.8	10.4 (Approximate mean flow)

Rio Ruidoso

The Rio Ruidoso has headwaters in the Sacramento Mountains on the eastern and southern flanks of Sierra Blanca. The major tributaries are Carrizo and Eagle Creek. Most of Eagle Creek is diverted to the Eagle Creek pipeline. The Rio Ruidoso at the gage just above the junction with the Rio Bonito has an average annual flow of about 19 cfs after diversions to Eagle Creek pipeline and to irrigate about 1,700 acres. The contributing area is 307 square miles. Selected flow-duration data show the following pattern:

Percent of time	Flow is equal to or greater than, cfs
62.9	3.0
49.2	7.0 (Approximate median flow)
22.4	20.0 (Approximate mean flow)

---

*At the University of New Hampshire, Durham, New Hampshire since July 1, 1964.

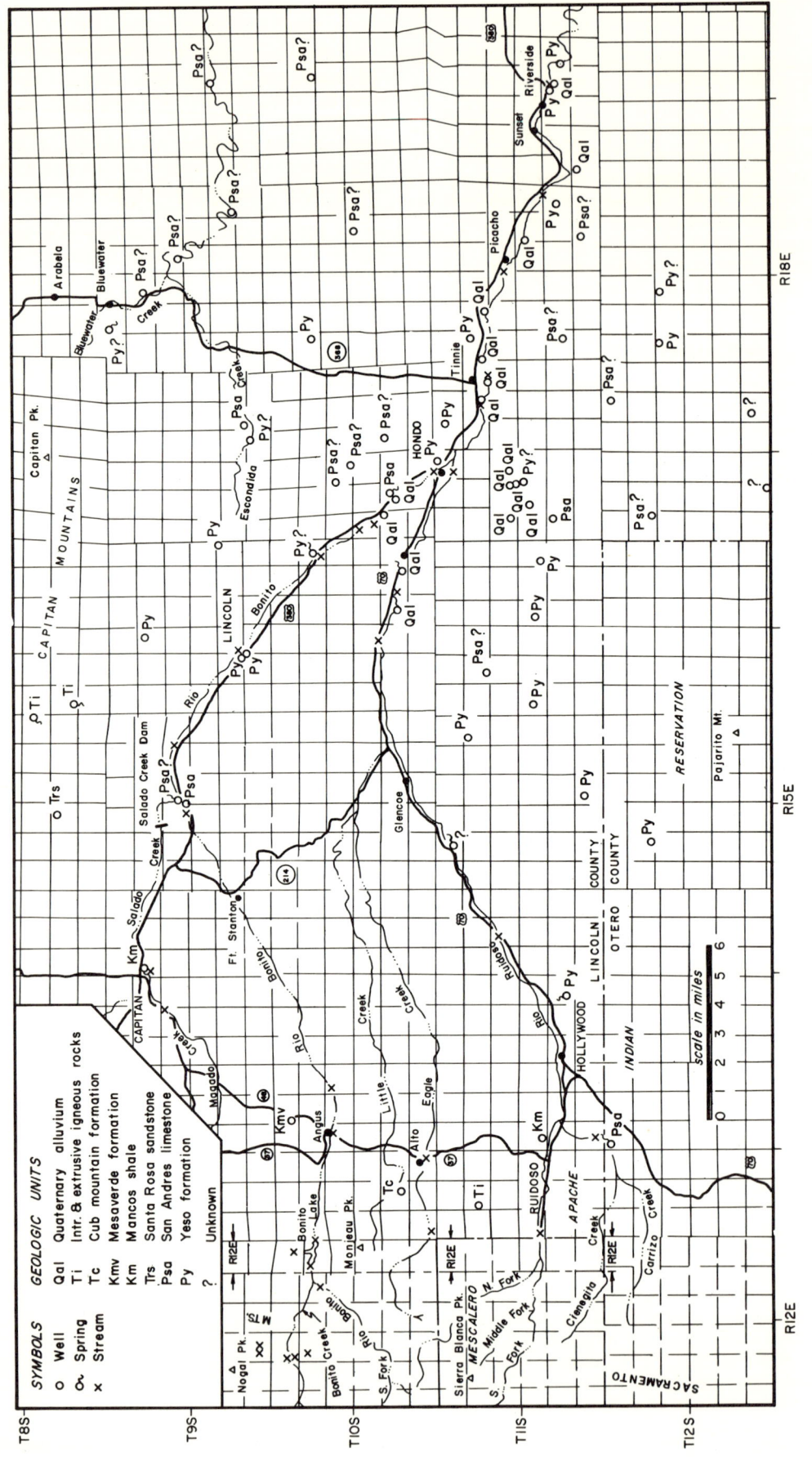

Figure 1. — Well, spring, and stream location map for a section of the eastern flank of the Sacramento Mountains, Lincoln and Otero Counties, New Mexico.

Rio Hondo

The Rio Hondo has no major tributaries between the confluence of its principal tributaries, Rio Bonito and Rio Ruidoso, and the eastern boundary of the area. The average annual flow at Picacho is about 40 to 50 cfs based on flow records at the Diamond A Ranch east of the area and on estimates of seepage loss below Riverside. Diversions for irrigation along the Rio Hondo are for about 3,000 acres. The contributing area below the confluence of Rio Bonito and Rio Ruidoso is 700 to 800 square miles.

GEOLOGY

The Sacramento and Capitan mountains consist of Tertiary intrusive and extrusive rocks. The remainder of the area has a sequence of sedimentary rocks abutting against the mountains and dipping gently eastward with some irregularities in dip due to faulting and folding. The sedimentary sequence includes Tertiary, Mesozoic, and Permian rocks close to the Sacramento Mountains; they in turn overlie older Permian rocks in most of the area east of the mountains. The uplands are mainly on the San Andres Limestone of Permian age, with the underlying Yeso Formation of Permian age exposed in the stream valleys. Downstream from Riverside, the Yeso is in the subsurface. Quaternary is found along the stream valleys. Table 1 taken from Mourant (1963, p. 15) summarizes the geologic section; in the present report the Glorieta Sandstone is included in the San Andres Limestone.

CHEMISTRY OF WATER

Most of the chemical analyses used in this study are published in reports of the U.S. Geological Survey (Mourant, 1963; Dinwiddie, 1963). Other analyses came from the files of the Geological Survey at Roswell and Albuquerque. Analyses of a few surface-water samples were made at the New Mexico Institute of Mining and Technology. The ranges of chemical constituents by source are summarized in table 2 and the sampling locations are shown in figure 1.

A rather arbitrary procedure was used in determining the ranges of constituents tabulated in table 2. When an analysis deviated greatly from the normal range from its source, it was not included in table 2. In all instances, the deviant analyses fitted the range of another source. The deleted analyses included one from Tertiary igneous rocks that closely resembled Mesaverde Formation or similar water, four analyses from the San Andres that resemble Yeso water, and four analyses from the Yeso that resemble San Andres water.

An expanded version of the trilinear graph (Piper, 1944) is used to display the chemical data. Figure 2 is for water from wells and springs, and figure 3 is for water from streams. A trilinear graph has a cation field in the lower left, an anion field in the lower right, and a combined field in the central diamond. Analyses are plotted on the graphs in percentage of equivalents per million (epm) in terms of 100 percent cations and 100 percent anions. The location in the central diamond can be indicated by a decimal number where the first part is percent calcium plus magnesium and the second part is percent carbonate plus bicarbonate. The decimal number is also useful for descriptive purposes. Some analyses used in this study do not plot in the anion field or central diamond, and these will be discussed in the text.

Chemical concentrations, ratios, and percentages are given in equivalents per million (epm). In the analyses given in this paper total dissolved solids in parts per

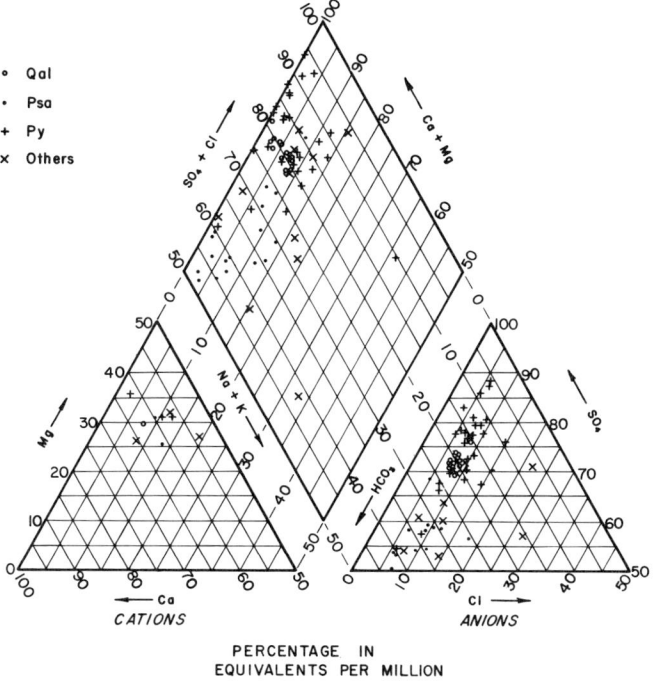

Figure 2. — Expanded Trilinear graph for well and spring samples

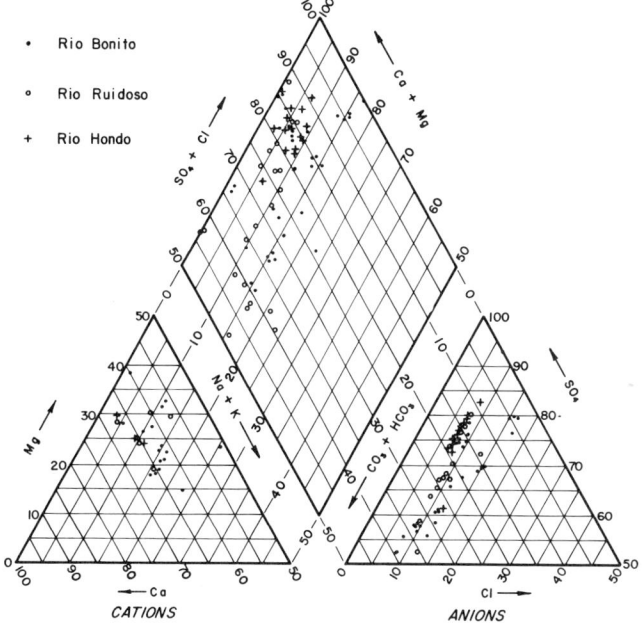

Figure 3. — Expanded Trilinear graph for stream samples

TABLE 1

GENERALIZED SECTION OF GEOLOGIC FORMATIONS IN THE
RIO HONDO DRAINAGE BASIN, CHAVES, LINCOLN, AND OTERO COUNTIES, NEW MEXICO
(From Mouránt, 1963, p. 15)

System	Stratigraphic Unit	Thickness (feet)	Physical Character
Quaternary	Alluvium	0-210±	Poorly sorted to well-sorted sand, gravel, and clay in lenses, stringers, and parallel beds.
	Alluvial fans	-	Mainly boulders and unsorted finer rock debris from intrusive igneous rocks.
Quaternary (?) and Tertiary (?)	Pediment gravel	0-50±	Unsorted angular to rounded fragments of igneous, sedimentary, and metamorphic rocks.
	——Unconformity——		
Tertiary (?)	Intrusive and extrusive igneous rocks	-	Andesite, diorite, microgranite, and rhyolite dikes, sills, and stocks.
	Cub Mountain Formation	0-500±	Red and white sandstone and chert pebble conglomerate; varicolored shale.
	——Unconformity——		
Cretaceous	Mesaverde Formation	0-540±	Gray, yellow, and buff quartzose sandstone; gray shale; coal; and carbonaceous shale.
	Mancos Shale	0-400±	Black fissile shale, thin-bedded limestone, and intercalated limestone and sandstone.
	Dakota Sandstone	0-130±	Ferruginous quartzose sandstone interbedded with gray shale and conglomerate.
	——Unconformity——		
Triassic	Chinle Formation	0-180±	Red and gray shale and white and gray dense limestone.
	Santa Rosa Sandstone	0-380±	Gray, yellow, and tan sandstone; thin-bedded limestone; red and gray shale; and chert pebble conglomerate.
Permian	Artesia Formation	0-450±	Gypsum, anhydrite, dolomite, impure limestone, siltstone, red shale and sandstone.
	——Unconformity——		
	San Andres Limestone	0-1,200	Mainly cherty limestone and dolomite; minor siltstone, sandstone, gypsum, anhydrite, and shale.
	Glorieta Sandstone	0-160	Mainly light-tan to dark-red, medium-grained quartz sandstone; minor silty limestone, siltstone, gypsum, and anhydrite.
	Yeso Formation	1,000± to 2,000±	Thin-bedded red and yellow siltstone; some limestone, sandstone, shale, gypsum, anhydrite, and salt.

TABLE 2
RANGE OF CHEMICAL COMPOSITION OF NATURAL WATERS IN EQUIVALENTS PER MILLION.

Aquifer or Stream	Number of Analyses	Ca^{++} plus Mg^{++}	Mg^{++}/Ca^{++}	Na^+ plus K^+	HCO_3^-	SO_4^-	Cl^-	Anion Total
Alluvium	17	14.40-21.60	.47[a]	.12-2.79	2.69-4.92	10.63-16.56	1.04-1.89	14.83-23.09
Tertiary Igneous Rocks	2[b]	1.06[c]	-	.27-.52	.56-.67	.60-.73	.17-.18	1.33-1.58
Cub Mountain Formation	1	-	-	-	4.64	7.72	2.03	14.39
Mesaverde Formation	1	17.52	.50	4.13	6.10	13.12	2.06	21.64
Mancos Shale	2	33.00-39.01	.56[a]	5.26-5.87	2.69-6.74	25.38-27.66	8.52-12.07	38.87-44.24
Santa Rosa Sandstone	1	12.80	-	2.59	4.07	9.88	1.44	15.39
San Andres Limestone	18[d]	6.08-11.60	-	0-2.13	2.43-4.95	1.96-6.74	.39-1.66	6.06-11.54
Yeso Formation	20[d]	13.10-29.40	.53-.58[e]	0-3.75	2.10-4.67	11.06-24.75	.68-4.37	14.26-30.14
Yeso Formation(?)	3[f]	37.60-50.40	-	0-1.60	2.44-3.44	32.86-44.30	1.80-2.85	38.19-50.32
Rio Bonito above Bonito Lake	10	1.24-4.34	.24-.41[g]	.37-.70	.39-1.59	.94-3.04	.23-.56	1.61-4.98
Rio Bonito-anomalous	4[h]	6.16-17.70	.33-.47	.88-6.00	0-4.39	2.83-21.86	.56-1.75	7.33-23.70
Rio Bonito below Bonito Lake	18	6.12-22.00	.48-.58[i]	.10-2.88	2.10-3.54	3.58-16.37	.56-3.44	6.24-22.67
Magado Creek	4	38.60-43.20	-	6.00-7.88	2.02-2.82	34.74-39.94	6.91-8.97	45.40-50.93
Rio Ruidoso-upstream	4	1.46-1.88	.39[a]	.01-.55	.57-.92	.85-1.18	.18-.31	1.61-2.37
Rio Ruidoso-downstream	11	5.46-25.00	.43[a]	.25-2.30	2.59-4.80	3.16-20.28	.68-2.06	6.53-26.23
Eagle Creek-upstream	5	1.98-3.03	.29-.52[e]	0-.51	.87-1.39	.67-1.62	.17-.94	2.01-3.38
Eagle Creek-downstream	1	5.46	-	1.07	2.69	3.16	.68	6.53
Carrizo Creek	1	13.78	.50	1.48	4.92	8.98	1.35	15.28
Rio Hondo	15	9.99-23.23	.34-.45[e]	.17-2.30	2.26-4.54	7.03-20.07	.70-2.00	10.62-25.33

Footnotes

a—One value
b—One analysis deleted
c—Two values
d—Four analyses deleted
e—Three values
f—Not like other waters from the Yeso
g—Seven values. One additional value at .64
h—From geochemical prospecting (Griswold and Missaghi, 1964)
i—Four values

million can be very roughly approximated by multiplying the cation or anion total in epm by 70. Individual constituents can be converted to ppm by multiplying by the proper combining weights.

Chemical Systems

A logical approach to the study of chemistry of natural waters is to consider the chemical processes that may occur in the rocks and to relate these to chemical systems and processes known from experimental work and theoretical calculations. If the chemical systems analogous to the rock types are known and solubility data are available, then theoretical compositions can be calculated for ideal conditions. Conversely, calculations can be made from analyses of natural waters to compare them with their theoretical compositions.

The main rock types present in the study area are intrusive and extrusive igneous rocks, limestone, dolomite, gypsum, anhydrite, and shale (table 1). The major process is chemical attack of rocks by water containing dissolved carbon dioxide and organic acids. The type and rate of reactions depend on length of time in contact, temperature, pressure, chemical composition, and surface area exposed to attack. Other processes such as oxidation - reduction and ion exchange may also take place. Before discussing equivalent chemical systems and theoretical compositions, however, three major problems affecting interpretation should be considered.
1. Rainfall, wind-blown dust, and human activities can provide extraneous sources of ions. Also, water may move from one rock type to another.
2. Bicarbonate content and pH are likely to change significantly between time of collection and time of analysis (Roberson and others, 1963). Therefore, good determinations of these characteristics can be obtained only in the field.
3. Most of the analyses are partials with concentrations only for calcium plus magnesium, sodium plus potassium, carbonate, bicarbonate, sulfate, and chloride. No analysis less complete than this was used in the study. About 25 percent of the analyses have individual determinations of calcium and magnesium, but with one exception they have no individual determinations for sodium and potassium. Some determinations are available for silica, nitrate, fluoride, iron, and boron but not enough for correlations with specific rock types.

Experimental data are available for calcium carbonate (calcite) and calcium sulfate (gypsum — $CaSO_4 \cdot 2H_2O$), both individually and in a combined system. Therefore, independent calculations can be made for the composition of water in a limestone and gypsum, a limestone, and a gypsum aquifer. If aragonite is present then the theoretical concentrations will be a little low as aragonite is more soluble than calcite. The solubility and phase relationships of gypsum and anhydrite are rather complex functions of temperature, pressure, and sodium chloride content. Anhydrite is more soluble at the pressures to be expected in the field and at temperatures lower than 40°C (Stewart, 1963). The calculations and discussions in this paper, however, are based on the simplifying but not necessarily correct assumptions that only calcite and gypsum are present in the aquifers. Calculations for dolomite are based on the assumption that dolomite solubility is the same as limestone solubility (Barnes and Back, 1964).

The approximate chemical compositions for the systems of limestone and gypsum and limestone alone are given in table 3 for three different partial, pressures of carbon dioxide (Pco_2). Gypsum solubility alone is unaffected by Pco_2. The values of Pco_2, in atmospheres, were selected on the following basis: 0.0003 is the average Pco_2 of the atmosphere and approximates that in rainfall; 0.02 is the average Pco_2 for many soils; and 0.1 is a reasonable maximum Pco_2 in soils.

The chemical compositions in table 3 allow some speculation as to the compositions of the more complex system of limestone and dolomite, dolomite and gypsum, and limestone, dolomite, and gypsum. Probably the best criterion for separating these is the magnesium/calcium (Mg^{++}/Ca^{++}) ratio which would range from zero in pure limestone and limestone and gypsum to one in dolomite. Ratios for the other systems would fall between zero and one. Waters from limestone rarely have a Mg^{++}/Ca^{++} ratio of zero but more commonly of 0.3 (White and others, 1963, table 6), indicating the presence of magnesium in the limestone. Waters from dolomite have a ratio of one in many instances with a range of from somewhat less than one to slightly greater than one (White and others, 1963, table 7).

The igneous rocks of the area are more or less highly silicic and in general range from diorite and andesite to granite and rhyolite. An analogous chemical system is water-carbon dioxide-silicates (mainly quartz and sodium-rich feldspars). Few calculations can be made for such a system at low temperatures and pressures. Waters from these rock types tend to have a low dissolved-solids content on the order of 150 to 300 ppm (about 2 to 4 epm); a sulfate-chloride ratio of about one with low concentrations; a sodium plus potassium content ranging from about 20 to 70 per cent of the cations; a Mg^{++}/Ca^{++} ratio on the order of 0.3 to 0.4; and bicarbonate making up about 70 percent of the anions (White and others, 1963, tables 1 and 2).

The probable composition of waters from shales cannot be calculated with any confidence. Many shales were deposited in saline environments and will reflect this in their chemical compositions (White and others, 1963, p. 6-7, table 5). In the study area, the shales are associated with rocks consisting of limestone, gypsum, dolomite, and anhydrite; therefore, waters from the shales are likely to be similar to waters from these rock types. Waters from the shales may have a higher chloride content and may be subject to cation exchange.

RELATIONSHIP TO ROCK TYPE

The relationship of chemical content of water to rock type is considered in terms of the geologic unit from which the ground-water sample was obtained or over which the surface water was flowing. Analyses are not available for the Artesia Formation, Chinle Formation, Dakota Sandstone, pediment gravel, and alluvial fans. These rocks are of limited areal extent, except for the last two which are more widespread. Water from the Artesia will probably resemble water from the

TABLE 3

ESTIMATED AND CALCULATED CHEMICAL COMPOSITIONS OF WATER IN SELECTED ROCK TYPES

Rock type	P_{CO_2}	Calcium			Magnesium			Bicarbonate			Sulfate		
		ppm	epm	%	ppm	epm	%	ppm	epm	%	ppm	epm	%
Limestone[1]	0.0003	20	1.00	100	-	-	-	61	1.00	100	-	-	-
	0.02	80	4.00	100	-	-	-	244	4.00	100	-	-	-
	0.1	160	8.00	100	-	-	-	488	8.00	100	-	-	-
Dolomite[2]	0.0003	10	.50	50	6	.50	50	61	1.00	100	-	-	-
	0.02	40	2.00	50	24	2.00	50	244	4.00	100	-	-	-
	0.1	80	4.00	50	48	4.00	50	488	8.00	100	-	-	-
Gypsum[3]		610	30.60	100	-	-	-	-	-	-	1,470	30.60	100
Limestone	0.0003	749	37.40	100	-	-	-	30	.50	1	1,772	36.90	99
and	0.02	679	33.89	100	-	-	-	178	2.92	9	1,487	30.97	91
Gypsum[4]	0.1	697	34.78	100	-	-	-	353	5.78	17	1,393	29.00	83

[1] Frear and Johnston, 1929
[2] Assuming dolomite solubility equals limestone solubility
[3] Shternina and Frolova, 1945
[4] Hall, 1963. Calculation at 0.0003 is a rough approximation

Yeso Formation; water from the Chinle Formation may be similar to water from the San Andres Formation; and water from the Dakota is probably similar to water from the Santa Rosa Sandstone. The pediment gravel and alluvial fan deposits are usually above the water table. Only one analysis each is available for the Santa Rosa Sandstone, Mesaverde Formation, and Cub Mountain Formation. These formations are of restricted extent, and the chemistry of water will not be discussed except to note that the three analyses resemble water from the San Andres or Yeso Formations (table 2).

Yeso Formation

Ground water from the Yeso Formation is of a pronounced calcium-sulfate type in the general decimal range of 75-100.5-25 in figure 2. The range of chemical constituents shown in table 2 for the three analyses listed as Yeso (?) are appreciably higher in content of calcium plus magnesium, sulfate, and total dissolved solids than the rest of the samples from the Yeso; however, they are within the Yeso decimal range in figure 2.

The Yeso Formation is of a mixed lithological character with thin-bedded siltstone, limestone, sandstone, shale, gypsum, and anhydrite. Limestone and gypsum appear to be the major contributors of dissolved constituents. A source of magnesium either in the limestone or from dolomite is indicated by the Mg^{++}/Ca^{++} ratios in table 2. Apparently, only a minor source of chloride is present, possibly in the form of isolated halite crystals or from meteoric-water recharge.

A comparison of waters from the Yeso Formation in table 2 with the limestone and gypsum system in table 3 suggests near saturation with regard to limestone and undersaturation with regard to gypsum. The lack of attainment of equilibrium probably can be explained in one of the following ways: (1) The Yeso does not fit the proposed system of limestone and gypsum; (2) insufficient gypsum is present to meet equilibrium requirements; or (3) there is insufficient time in contact to reach equilibrium. The third possibility seems the most plausible, as explained below, but the other two cannot be completely disproved.

The three analyses listed as Yeso Formation (?) in table 2 are supersaturated with respect to gypsum. The analyses are not like the rest of the Yeso in concentrations, nor do they resemble samples from the other aquifers. The sample locations are NE¼NW¼NW½ sec. 32, T. 11 S., R. 15 E. (two samples) and SE¼SE¼NW¼ sec. 19, T. 11 S., R. 16 E. The waters could have come only from the Yeso, or possibly the San Andres Limestone which is not likely. The supersaturation might be due to contact with anhydrite at lower than normal temperatures, but this would be hard to explain. A possible mechanism suggested by S. W. West, U.S. Geological Survey, (personal communication) is that these types of waters have been in a more highly saline environment and then migrated out of the environment with chloride being held behind by shale layers acting as selective membranes.

A comparison of sulfate content with distance from the western side of the area shows that the waters range from lowest in the west to highest in the east. Chloride content also shows the same trend, but bicarbonate is relatively unaffected by distance. The relationship of increasing sulfate content with distance toward the east is good reason for believing that the lack of equilibrium is due to inadequate contact time.

The courses of the Rio Bonito, Rio Ruidoso, and Rio Hondo east of the mountains are cut for a considerable distance into the Yeso Formation, and waters from these reaches have compositions very similar to waters from the Yeso (fig. 3). Figure 4 is a graph of river distance above the point at which the Rio Hondo leaves the area versus sulfate content based on spot samples and estimated flows (Mourant, 1963, table 4). Where possible, approximate lines are drawn for equal flow rates to put the gain in sulfate on a comparative basis. The trend of increase of sulfate in the streams is similar to that of the ground water in the Yeso. The rate of increase along the Rio Hondo is smaller than for the other streams. The reasons for this are not clear but might be due to the fact that toward the east, the top of the Yeso is dipping beneath the valley of the Rio Hondo.

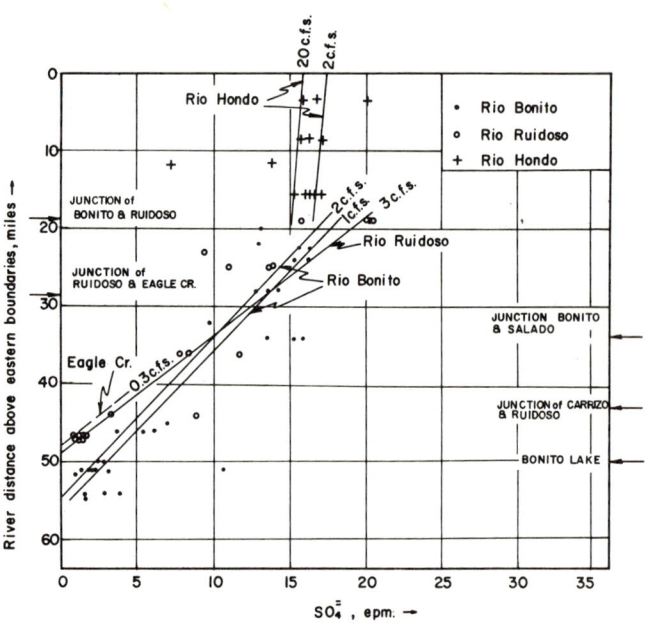

Figure 4. — Graph of sulfate content versus river distance for stream samples.

San Andres Limestone

Water from the San Andres Limestone is of a calcium sulfate to calcium bicarbonate-sulfate type with a general decimal range of 85-100.25-55 (fig. 2). A number of analyses do not plot in the anion field and a few do not plot in the central field of Figure 2. The reasons for this are a bicarbonate content of slightly greater than 50 per cent and a sulfate content slightly less than 50 per cent. The ranges of constituents in water from the San Andres are given in Table 2.

The San Andres Limestone consists mainly of cherty limestone and dolomite with some sandstone, gypsum, and anhydrite (table 1). No magnesium determinations are available, but the Mg^{++}/Ca^{++} ratio is probably on the order of 0.5. The sulfate range is much too low for equilibrium with gypsum, but too much calcium is present for equilibrium with limestone (table 3). Chloride content is lower than in the Yeso Formation. A comparison of sulfate and bicarbonate content with distance from the western side of the area shows little or no correlation between distance and content. The lack of equilibrium with gypsum probably is caused by a small gypsum content in the San Andres. Therefore, the San Andres Limestone can be considered nearly to fit the limestone system of Table 3 but with too much calcium from gypsum for equilibrium.

Mancos Shale

Analyses are available for two ground-water samples and four surface-water samples taken from Magado Creek in the outcrop area (samples from secs. 17 and 18, T. 9 S., R. 14 E.). The ground-water samples under the "others" category (fig. 2) are at 85.07 and 88.15, and the surface-water samples under the Rio Bonito category (fig. 3) cluster around 85.05. Magado Creek drains to the Rio Bonito by way of Salado Creek, but the volume of flow must be small as there is no perceptible effect on the Rio Bonito. The water is a calcium sulfate type with a high chloride and total dissolved-solids content.

The Mancos Shale consists of black shale, limestone, and sandstone (table 1). The ground-water samples are supersaturated in gypsum, and the surface-water samples are undersaturated in gypsum. The problems of gypsum-anhydrite phases and the suggested cause of supersaturated of the Yeso(?) Formation samples may apply to the Mancos as well, but the discrepancies are difficult to understand on the basis of such limited data. The high chloride content is very likely due to water entrapped during deposition or to salts precipitated by evaporation during deposition in a saline or brackish water environment. The surface-water analyses are at 42 and 43 miles above the eastern boundary of the area, but they are too high in sulfate to be in figure 4.

Tertiary Igneous Rocks

Analyses are available for ony two ground-water samples from the Tertiary igneous rocks; however, the surface-water samples listed in table 2 as Rio Bonito above Bonito Lake, Rio Bonito-anomalous, Rio Ruidoso-upstream, and Eagle Creek-upstream were all collected within the outcrop area of the Tertiary igneous rocks. The waters are in the compositional range of calcium bicarbonate to calcium sulfate with a decimal range in figure 3 of 75-100.25-60 which is close to the decimal range of the San Andres Limestone. The two ground-water analyses fall within the same range. A few analyses do not plot in figure 3 because of high bicarbonate and low sulfate.

The tertiary igneous rocks are both intrusive and extrusive with complex relationships in many areas. The main rock types on the Rio Bonito are syenodiorite, diorite, and basaltic andesite (Griswold and Missaghi, 1964). The rocks on the Rio Ruidoso and Eagle Creek are not so well known, but they are similar to the Rio Bonito (table 1). The composition of the waters is more or less what might be expected from the igneous rocks except that the calcium and sulfate contents are quite high and the sodium content is low. The Mg^{++}/Ca^{++} ratio has a range of 0.24 to .58.

The samples listed in table 2 as Rio Bonito-anomalous were collected during a geochemical prospecting program (Griswold and Missaghi, 1964); most of them were collected near oxidizing sulfide mineral deposits. One sample (from $NE\frac{1}{4}SE\frac{1}{4}$ sec. 34, T. 9 S., R. 11 E.) has 21.86 epm sulfate, no bicarbonate, and a ph of 3.3. In figure 4 all of the values to the right of the Rio Bonito curves above 50 miles are from the geochemical program. Trace amounts were found of molybdenum, copper, and zinc in some of the samples. The waters in the main Rio Bonito do not appear to show much addition of sulfate from the oxidizing sulfides. Therefore, oxidizing sulfides probably are not a major source of sulfate.

The major source of the high calcium-sulfate content and possibly some calcium carbonate is probably wind-blown dust from the east. A point of interest in this regard is that waters from the Tertiary igneous rocks and the San Andres Limestone are quite similar in composition and fall within the same decimal range. The only major difference appears to be the higher dissolved-solids content of the San Andres.

Quaternary Alluvium

Waters from the alluvium are of a calcium sulfate type with a decimal range of 87-99.15-22 (fig. 2). The chemical composition and decimal range fall within those for the Yeso Formation. This indicates that the alluvium receives water from the Yeso in many reaches. The samples from the alluvium show the same trend of increasing content of sulfate toward the east. The waters from the alluvium also closely resemble waters from the streams east of the igneous rocks. The samples in the alluvium show the same pattern of undersaturation in gypsum as do waters from the Yeso Formation and from the streams. Insufficient time in contact seems to be the best explanation for this.

SUMMARY AND CONCLUSIONS

The ground and surface waters on the eastern flank of the Sacramento Mountains are predominantly calcium sulfate to calcium bicarbonate-sulfate types characterized by waters from the Tertiary igneous rocks, the San Andres Limestone, and the Yeso Formation. Sedimentary rocks of Mesozoic and Tertiary age are of rather limited extent, and waters from them more or less resemble one of the main types. The only exception is water from the Mancos Shale which is a calcium-sulfate water but with a fairly high chloride content. The waters can be summarized as follows:

1. *Tertiary igneous rocks.* Calcium sulfate to calcium bicarbonate waters with a low dissolved-solids content. The general composition is what might be expected from the igneous rocks except for the high content of sulfate and calcium. Some sulfate is derived from oxidizing sulfides, but wind-blown dust probably is the major source. Ground water and surface water is from

the area of the upstream reaches of the Rio Bonito, Rio Ruidoso, and Eagle Creek.

2. *San Andres Limestone.* Calcium sulfate to calcium bicarbonate-sulfate water of a moderate dissolved-solids content. The water is too high in calcium to be in equilibrium with limestone but is too low in sulfate to be in equilibrium with limestone and gypsum. The lack of equilibrium appears to be due to a small gypsum content in the San Andres. The chemical composition of water from the San Andres is similar to water from the Tertiary igneous rocks except for a higher dissolved-solids content.

3. *Yeso Formation.* Calcium-sulfate water of moderate to fairly high dissolved-solids content. With few exceptions, however, the samples are undersaturated with respect to gypsum. The undersaturation is probably due to insufficient time in contact to attain equilibrium. Waters from the Quaternary alluvium, the Rio Hondo, and the downstream parts of the Rio Bonito and Rio Ruidoso are all quite similar to water from the Yeso.

REFERENCES CITED

Barnes, Ivan, and Back, William, 1964, Dolomite solubility in ground water: U.S. Geol. Survey Prof. Paper 475-D, p. 179-180.

Dinwiddie, G. A., 1963, Municipal water supplies and uses, southeastern New Mexico: New Mexico St. Engr. Tech. Rept. 29A.

Dorroh, J. H., Jr., 1946, Certain hydrologic and climatic characteristics of the Southwest: Univ. New Mexico Pub. in Engrng., no. 1.

Frear, G. L., and Johnston, J., 1929, The solubility of calcium carbonate (calcite) in certain aqueous solutions at 25°C.: Amer. Chem. Soc. Jour., v. 51, p. 2082-2093.

Griswold, G. B., and Missaghi, F., 1964, Geology and geochemical survey of a molybdenum deposit near Nogal Peak, Lincoln County, N. Mex.: N. Mex. Inst. Min. and Tech., State Bur. Mines and Min. Res. Circ. 67.

Hall, F. R., 1963, Calculated chemical composition of some sulfate-bearing waters: Internl. Assn. of Sci. Hydro. Pub. no. 64, p. 7-15.

Mourant, W. A., 1963, Water resources and geology of the Rio Hondo drainage basin, Chaves, Lincoln and Otero Counties, N. Mex.: New Mexico St. Engr. Tech. Rept. 28,

Piper, A. M., 1944, A graphic procedure in the geochemical interpretation of water analyses: Trans. Amer. Geophys. Un., v. 25, p. 914-923.

Reiland, L. J., and Haynes, G. L. Jr., 1963, Flow characteristics of New Mexico streams: N. Mex. St. Engr. Spec. Rept.

Roberson, C. E. and others, 1963, Differences between field and laboratory determinations of pH, alkalinity, and specific conductance of natural water: U.S. Geol. Survey, Prof. Paper 475-C, p. 212-215.

Shternina, E. B. and Frolova, E. V., 1945, Solubility in the system $CaCO_3$-$CaSO_4$ $NaCl$-CO_2-H_2O at 25°C.: C. R. (Doklady) de l'Académie des Sciences de l'URSS, v. 47, no. 1, p. 33-35.

Stewart, F. H., 1963, Marine evaporites, Chapter Y in Data of geochemistry, 6th ed.: U.S. Geol. Survey Prof. Paper 440-Y, p. 13-14.

White, D. C., and others, 1963, Chemical composition of subsurface waters, Chapter F in Data of geochemistry, 6th ed.: U.S. Geol. Survey, Prof. Paper 440-F.

✗ ✗ ✗

SOME ASPECTS OF THE NATURAL HISTORY OF THE CAPITAN AND JICARILLA MOUNTAINS, AND SIERRA BLANCA REGION OF NEW MEXICO

William C. Martin*
University of New Mexico

INTRODUCTION

In this article certain aspects of the natural history of the Capitan and Jicarilla Mountains and Sierra Blanca region of southcentral New Mexico are discussed and some items of interest regarding this area are indicated. The primary interest and experience of the author is developed along botanical lines. Therefore, the plant life of this region is given the most attention, but some mention also is made of the animal life, primarily that of the mammals. Appreciation is extended to Dr. Clyde Jones, Assistant Curator, Museum of Southwestern Biology, for his comments and helpful criticism of the manuscript.

For a long time the Capitan and Jicarilla Mountains, Sierra Blanca, the surrounding plains, and the lowlands have continued to arouse the interest of naturalists and biologists. Botanists, in particular, have long recognized this region as one possessing unusual floristic characteristics. For example, a number of taxa described from this area in the late nineteenth century and the early twentieth century are recognized as being endemic to this part of the State. This relatively high proportion of endemics is probably a reflection of long-time isolation of this group of mountains from other mountain masses, thus providing many taxa with the opportunity to evolve independently from their counterparts elsewhere.

The Capitan and Jicarilla Mountains, and Sierra Blanca are of additional interest due to an ecological potential for the development of a very diversified flora and fauna. Few areas anywhere have such a variety of habitats to offer, and rarer still are those places that exhibit as many life zones in so small a space. Altitudes range from 4,500 feet in the vicinity of Tularosa and the Tularosa Basin to more than 12,000 feet at the top of Sierra Blanca Peak—called "Old Baldy" by natives of the region. Extensive areas, such as the ridge of the Capitan Mountains and other peaks in the vicinity reach altitudes considerably above 9,000 feet.

The amount and distribution of precipitation throughout this area also is an important factor in the development of the widely diversified flora and fauna as are found here. Rainfall certainly is not especially plentiful anywhere in this region, but the Jicarilla and Capitan Mountains are somewhat more xeric than Sierra Blanca. This condition is probably due to the lower altitude reached by both the Jicarillas and the Capitans and partly to the smaller masses of these ranges. In addition, both ranges seem to be located somewhat in the rain shadow of the higher Sierra Blanca to the south.

Additional geographic features of the area include several relatively small mountains such as Carrizo Peak more than 9,600 feet high, Potos Mountain, approximately 8,400 feet, and several lower masses such as the Godfrey Hills lying between Sierra Blanca and Tularosa Basin to the west. Thus, the general character of this region is that of a series of peaks, ridges, and hills separated by high plateaus.

It is important to keep some continuity between types of organisms mentioned and certain measurable features of the terrain such as altitude. Therefore, the approach in this article is that of characterizing or listing a variety of the organisms that can be expected to exist in each of several altitudinal associations or zones. These associations can be roughly compared with the well-known life zones but no special attempt is made here to follow the life-zone concept with any degree of exactness because certain features, such as direction of exposure and availability of moisture, greatly modify the altitudinal range in which organisms can exist.

The associations discussed in this paper are based primarily on vegetational as well as altitudinal criteria, and include the desert grassland, pinyon-juniper, transition, spruce-fir, and alpine associations. This paper presents first the desert grassland association and proceeds step-by-step through successively higher associations to the alpine situation. A map of the area (fig. 1) is included to give the reader a general idea of the extent and distribution of the associations under discussion. The map indicates the position of the major peaks and their approximate altitudes, as well as other points of reference. The crosssection (fig. 2) shows the vertical extent and briefly summarizes the important biological characteristics of each association.

DESERT GRASSLAND ASSOCIATION

A relative small section of the study area is in the so-called desert grassland association, mostly west of the main mountain mass. The desert grassland includes the territory between an altitude of 4,500 feet at the edge of the Tularosa Basin and an altitude of 6,000 feet at the base of the Jicarilla Mountains to the north and in the vicinity of Bent to the south. A few areas east of Sierra Blanca can (also roughly) be designated as desert grassland, but, for the most part, these are located near the upper limits of the altitudinal range indicated for this association.

The section of the desert grassland bordering in the Tularosa Basin, although almost treeless, supports a num-

---
*Associate Professor of Biology, Curator of the Herbarium, Museum of Southwestern Biology.

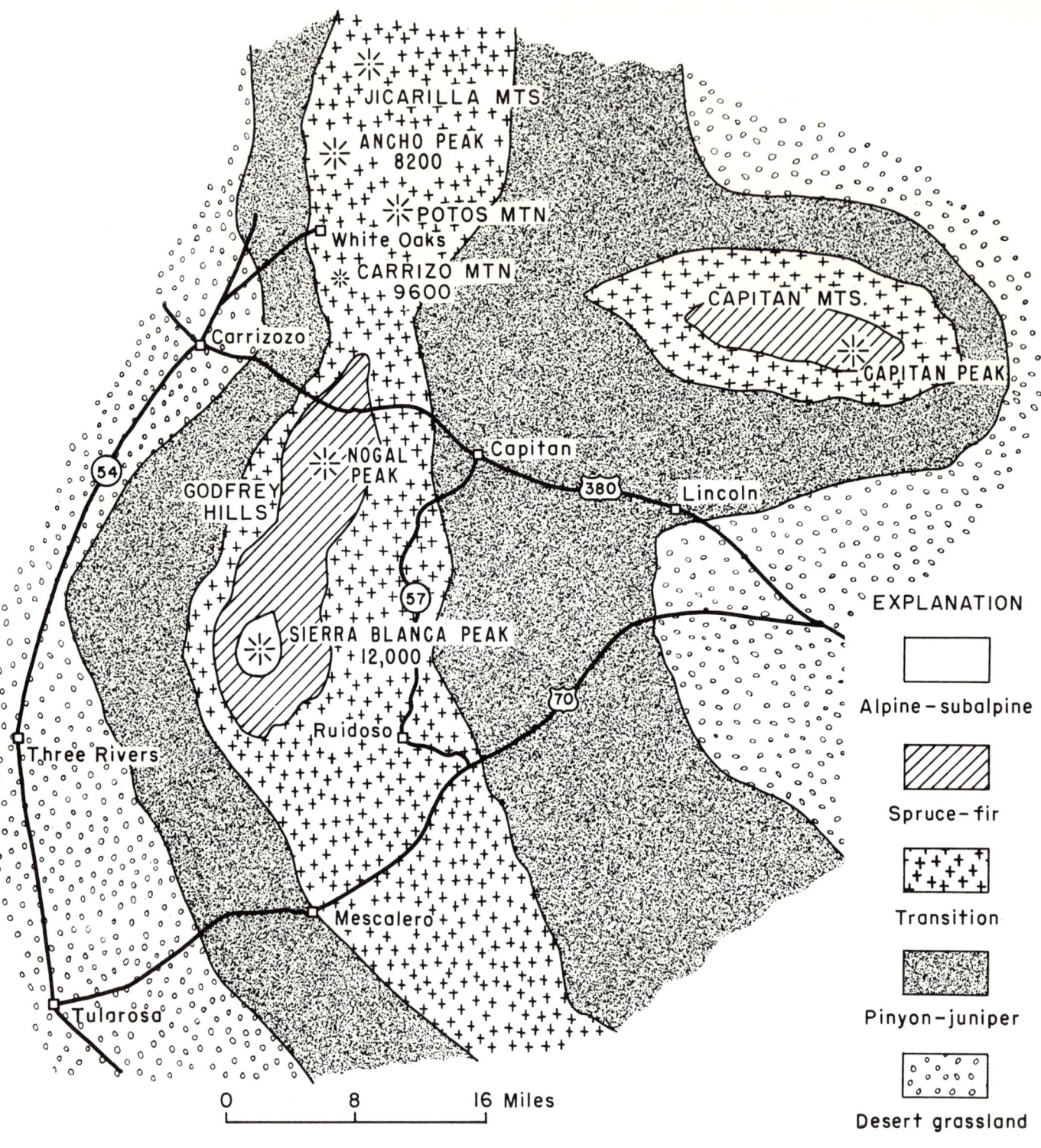

Figure 1. — Map showing the general distribution of life associations in Sierra Blanca and the Jicarilla and Capitan Mountains of New Mexico.

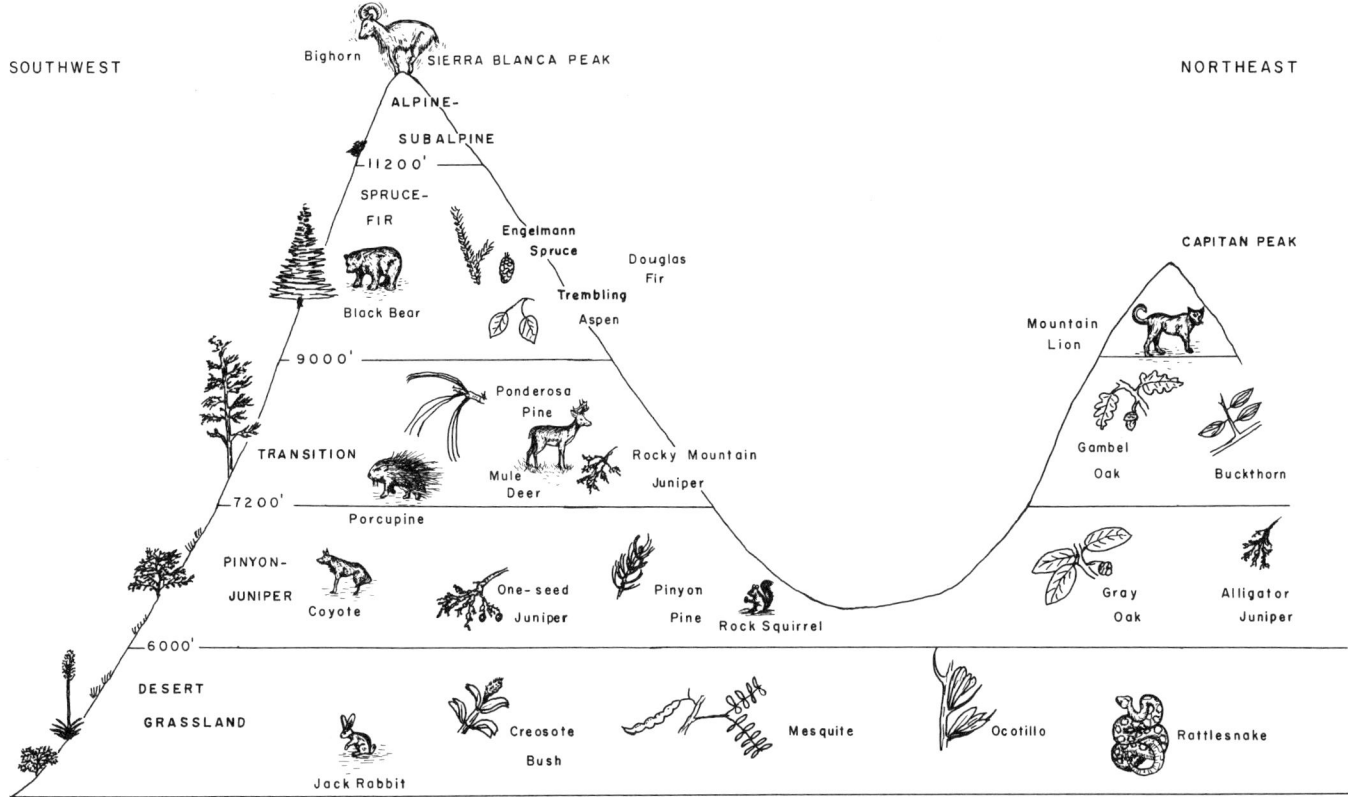

Figure 2. — A diagramatic cross-section through Sierra Blanca Peak and the Capitan Mountains showing the approximate vertical distribution and characteristic members of life associations. View is looking northwestward.

ber of important shrub species including the well-known creosote bush (*Larrea tridentata*), the soapweed yucca (*Yucca elata*), the joint-fir (*Ephedra torreyana*), several members of the legume family including catclaw acacia (*Acacia greggii*), whiteball acacia (*Acacia angustissima*), and honey mesquite (*Prosopis glandulosa*), and some shrubby composites such as the low-growing snakeweed (*Gutierrezia sarothrae*), and tarbush (*Flourensia cernua*). A number of succulents belonging mainly to the genus *Opuntia* in the cactus family also grow in this association.

Although the lower part of the area occupied by the desert grassland association is very dry, many herbaceous plants make their home here. Some of the most spectacular wild flowers in New Mexico are to be found here, such as the stickleaf or blazing star (*Mentzelia* spp.) with its silvery white stems and huge, lemon-yellow flowers, the desert marigold (*Baileya multiradiata*) with bright yellow-orange flower heads and densely white-wooly stems, the widely distributed orange-red globe mallow (*Sphaeralcea coccinea*), and the straggly-stemmed, purple-flowered desert four-o-clock (*Boerhaavia* spp.). Other well known herbaceous dicots common to this area are wild zinnia (*Zinnia grandiflora*), hogpotato (*Hoffmanseggia densiflora*), doveweed croton (*Croton texensis*), various legumes known generally as loco weeds (*Astragalus* spp.), a relative of the nightshade, the horse nettle (*Solanum elaeagnifolium*), paper daisy (*Psilostrophe tagetina*), so called because of the papery texture of the large yellow rays, and finally, a mustard called spectacle pod (*Dithyrea wislizenii*).

As in other associations, grasses play a major role in the vegetational cover of the desert grassland. Many species of the grass family grow here, but mention of a few of the more common ones will suffice. At lower levels are found sand dropseed (*Sporobolus flexuosus*), mesquite grass (*Muhlenbergia porteri*), three-awn (*Aristida* spp.), burro grass (*Scleropogon brevifolius*), and vine-mesquite (*Panicum obtusum*). In flat places or low swales, alkali sacaton (*Sporobolus airoides*) is often present as well as some grasslike plants from the rush family, for example, the Torrey rush (*Juncus torreyi*).

Toward the upper levels of the desert grassland, especially on low, rocky ridges and hills, the plant complement undergoes a definite change, giving away to additional species with a corresponding decrease in the frequency of plants common to lower altitudes. Among the shrubs making a first appearance are apache plume (*Fallugia paradoxa*), ocotillo (*Fouquieria splendens*), and the not-very-shrublike beargrass (*Nolina microcarpa*). For the most part, additional herb species belong to the composite family, but several new euphorbias of the spurge family are also common as well as a member of the geranium family, the cranesbill (*Erodium cicutarium*), a low-growing plant with deeply dissected leaves and strikingly elongated fruit capsules. Of all the plants of the arid regions, none attracts more attention than does the above mentioned ocotillo, with its large, terminal panicles of bright scarlet flowers and stiff, spiny stems densely covered with fascicles of spatulate leaves when there is sufficient soil moisture. These leaves fall quickly when very dry conditions prevail. Therefore, much of the year, this shrub is characterized only by its tall, slender, spiny, leafless stems.

Surprisingly enough, the desert grassland association abounds with animal life. Many kinds of reptiles as well as several species of mammals are able to tolerate the arid conditions. A few examples of mammals to be expected here are the hispid pocket mouse (*Perognathus hispidus*), rock pocket mouse (*Perognathus intermedius*), western harvest mouse (*Reithrodontomys megalotis*), cactus mouse (*Peromyscus eremicus*), hispid cotton rat (*Sigmodon hispidus*), desert cottontail (*Sylvilagus audubonni*), black-tailed jack rabbit (*Lepus californicus*), and an occasional hog-nosed skunk (*Conepatus leuconotus*). From this list, it would seem that the majority of the mammal life in this area belongs to the rodent order.

PINYON-JUNIPER ASSOCIATION

In the pinyon-juniper association which occurs generally between the altitudes of 6,000 and 7,200 feet, (an area corresponding roughly to the pinyon-juniper zone), the vegetation includes, in addition to grass and shrub cover, some arborescent forms. Throughout this association, prevailing low tree forms are one-seed juniper (*Juniperus monosperma*) and nut pine or pinyon (*Pinus edulis*). At the lower levels of the altitudinal range, the one-seeded juniper is the predominating tree form while, at higher altitudes, the pinyon pine is more common, in some areas practically to the exclusion of juniper. Another fairly common juniper toward the upper limits of the association is the alligator-bark juniper (*Juniperus deppeana*); the regular, rectangular, much-thickened bark scales giving the bark an appearance somewhat similar to the skin of the alligator. In rocky canyons and on rocky hillsides, the oaks begin to appear, principally the scrubby gray oak (*Quercus grisea*). This oak is one of the most common and certainly the most variable of the oaks in New Mexico.

Still apparent among the shrubby plants of the pinyon-juniper zone are apache plume, yucca, beargrass, joint-fir, and, of course, the cacti (*Opuntia* and *Mammalaria* spp.). A number of other shrubs begin to appear in the pinyon-juniper association, some of which are occasionally found in the upper part of the desert grassland association. The familiar catclaw mimosa (*Mimosa borealis*), the aromatic skunkbush sumac (*Rhus trilobata*), characterized by three-parted pinnately compound leaves, the spiny-leaved barberry (*Berberis haematocarpa*), and at least two species of rabbit brush (*Chrysothamnus* spp.) are noted along draws and dry hillsides.

As might be expected, grass species are liberally represented in the pinyon-juniper association and along with the shrub and tree cover are found throughout this area. Some of the important grass species are purple hair grass or sandhill muhly (*Muhlenbergia pungens*), mesquite grass (*Muhlenbergia porteri*), mountain muhly (*Muhlenbergia montana*), mesa muhly (*Muhlenbergia monticola*), sand bunchgrass (*Oryzopsis hymenioides*), scratchgrass (*Sporobolus asperifolius*), sacaton (*Sporobolus wrightii*), alkali sacaton (*Sporobolus airoides*), wiregrass (*Aristida longiseta*), arizona three-awn (*Aristida arizonica*), wolftail or Texas timothy (*Lycurus phleoides*), galleta (*Hilaria jamesii*), and tobosa grass (*Hilaria mutica*); this is the approximate northern limit for tobosa. Also common are Texas crab grass (*Schedonnardus paniculatus*), sideoats grama (*Bouteloua curtipendula*), six-weeks grama (*Bouteloua barbata*), black grama (*Bouteloua eriopoda*), Mexican lovegrass (*Eragrostis mexicana*), bluestem wheatgrass (*Agropyron smithii*), squirrel tail (*Hordeum jubatum*), and wild rye (*Elymus canadensis*), and blue grama (*Bouteloua gracilis*) which is beginning to appear at this altitude.

The dicot herbs are not as obvious here as at other locations but are usually represented by a large number of Compositae in late summer and autumn. An interesting herb of this area is Indian paint brush (*Castilleja integra*), characterized by its very irregular tubular flowers and bright red floral bracts. This is among the most colorful of all the plants of the association. Other herbs include species of globe mallow (*Sphaeralcea* spp.), daisy fleabane (*Erigeron* spp.), goldenrod (*Solidago* spp.), gum weed (*Grindelia aphanactis*), ground sorrel (*Senecio longilobus*), wild buckwheat (*Eriogonum* spp.), including both herbaceous and suffrutescent species, and here and there prickly poppy (*Argemone intermedia*).

The animal life of the pinyon-juniper association is diverse and includes the kit fox (*Vulpes velox*), coyote (*Canis latrans*), bobcat (*Lynx rufus*), rock squirrel (*Citellus variegatus*), spotted ground squirrel (*Citellus spilosoma*), pocket gopher (*Thomomys bottae*), Mexican pocket gopher (*Cratogeomys castanops*), silky pocket mouse (*Perognathus flavus*), Ord's Kangaroo rat (*Dipodomys ordi*), banner-tail kangaroo rat (*Dipodomys spectabilis*), northern grasshopper mouse (*Onychomys leucogaster*), western harvest mouse (*Reithrodontomys megalotis*), pinyon deer mouse (*Peromyscus truei*), long-tailed deer mouse (*Peromyscus maniculatus*), brush deer mouse (*Peromyscus boylei*), possibly the southern plains woodrat (*Neotoma micropus*), white-throated woodrat (*Neotoma albigula*), hispid cotton rat (*Sigmodon hispidus*), desert cottontail (*Sylvilagus auduboni*), black-tailed jack rabbit (*Lepus californicus*), and the hog-nosed skunk (*Conepatus leuconotus*). A number of the species mentioned in this list are also present in the desert grassland.

TRANSITION ASSOCIATION

The transition association occurs above the pinyon-juniper association approximately between altitudes of 7,200 to 9,000 feet. In this zone, which is broken into several isolated units, the tree species for the first time become major features of the vegetation, and at least one important timber tree is found throughout this association. There are a few hold-over trees from the pinyon-juniper association such as an occasional one-seed juniper, which is seldom of any importance in the transition association and gray oak (*Quercus grisea*), still appearing on dry, rocky slopes of the lower part of this area.

The alligator-bark juniper, often making its appearance in the upper part of the pinyon-juniper level, is often well represented in the lower part of the transition association. Another juniper, the Rocky Mountain juniper (*Juniperus scopulorum*), is common here and, at higher altitudes, gradually replaces the other junipers. The Rocky Mountain juniper can be recognized by its slender, drooping, gray-green foliage, having none of the stiff, clustered appearance of either the one-seed or alligator-bark junipers. The juniper picture usually becomes somewhat confusing in the lower part of the transition association, as hybridization is common between all of these species.

The really important tree of this area and association is the ponderosa pine (*Pinus ponderosa*), one of the more valuable timber trees of the west. This one is the typical three-needled variety; apparently the five-needled var. *arizonica* does not extend this far east. While the ponderosa pine is common throughout the transition association, it is gradually replaced by douglas fir and white fir toward the upper limits of the association. Other trees of less importance include the southwestern chokecherry (*Prunus virens*), the black choke cherry (*Prunus virginiana* var. *melanocarpa*) in canyons and other mesic areas, and the western black walnut (*Juglans major*) common to gravelly outwash areas on canyon floors. Principal trees of riparian habitats are the narrow-leaved cottonwood (*Populus angustifolia*), ash-leaf maple (*Acer negundo*), and the Rocky Mountain maple (*Acer glabrum*). In addition to the gray oak, two other oak species also grow here. Gambel oak (*Quercus gambellii*) is common at this altitude over much of the state but tends to inhabit canyons or damp slopes. The chestnut oak (*Quercus muhlenbergii*), not a common tree in this part of the state, is reported from the slopes of the Capitan Mountains. It is so called because the leaves resemble those of American chestnuts.

The shrub complement of the transition association includes the spiny-leaved barberry (*Berberis haematocarpa*), apache plume (*Fallugia paradoxa*), skunkbush sumac (*Rhus trilobata*), mountain mahogany (*Cercocarpus montanus*), buckthorn (*Ceanothus fendleri*), and western mock orange (*Philadelphus microphyllus*) on generally open, rocky slopes or in dry thickets. In shaded areas bush rockspiraea (*Holodiscus dumosus*), mescalero currant (*Ribes mescalerium*), creeping barberry or Oregon grape (*Berberis repens*), and wild grape (*Vitis arizonica*) are common. Along streams the willows such as blue-stem willow (*Salix irrorata*), and coyote willow (*Salix exigua*) predominate.

Many shade-loving herbaceous plants occur in this association. In partially shaded areas are common vetch (*Vicia americana*) in the legume family; several daisy fleabanes (*Erigeron* spp.), and a number of asters (*Aster* spp.) in the composite family; fireweed (*Epilobium angustifolium*), and evening primrose (*Oenothera* spp.), both in the evening primrose family; western wallflower (*Erysimum capitatum*), and wild geraniums (*Geranium* spp.). Herbs growing along streams include several species of monkeyflower (*Mimulus* spp.) and coneflower (*Rudbeckia laciniata*). Species tending to prefer open or sunny areas are Indian paint brush (*Castilleja* spp.), some members of the mustard family, whitlow grass (*Draba* spp.), bladderpod (*Lesquerella fendleri*), peppergrass (*Lepidium montanum*), and others such as Rocky Mountain bee plant (*Cleome serrulata*), wild onion (*Allium* spp.), lambsquarters (*Chenopodium* spp.), and the amaranth or pigweed (*Amaranthus retroflexus*), Indian hemp (*Apocynum cannabinum*), four-o-clock (*Mirabilis multiflorus*), little primrose (*Gaura coccinea*), lupine (*Lupinus* spp.), and one of the most popular of our wild flowers, the orange-flowered milkweed or butterfly weed (*Asclepias tuberosa*), so called because hordes of butterflies are attracted to the flower.

Fewer species of grasses might be expected in the transition association than in lower areas, but the importance of grasses in the overall cover here should not be underestimated. Some commonly noted grasses include prairie junegrass (*Koeleria cristata*), several muhly grasses such as spikemuhly (*Muhlenbergia wrightii*), bullgrass (*Muhlenbergia emersleyi*), and deergrass (*Muhlenbergia rigens*), three-awn (*Aristida* spp.), Arizona fescue (*Festuca arizonica*), nodding brome (*Bromus anomalus*), Kentucky bluegrass (*Poa pratensis*), Bigelow bluegrass (*Poa bigelovii*) several wheat grasses, some of them introduced (*Agropyron* spp.), squirreltail (*Sitanion hystrix*), foxtail barley (*Hordeum jubatum*), grama grasses, blue grama and side-oats grama, already mentioned for the upper level of the pinyon-juniper association, red top (*Agrostis alba*), sleepy grass (*Stipa vaseyi*), and wild rye (*Elymus canadensis*). In wet areas and along the edges of marshes, a number of sedges are expected, these, for the most part, belonging to three genera (*Carex, Cyperus,* and *Scirpus*).

The transition association provides many habitats for a diversified population of animal life, but some of those noted for the pinyon-juniper association are also present here. These are the bobcat, rock squirrel, golden mantle ground squirrel, valley pocket gopher, long-tailed deer mouse, and brush deer mouse. Other mammals found in this association are the Mexican vole (*Microtus mexicanus*), porcupine (*Erethizon dorsatum*), a very serious pest of young pine stands, muledeer (*Odocoileus hemionus*), white-tailed deer (*Odocoileus virginianus*), mountain lion (*Felis concolor*), to be looked for at almost any altitude, striped skunk (*Mephitis mephitis*), long-tailed weasil (*Mustela frenata*), ranging from the upper part of the transition, raccoon (*Procyon lotor*), and black bear (*Ursus americanus*).

SPRUCE - FIR ASSOCIATION

The spruce-fir association, ranging from altitudes of 9,000 feet to more than 11,000 feet, is often divided into two levels. At the lower level, the predominant trees are douglas fir (*Pseudotsuga taxifolia*), and white fir (*Abies concolor*), although a scattering of ponderosa pine may appear here and there. Higher in this association the spruce becomes dominant and the limber pine (*Pinus flexilis*) makes an appearance on the drier slopes and ridges. Blue spruce (*Picea pungens*), and Engelmann spruce (*Picea engelmannii*) make up the bulk of the spruce level. Blue spruce seems to be somewhat more restricted as to distribution, preferring canyons and moist areas, while Engelmann spruce seems to be more tolerant of a wide range of habitats. In riparian associations the Rocky Mountain maple, several willow species, among them Bebb willow (*Salix bebbiana*), and the alder (*Alnus oblongifolia*) are to be expected. Another common tree found almost anywhere in the spruce-fir zone is the quaking aspen (*Populus tremuloides* var. *aurea*). It generally grows along small streams or ravines or cool, damp hillsides and is considered to be a rather fast-growing but short-lived tree. It is one of the first plants to enter an area after a burn and quickly develops a thick stand which acts as a nurse crop to allow the slower growing conifers to become established.

In the often dense tree cover of the spruce-fir association, shade tolerant shrubs are numerous. In shaded or partially shaded situations are the thimble berry (*Rubus parviflorus*), Rocky Mountain clematis (*Clematis pseudoalpina*), bush rockspiraea (*Holodiscus dumosus*), ninebark (*Physocarpus monogynus*), the low growing evergreen myrtle boxleaf (*Pachystima myrsinites*), orange gooseberry (*Ribes pinetorum*), Rothrock currant (*Ribes wolfii*), mescalero currant (*Ribes mescalerium*), this currant also is found in transition areas and appears to be endemic to this part of the state, New Mexican elder (*Sambucus neomexicana*), and black bead elder (*Sambucus melanocarpa*). The New Mexican elder often attains tree-like proportions. Shrubs that generally inhabit clearings or open, rocky areas are cliff jamesia (*Jamesia americana*), roundleaf snowberry (*Symphoricarpos rotundifolius*), shrubby cinquefoil (*Potentilla fruticosa*), and New Mexican locust (*Robinia neomexicana*), the last usually common in upper transition and lower spruce-fir associations and characterized by pinnately-compound leaves and large, drooping panicles of reddish purple flowers in early summer.

The spruce-fir association supports a lush understory of herbs such as wafer parsnip (*Pseudocymopterus montanus*), wild strawberry (*Fragaria bracteata*), blue flag (*Iris missouriensis*), horsemint (*Monarda menthaefolia*), red columbine (*Aquilegia elegantula*), rock jasmine (*Androsace septentrionalis*), yarrow (*Achillea lanulosa*), Rusby primula (*Primula rusbyi*), valerian (*Valeriana acutiloba*), owl's claws (*Helenium hoopsii*), cohosh (*Actaea viridiflora*), Canada violet (*Viola canadensis*), cardinal flower (*Penstemon cardinalis*), Jacob's ladder (*Polemonium filicinum*), Gray's lousewort (*Pedicularis grayi*), buttercups (*Ranunculus* spp.), camas or wand lily (*Zygadenus elegans*), bluebell (*Campanula rotundifolia*), bog orchis (*Habenaria brevifolia*), and fairy slipper (*Calypso bulbosa*).

Grasses common to the spruce-fir association of these mountains include mountain brome (*Bromus marginatus*), bearded wheatgrass (*Agropyron subsecundum*), slender wheatgrass (*Agropyron trachycaulum*), thurber fescue (*Festuca thurberi*), Columbia needlegrass (*Stipa columbiana*), mountain timothy (*Phleum alpinum*), timber danthonia (*Danthonia intermedia*), tufted hairgrass (*Deschampsia caespitosa*), bull wildrye (*Elymus glaucus*), New Mexican bluegrass (*Poa occidentalis*), melic grass (*Melica porteri*).

In addition to animals normally present in this association such as the pocket gopher, bobcat, chipmunk, mountain lion, long-tailed vole and black bear, we can add the dusky shrew (*Sorex vagrans*) to the list.

ALPINE ASSOCIATION

There is no doubt some room for argument as to the extent of the alpine association in this region. None of the peaks except Sierra Blanca are high enough to support anything resembling alpine vegetation. Since Sierra Blanca Peak reaches an altitude of more than 12,000 feet, it seems logical that at least a small portion at the top of the peak should fall into the alpine category. The alpine zone is not as clear-cut on Sierra Blanca Peak, however, as on comparable peaks farther north. The alpine association generally is regarded as beginning at about 12,000 feet on most peaks of the Sangre de Cristo range, but the alpine limit theoretically should begin somewhat lower on these peaks than on Sierra Blanca Peak owing to climatic changes associated with latitude and relative size of surrounding mountain masses. Although there is evidence of glaciation having occurred on Sierra Blanca Peak, the time of permanent snow fields on this peak is apparently long past.

At any rate, a small area of the top of the peak seems to have some characteristics of an alpine situation. However, many species of plants common to the alpine region of the Sangre de Cristo range have no representatives on Sierra Blanca Peak.

The shrub cover which could be classed as alpine would be represented only by arctic willow (*Salix petrophila*), while herbs include campion (*Silene* spp.), avens (*Geum turbinatum*), sandwort (*Arenaria obtusiloba*), White Mountain cinquefoil (*Potentilla sierrae-blancae*), gentian (*Gentiana strictiflora*), and bitterweed (*Hymenoxys grandiflora*). Rushes and sedges make up an important part of the vegetation here; the majority belong to two genera (*Luzula* and *Carex*).

SELECTED REFERENCES

Harris, A. H., 1956, A distributional check-list of New Mexican mammals: Univ. New Mexico unpub. Masters thesis, 463 p.

Hitchcock, A. S., 1950, Manual of the grasses of the United States. 2d ed., revised by Agnes Chase: U.S. Dept. Agr. Pub. 200, 1051 p.

Kearney, T. H., and Peebles, R. H., 1960, Arizona flora, 2d ed. with supplement by J. T. Howell, E. McClintock and collaborators: Berkeley and Los Angeles, Univ. Calif. Press, 1085 p.

Martin, W. C., and Castetter, E. F., 1964, A checklist of gymnosperms and angiosperms of New Mexico: Univ. New Mexico Pub. Biol. In press.

Wooton, E. O., and Standley, P. C., 1915, Flora of New Mexico: U.S. Natl. Herbarium Contr. v. 19, 794 p.

PETROGLYPHS OF THE SIERRA BLANCA

Robert H. Weber

New Mexico Bureau of Mines and Mineral Resources
New Mexico Institute of Mining and Technology
Socorro, New Mexico

INTRODUCTION

The distribution of petroglyphs in the foothills of the Sierra Blanca indicates widespread usage of the region by prehistoric Indian cultures that are as yet only poorly known. The natural advantages offered by streams in the mountain canyons, numerous springs scattered across the surrounding slopes, an abundance of game animals and birds, a wide variety of wild plant foods, fibers, and timber, useful rocks and minerals for the manufacture of implements, and arable land along floodplains and alluvial terraces must have proved highly attractive to both nomadic and sedentary groups.

Many of the topographic promontories of the area are capped by Tertiary dikes and sills, and by resistant Cretaceous sandstones. The dark gray to black or brown weathered surfaces of these rocks, beneath which a contrastingly paler-hued layer was exposed readily by pecking, incising, and grinding, provided an enduring medium for recording figures of geometric and animalistic forms. Some of these figures must be products of artistic impulses inherent in man, as indicated by similarities with designs on pottery, basketry, and textiles. Others appear related to religious and secular symbolism, the principal lifeways of the people, and perhaps charms connected with hunting. Some are as informal and abstract as modern doodling.

Although several of the more conspicuous sites show some use as workshops for the chipping of implements and preparation of food, many bear little evidence of use aside from that of the inscription of petroglyphs. Locations near springs, passes, and probable game trails were obviously favored, but some sites appear to have been attractive because of their location as convenient lookouts, providing unimpeded views of the surrounding area.

Only a few of the sites west of the Sierra Blanca between Three Rivers and Carrizozo are described here. There are undoubtedly other noteworthy ones within this same area, and many more along the ridges and canyons east of the Sierra Blanca. Gebhard (1957) described and illustrated pictographs from the eastern slope of the range, suggesting that they are the work of the Mescalero Apache. Only the square-shouldered figure in the lower left corner of figure 3 was chalked for greater clarity; all of the other figures and designs shown in the photographs accompanying this paper are not chalked.

THE THREE RIVERS PETROGLYPHS

The most impressive display of petroglyphs is 4 miles northeast of Three Rivers, in secs. 16 and 21, T. 11 S., R. 9½ E. An Official Historic Marker on U.S. Highway 54 at Three Rivers carries the following information: "THREE RIVERS PETROGLYPHS. A mile-long array of pictures pecked into the solid rock walls of a volcanic ridge. They include both geometric and animal forms. Most were made by prehistoric Indians. May be contemporary with a nearby Mimbres site, dating from 900-1000 A.D. Follow road three miles east." The distance is actually 5.1 miles but, by following signs placed along the route, little difficulty will be had in finding the locality.

The "volcanic ridge" trends northerly for a distance of a little over one mile, and consists of a thin eastward-dipping hornblende-biotite lamprophyre sill intrusive into sandstones of the Mesaverde Group. The rock tends to weather to smooth, rounded surfaces coated with a dark gray to lustrous black desert varnish. Petroglyphs are distributed throughout the length of the sill on both outcrop and talus boulders, with noteworthy concentrations at the southern and northern ends. The figures are highly varied and may be of more than one age (figures 1 and 2. Among the forms noted are realistic, stylized and surrealistic animal figures; various representations of human figures, heads, handprints, footprints, and possible mythical beings; corn plants; curvilinear and rectilinear geometric patterns that include various embellishments of circles, spirals, dots, triangles, rectangles, stepped terraces, parallel zigzag and wavy lines, and aimless(?) meandering and looping lines. Among the animal figures are birds in flight and at rest (a highly realistic quail, roadrunners, turkeys, possible macaws, and others), lizards, frogs, turtles, snakes, beetles, butterflies, worms, fish, deer (a spotted fawn is especially noteworthy), rabbits, chipmunk, skunk, mountain lions, and mountain sheep. Tracks of birds are common; some are aligned in trails that trip lightly across the tops of boulders. The X-shaped track of the roadrunner is faithfully portrayed. Tracks of bear and wolf are also clearly delineated, Human figures are largely stylized stick and solid forms of considerable variety. Goggle-eyed faces are repeated at several places, as is the ingenious use of corners of rocks to provide depth in portrayals of human heads as shown in the lower left photograph in figure 2. Some of these faces are enhanced by pecked shading of features on one side. Masks and headdresses are indicated on several figures.

Cultural affiliations of the Three Rivers petroglyphs have not been established, but Puebloan styles are strongly indicated. The exhuberant depiction of animals and frequency of geometric patterning of animal bodies are highly suggestive of Mimbres pottery designs. The site is within the area occupied by the Jornada Branch of the Mogollon, of which one of the northern variants, the Three Rivers Phase (circa 1100-1200 A.D.), was defined from sites in this vicinity (Lehmer, 1948). The results of excavations in 1925 of 10 rooms of a nearby pueblo unfortunately have not been published. Some

Figure 1. — Petroglyphs at the Three Rivers site.

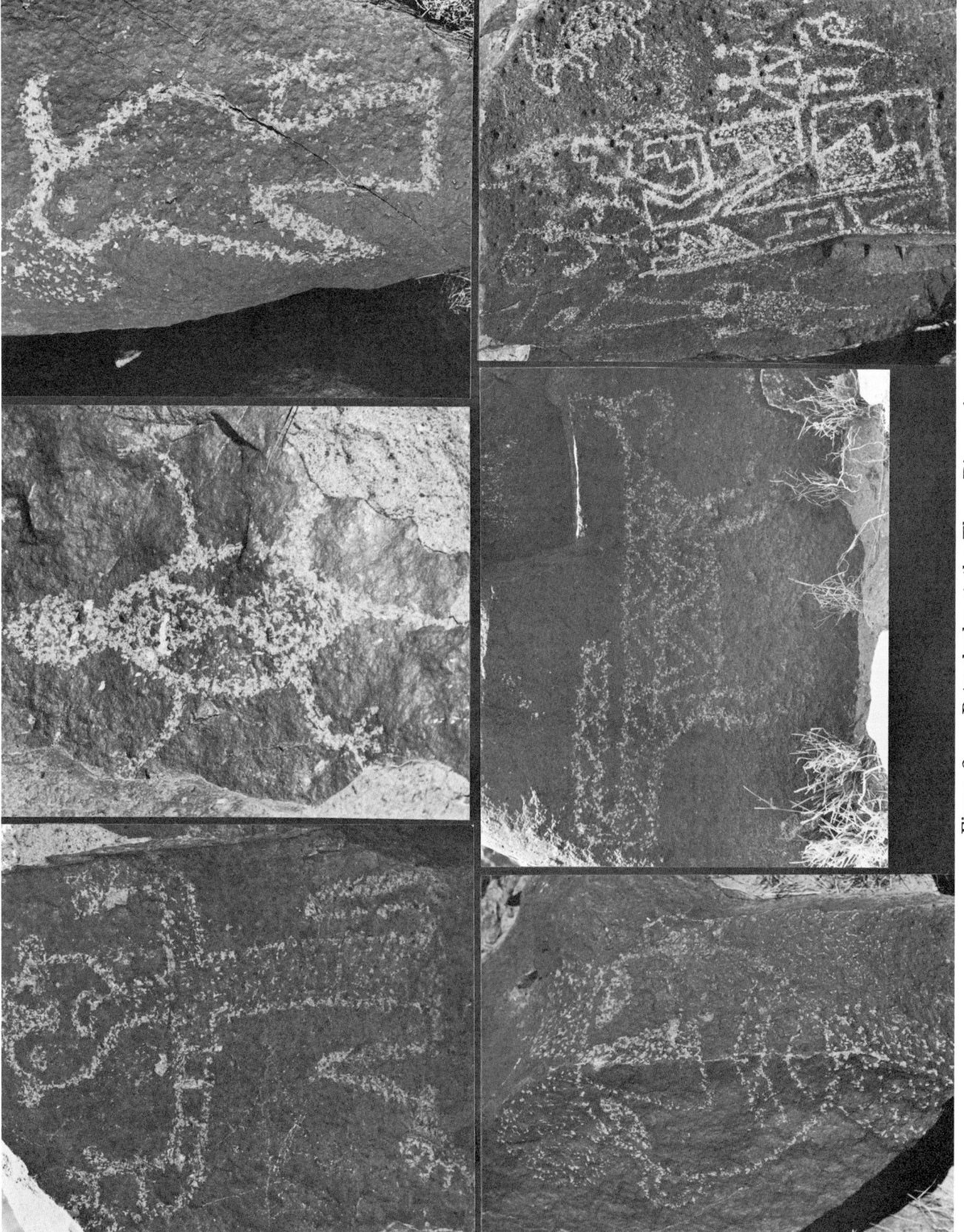

Figure 2. — Petroglyphs at the Three Rivers site.

Figure 3. — Petroglyphs at the Willow Hill site; geology pick indicates scale.

of the fresher-appearing figures may be attributable to the modern Apache, who now occupy the adjacent Mescalero Apache Indian Reservation.

North of the Three Rivers site, a series of sill-capped hills extends northeastward along a structural trend dominated on the south by Malagro Hill. Petroglyphs were noted locally on black patinated sill outcrops in the vicinity of Malagro Springs, above which there are indications of a fairly extensive village site. Both sills and adjacent sandstones of the Mesaverde Group in smaller hills in secs. 1, 2, and 3, T. 9 S., R. 9 E. bear isolated clusters of petroglyphs.

THE WILLOW HILL PETROGLYPHS

Turning eastward through the canyon between Cub Mountain and Willow Hill, past Willow Springs, a basaltic dike of west-northwesterly trend rises as a conspicuous wall above a spring near the southern edge of the SE 1/4 sec. 35, T. 8 S., R. 10 E. The jointed, weathered surfaces of the dike are decorated for a distance of several hundred feet with large panels of petroglyphs. Looping, meandering lines, tally marks, and rows of human figures holding hands are conspicuous design elements, accompanied by various animal motifs (fig. 3). This site is in all probability on an old trail connecting the Tularosa Valley on the west with the Sierra Blanca on the east, where wild game, pinyon, and other food resources were exploited. It would have served admirably as an ambush for game watering at the springs. Minor lithic sites, possibly representative of the Hueco Phase of the Jornada Branch, are scattered along terraces in this area. Sparse shards of brownware indicate continued occupation in later pottery-bearing phases.

Small groups of petroglyphs are present at scattered localities along the western slope of Willow Hill and the eastern edge of the Carrizozo Malpais, but none of these are as impressive as those described above.

REFERENCES CITED

Gebhard, David, 1957, Pictographs in the Sierra Blanca Mountains: El Palacio, v. 64, p. 215-222, 3 photographs.

Lehmer, D. J., 1948, The Jornada Branch of the Mogollon: Univ. Ariz. Bull., v. 19, no. 2; also Soc. Sci. Bull. no. 17, 99 p

CAVES OF THE FORT STANTON AREA, NEW MEXICO

Donald E. Hallinger

Sunray DX Oil Company
Abilene, Texas

INTRODUCTION

There are a number of caves in the Fort Stanton area of New Mexico. These caves, some of which are well known, occur in the San Andres Limestone of Permian age. The caves are of interest because of the speliothems (secondary mineral deposits formed in caves) they contain and because of their past usage by man. In this paper the development of the caves and their usage by man is discussed.

HISTORY OF THE DEVELOPMENT OF THE CAVES

The caves probably were formed shortly after the origin and development of the present surface drainage. Although it is commonly thought that caves generally are developed by waters in either the phreatic or the vadose zone, my studies indicate that the action of vadose water combined with some erosion by underground streams has formed the caves in the Fort Stanton area. This is suggested by the following facts:

1. The passageways, although somewhat affected by joint systems, appear to conform in general to the present surface drainage patterns.
2. One domal room of considerable magnitude in Fort Stanton Cave contains a characteristic heap of "breakdown" which is cemented at its base by the same type of clay fill that is found in all of the nearby caves. Attached to several pieces of this deposit of "breakdown" are fragments of speliothems indicating that speliothems formed on the ceilings prior to breakdown, and thus prior to the deposition of the cave fill. Many of the blocks of breakdown bear the marks of erosion, not solution. Some of these marks are covered by the clay fill, suggesting that prior to its deposition, the process actively removing the breakdown and therefore modifying the cave itself, was an underground stream.
3. Several curtains of speliothems that developed under water before the clay fill was deposited are present in Fort Stanton Cave.
4. The walls of a number of the main passageways in Fort Stanton Cave exhibit two features of a passage modified by moving water. Several distinct water levels occur on the walls. Below each succeeding lower wall level more of the wall rock was removed then above that line creating typical inverted step walls. These features also predate the cave fill.
5. At two slight bends in the passageways, a terraced mound is superimposed on the bedrock, with the highest development of the mound at the inside of the passageway along the wall. The mounds slope down towards the outside of the bend of the passageway, just as a meander scar would develop.

The second step occurred when the passageways were filled with clay and gravel. The composition of the gravels indicates that at least one surface stream emptied into Fort Stanton Cave after the cave formed, as a significant number of the pebbles in the gravel are of igneous origin. Apparently these pebbles were derived from nearby igneous bodies. Some passages in the cave were filled completely with clay and gravel while others were only partially filled.

The third step was the partial excavation of the clay and gravel in the passages by streams originating on the land surface as suggested by the many igneous pebbles found in the stream beds. These pebbles have a greater degree of rounding than the pebbles in the clay and gravel fill.

The fourth, most recent, most interesting, and sometimes most destructive step in the history of the present caves, is the work of humans. The earliest record of human habitation is found in Feather Cave and the several shelter caves nearby.

Vandalism by modern man has been extensive in the caves of the Fort Stanton area. It is virtually impossible in exploring new passages in a cave to keep from breaking some speliothems. However, the wholesale and systematic breakage of all speliothems for monetary reasons is hardly in the same class. Because of the long time of development, and unreproducible conditions of speliothems every broken one represents a loss for us and our descendants. Thus as one walks through the first one or two miles of Fort Stanton Cave, all that can be seen are bare walls with the remnants of broken speliothems. This is what other "collectors" have left for you to see. The only parts of Fort Stanton Cave that still contain pretty speliothems are the "new sections" at the back of the generally known cave. And even with the little publicity they have received, the new sections are being vandalized.

There is some evidence that Fort Stanton Cave was known and frequented by the Indians. In 1862, a company of the U.S. Cavalry chased a group of Indians into the mouth of Fort Stanton Cave. The troopers pitched camp outside and decided to starve the "redskins" out. A few days later, the same Indians were seen stealing the troopers' horses. These Indians knew of a second entrance, something which modern explorers have failed to locate.

SPELIOTHEMS

One of the most intriguing features of caves are the speliothems they contain. After once having created the long winding passageways and the high vaulted rooms, Mother Nature is not satisfied until she has decorated these chambers with sparkling crystal needles and pendants formed of calcium carbonate or calcium sulfate. Speliothems may be divided into two major groups: 1) those formed in air filled chambers; and 2) those formed in water filled chambers. Speliothems formed in an air filled chamber occur either as pendants hanging from the ceiling or walls (stalactites or helictites), or rising from the floors (stalagmites), or as a covering on the wall or floor known as flowstone.

The most impressive speliothems are the massive stalactites suspended from the ceiling, and their floor based counterparts, stalagmites. Stalactites will form only if the evaporation rate in the cave is higher than the amount of water present otherwise, stalagmites will develop. Stalagmites form because the water, not being able to deposit all of its dissolved salts on the ceiling, falls to the floor and deposits the remaining dissolved salts as evaporation occurs.

Though evaporation is not the only variable which determines the rate of deposition of speliothems it is easy to see that all stalagmites and stalactites do not necessarily form in the same length of time. The differences become even more apparent when the caves of arid New Mexico are compared to the caves in southwestern Virginia, where there is heavy annual rainfall. The speliothems in the New Mexico caves are quite often "dead" and dry, whereas the speliothems in the caves of southwestern Virginia are generally wet and "alive." In several caves, samples have been taken of huge speliothems and accompanying water and it has been determined how much volume is being added to the speliothems in that area at present. At one tested commercial cave in Maryland, the proprietor proudly proclaims that as it takes 100,000 years to deposit one cubic inch of speliothem material and as the volume of that particular speliothem is 700 cubic inches, the formation is approximately 700 million years old. The cave is formed in Upper Ordovician limestone indicating that, this speliothem and at least part of the cave would have been formed about 200 million years before the surrounding rocks were deposited if the rate of deposition had been constant.

Actually, deposition rates of $CaCO_3$ varies considerably, from the quoted rate of 1 cubic inch per 100,000 years, to as much as 4 cubic inches per year, as has been observed by the author in the Washington, D. C. area.

The shape of speliothems is the basis for their common names. Pillars are stalactites and stalagmites that have grown together into massive columns. "Broom sticks" are very slender pillars, about 2 to 4 inches in diameter. "Soda straws" are very slender stalactites, which look like long straws suspended from the ceiling. Quite often a sloping ceiling will have "curtains" developed on it. "Curtains," "drapes," or "bacon rind," as they may be called, are formed when water, instead of dropping from the ceiling, runs down an inclined surface, depositing $CaCO_3$ as it goes. These speliothems are quite often banded parallel to their edge, leading to the name "bacon rind."

Helictites are a type of pendant formation that do not respond in the normal way to gravity as they may grow in any direction and usually change directions. Helictites are composed of $CaCO_3$ and/or $CaSO_4 \cdot 2H_2O$. The name helictite generally is applied to any clump of stalactites or stalagmites that do not hang straight down from the ceiling or point straight up from the floor. Gypsum flowers are a type of helictite.

The most commonly encountered type of flowstone is the frozen waterfall. Frozen waterfalls are composed of overlapping sheets of $CaCO_3$ that were deposited on a wall or inclined floor.

There are several other types of speliothems which can be deposited in an air filled chamber, but they are not known to occur in the caves of the Fort Stanton area and therefore are not discussed here.

The second major group of speliothems, those formed in water filled chambers, are quite varied and include such features as calcite rafts, lily pads, and rimstone pools. They are usually associated with a noticeable water level mark below which all surfaces are covered with individual crystals that are larger than those formed in air filled chambers. A stalactite covered with these crystals is generally larger at its base than at its apex and has the appearance of a club hanging from the ceiling. These speliothems are known as "war clubs," and passages containing an abundance of them are often called war club rooms.

One of the most striking features of speliothems is their color. In most caves, they stand out as stark white forms, against a drab brown or gray background. However other colors occur in one of the caves in the Fort Stanton area.

THE CAVES

The caves in the Fort Stanton area can be divided into two groups on the basis of size. One group includes caves which are deep enough for a man to get out of sight of the sun. The two best known caves of this type, although there are others, are Fort Stanton Cave and Feather Cave. The second group includes the shallow shelter caves which generally occur at the base of steep bluffs.

Fort Stanton Cave is located on the south side of Highway 380 about midway between Lincoln and Capitan, New Mexico. The entrance is a steep-sided sinkhole. The rubble in the sinkhole has effectively divided the original cave into separate caves. The main cave has several miles of known passageways. The first 1 to 2 miles are devoid of speliothems. In the "new section," all of the different types of speliothems mentioned earlier are present.

Two rare types of selenite crystals are found in Fort Stanton Cave. One is a selenite twin crystal form that occurs in the Crystal Passage. These crystals look like long flat needles with a decidedly concave prism face (Hills, 1895). In 1939 mention of these crystals appeared in another article (Wheeler, 1939) in which a collecting expedition to Fort Stanton Cave was reported. The practice of collecting these crystals to sell has gone on for some time. So much so, that today there are more crystals, the majority of them broken, around the entrance of the cave and for sale in local souvenir shops, than there are in the cave.

The second rare type of selenite crystal has not been described in the literature, and is known from only one other cave (Crystal Cave, Indiana), besides Fort Stanton Cave. These crystals occur individually as 1½-inch long needles, terminated on both ends by a 6-sided pyramid. The needles have 6 equal sides and are 1/40 inch wide.

Some of the speliothems in Fort Stanton Cave are unusual because of their color. One seldom observed color in speliothems is bluish black. Flowstone of this color occurs in Fort Stanton Cave and looks like velvet. This flowstone has been analysed and found to have a high manganese content. Other flowstone in the cave is carmel colored; the impurity causing this particular color is unknown.

It has been reported that in the early 1900's it was necessary to use a boat to visit the middle part of the known Fort Stanton Cave. At that time the Federal Government had the first mile of the cave surveyed in order to determine if the water in it flowed toward the nearby Government Springs. The findings indicated that this was the case and the water level in the caves was 37 feet higher than the spring. The spring still flows intermittently although all of the known passages in Fort Stanton Cave are dry today, except after an especially rainy season. It is thought that this recent drying of the cave may be a reflection of a regional lowering of the water table. Two of the known passageways of Fort Stanton Cave end in breakdown within several hundred feet of Government Spring. On several occasions running water has been heard through this breakdown, suggesting that there are passageways containing water behind and below it.

Feather Cave is across the highway from Fort Stanton Cave. It has a shallow sinkhole entrance. From the entrance, a rubble covered slope leads down to a fairly flat room approximately 200 feet long and 50 feet wide. The floor is quite dissected and the trenches of the archaeologists are still visible. The most striking feature of Feather Cave is the utterly black appearance of the walls and ceilings. This color was caused by soot from countless cooking fires kindled by the early inhabitants of the cave.

Feather Cave has been partially excavated by University of New Mexico archaeology students. In the literature published by this group, the cave was given a new name, Dan's Cave, in honor of one of the researchers. Prior to that time, the people in the area knew this cave as Feather Cave, or Outlaw Cave. The cave was studied for an entire summer by a group of University of New Mexico students, and was subsequently visited by many hundreds of people. However in spite of this careful study of a room barely 200 feet long and 50 feet wide, a new room was discovered a few months ago behind the breakdown at the end of the cave. This new room contained many well preserved Indian artifacts which will be described in the near future.

There are several small shelter caves in the bluffs across the highway from Fort Stanton Cave and near Feather Cave (fig. 1). Some of these caves contain speliothem development. Shards of pottery and faded pictographs have been found in some of these caves. At least one of the shelter caves is the home of cave swallows, a bird of somewhat restricted range in New Mexico.

Almost every trip made to the Fort Stanton area in the last two years has resulted in new discoveries, either in additional passages to known caves, or in the discovery of new caves. All have been partially excavated, although some have not been fully opened. All of the newly discovered caves, as far as they have been explored to date, are above the level of Fort Stanton Cave, and like Fort Stanton Cave show the same alignment to the surface drainage.

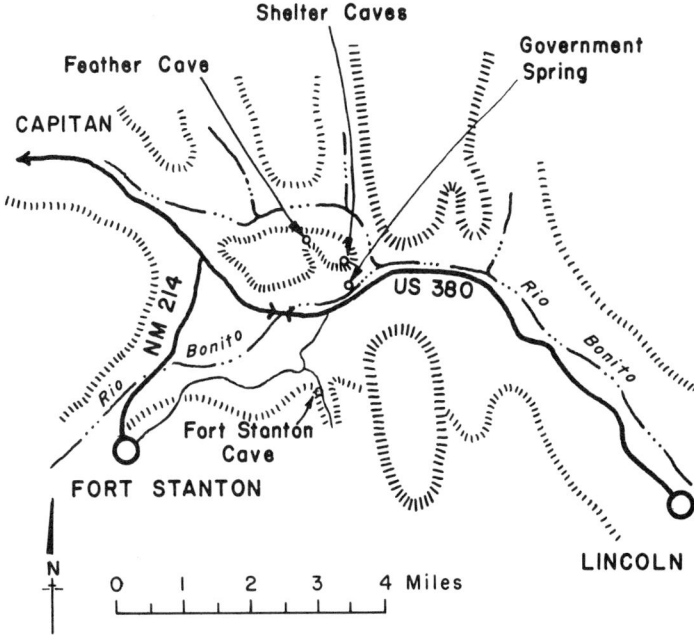

Figure 1. — Sketch map of the Fort Stanton Cave area, New Mexico.

A sketch map (fig. 1) indicates the general location of some of the caves discussed here. There are many known caves in the area covered by figure 1 in addition to these marked. The locations of these caves are purposely not shown because several would be quite dangerous for a novice; several are merely tunnels dug into the clay and gravel fill blocking the cave entrances; and at least two of the unmarked caves have not been fully explored and it is not advisable for a novice to attempt to explore them. The two caves that are marked on the sketch map are quite interesting, safe, and contain several miles of mapped passageways.

SUGGESTIONS TO SPELUNKERS

Caving can be fun as well as informative and interesting. There are many cavers that visit caves to gather data to enable them to better understand the caves and the flora and fauna they contain. These people are called "speleologists." Those people that visit caves for fun and enjoyment are called "spelunkers." To them belongs the thrill of finding a room with no signs of human passage, a room never seen by man before. As a matter of fact, the parent body of organized caving in this country; the National Speleological Society, started as just such a group, a hiking group that had couarge and curosity enough to poke their heads into holes in the ground.

There are laws protecting the caves of the Fort Stanton area, because it is on Federal land. However, owing to excessive vandalism, it is quite possible that in the near future a locked gate may be placed at the entrance to protect the cave from people. As a prospective visitor to the wonders of subterranean worlds, you may forestall such measures by being cognizant of and following the simple conservation practice of removing nothing from a cave but pictures, and leaving nothing behind but foot prints.

If you do plan to visit some of the caves in this area, there are a few simple precautions to follow:

1. Have alternate sources of light. Matches may become wet, just as batteries run down. So have both matches and flashlights, as well as spares.
2. Quite often a hard hat is necessary to protect yourself from low ceilings.
3. An accident in a cave may be quite serious, so tell some reliable friends where you are going, and never go alone.
4. All accidents in caves that have been reported were due to the carelessness of the individuals involved. Caves hold no hidden pit falls or traps, only beauty and different forms of life than those seen on top of the ground.
5. In order to preserve the beauty for others that will follow, remember—Take only pictures, and leave only foot prints.

BIBLIOGRAPHY

Hassemer, Jerry, 1963, Fort Stanton Cave — past and present: National Speleological Soc. News, v. 21, no. 2, p. 12-13.

Hills, R. C., 1895, Twin crystals of selenite (From near Fort Stanton): Colorado Sci. Soc. Proc., v. 4, p. 32.

Mowat, George D., 1962, Progressive changes of shapes by solution in the labratory: Cave Notes, v. 4, no. 6, p. 45-49.

de Sausaure, R., 1963, The general formation and development of limestone caves: Cave Notes, v. 5, no. 1, p. 1-5.

Wheeler, Verne C., 1939, Collecting in a cave: Rocks and Minerals, v. 13, p. 352-356.

ABSTRACTS OF TECHNICAL PAPERS

Presented at the 18th Annual Meeting

Silver City, April 23-24, 1964

UPPER TRIASSIC PLANTS OF NEW MEXICO AND ARIZONA

Sidney R. Ash

U.S. Geological Survey, Albuquerque, New Mexico*

The Chinle Formation (Upper Triassic) of New Mexico and Arizona contains plant fossils at a number of localities. Although the celebrated silicified logs in the Petrified Forest of Arizona are the most widely known of these fossils, the formation also contains pollen, spores, and leaf impressions. The last comprehensive study of any of these floras published in 1941 and primarily concerned a collection of leaves from the Petrified Forest.

Recently the author collected well preserved leaves and wood from the Chinle Formation of western New Mexico. His collection, and others made in the same area, contain some species that are identical with those previously described from Arizona and others that have not been reported from that area. Particularly interesting are several undescribed fertile structures. Thus far, representatives of most major groups of plants, including the fungi, lycopods, horsetails, ferns, cycads, and conifers have been found in the Triassic rocks of New Mexico and Arizona.

*Publication authorized by the Director, U.S. Geological Survey

THE CRETACEOUS-TERTIARY BOUNDARY, SAN JUAN BASIN, NEW MEXICO

Elmer H. Baltz and Sidney R. Ash

U.S. Geological Survey, Albuquerque, New Mexico*

During studies of the distribution of the Ojo Alamo Sandstone and its water-bearing capabilities in the San Juan Basin, northwestern New Mexico, the authors found new evidence concerning the stratigraphy and age of this unit. At its type locality the Ojo Alamo Sandstone was defined by C. M. Bauer in 1917 to consist of a thin basal conglomerate, a medial dinosaur-bearing shale, and an upper conglomeratic sandstone that contains numerous large silicified logs. Bauer reported that these units were conformable with each other, and that the medial shale is a lens enclosed between the upper and lower conglomerates which were said to merge into one unit of sandstone away from the type of locality. The dinosaur fauna in the medial shale is of Montana age; thus the Ojo Alamo was said to be Late Cretaceous in age. The Ojo Alamo was reported to be conformable with the underlying Kirtland Shale of Late Cretaceous (Montana) age, and unconformable with the overlying Nacimiento Formation that contains early Paleocene (Puerco) mammals.

A restudy of the type region of the Ojo Alamo Sandstone indicates that the upper conglomeratic sandstone rests on a deeply channeled erosion surface cut in the medial dinosaur-bearing shale which is a persistent unit, rather than being a lens as reported by Bauer. The upper conglomeratic sandstone also intertongues with the Nacimiento Formation, and contains a microflorule identical to a microflorule from the beds of the Nacimiento that contain Puercan mammals. Thus, the upper part of Bauer's Ojo Alamo is Paleocene and rests unconformably on the middle part which is Late but not latest Cretaceous. These facts indicate that the Ojo Alamo Sandstone should be redefined, and concepts on the nature and stratigraphic position of the Cretaceous-Tertiary boundary in the San Juan Basin should be revised.

*Publication authorized by the Director, U.S. Geological Survey

GEOLOGY OF THE NORTHERN AND EASTERN PORTIONS OF THE LADRON MOUNTAINS, SOCORRO COUNTY, NEW MEXICO

Bruce A. Black

Shell Oil Company, Bakersfield, California

The Ladron Mountains are a westward-tilted fault block and an important western bounding structure of the Rio Grande depression in the Albuquerque-Belen basin. The main massif is a complex of igneous and metamorphic Precambrian rocks. The complex consists of a thick sequence of steeply east-dipping quartzites and schists which are predominantly a product of low- to medium-grade regional Precambrian metomorphism. Abundant schist remnants which have been invaded lit-par-lit by granite gneiss occur in a large area on the eastern flank of the mountains and represent an ultrametamorphic product of anatexis. All metamorphic rocks have been invaded by two Precambrian granites. The second of these intrusions has produced much migmatite in the northern part of the mountains.

The mountains are bounded by a roughly triangular shaped system of faults or fault zones. On the west and southwest is the Ladron fault, and on the east and southeast the Cerro Colorado fault zone. A buried fault zone on the north completes the triangle.

The Ladron fault is a high-angle normal fault along which down-faulted Paleozoic limestones form an impression north-trending hogback. The Cerro Colorado fault zone is a complex of north-northeast trending normal faults. Occasional wedges of Mesozoic and Paleozoic sediments are found caught as slivers between adjacent faults in this zone. The northern fault zone is almost completely buried beneath pediment gravel and is presumed to be composed of high-angle normal faults trending northwesterly.

Two unusual structural features are found on the eastern flank of the range. The first of these, the Jeter fault, seems to be a low-angle fault above which a thin plate of Cenozoic sediments, including the Tertiary Baca, Popotosa, and Santa Fe Formations, have been thrust westward over Precambrian gneiss.

The second unusual feature, and perhaps an even more important clue to the geomorphic history of the area, is the occurrence of a thin plate of highly disturbed

Paleozoic limestone that rests in low-angle discordance on the Precambrian gneiss and the Tertiary Popotosa Formation, and lies across the Jeter fault. Foraminiferal thin sections helped to identify this limestone as part of the Atrasado Member of the Madera Limestone.

The origin of this plate is debatable, but it seems most likely to have formed as a gravity slide from Pennsylvanian limestones that at one time capped the rising Ladron uplift in much the same manner as the present Sandia and Los Pinos uplifts are capped. This klippe was preserved under Santa Fe fanglomerate until exhumed by recent erosion.

Mineralization in the Ladrons has generally been confined to the major bounding fault zones and the Jeter fault. Copper and uranium are concentrated along a 10- to 15-foot sheared, reddish-brown and black, gouge zone of the Jeter fault. The zone contains fragments of Paleozoic, Mesozoic, and Cenozoic sediments which have been dragged into the zones as the plate has passed over these rocks.

CONODONTS FROM THE SOUTHERN SACRAMENTO MOUNTAINS, OTERO COUNTY, NEW MEXICO

Robert C. Burton
West Texas State University, Canyon, Texas

Biostratigraphic boundaries within the Mississippian System, based on conodonts, coincide with physical boundaries recognized by Laudon and Bowsher (1949) in the Southern Sacramento Mountains of New Mexico. The fauna of the Caballero Formation (Kinderhookian) is typified by *Siphonodella* (Branson and Mehl, 1934) and *Solenodella* (Branson and Mehl, 1934). The lower 15 feet of the Andrecito member of the overlying Lake Valley Formation (Osagean) contains *Siphonodella* (a diagnostic Kinderhookian form) and the first occurrence of *Pseudopolygnathus lanceolata* (Hass, 1959), which serves to distinguish the zone but makes the age questionable. *Apatognathus lipperit* (Bischoff, 1956) and *Nothognathella* (Branson and Mehl, 1934) are restricted to the Alamogordo member of the Lake Valley. The lower 5 feet of the Tierra Blanca member contains *Staurognathus cruciformis* (Branson and Mehl, 1941). Polygnathids make up approximately 30 percent of the fauna of the lower half of the unit whereas Gnathodids make up 25 percent of the fauna in the upper half. The Arcente member of the Lake Valley is barren although *Gnathodus texanus* (Roundy, 1926) constitutes 35 percent of the overlying Dona Ana member fauna. The lower 25 feet of the Rancheria Formation (Meramecian) yields a small, reworked fauna with *Cavusgnathus* (Harris and Hollingsworth, 1933) making its first appearance. The upper 20 feet of the Helms Formation (Chesterian) has a small fauna characterized by the relative abundance of *Cavusgnathus* and the first absence of *Polygnathus* (Hinde, 1879). Broader zonation based on variations in the blade and platform of *Polygnathus communis* (Branson and Mehl, 1934) is possible from the Caballero Formation (Kinderhookian) through the Rancheria Formation (Meramecian).

The Mississippian conodont fauna from the Sacremento Mountains contains 40 of 47 forms present in the Chappel Limestone of Texas. Sixty-three percent of the Caballero-Lake Valley fauna correlates with the Bushberg-Hannibal horizon in Oklahoma, while 53 percent matches the Bushberg-Hannibal fauna of Missouri. The Alamogordo, Tierra Blanca faunas contain 7 species which are present only in German faunas.

In New Mexico conodonts have also been found by the author in the Valmont and Montoya Formations (Ordovician), in the Devonian, and in the Gobbler Formation (Pennsylvanian). Ash's prediction (1962) that conodonts would become important stratigraphic tools in New Mexico is justified and continued study of conodonts in New Mexico is warranted.

HYPOGENE ZONING IN THE LORDSBURG MINING DISTRICT, HIDALGO COUNTY, NEW MEXICO

Kenneth F. Clark
University of New Mexico, Albuquerque, New Mexico

Hypogene zoning has been established in vein deposits related to a granodiorite stock that intruded basalts in late Cretaceous or early Tertiary time in the Lordsburg mining district.

The mining district is divided into two subdistricts, the Virginia subdistrict in the northern part and the Pyramid subdistrict in the southern part.

In the Virginia, subdistrict, the association tourmaline-chalcopyrite-pyrite-specularite is predominant in a subsurface core zone at a depth of 700 feet, and is surrounded by a central zone characterized by chalcopyrite-pyrite-specularite, an intermediate zone of galena-sphalerite, and a peripheral zone of fluorite-calcite-barite. In the Pyramid subdistrict the core zone is absent, the central zone is represented by the association chalcopyrite-bornite, the intermediate zone by silver-rhodochrosite-barite, and the peripheral zone by fluorite-calcite-barite.

The Pyramid subdistrict is genetically related to the Virginia subdistrict, but whether or not it had a separate center of mineralization remains uncertain.

Six stages of mineralization were recognized by Lasky in the Virginia subdistrict. The zone minerals tourmaline and specularite are found in stage one; pyrite, chalcopyrite, sphalerite, galena, and barite, in order of appearance, in stage two; pyrite and chalcopyrite in stage three; calcite and minor amounts of chalcopyrite in stages four and five; and calcite and fluorite in stage six. Six stages of mineralization have also been established in the Pyramid subdistrict. Zone minerals consist of minor amounts of hematite in stage one; chalcopyrite, bornite, barite and fluorite in stage two; rhodochrosite, barite, and calcite in stage three; calcite in stages four and five; and calcite and fluorite in stage six.

In the central zone of the Pyramid subdistrict a maximum temperature of formation of 550° to 580°C is indicated by sphalerite geologic thermometry. Similar maximum temperatures of formation prevailed in the Virginia subdistrict. Qualitative X-ray fluorescence analysis for trace elements in sphalerite, galena, and chalcopyrite, shows that cadmium and germanium are present in ores of the intermediate zone of the Virginia subdistrict. Traces of tin are present in ore from the central zone, collected on the 1300 level of the Banner mine.

The core and central zones were nearest the source of mineralizing fluids. Minerals with high temperatures of formation tended to be deposited nearer the source, whereas the lower-temperature assemblages were not deposited until the fluids had cooled by traveling upward and outward for considerable distances. There is a broad relationship between zoning and paragenesis, as minerals of the earlier stages are mainly confined to the inner zones.

Zoning is both horizontal and vertical in the Virginia subdistrict. In the Anita mine, all four zones are represented and provide a good example of vertical "telescoping." The changes from the core zone to the peripheral zone takes place in less than 1,000 feet vertically; a similar horizontal transition extends over 1 mile. Telescoping is evidence that mineralization took place at relatively shallow depths. The combination of initial high temperatures of formation and shallow depth of emplacement suggests that the copper-tourmaline deposits of the Lordsburg district can be assigned to the xenothermal class.

THE DETERMINATION OF THE GALLIUM-ALUMINUM RATIO IN ROCKS AND THE POSSIBLE PETROGENIC SIGNIFICANCE OF THIS RATIO

K. A. Grace
New Mexico Institute of Mining and Technology,
Socorro, New Mexico

Spectrographic methods have been developed for the analysis of gallium and aluminum in rock samples, and the determination of the gallium-aluminum ratio in igneous, sedimentary and metomorphic rocks. Gallium follows aluminum in silicate minerals during magmatic crystallization. In the process of weathering and subsequent transport, however, some separation occurs, and a change occurs in the gallium-aluminum ratio in the sedimentary deposits. The ratio of these two elements suggests a possible tool in determining whether a granite is of metasomatic or truly igneous origin.

SEDIMENTARY FRAMEWORK OF THE PRE-CENOZOIC ROCKS IN SOUTHWESTERN NEW MEXICO

Frank E. Kottlowski
New Mexico Bureau of Mines and Mineral Resources,
Socorro, New Mexico

Pre-Pennsylvanian strata in the southwestern quarter of New Mexico were deposited in shallow shelf seas and are mainly carbonate rocks except for 1) a basal Paleozoic clastic unit, the Cambrian-Ordovician Bliss Sandstone, 2) the Cable Canyone Sandstone, 3) the Devonian shales and siltstones, 4) the shaly early Mississippian strata, and 5) arenaceous Late Mississippian rocks, the Paradise and Helms Formations. The first four of these clastic facies overlie pronounced erosional surfaces and, except for the Bliss Sandstone, their clastic materials were derived from afar, probably chiefly from the northwest. The Late Mississippian clastic sediments reflect the beginning of widespread erosion in central and northern New Mexico that culminated in early Pennsylvanian time.

North-south-trending geographical features were formed in Pennsylvanian time, superimposed on the earlier east-west trends. The Pedernal landmass rose slowly and intermittently on the northeast to its climax in late Pennsylvanian-early Permian time, flanked on the west by a zeugogeosyncline, the Orogrande basin. This basin connected northward toward the Paradox basin via a series of autogeosynclines; a large autogeosyncline, the Pedregosa basin, lay in the southwestern corner of the region. Permian rocks reflect the mingling of north-south and east-west sedimentational features, the basal unit being the Abo Redbeds that grade southward into the Hueco Limestone.

The early Mesozoic was a full time of uplift and erosion accelerated during Early Cretaceous time when all Paleozoic strata were stripped from the Burro uplift in western Grant County and all of the upper Permian beds removed throughout large areas of southwestern New Mexico. Early Cretaceous strata may be more than 17,000 feet thick south of the Burro uplift. They consist of red beds, shoreline sandstones, nearshore conglomerates, fossiliferous limestones, and volcanic detritus.

To the northeast, Late Cretaceous beds, the Dakota Sandstone, Mancos Shale, and Mesaverde Formation, rest on middle Permian rocks or on a thin northward-tapering edge of Early Cretaceous strata. The southward change from marine to nearshore facies is shown by southward gradation from black Mancos Shale into shaly Eagle Ford sandstones. Latest Cretaceous rocks are local thick sequences of conglomeratic and volcanic detritus marking the beginning of Laramide deformation.

THE SEARCH FOR ORE DEPOSITS

Harrison A. Schmitt, Consultant
Silver City, New Mexico

It would seem that an exposition on the search for ore deposits must be largely subjective. No one person's experience can have covered the entire mining field in one lifetime nor could the gaps have been filled by the literature which is incomplete and to some extent biased.

Intensive mining activity in the western United States during the last quarter of the 19th century motivated wide interest in the theory of mineral deposition. The work prior to 1900 is best covered in "The Genesis of Ore Deposits" published by the AIME in 1901. One gets the impression that the broader aspects of ore deposit theory had been outlined by that time.

It is nearly impossible to make an estimate of the application of geology to ore finding before 1900. While certainly some ore finding was done through this theory, the burden of new discovery fell largely to the prospector and his cut and try methods.

After 1900 there was an increased awareness of the need for surface and underground maps. Intensive surface mapping by the U.S. Geological Survey has partially filled this need. Individual underground mapping projects also aided in solving basic problems in ore finding during the first two decades of the century.

The advent of interest in "porphyry coppers" further advanced the state of the art as did the flood of papers during the 1930's when many technical men returned to college.

Professional relationships between operators, mining engineers and geologists were poor as late as 1941. However, the importance of geological work in many districts has been increasingly recognized since that time. While laboratory aids to field work have been investigated in the fields of geophysics and geochemistry, effective application has been slow in developing. The schism between geophysicists and geologists is slowly narrowing and there are examples of close cooperation.

As the search for ore becomes more and more difficult, reliance on geophysical methods to pinpoint areas for study increases. Recent discoveries indicate this to be the case.

Equally important is the application of geology and geophysics in the field of operating economics, particularly in evaluation of prospects where limited data is available.

The overall picture shows the necessity for an ever greater background in the general sciences for the geologist. Education seems to be meeting this need. Unfortunately, because of present conditions in the mining industry, most modern geologists can seldom experience the discipline gained in mapping miles of underground workings and that of tying the geologic work to the facts of mine economics.

We are witnessing a marriage of the fields of geology and applied geophysics and much more cooperation between operations and exploration staffs. Although there is still a place for bold individual initiative, even for the lone explorer, the need for teams of specialists is more and more evident.

THE GEOLOGY OF THE SOUTH MOUNTAIN AREA, BERNALILLO, SANDOVAL, AND SANTA FE COUNTIES, NEW MEXICO

Tommy B. Thompson
University of New Mexico, Albuquerque, New Mexico

South Mountain is approximately 30 miles northeast of Albuquerque in the southern end of the San Pedro-Ortiz porphyry belt. It is a Tertiary monzonite laccolith that intrudes the Permian Abo and Yeso Formations and, in places, the Permian Glorieta Sandstone. The base of the laccolith lies on the Abo except in the southeastern part where it overlies the Meseta Blanca Member of the Yeso. The incompetence of the Yeso appears to have allowed the monzonitic magma to spread laterally throughout the stratigraphic interval up to the Glorieta Sandstone which was more resistant and broken only locally by the intrusion. The Yeso was apparently shoved aside by magmatic forces and, at the same time, added to the doming of overlying sediments caused by the intrusion. The Abo and underlying formations were folded into a basin apparently by the intrusion. In the southwestern part of the laccolith a small circular quartz monzonite stock intruded the monzonite with little shattering or brecciation along the contact. This seems to indicate that crystallization of the monzonite had not been completed.

Northwest of South Mountain a latite-andesite porphyry laccolith intruded the Pennsylvanian Sandia Formation. It overlies a conglomerate at the base of the Sandia Formation and is overlain by massive limestone of the Madera Limestone.

North of South Mountain a series of rhyolite sills intrude the Madera Limestone. The sills can be traced to the San Pedro Mountains. The feeder for the sills seems to be a dike around which there is zoning of mineral deposits.

There probably were at least two periods of faulting: 1) contemporaneous with intrusion, and 2) post-intrusion. The dominant trend of faulting is to the northeast while minor trends are southeasterly and easterly. Most of the faults belong to the Tijeras fault system which is of regional extent.

Mineral deposits include: 1) a small contact-metasomatic magnetite deposit, 2) many small supergene iron deposits, 3) a fissure vein of magnetite-specularite, and 4) a fissure vein of galena, sphalerite, chalcopyrite, and pyrite. These deposits are small and not economically important.

Ground water is usually available in the Madera Limestone or in Quaternary alluvium at a depth no greater than 200 feet.

GROUND WATER IN RELATION TO THE ECONOMY AND GEOLOGY OF GRANT COUNTY, NEW MEXICO

Frederick D. Trauger
U.S. Geological Survey, Albuquerque, New Mexico*

Ground water is the most important commodity and natural resource in Grant County. Surface water supplies are limited; they are available locally, but not where the need is greatest and they have been insufficient to meet all the needs for water. Ground water generally is available within economic distances of the point of need.

Ore deposits associated with intrusive rocks of Cretaceous and Tertiary age determined the location of the urban centers. Growth of the cities and development of the mines created a demand for large amounts of water that, with few exceptions, could be supplied only from underground.

The livestock industry generally is dependent upon ground water for a year-round supply. Water for irrigation in the Gila and Mimbres Valleys is available from surface flow but many irrigators supplement surface watter with ground water and some are entirely dependent upon ground water.

The principal aquifer in Grant County is the unconsolidated alluvium and bolson fill of Quaternary age. Thicknesses range from a few feet in upland stream channels to hundreds of feet in the lowland areas. Well yields range from less than 1 gpm (gallon per minute) to 2,200 gpm.

The Gila Conglomerate of Pliocene and Pleistocene age is an important aquifer because it is essentially the only aquifer underlying the best rangelands. The varied thickness and lithologic character of the Gila result in varied water-bearing characteristics. Well yields range from less than 1 gpm to 2,000 gpm depending on the degree of consolidation.

The Colorado Shale of Cretaceous age crops out in an area increasingly popular for suburban living. The formation contains little water whose occurrences are erratic.

Rocks of Paleozoic age, mostly limestone, locally yield as much as 250 gpm of water to wells. About 2,000 feet of Paleozoic rocks have been drilled in test wells in the vicinity of Hurley.

Intrusive and volcanic rocks furnish little water to wells. Yields as large as 20 gpm have been obtained locally from fractured and weathered granite. The Datil Formation of Tertiary age, generally a poor aquifer, is reported to yield as much as 400 gpm to wells at Apache Tejo.

Abrupt changes in the shape of the water table and in the yield characteristics of wells are indicative of significant changes in the lithology that are not always apparent at the surface.

Development of ground water for municipal, industrial, and irrigation supply has created local shortages of ground water, resulted in contamination of some ground-water supplies, and raised legal questions.

*Publication authorized by the Director, U.S. Geological Survey

GEOLOGIC CONTROLS OF SILVER-LEAD-ZINC REPLACEMENTS IN EUREKA MINING DISTRICT, SOUTHWESTERN NEW MEXICO

Robert A. Zeller, Jr., Consulting Geologist
Hachita, New Mexico

The Eureka mining district in southernmost Grant County produced high-grade silver ore from shallow mines during early operations. Deeper sulfide ores of silver, lead, and zinc have been produced in recent years from the Hornet and American mines. Detailed geologic mapping and study of these mines have revealed the principal geologic controls of ore emplacement in the district.

In each mine, ore formed as replacement bodies in the same massive Lower Cretaceous reef limestone. Mineralizing solutions ascended along the northeast-striking high-angle Hornet and American faults. In the Hornet mine, ore bodies formed adjacent to the fault in the limestone immediately below a thin shale bed and andesite flows, which apparently acted as barriers to rising solutions. Rolls in the bedding also influenced ore deposition; where the bedding attitude is concave downward, large (30 ft. diameter) ore bodies were formed.

The principal ore bodies in the American mine are within the reef limestone and are confined to two overlapping zones — one in the footwall and the other in the hanging wall of the American fault. These represent ore replacements in a particular favored limestone startum offset by the fault prior to mineralization. Cross factures in the wall rock adjacent to bends in the American fault facilitated replacement; the greatest fracturing and the largest ore bodies (40 ft. diameter) are on the convex sides of the bends.

Discovery of factors controlling ore distribution provides challenging exploration targets in the Eureka district.

PAINTINGS BY PETER HURD

The New Mexico Geological Society is proud to present photographs of six paintings by the renowned artist Peter Hurd as the concluding feature of this guidebook. It is especially fitting that a few of Peter Hurd's paintings be included because the hills and valleys of the field conference area and many other parts of New Mexico appear in so many of his paintings. Although some of the paintings reproduced here are not as well known as others, readers will agree that Peter Hurd certainly has caught the spirit of New Mexico in all of them.

The Society wishes to thank Peter Hurd who lives in San Patricio, Hondo Valley, New Mexico, for permission to reproduce his paintings. Also the Society is indebted to Mr. Eugene A. Smith, Director of the Roswell Museum, who kindly permitted the Society to use Mr. Hurd's "self-portrait" and to Mr. Patrick J. Leonard, Vice-President of the Leonard Oil Company for allowing the Society to reproduce "Sheep Camp." This painting is on display in the Security National Bank of Roswell. All of the photographs were taken by Mr. Kenyon Cobean, commercial photographer, Roswell, New Mexico.

Self Portrait (1956). In the background are some of the hills in the Hondo Valley near San Patricio, New Mexico.

Sheep Camp.

La Capitan

Rain Shower Over Los Alamos, New Mexico.

Villanueva in Springtime. Villanueva is on the Pecos River south of Las Vegas, New Mexico.

The Young Marksman (1960). Marksman is Peter Hurd's son Michael.

Business and Professional Directory

Bankers to the New Mexico Geological Society

FIRST STATE BANK

Member F.D.I.C.

Socorro, New Mexico

RESOURCES ARE OUR BUSINESS

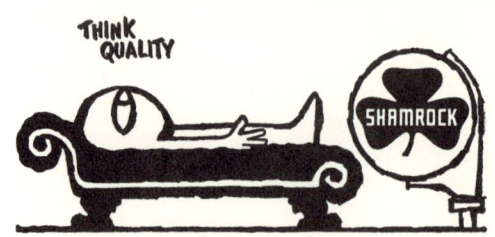

The Shamrock Oil and Gas Corporation

RETAILERS OF:
MAPS, GLOBES, ATLASES, BOOKS
DRAFTING ACCESSORIES & EQUIPMENT
TELESCOPES & BINOCULARS

AUTHORIZED AGENTS FOR SALE OF:
USGS MAPS
USC & GS AVIATION CHARTS
US GOV'T. PRINTING OFFICE PUBLICATIONS

MAPS - **TECHNICAL BOOKS** — **DRAFTING SUPPLIES**

HOLMAN'S
The House of Maps
401 WYOMING BLVD. NE
ALBUQUERQUE, NEW MEXICO
PHONE 265-7982

Consider This a Personal Invitation to...

Drop in and See Us Whenever You're in Albuquerque

ALBUQUERQUE NATIONAL BANK
Albuquerque's oldest and largest

HEAD OFFICE—SECOND AND CENTRAL
E. CENTRAL OFFICE—4401 CENTRAL AVE. NE
N. FOURTH OFFICE—1610 FOURTH ST. NW
SIMMS BLDG. OFFICE—FOURTH AND GOLD
MENAUL OFFICE—5400 MENAUL BLVD. NE
WINROCK OFFICE—115 WINROCK CENTER
DRIVE-IN—SECOND AND COPPER
MEMBER FDIC

Business and Professional Directory

Oil & Gas Reporting Services
Covering the Rocky Mountain Region, the Appalachian, Illinois and the Michigan Basins.

Completion Cards
Covering the Rocky Mountain Region, the Appalachian, Illinois and the Michigan Basins.

Up-to-date Oil & Gas Maps
In the Rocky Mountain Region and the active areas of Ohio. Wall Maps of the Rocky Mountain Region and of the Midwestern & Northeastern U.S. are available.

Oil & Gas Production Reports
Covering the Rocky Mountain Region, the Illinois Basin, Ohio (Deep Production only) and the Gulf Coast States.

Annual Resumes of the Oil and Gas activity
in the Rocky Mountain Region including back issues.

Lockwood Source Books of Petroleum Statistics
Covering Texas, Louisiana, Arkansas, Mississippi, Alabama and Florida - write for a schedule of prices and services.

 Petroleum Information CORPORATION

1610 Grant Street, P.O. Box 2612, Phone: 825-2181, Denver, Colorado
BILLINGS • CASPER • DURANGO • EVANSVILLE • HOUSTON

BEST WISHES!

15TH FIELD CONFERENCE
NEW MEXICO GEOLOGICAL SOCIETY

Kermac Nuclear Fuels Corp.
GRANTS, NEW MEXICO

ESTABLISHED 1880   30 SOUTH MAIN

JACOBS ASSAY OFFICE
REGISTERED ASSAYERS

PHONE MAin 2-0813   P. O. BOX 1889

TUCSON, ARIZONA

HOW TO S-T-R-E-T-C-H
your exploration dollar

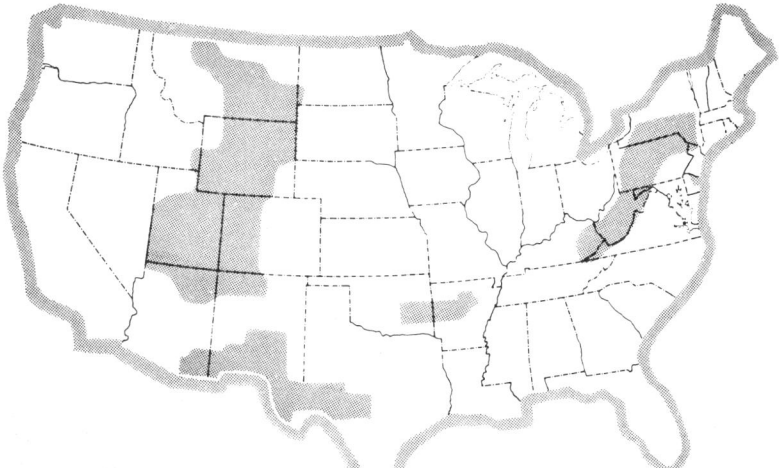

GEOPHOTO has available for immediate delivery detailed photogeologic maps in important petroleum provinces including Rocky Mountains, Sonora-Las Cruces Basins, Southeast New Mexico, Delaware Basin, Marfa Basin, Val Verde Basin, Kerr Basin, Arkoma Basin and Appalachian Area. Geology is ink drafted to copyrighted Geophoto planimetric bases compiled from township plats. You may inspect any of these maps. Price quotations gladly provided. Discounts for quantity purchases.

Investigate These Other GEOPHOTO Services • Quantitative Photogeology • Structural Contouring • Topographic Mapping • Detailed Stratigraphic Studies • Contract Surface Parties • Comprehensive Geomorphic Studies

 **GEOPHOTO SERVICES INC.**
BOX 22293 • 2149 SOUTH HOLLY STREET • DENVER, COLORADO 80222

Business and Professional Directory

Humble works wonders with oil

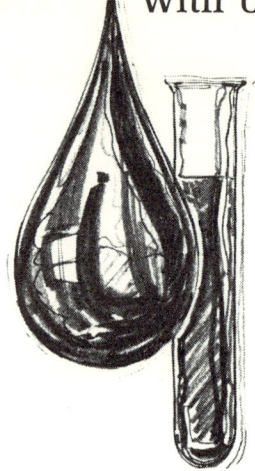

HUMBLE Oil & Refining Company
America's Leading ENergy COmpany

FOR YOUR CONVENIENCE...

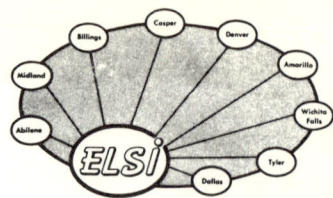

...All ELSI offices are interconnected by direct-wire teletype. Through any ELSI office, you have access to the complete facilities of the entire organization — at no additional cost to you.

West Texas Electrical Log Service
Rocky Mountain Well Log Service
Panhandle Electrical Log Service
North Texas Well Log Service
East Texas Well Log Service
Bess Mason Log Service

Offering the best possible source of reduced prints of electrical, radioactivity and hydrocarbon logs...

- We are engaged exclusively in the gathering and distribution of logs, with 18 years experience in this field.
- Our maintenance of print libraries in important oil centers, available for immediate delivery, assures easy access and rapid distribution.

CONTACT THE OFFICE NEAREST YOU OR WRITE TO:

 ELECTRICAL LOG SERVICES, INC.
1407 ROSS AVENUE • DALLAS 2, TEXAS

YOU'RE ALWAYS AMONG FRIENDS

Central at Third Downtown
North Fourth at Candelaria
East Central at San Mateo
Hoffmantown Shopping Center
828 Bridge Boulevard, SW
Winrock Shopping Center

Business and Professional Directory

American Stratigraphic Company

- STRATIGRAPHIC STUDIES
- SAMPLE LIBRARIES
- WELL-SITE CONSULTING

CASPER, WYOMING
524 EAST YELLOWSTONE

BILLINGS, MONTANA
17 NORTH 31ST STREET

DENVER, COLORADO
1820 BROADWAY

ANCHORAGE, ALASKA
BOX 2127

CANADIAN STRATIGRAPHIC SERVICE, LTD.
705 11TH AVENUE WEST
CALGARY, ALBERTA

CANADIAN STRATIGRAPHIC SERVICE, LTD.
1840 McINTYRE ST.
REGINA, SASKATCHEWAN

AMERICAN SMELTING AND REFINING COMPANY

Miners, smelters and refiners of major base metals and precious metal ores.

MAIN OFFICE:
American Smelting and Refining Company
120 Broadway, New York 10005

SOUTHWESTERN OFFICE:
American Smelting and Refining Company
Valley National Bank Bldg., Tucson, Arizona

Please Contact

Homestake-Sapin Partners

P. O. Box 98
Grants, New Mexico

for

New & Used Mine & Mill Equipment & Supplies

Business and Professional Directory

Phelps Dodge Corporation Copper Concentrator at Morenci, Arizona
(Ball-Mill and Classifier Section)

The Morenci Concentrator is considered the largest copper concentrator in the world. This view shows the 30 grinding ball-mills and 60 spiral classifiers in operation. Approximately 60,000 tons of ore are ground and treated daily in this plant.

PHELPS DODGE CORPORATION

Ajo   Bisbee   Douglas   Morenci

Business and Professional Directory

KOOGLE & POULS ENGINEERING, INC.
5115 Copper N.E., 87108
Albuquerque, New Mexico

PHOTOGRAMMETRIC ENGINEERS

Serving the Southwest SINCE 1890

FULL SERVICE BANK

THE FIRST NATIONAL BANK OF ROSWELL

Member F.D.I.C.

CABLE TV

RUIDOSO, N.M.

RUIDOSO'S FINEST MOTEL

Phone 257-4078   "Where Most People Stay"   P.O. Box 460

Ed and Bess Anderson, Hosts

DUVAL CORPORATION

Producers of High Grade Muriate of Potash

CARLSBAD   NEW MEXICO

COMPLIMENTS OF YOUR HOST

The Chaparral Motor Hotel

Ruidoso Downs, New Mexico

—NOTES—

—NOTES—

NOTES